GATE-CY

A Detailed Manual Solution of Organic Chemistry

(Reagents and Reactions Mechanism in Organic Chemistry)

Dr. Ajeet Chandra

CLEVER FOX PUBLISHING
Chennai, India

Published by CLEVER FOX PUBLISHING 2022

Copyright © Dr. Ajeet Chandra 2022
All Rights Reserved.

ISBN 978-93-56481-33-6

This book has been published with all reasonable efforts taken to make the material error-free after the consent of the author. No part of this book shall be used, reproduced in any manner whatsoever without written permission from the author, except in the case of brief quotations embodied in critical articles and reviews.

The Author of this book is solely responsible and liable for its content including but not limited to the views, representations, descriptions, statements, information, opinions and references ["Content"]. The Content of this book shall not constitute or be construed or deemed to reflect the opinion or expression of the Publisher or Editor. Neither the Publisher nor Editor endorse or approve the Content of this book or guarantee the reliability, accuracy or completeness of the Content published herein and do not make any representations or warranties of any kind, express or implied, including but not limited to the implied warranties of merchantability, fitness for a particular purpose. The Publisher and Editor shall not be liable whatsoever for any errors, omissions, whether such errors or omissions result from negligence, accident, or any other cause or claims for loss or damages of any kind, including without limitation, indirect or consequential loss or damage arising out of use, inability to use, or about the reliability, accuracy or sufficiency of the information contained in this book.

PREFACE

This book is completely focused on organic chemistry on the topic of one-pot steps and multistep reactions. Also, primarily intended for graduate as well as post-graduate students for organic chemistry and broadly focuses on the topics of single-step/multistep reaction, name reactions, reagents, anomeric effects, and conformational analysis from competitive GATE-exam questionnaires are largely derived. Detailed solutions for 'GATE-CY: A Detailed Solution Manual of Organic Chemistry' papers of the previous years from 2005 to 2022 has been provided. Great efforts have been made to equip students with ample knowledge of organic chemistry, which will enable them to solve questions in various qualifying examinations. Aspiring researchers of synthetic chemistry will also find the subjects covered herein to be very useful in their proposed research areas.

References for scientific journals and books have been added as and when required in the text, in keeping with contemporaneous research. Three-dimensional illustrations for reaction mechanisms have been provided wherever possible for greater understanding and depth. The readers should also note that there might be slight variations in the operating mechanism for the same reaction at different points in the book, as these have been sourced from research publications spanning multiple decades.

The author would greatly appreciate critical feedback from readers if they find any discrepancies in the mechanisms discussed in this book, which will also serve as updates for the next edition. This book can be used for the clamming answers for the given wrong answers by any examinations if references are available. The author has doubts in the case of a few astricts marked questionnaires. Thus, I would like to thank the readers in advance, if they can provide the references for the astricts marked questionnaires that can be edited in the next edition.

It consists of basic and advanced levels of a detailed solution manual of organic chemistry problems based on synthetic transformations, named reaction, reagents basis, and stereochemistry which can also be more beneficial for the researchers. This book will give a good knowledge and a better logical approach to thinking in the area of Organic Chemistry. I was aiming to help and encourage the students who wanted to work in the area of chemistry. I have done my best in the writing of this book to provide good knowledge of organic chemistry and tried my best to make three-dimensional views of the reaction mechanism. During writing these books, I have cited books and scientific journals to update them, and also, in some places, you may get different reaction mechanisms because I have taken from both old and newly written mechanisms. Hence, all the reaction mechanisms are correct. I will be thankful to all readers of this book; if you have doubt that the reaction mechanism is wrong or not written perfectly, please let me know, and I will update it in the next edition of the book.

ACKNOWLEDGMENT

Firstly, I would like to thank my parent for their moral and financial support throughout my educational journey. I would like to express my heartfelt gratitude to my research supervisors, Prof. J. N. Moorthy/ Prof. R. Gurunath and Prof. I. N. Namboothiri for giving me a great opportunity to pursue my research under their fruitful guidance. During my stay at IITs, my knowledge of advanced organic chemistry has vastly improved under the tutelage of Prof. N. G. Ramesh, Prof. R. Ramapanicker, and Prof. V. K. Yadav. I am greatly indebted to Prof. L. D. S. Yadav, Prof. Jagdamba Singh, and Prof. I. R. Siddiqui for facilitating my greater understanding of a logical and systematic approach to organic chemistry. Prof. Singh's books, mainly, is vital for every thoughtful chemistry student who wants to understand the governing mechanism of organic reactions. My research work experience and expertise in synthetic chemistry have fostered my skills to work independently and in a team. During my graduate study at IIT Kanpur, I worked on hypervalent iodine(V) mediated oxidative transformations. As a Pre-PhD research experience at IIT Delhi, I worked on various peptides and dendrimer molecules. As a postdoctoral fellow, I am working in the area of sulfonyl phthalides chemistry and aim to explore new synthetic methodology with novel applications, also have gained experience in asymmetric catalysis as well and have done the PG degree with a specialization in organic chemistry at the University of Allahabad, Prayagraj (Allahabad). Also, my undergraduate teachers, especially; Prof. Krishna K. Singh and Dr. Krishna Kumar Singh and all other professors of TDPG Collage, Jaunpur, deserve special thanks. I enjoyed a lot by learning the concepts and logical approaches from all the IITs mentioned above, University and college teachers of the Department of Chemistry.

I am grateful to Dr. Abhishek R. Tiwari for his invaluable assistance during the revision of my book. I would like to thank my senior and junior colleagues, Prof. Vishnu P. Shrivastava, Prof. Rohan R. Erendey, Prof. Dheeraj Kumar, Prof. Suresh C. Yadav, and Prof. Santosh Singh. Special thanks to my present and past labmates at IIT Kanpur (years: 2014-2020) and IIT Bombay (years: 2021-2022). Also, I would like to thank the graduate aptitude test in engineering (GATE) organizing institutes; especially, IITs and IISc Bangalore for their cooperation in providing the question papers with answer keys for the public domain. This book promotes the GATE-CY exam and other competitive examinations for chemistry. I am sure that this book will be helpful for the upcoming students to grow-up their knowledge in chemistry. Finally, I also would like to thank all the readers for their insightful comments and suggestions, especially Dr. Pravin, Dr. C. Siva Sankara, Mr. Deepak, Mr. Banamali, Ms. Rajni, and Ms. Snehal, and all the other friends.

CONTENTS

Abbreviation, Name and Chemical Structure of Organic Compounds

S. N.	Abbreviation	Full name	Chemical structure
1.	Ac	Acetyl	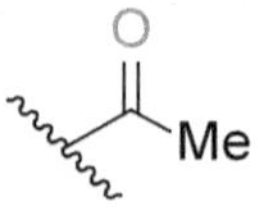
2.	AcO	Acetate	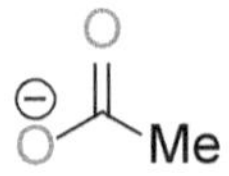
3.	Ac_2O	Acetic anhydride	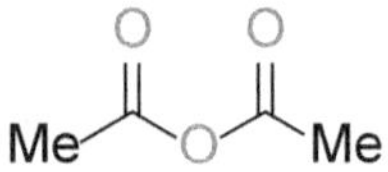
4.	acac	Acetylacetone (ligand)	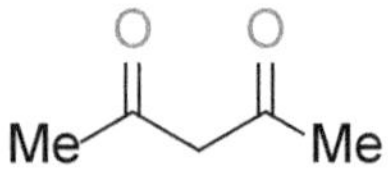
5.	AIBN	Azobis(isobutyronitrile)--radical initiator	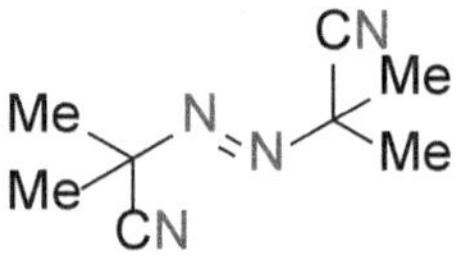
6.	All	Allyl	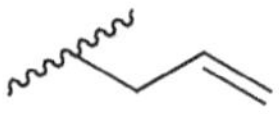
7.	Ph	Phenyl	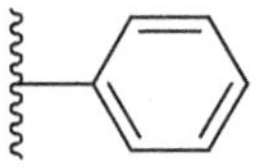
8.	9-BBN-H	9-Borabicyclo[3.3.1]nonane	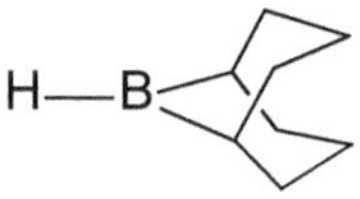
9.	Bn	Benzyl	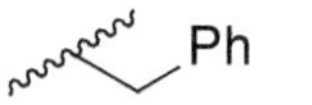
10.	BHT	Butylated hydroxy toluene (2,6-di-*tert*-butyl-4-methylphenol)	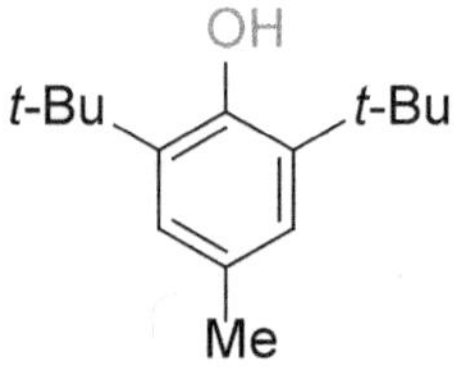
11.	bipy or bpy	2,2'-bipyridyl	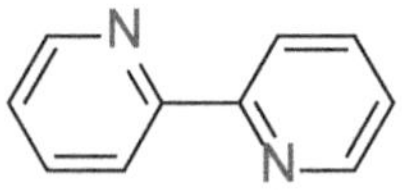
12.	BMS	Borane dimethylsulfide	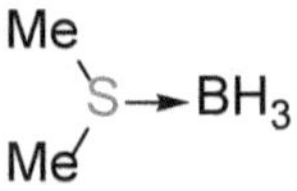
13.	Boc	*t*-Butyloxycarbonyl	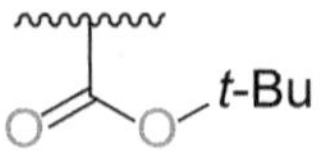

14.	BOM	Benzyloxymethyl (alcohol protection)	
15.	Bs	Brosylate	
16.	Bz	Benzoyl	
17.	Bu or *n*-Bu	*normal*-Butyl	
18.	*s*-Bu	*secondary*-Butyl Or sec-Butyl	
19.	*t*-Bu	*tertiary*-butyl Or *tert*-butyl	
20.	CAN	Ceric Ammonium Nitrate	
21.	Cbz or Z	Carbobenzyloxyl Or Benzyloxycarbonyl	
22.	Chloranyl	2,3,5,6-tetrachlorocyclo-hexa-2,5-diene-1,4-dione	

23.	COT	Cyclooctatetraene	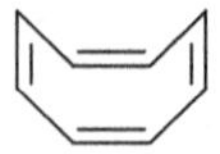
24.	Cp	Cyclopentadienyl where # = Cation, Radical or Anion	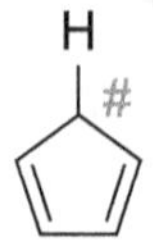
25.	Cp*	Pentamethylcyclopentadienyl where # = Cation, Radical or Anion	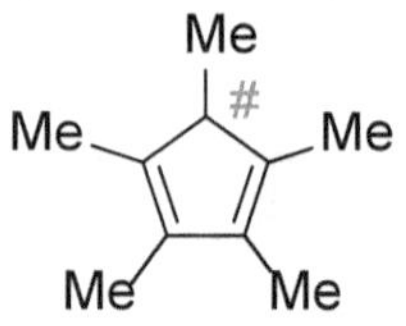
26.	CSA	Camphorsulfonic Acid	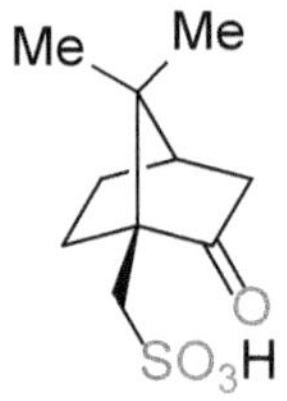
27.	CSI	Chlorosulfonyl Isocyanate	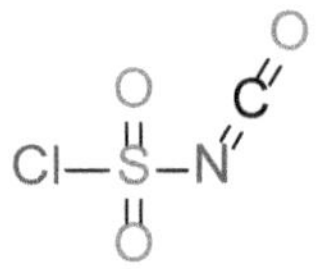
28.	CTAB	Cetyltrimethylammonium bromide	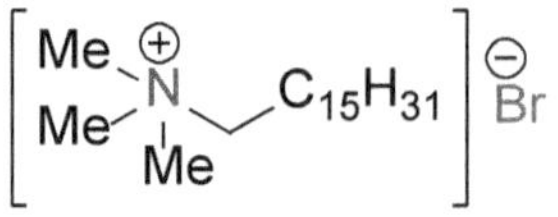
29.	Cy	Cyclohexyl	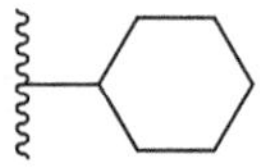
30.	DABCO	1,4-Diazabicyclo[2.2.2]octane	
31.	DBN	1,5-Diazabicyclo[4.3.0]non-5-ene	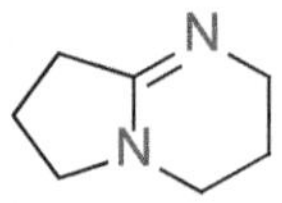
32.	DBU	1,8-Diazabicyclo[5.4.0]undec-7-ene	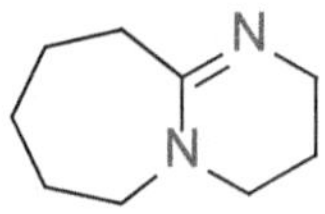
33.	DCC	Dicyclohexyl Carbodiimide	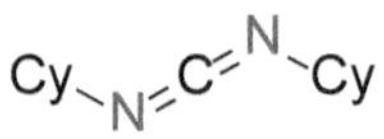

34.	DDQ	2,3-Dichloro-5,6-dicya-no-1,4-benzoquinone	
35.	DEADCAT Or DEAD	Diethyl azodicarboxylate	
36.	DET	Diethyl Tartrate	
37.	DIAD	Diisopropyl azodicarboxylate	
38.	DIBAL or DIBAH	Diisobutylaluminum Hydride	
39.	Diglyme	Diethylene glycol dimethyl ether	
40.	DIPT	diisopropyl tartrate	
41.	DHP	Dihydropyran (as a 'O' protection group)	
42.	DMA	Dimethoxyacetone	
43.	DMAD	Dimethyl Acetylenedicarboxylate	
44.	DMAP	4-Dimethylaminopyridine (base catalyst)	

45.	DMDO	Dimethyldioxyrane	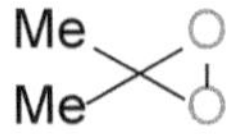
46.	DME	1,2-Dimethoxyethane	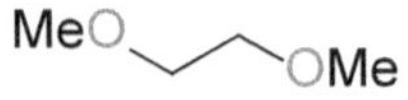
47.	DMF	Dimethylformamide	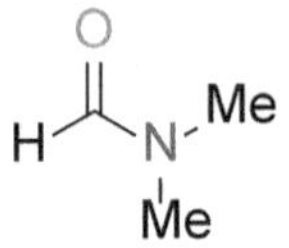
48.	DMSO	Dimethyl sulfide	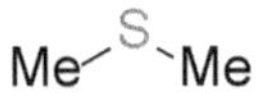
49.	DMSO	Dimethyl sulfoxide	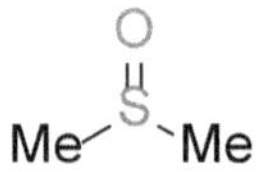
50.	$DMSO_2$	Dimethyl Sulfone	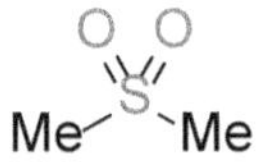
51.	DMT	Dimethyl tartrate	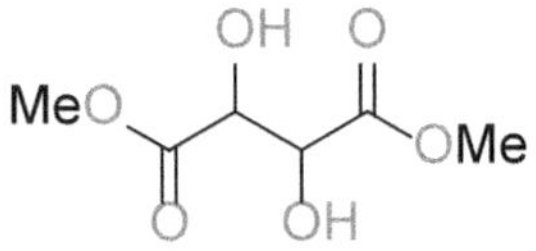
52.	DNP	Dinitrophenylhydrazine	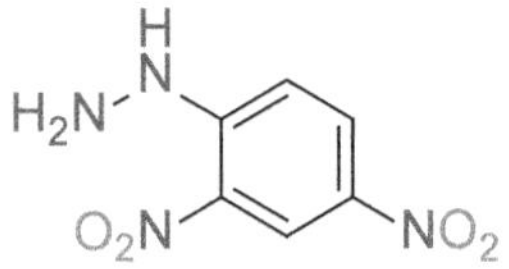
53.	DNPBA	2,4-Dinitroperbenzoic acid	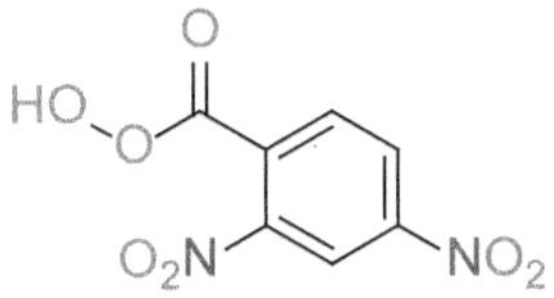
54.	DPS	tert-butyldiphenylsilyl	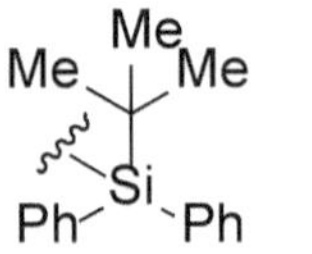
55.	E	Methoxycarbonyl	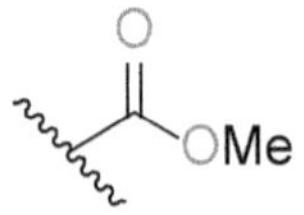
56.	EDTA	Ethylenediaminetetraacetic acid	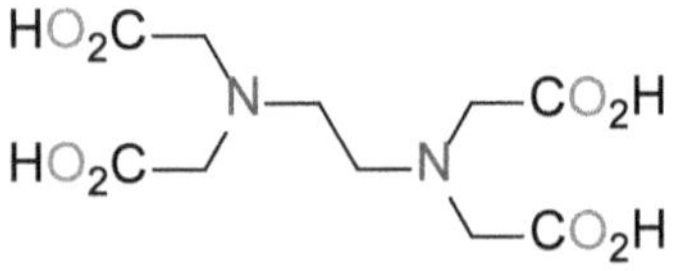

57.	EE	1-Ethoxyethyl (alcohol protection)	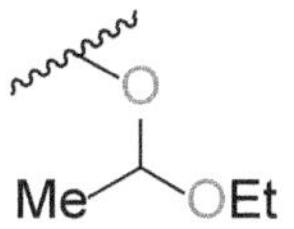
58.	en	Ethylene Diamine	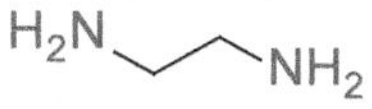
59.	Et	Ethyl	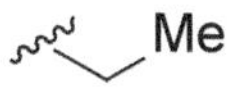
60.	Fmoc	9-Fluorenylmethoxycarbonyl	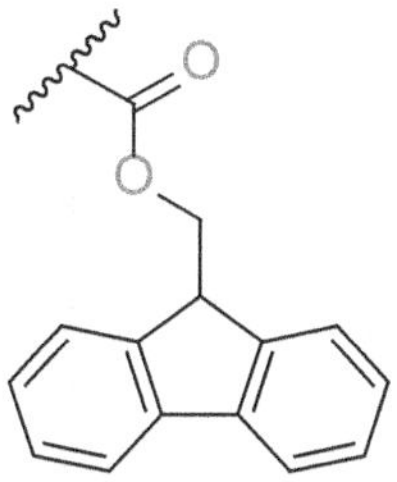
61.	HBT	Hydroxybenzotriazole	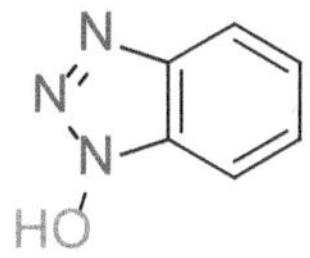
62.	HMDS	Hexamethyldisilazide	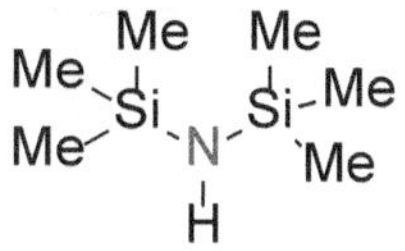
63.	HMPA Or HMPT	Hexamethylphosphorictriamide	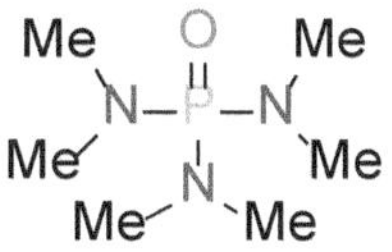
64.	IBX	2-Idoxybenzoic acid	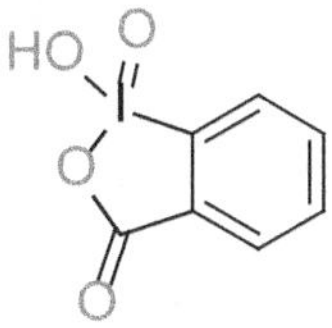
65.	Ipc$_2$BH	Bis(isopinocampheylborane)	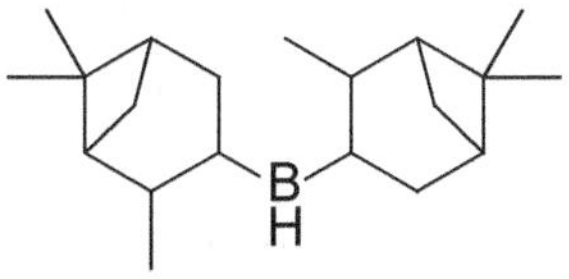
66.	LAH	Lithium Aluminum Hydride (LiAlH$_4$)	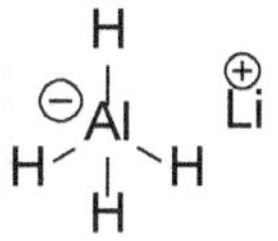

67.	LDA	Lithium Diisopropylamide	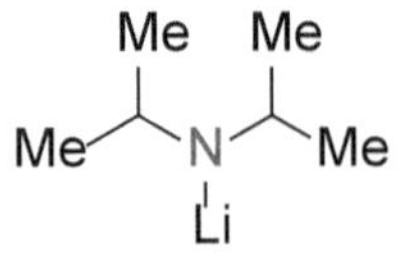
68.	LHMDS	Lithium hexamethyldisilazide Or Lithium bis(trimethylsilyl) amide	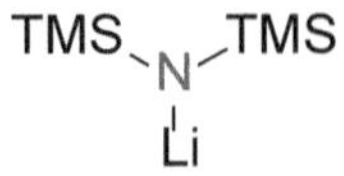
69.	LICA	Lithium *N*-isopropylcyclohexyl- amide	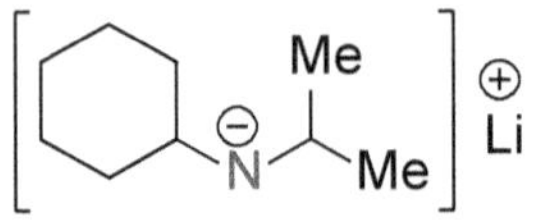
70.	LiDBB	Lithium di-*tert*-butylbiphenyl (electron transfer species)	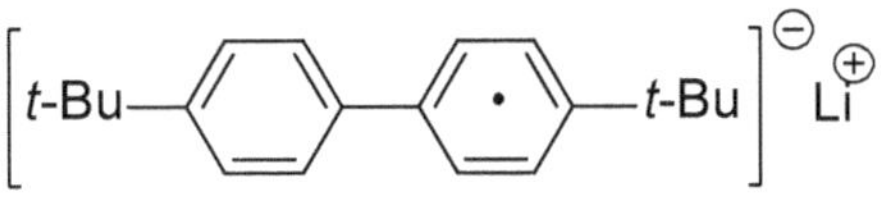
71.	LiTMP	Lithium tetramethylpiperidide	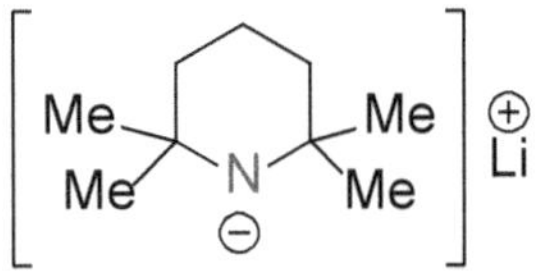
72.	LTA	Lead tetraacetate	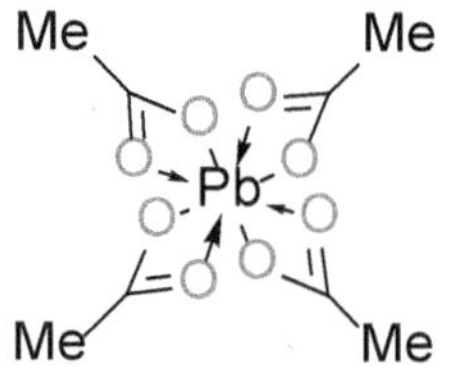
73.	MA	Maleic anhydride	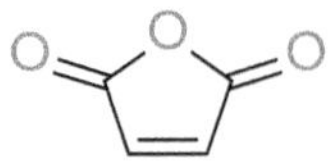
74.	*m*-CPBA	*meta*-Chloroperoxybenzoic acid	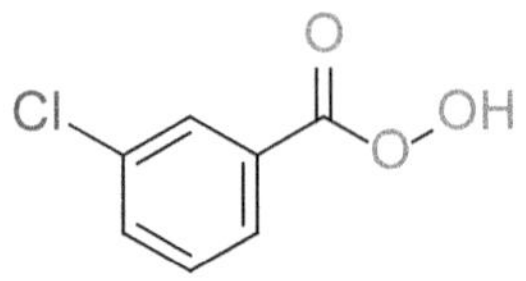
75.	Me	Methyl	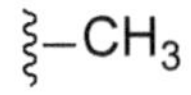
76.	MEM	2-Methoxyethoxymethyl (alcohol protection)	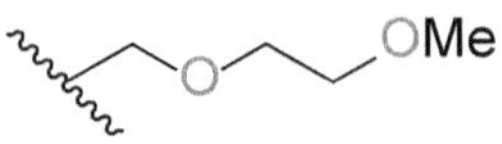
77.	Mes	Mesityl Or 2,4,6-trimethylphenyl	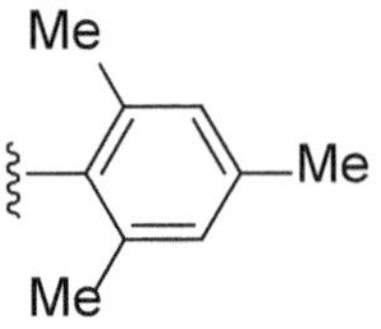

No.	Abbreviation	Name	Structure
78.	MOM	Methoxymethyl (alcohol protection)	
79.	Ms	Methanesulfonyl Or Mesyl	
80.	MTBE	methyl *tert*-butyl ether or (+,–)-ether	
81.	MVK	Methyl vinyl ketone (MVK) Or 3-Butene-2-one	
82.	NBS, NCS	*N*-Bromosuccinimide & *N*-Chlorosuccinimide	
83.	NIS	*N*-Iodosuccinimide	
84.	NMO	*N*-Methylmorpholine-*N*-oxide	
85.	NMP	*N*-Methylpyrrolidone	
86.	Ns	*p*-Nitrobenzenesulfonyl	
87.	PCC	Pyridinium chlorochromate	
88.	PDC	Pyridinium dichromate	

89.	PMB	*p*-Methoxybenzyl	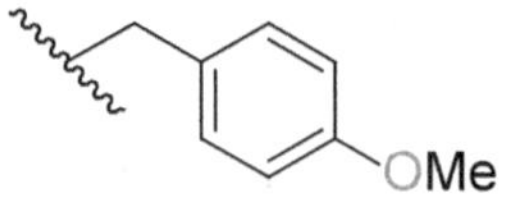
90.	PNB	*p*-Nitrobenzoate	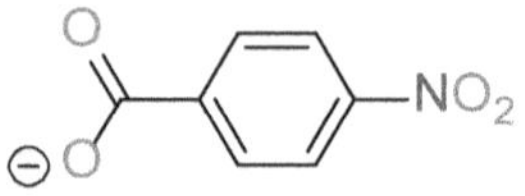
91.	PPTS	Pyridinium *p*-toluenesulfonate	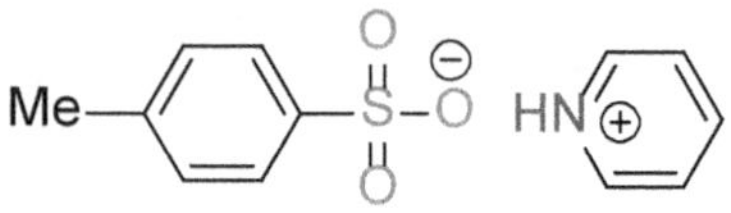
92.	n-Pr	*n*-Propyl or normal propyl	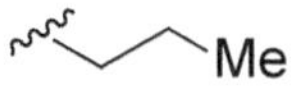
93.	i-Pr	*i*-Propyl or isopropyl	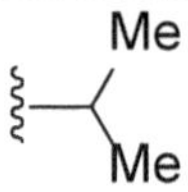
94.	Pv	Pivaloyl	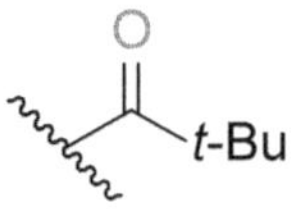
95.	Py	Pyridine	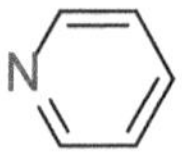
96.	Sia$_2$BH	Disiamylborane	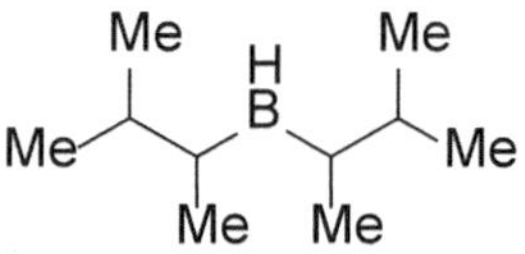
97.	TBAC	tetra-*n*-butylammonium chloride	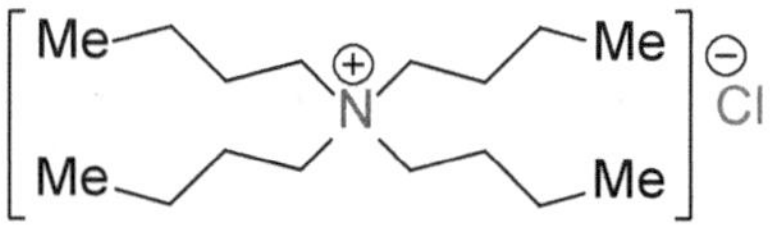
98.	TBAF	tetra-*n*-butylammonium fluoride	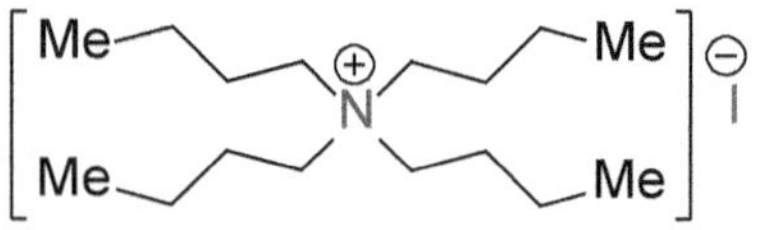
99.	TBDMS Or TBS	*t*-Butyldimethylsilyl (alcohol protection)	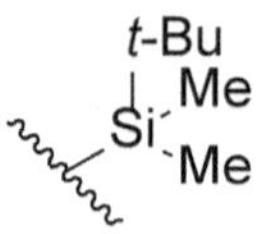
100.	TBDPS	*t*-Butyldiphenylsilyl (alcohol protection)	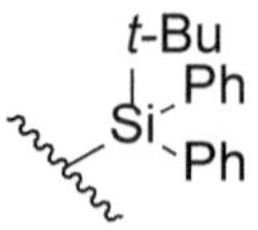
101.	TBHP	*t*-Butylhydroperoxide	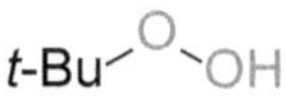

No.	Abbreviation	Name	Chemical Structure
102.	TEA	Triethylamine	Et–N(Et)Et
103.	TEAB	tetraethylammonium bromide	[Et₄N]⁺ Br⁻
104.	TES	Triethylsilyl	–Si(Et)(Et)Et
105.	Tf	Triflate	–SO₂CF₃
106.	TFA	Trifluoroacetic acid Or Trifluoroacetyl Chloride	HOC(O)CF₃ and ClC(O)CF₃
107.	TFAA	Trifluoroacetic anhydride	CF₃C(O)–O–C(O)CF₃
108.	Th	Thexyl borane	H₂B–C(Me)₂CH(Me)Me
109.	TIPS	Triisopropylsilyl (alcohol protection)	Si(CHMe₂)₃
110.	TMAI	Tetramethylammonium iodide	[Me₄N]⁺ I⁻
111.	TMEDA	*N,N,N',N'*-Tetramethylethylene-diamine	Me₂N–CH₂CH₂–NMe₂
112.	TMS	Tetramethylsilane and Trimethylsilyl	Me–Si(Me)(Me)Me and –Si(Me)(Me)Me

113.	TMSCl and TMSI	Trimethylsilyl chloride & Trimethylsilyl Iodide	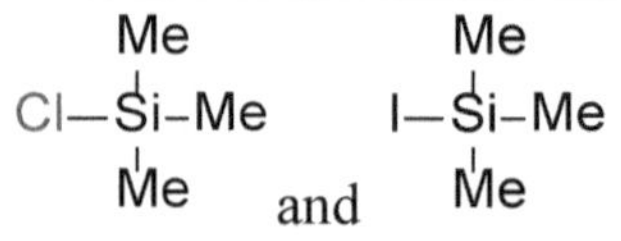
114.	*p*-Tol	*p*-Tolyl	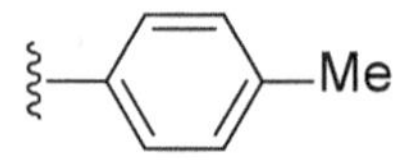
115.	TPAP	Tetra-*n*-propylammonium Perruthenate	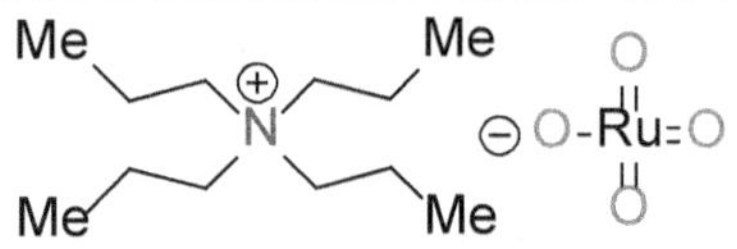
116.	Tr	Triphenylmethyl (Trityl)	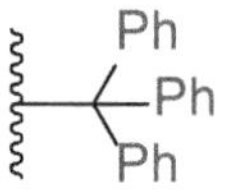
117.	Troc	Trichloroethyloxycarbonyl	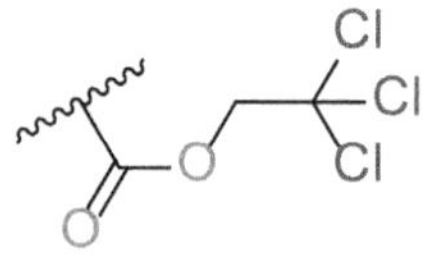
118.	Ts	Tosyl	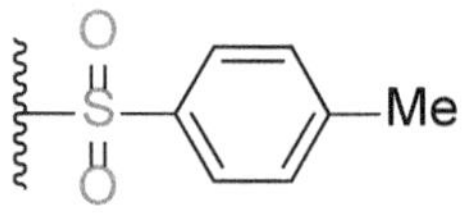
119.	Vitride®	Sodium bis(2-methoxyethoxy) aluminium hydride	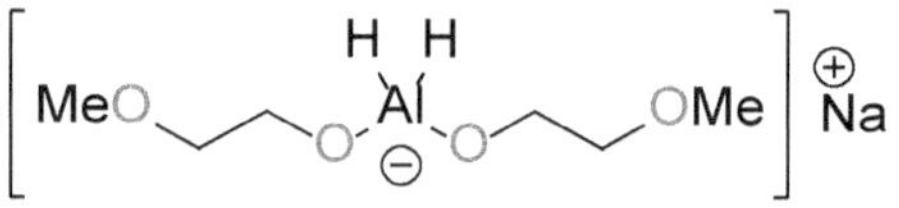

S. N.	Spectroscopic Terms and tools	Separation Acronyms
1.	δ	Chemical shift (NMR)
2.	CD	Circular Dichroism
3.	CI	Chemical Ionization (mass spec)
4.	CIDNP	Chemically Induced Dynamic Nuclear Polarization
5.	CMR	Carbon-13 Magnetic Resonance
6.	COSY	Correlation Spectroscopy (NMR)
7.	DEPT	Distortionless Enhancement by Polarization Transfer (NMR)
8.	DNMR	Dynamic NMR EI Electron Impact (MS)
9.	ENDOR	Electron Nuclear Double Resonance
10.	ESR (EPR)	Electron (Paramagnetic) Spin Resonance
11.	FT	Fourier Transform
12.	GLC	Gas-liquid Chromatography (VPC)
13.	HETCOR	Heteronuclear correlation (NMR)
14.	HPLC	High Performance Liquid Chromatography
15.	INEPT	Insensitive Nuclei Enhanced by Polarization Transfer (NMR)
16.	IR	Infrared
17.	J	Coupling Constant (NMR)
18.	LC	Liquid Chromatography
19.	LIS	Lanthanide Induced shifts (NMR)
20.	MS	Mass spectrum
21.	NMR	Nuclear Magnetic Resonance
22.	NOE(SY)	Nuclear Overhauser Effect (Spectroscopy)
23.	Rf	Retention Factor (chromatography)
24.	ROESY	Rotating Frame Nuclear Overhauser Spectroscopy (NMR)
25.	TLC	Thin Layer Chromatography
26.	UV	Ultraviolet spectroscopy
27.	VPC	Vapor Phase Chromatography (GLC)
28.	XPS	(ESCA) X-Ray Photoelectron Spectroscopy

S.N.	Name Of the Books	Authors
1.	Advanced Organic Chemistry	J. Singh and L. D. S. Yadav
2.	Organic Synthesis	J. Singh and L. D. S. Yadav
3.	Advanced Organic Chemistry-Reactions & Mechanics	M. S. Singh and K. Raghuvanshi
4.	Organic Chemistry	J. Clayden, N. Greeves, and S. Warren
5.	March's Advanced Organic Chemistry: Reactions, Mechanisms, and Structure	Michael B. Smith
6.	Advanced Organic Chemistry: Part A: Structure and Mechanisms	F. A. Carey and R. J. Sundberg
7.	Advanced Organic Chemistry: Part B: Reaction and Synthesis	F. A. Carey and R. J. Sundberg
8.	Modern Methods of Organic Synthesis	W. Carruthers and I. Coldham
9.	Reactive Intermediates in Organic Chemistry: Structure, Mechanism, and Reactions	M. S. Singh
10.	Intermediates for Organic Synthesis	V. K. Ahluwalia, P. Bhagat, R. Aggarwal, and R. Chandra
11.	Photochemistry and Pericyclic Reactions	Jagdamba Singh and Jaya Singh
12.	Fundamentals of Photochemistry	K. K. Rohatgi and K. K. Mukherjee
13.	Pericyclic Reactions & Organic Photochemistry	S. Dey and N. K. Hazra
14.	Introduction to Organic Photochemistry	J. D. Coyle
15.	Organic Photochemistry	A. Padwa
16.	Principles of Molecular Photochemistry	N. J. Turro, V. Ramamurthy and J. C. Scaiano
17.	Principles and Applications of Photochemistry	Brian Wardle
18.	Stereochemistry with Applications to Organic Reactions	Jagdamba Singh, L. D. S. Yadav, Jaya Singh, and Santosh Singh
19.	Stereochemistry of Organic Compounds	E. L. Eliel and S. H. Wilen
20.	Organic Spectroscopy Principles, Problems and their Solutions	Jagdamba Singh and Jaya Singh
21.	Spectroscopy of Organic Compounds	P. S. Kalsi
22.	Elementary Organic Spectroscopy	Y. R. Sharma
23.	Spectrometric Identification of Organic Compounds	R. M. Silverstein, F. X. Webster, D. J. Kiemle, and D. L. Bryce
24.	Introduction to Spectroscopy	Donald L. Pavia
25.	Organic Spectroscopy (Structures from Spectra Theory, Instrumentation, Interpretation)	William Kemp

Question No-4: The metal present at the active site of the protein carboxypeptidase **A** is

  A. Zn   **B.** Mo   **C.** Mg   **D.** Co

Answer: A. The metal present at the active site of the protein carboxypeptidase **A** is Zn.

Question No-9: Out of the following, the one which is not an excitation source for IR spectrometer is

  A. Tungsten filament lamp   **B.** Nernst glower

  C. Deuterium lamp   **D.** Mercury arc

Answer: D. Among these, mercury arc is not an excitation source for IR spectrometer.

Question No-11: Among the following, the optically inactive compound is

  A. 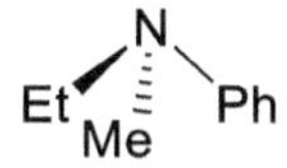   **B.** 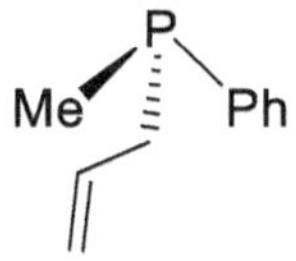   **C.** 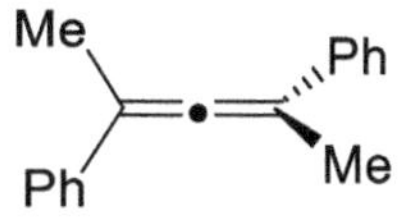   **D.**

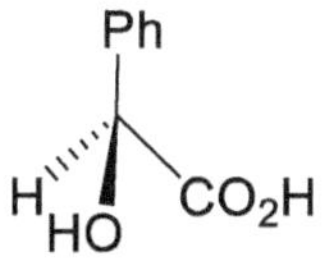

Answer: A. Among these, the optically inactive compound is *N*-ethyl-*N*-methylaniline. The rapid conversion of one enantiomer to another enantiomer *via* planar transition state (rapidly inverts of its configuration; umbrella or Walden inversion).

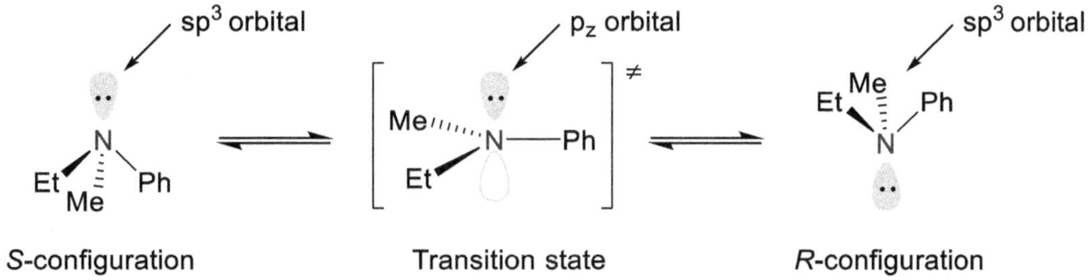

sp^3 orbital p_z orbital sp^3 orbital

S-configuration   Transition state   *R*-configuration

Question No-12: Match the following compounds with their respective classes

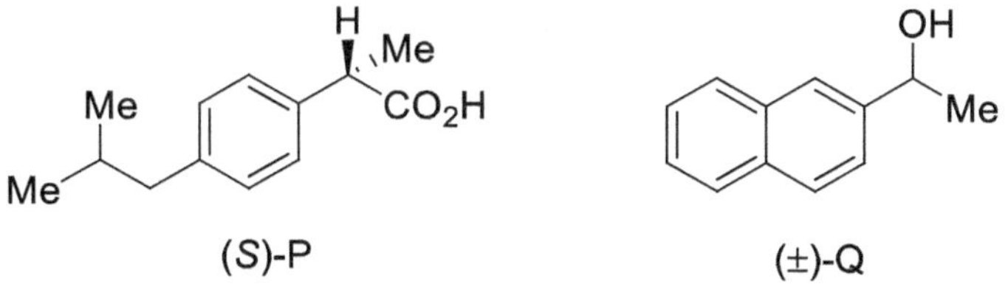

(*S*)-P   (±)-Q

  A. only one enantiomer   **B.** a mixture of diastereomers

  C. a mixture of enantiomers   **D.** only one diastereomer

Answer: B. The reaction on the given compounds **P** and **Q** furnishes a mixture of diastereomers.

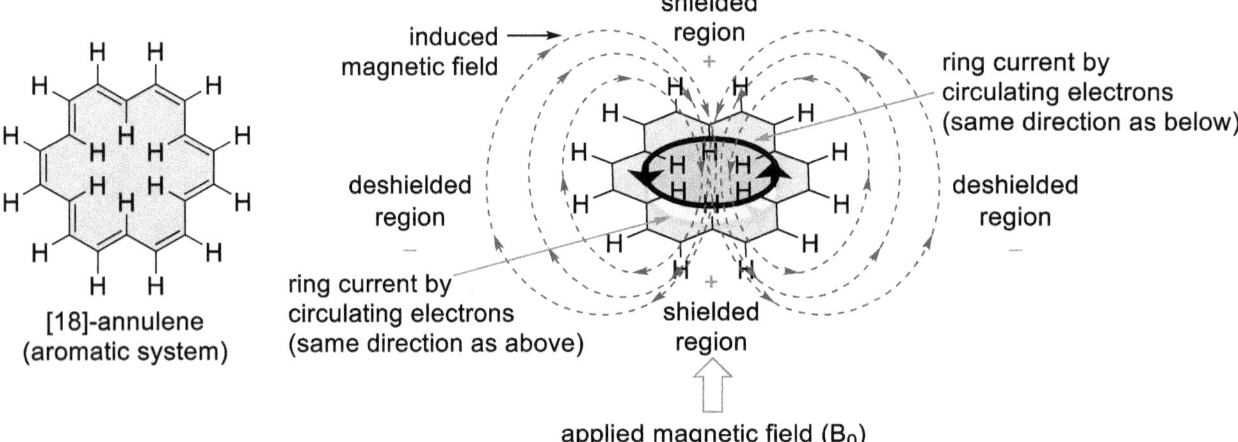

Question No-13: ^{1}H NMR spectrum of [18]-annulene shows

A. Only one peak at δ 7.2 (18 H)   B. Only one peak at δ 5.0 (18 H)

C. Two peaks at δ 9.0 (12 H) and δ -3.0 (6 H)   D. Two peaks at δ 9.0 (6 H) and δ -3.0 (12 H)

Answer: C. ^{1}H NMR spectrum of [18]-annulene shows two peaks at δ 9.0 (12 H) and -3.0 (6 H) ppm. The inner six protons are coming up-fielded (shielding effect) due to the opposite of the induced magnetic field (generated by ring current of the aromatic resonating electrons) with the applied magnetic field whereas outer protons are in parallel to it (coming down-fielded). This phenomenon is known as the Anisotropic effect.

Question No-14: The compound formed on methanolysis of **P** is

P

A.   B.   C.   D.

Answer: D. The compound formed on methanolysis of **P** is 3-chloro-2-methoxytetrahydro-2H-pyran.

Question No-15: The pKa values for the three ionizable groups **X**, **Y** and **Z** of glutamic acid are 4.3, 9.7 and 2.2, respectively.

The isoelectric point for the amino acid is

A.   7.00   B.   3.25   C.   4.95   D.   5.95

Answer: B. The glutamic acid is an acidic one suggesting its isoelectric point to come into the more acidic region (pKa value of 9.7 represents amino acid to be of nature).

The isoelectric point for the glutamic acid = (pKa$_1$ + pKa$_2$)/2 = (4.3 + 2.2)/2 = 3.25.

Question No-16: Bridge-head hydrogen of the conformer of *cis*-decalin is positioned as

[a = axial; e = equatorial]

A.   a, a   B.   e, e   C.   a, e   D.   pseudo-a, pseudo-e

Answer: C. Bridge-head hydrogen of the conformer of *cis*-decalin is positioned as axial and equatorial.

cis-decalin   *trans*-decalin

Question No-17: The major product of the acetylation of salicylic acid with Ac$_2$O/H$^+$ followed by heating with anhydrous AlCl_3 is

Answer: B. The major product of the acetylation of salicylic acid with Ac_2O/H^+ gives Aspirin which further undergoes Fries rearrangement yielding the major product 5-acetyl salicylic acid.

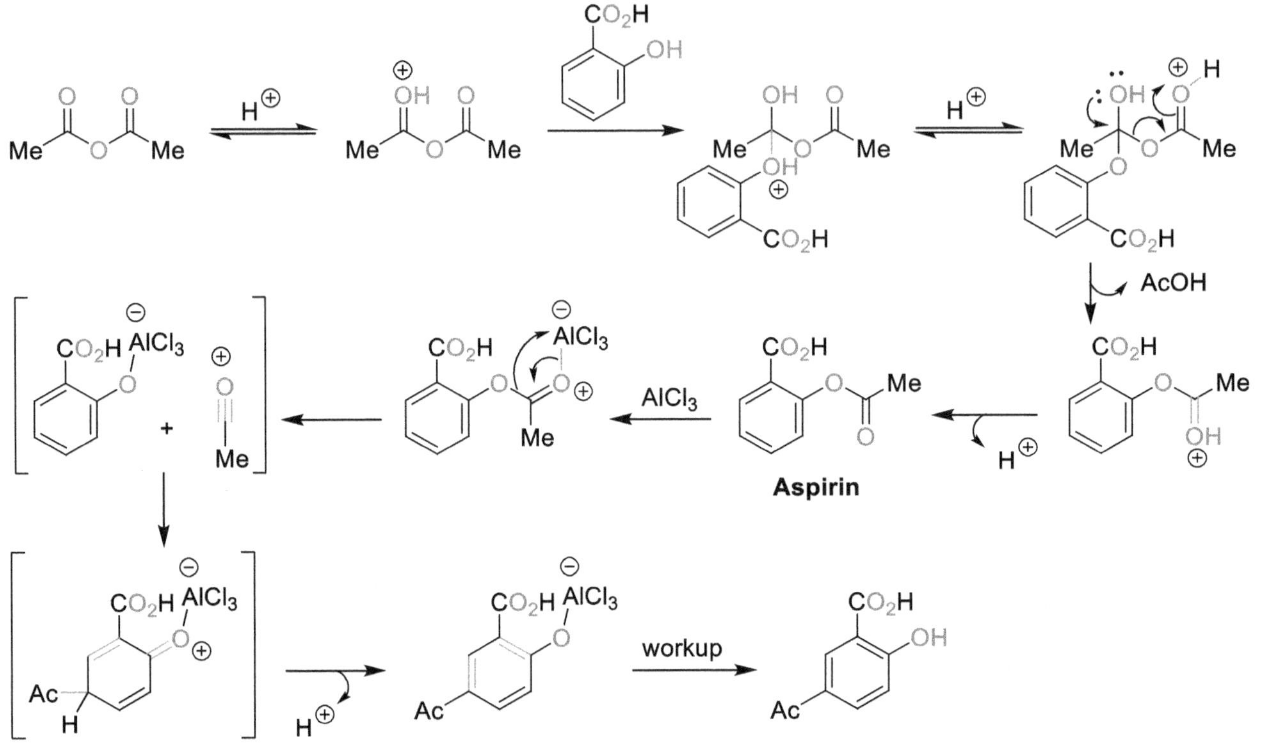

Note. The 3-acylation will be a minor product due to steric crowding.

Question No-18: Order of reactivity of the following dienes **X, Y** and **Z** in the Diels-Alder reaction is

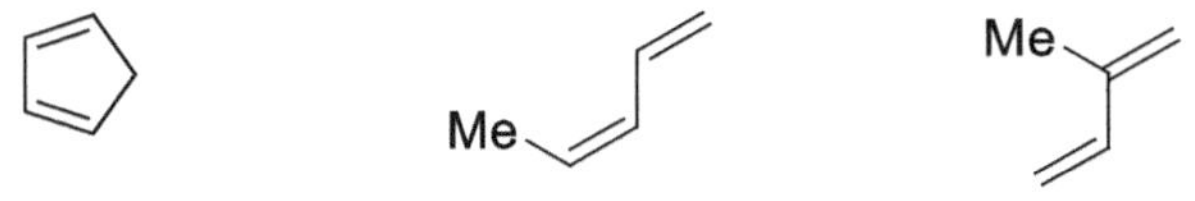

X   Y   Z

Code

A. $X > Z > Y$ B. $Y > X > Z$ C. $Y > Z > X$ D. $X > Y > Z$

Answer: A. Order of reactivity of the following dienes **X, Y** and **Z** in a Diels-Alder reaction is $X > Z > Y$.

Question No-19: The major product **P** of the following reaction is

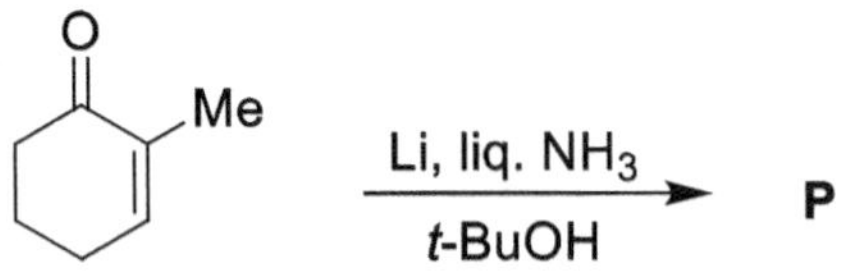

A. (structure: cyclohexanone with Me and NH_2 substituents)

B. (structure: cyclohexanone with Me and O-*t*-Bu substituents)

C. (structure: cyclohexanone with Me substituent)

D. (structure: cyclohexene with O-*t*-Bu and Me substituents)

Answer: C. The major product **P** formed in the given Birch reaction is 2-methylcyclohexanone.

Note. Alcoholic metal-ammonia can also reduce ketone while it cannot reduces its enolate.

Question No-20: Among the following, the most stable isomer for 3-methoxycyclohexanol is

A. (structure: cyclohexane with OMe and HO)

B. (structure: cyclohexane with OH and OMe)

C. (structure: cyclohexane with OMe and OH)

D. (structure: cyclohexane with OH and OMe)

Answer: D. Among these, both the axially oriented –OMe and –OH groups are the most stable isomer for 3-methoxycyclohexanol because of the hydrogen bonding.

less stable conformer   preferred conformer

Questions 41-47: Required matching of items of **Column 1** with the appropriate items in **Column 2**. Choose the correct one from the alternative **A, B, C** and **D**.

Question No-41:

	Column 1		Column 2
P.	Cytochrome-C	(I)	Molybdenum
Q.	Calmodulin	(II)	Potassium
R.	Chlorophyll	(III)	Magnesium
S.	Alcohol dehydrogenase	(IV)	Zinc

(V)	Iron
(VI)	Calcium

Codes

A.	P-V, Q-VI, R-III, S-IV	B.	P-II, Q-III, R-IV, S-VI
C.	P-III, Q-IV, R-VI, S-III	D.	P-IV, Q-V, R-II, S-IV

Answer: A. The correct match of **Column 1** with **Column 2** is P-V, Q-VI, R-III, S-IV.

Question No-42:

	Column 1		Column 2
P.	Atomic absorption	(I)	Transition time
Q.	Chronopotentiometry	(II)	Cell constant
R.	Spectrophotometry	(III)	Coulomb
S.	Conductometry	(IV)	Molar absorptivity
		(V)	Limiting current
		(VI)	Hollow cathode lamp

Codes

A.	P-I, Q-III, R-IV, S-V	B.	P-VI, Q-I, R-IV, S-II
C.	P-II, Q-III, R-IV, S-V	D.	P-V, Q-VI, R-II, S-IV

Answer: B. The correct match of **Column 1** with **Column 2** is P-VI, Q-I, R-IV, S-II.

Question No-43: Require matching of items of **Column 1** with the appropriate items in **Column 2**. Choose the correct one from the alternatives **A**, **B**, **C** and **D**.

	Column 1		Column 2
P.	Wilkinson's catalyst	(I)	*trans*-IrCl(CO)(PPh$_3$)$_2$
Q.	Speier's catalyst	(II)	Hydrosilylation
R.	Water gas shift catalyst	(III)	RhCl(PPh$_3$)$_3$
S.	Zeolite ZSM-5 catalyst	(IV)	Synthetic gasoline
		(V)	Hydroformlylation
		(VI)	Zinc-copper oxide

Codes

A.	P-III, Q-II, R-VI, S-IV	B.	P-I, Q-V, R-III, S-IV
C.	P-V, Q-II, R-VI, S-IV	D.	P-III, Q-VI, R-IV, S-II

Answer: A. The correct match of **Column 1** with **Column 2** is P-III, Q-II, R-VI, S-IV.

Question No-44:

	Column 1		Column 2
P.	Ostwald process	(I)	Manufacture of nickel
Q.	Solvay process	(II)	Manufacture of nitric acid
R.	Mond process	(III)	Manufacture of Na_2CO_3
S.	Frasch process	(IV)	Manufacture of silicones
		(V)	Manufacture of caustic soda
		(VI)	Mining of elemental sulfur

Codes

A. P-I, Q-III, R-II, S-VI

B. P-II, Q-III, R-I, S-VI

C. P-II, Q-I, R-IV, S-V

D. P-III, Q-II, R-V, S-VI

Answer: B. The correct match of **Column 1** with **Column 2** is P-II, Q-III, R-I, S-VI.

Question No-45:

	Column 1 (Compounds)		Column 2 (Carbonyl stretching frequency (cm^{-1}))
P.	cyclohexanone	(I)	1910
Q.	cyclopentanone	(II)	1715
R.	cyclobutanone	(III)	1813
S.	cyclopropanone	(IV)	1650
		(V)	1780
		(VI)	1745

Codes

A. P-I, Q-II, R-III, S-IV

B. P-II, Q-VI, R-V, S-III

C. P-VI, Q-V, R-IV, S-III

D. P-I, Q-V, R-IV, S-III

Answer: B. The correct match of **Column 1** with **Column 2** is P-II, Q-VI, R-V, S-III.

Compounds	cyclohexanone	cyclopentanone	cyclobutanone	cyclopropanone
IR Stretching frequencies	$1715\ cm^{-1}$	$1745\ cm^{-1}$	$1780\ cm^{-1}$	$1813\ cm^{-1}$

Question No-46:

	Column 1		Column 2
P.	Many electron wave function	(I)	Adiabatic demagnetization
Q.	Low temperature	(II)	Slater determinant
R.	Mean speed	(III)	Partition function

S.	Molecular ensemble	(IV)	Maxwellian distribution
		(V)	LCAO-MO
		(VI)	Photoejection

Codes

A. P-IV, Q-I, R-VI, S-III

B. P-II, Q-I, R-IV, S-III

C. P-II, Q-V, R-VI, S-IV

D. P-VI, Q-IV, R-III, S-II

Answer: B. The correct match of **Column 1** with **Column 2** is P-II, Q-I, R-IV, S-III.

Question No-47:

	Column 1		Column 2
	(Spectral Technique)		(Selection rule)
P.	Rotational transition	(I)	$\Delta v = \pm 1$
Q.	Vibrational transition	(II)	$\Delta J = 0$
R.	Electronic transition in atoms	(III)	$\Delta J = \pm 1$
S.	Molecular ensemble	(IV)	$\Delta L = \pm 1$
		(V)	$\Delta m_l = \pm 1$
		(VI)	$\Delta v = 0$
		(VII)	$\Delta L = 0$

Codes

A. P-I, Q-VI, R-VII, S-V

B. P-II, Q-I, R-IV, S-V

C. P-III, Q-I, R-IV, S-V

D. P-I, Q-VI, R-VII, S-V

Answer: C. The correct match of **Column 1** with **Column 2** is P-III, Q-I, R-IV, S-V.

Question No-49: The major product **P** formed in the given

$$\text{(Me, Ph, H, Me, H — OTs)} \xrightarrow[\text{EtOH}]{\text{NaOEt}} \textbf{P}$$

A.

B.

C.

D.

Answer: D. The major product **P** formed in the given elimination is (*E*)-but-2-en-2-ylbenzene.

$$\text{(Me, Ph, H, Me, H — OTs)} \xrightarrow{\text{NaOEt}} \textbf{P} \; + \; \text{EtOH} \; + \; \text{TsONa}$$

Question No-50: The order of reactivity towards acid catalyzed hydrolysis of the following cyclic acetals is

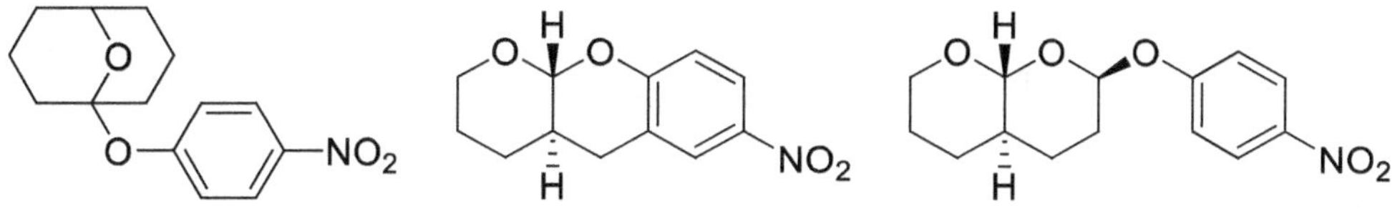

X Y Z

Code

A. $Z > Y > X$ B. $X > Y > Z$ C. $X > Z > Y$ D. $Z > X > Y$

Answer: D. The order of reactivity towards acid-catalyzed hydrolysis of the following cyclic acetals is $Z > X > Y$.

Explanation. In the case of compound **X**, each conformer X_1 and X_2 have one anomeric effect that enhances the rate of hydrolysis than compound **Y** (undergoes normal hydrolysis due to lack of the same).

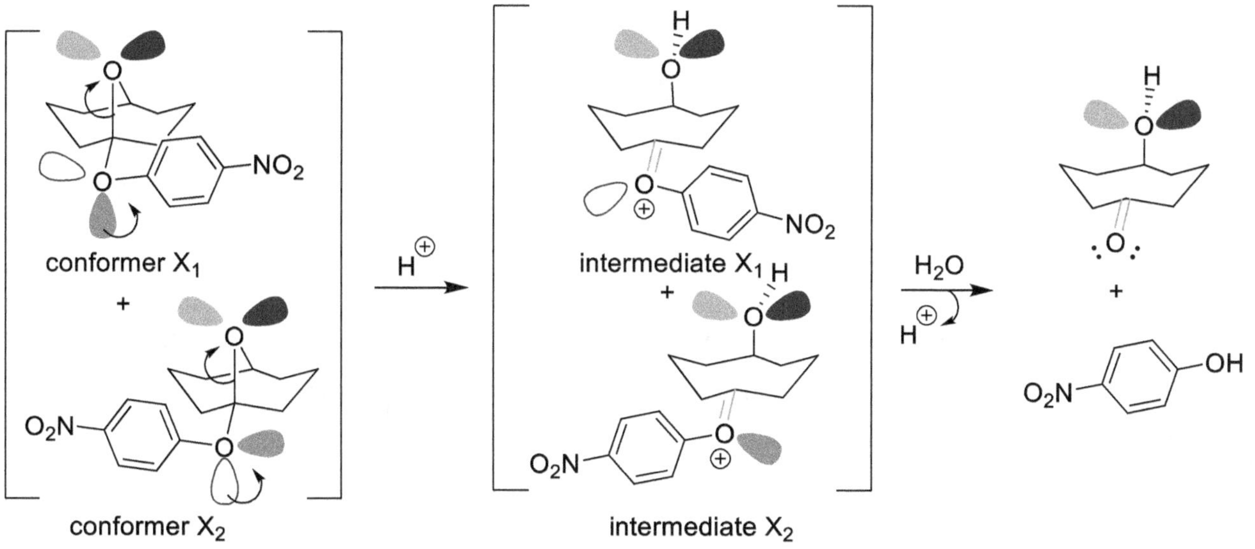

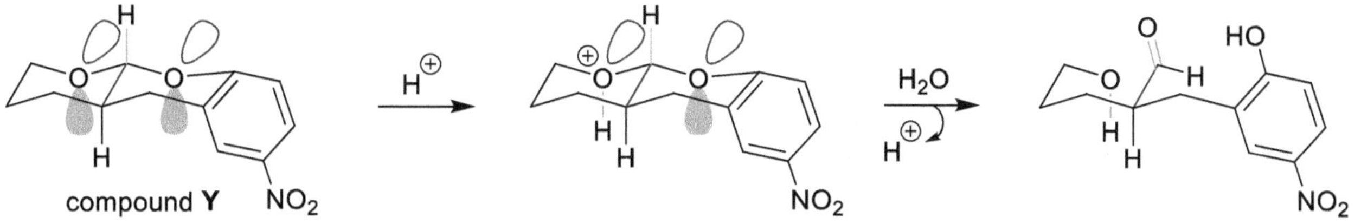

In the case of compound **Z**, each conformer Z_1 and Z_2 have additional anomeric effects *via* phenolic oxygen and tetrahydropyran oxygen that helps in the faster rate of hydrolysis than compound **X**.

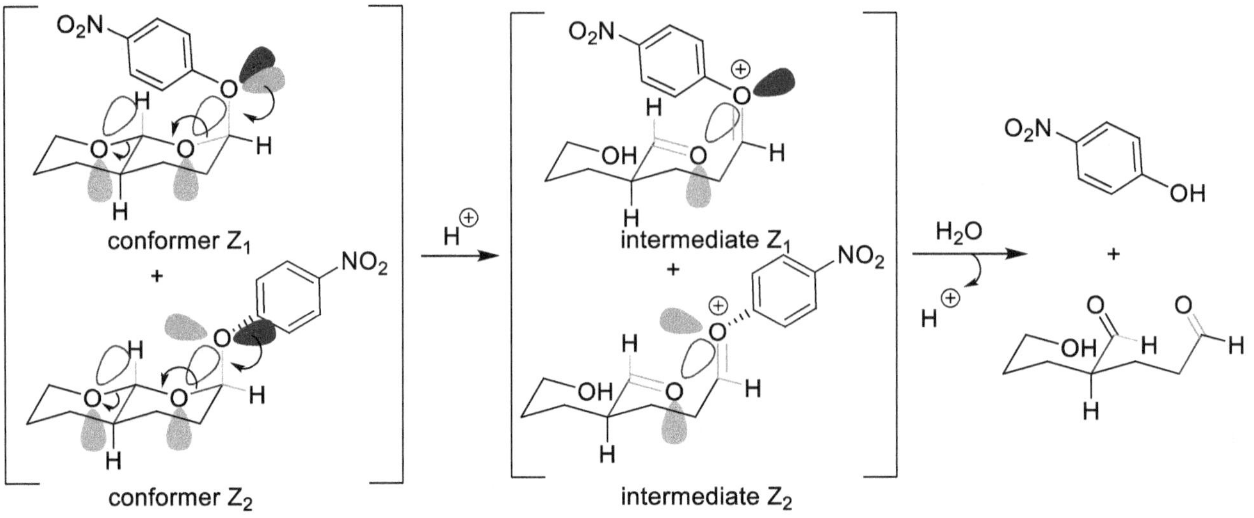

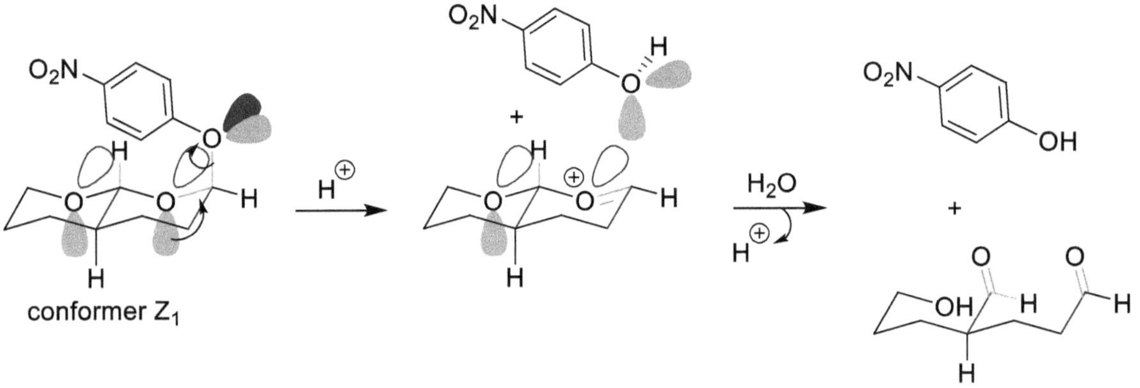

Note. Similarly, conformer $\mathbf{Z_2}$ can also undergo hydrolysis. The compounds $\mathbf{X}$ and $\mathbf{Z}$ can also exhibit conformers $\mathbf{X_3}$ and $\mathbf{Z_3}$, in which lone pair electrons cannot be present in anomeric relation.

Question No-51: The binaphthol (Bnp) is

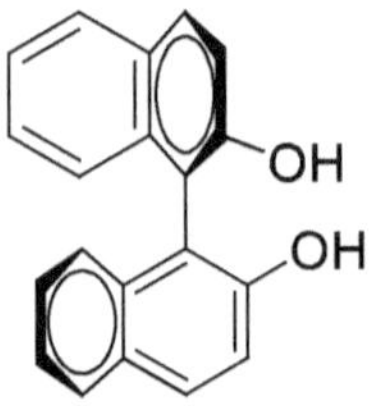

A. An optically active compound with (R)-configuration

B. An optically inactive compound

C. A *meso*-compound

D. An optically active compound with (S)-configuration

Answer: A. The binaphthol (Bnp) is an optically active compound with (R)-configuration.

Question No-52: In the given reactions, identify the correct combination of their major products **P** and **Q**

[LDA = LiN(i-Pr)$_2$]

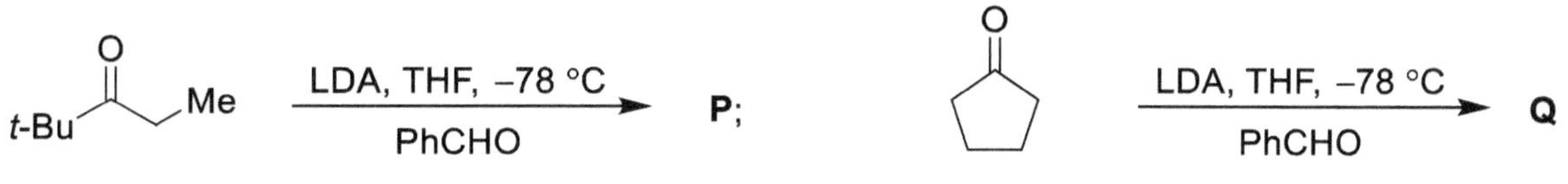

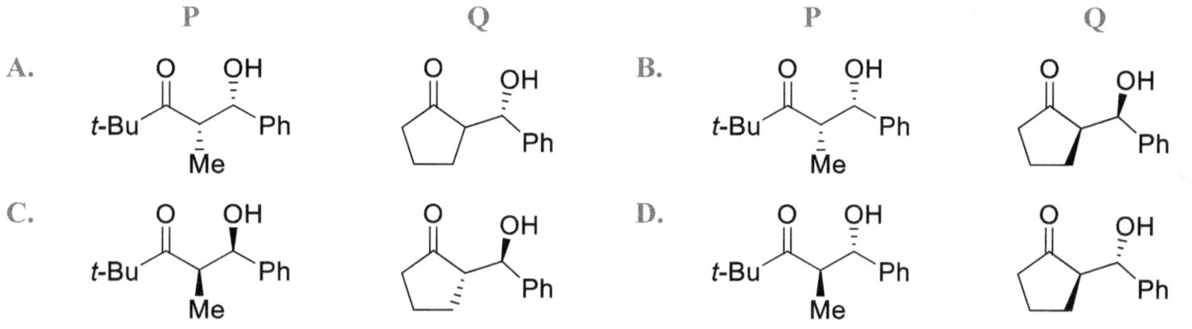

Answer: C. The *tert*-butyl ethyl ketone with LDA offers *Z*-enolate, which on further reaction with benzaldehyde produces *syn*-aldol product i.e.1-hydroxy-2,4,4-trimethyl-1-phenylpentan-3-one (a pair of enantiomer). The stereochemistry can easily be visualized by the Zimmerman-Traxler transition state.

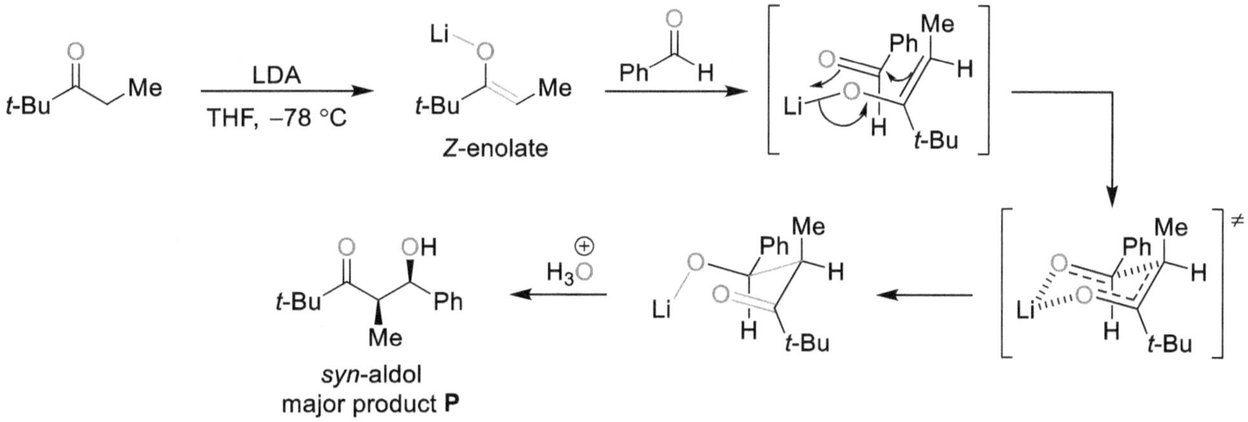

The LDA abstract proton from the cyclopentanone gives *E*-enolate, which further reacts with benzaldehyde to offer *anti*-aldol as the major product i.e. 2-(hydroxy(phenyl)methyl)cyclopentan-1-one (with a pair of enantiomer).

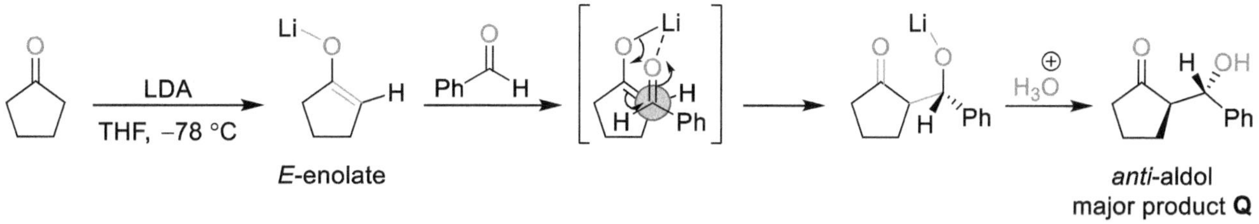

Question No-53: The major stereoisomer obtained in the reaction of (*S*)-2-phenylpropanal with MeMgBr is

A.
$$\begin{array}{c} Me \\ HO\!-\!\!|\!\!-\!H \\ Ph\!-\!\!|\!\!-\!H \\ Me \end{array}$$

B.
$$\begin{array}{c} Me \\ HO\!-\!\!|\!\!-\!H \\ H\!-\!\!|\!\!-\!Ph \\ Me \end{array}$$

C.
$$\begin{array}{c} Me \\ H\!-\!\!|\!\!-\!OH \\ H\!-\!\!|\!\!-\!Ph \\ Me \end{array}$$

D.
$$\begin{array}{c} Me \\ H\!-\!\!|\!\!-\!OH \\ Ph\!-\!\!|\!\!-\!H \\ Me \end{array}$$

Answer: C. The major stereoisomer obtained in the reaction of (*S*)-2-phenylpropanal with MeMgBr is *erythro*-(2*S*,3*S*)-3-phenylbutan-2-ol.

Explanation. Later, I will also be discussing that the diastereoselective reactions based on the Felkin model. Herein, I shall discuss the given diastereoselective reaction using another non-chelate Cram's rule by obeying: (i) the fixed configuration (the chirality) of the given starting compound should not be changed from any projections to Newman projection, (ii) the larger substituents should be anti-parallel to the carbonyl group, (iii) the attack of nucleophile (Grignard reagent *via* major route) should be preferred from the smaller substituent site (H). The attack from the smaller site will offer the major product, but the unfavored attack from the medium substituent site (Me) will offer the minor product.

Note. Felkin-Anh model is an updated version of Cram's rule in the terms of the mode of attack of nucleophile (more than **107°** i.e. *Bürgi–Dunitz angle*), steric electronic repulsion (between carbonyl and nucleophile) and conformer of the product (staggered).

Question No-54: The major product **P** formed in the following reaction is

A.

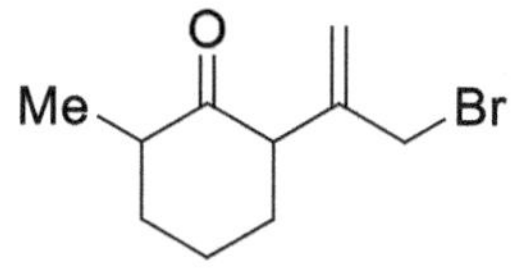

B.

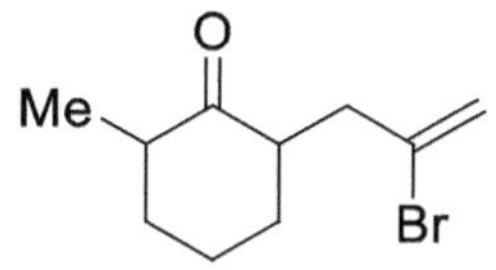

C.

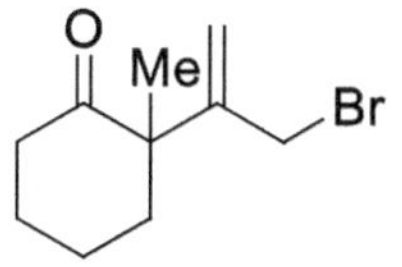

D.

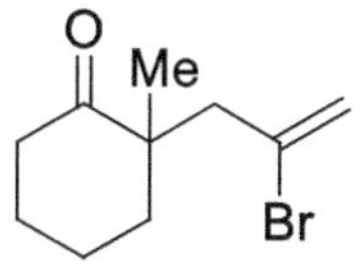

Answer: B. LDA is a hindered base and abstract proton from the less substituted position of the 2-methylcyclohexanone to form an *E*-enolate derivative, which on further allylation using 2,3-dibromoprop-1-ene gives kinetically controlled *trans*-2-(2-bromoallyl)-6-methylcyclohexanone as the major product.

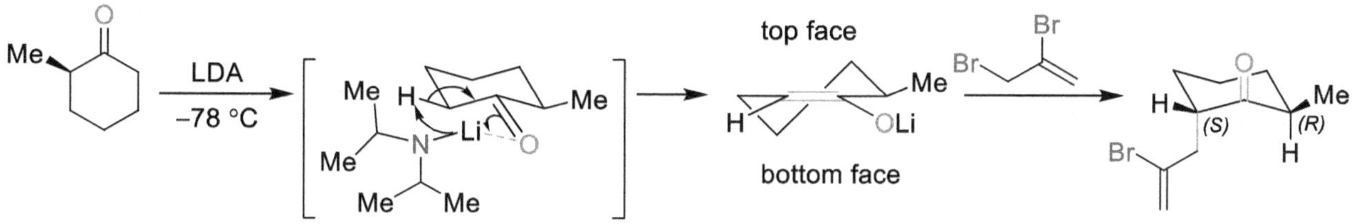

Note. The formation of the product takes place *via* the axial attack approach of the allyl bromide derivative to give a chair conformer (bottom face approach) rather than the more strained and high-energy boat conformer (top face approach).

Question No-55: Iodolactonization of β,γ-unsaturated carboxylic acid **X** with I$_2$ and NaHCO$_3$ gives

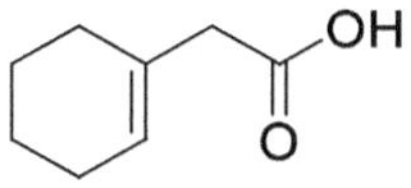

X

A.

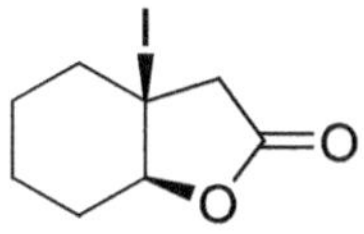

B.

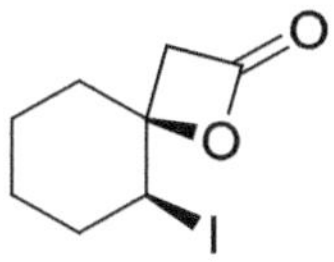

C.

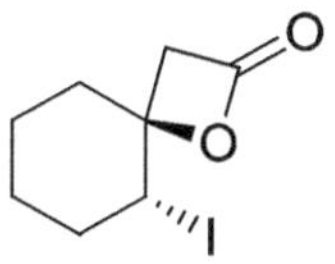

D.

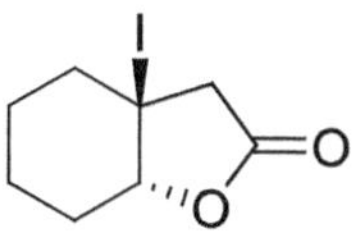

Answer: D. The iodolactonization of β,γ-unsaturated carboxylic acid **X** with I$_2$ and NaHCO$_3$ gives fused bicyclic lactone derivative. As earlier, the bottom face attack on iodine is favored than the top face.

Question No. 56: The major stereoisomer **P** obtained in the following reaction is

$$\xrightarrow[\text{DCM, H}_2\text{O}]{\text{Ph}_3\text{P, I}_2} \quad \textbf{P}$$

A. *t*-Bu

B. *t*-Bu

C. *t*-Bu

D. *t*-Bu

Answer: C. The major stereoisomer **P** obtained in the given reaction is (1*R*,2*R*,4*S*)-4-(*tert*-butyl)-2-iodocyclohexan-1-ol.

$$\text{Ph}_3\text{P} + \text{I}_2 \rightleftharpoons \text{I}{-}\overset{I}{\underset{I}{>}}\text{PPh}_3 \rightleftharpoons \left[\text{I}{-}\overset{\oplus}{\text{PPh}_3}\right]\overset{\ominus}{\text{I}} \xrightarrow[\text{then workup}]{} $$

Question No-57: The major product **P** of the following reaction is

$$\xrightarrow[\text{dark}]{\text{Br}_2} \quad \textbf{P}$$

A.

Me Me Br Br

B.

Br Br Me Me

C.

Br Me Br Me

D.

Me Me Br Br

Answer: D. The major product **P** of the given reaction is 2,4-dibromopentane which is formed *via* an ionic mechanism, whereas the presence of light offers monobrominated product **Q** *via* a free radical mechanism.

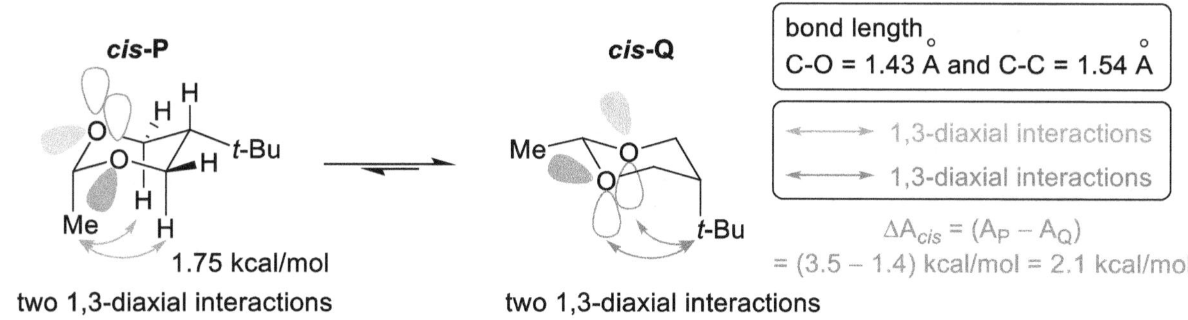

Note. Cyclopropane has a high ring strain (bond angle should be 60°; theoretically) which is drastically lowered by banana bond (bond angle ≈ 104°; experimentally). The bent/banana bond is more stable than π-bond and less stable than σ-bond because it has the hybrid character of both (σ and π) which makes it more reactive than the other cycloalkanes.

Question No-58: *Cis-* and *trans-*2-methyl-5-*t*-butyl-1,3-dioxane each can exist as two conformers as shown below

The preferred conformations for the *cis-* and *trans-*compounds will be

A. P, R   B. Q, S   C. P, S   D. Q, R

Answer: B. For the given compound, the preferred conformations are *cis-***Q** and *trans-***S**.

Explanation. The *cis-*2-methyl-5-*t*-butyl-1,3-dioxane **Q** is a more stable conformer than conformer *cis-***P** (shorter C-O bond length) due to poor 1,3-diaxial strains in the previous one which is lowered by the energy of ≈ 2.1 kcal/mol from (3.5 − 1.4) kcal/mol.

In the case of the *trans-*2-methyl-5-*t*-butyl-1,3-dioxane **R** is a more stable conformer than the *trans-***S** due to the absence of 1,3-diaxial strains.

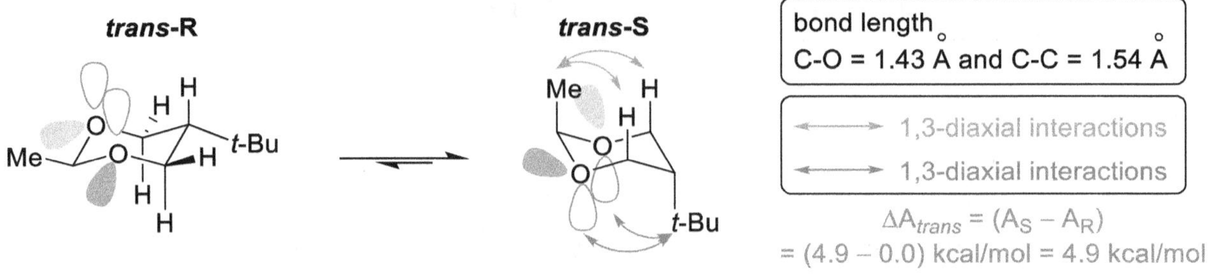

lack 1,3-diaxial interactions
(A_R) = 0.0 kcal/mol

four 1,3-diaxial interactions
(A_S) = (2 × 1.75 + 2 × 0.7) kcal/mol = 4.9 kcal/mol

Hence, the increasing order of the stability of the given conformers = *trans*-**S** < *cis*-**P** < *cis*-**Q** < *trans*-**R**.

Zweifel, G. S.; Nantz, M. H. Stereochemical Considerations in Planning Syntheses. In *Modern Organic Synthesis: An Introduction.* 1st Ed.; W. W. Freeman And Company, New York, 2007; p 40.

Question No-59: The major product **P** of the given reaction is

Answer: D. The major product **P** formed in the given reaction *via* Oxy-Cope rearrangement is (4a*R*,8a*S*)-3,4,4a,7,8,8a-hexahydronaphthalen-2(1*H*)-one.

Note. It is believed that the Oxy-Cope rearrangement (flow of 6π-electrons would be in the same direction) have a faster rate of progression than normal Cope rearrangement due +*R*-effect exerted by the anionic oxide group.

Question No-60: The major product **P** formed in the following photochemical reaction is

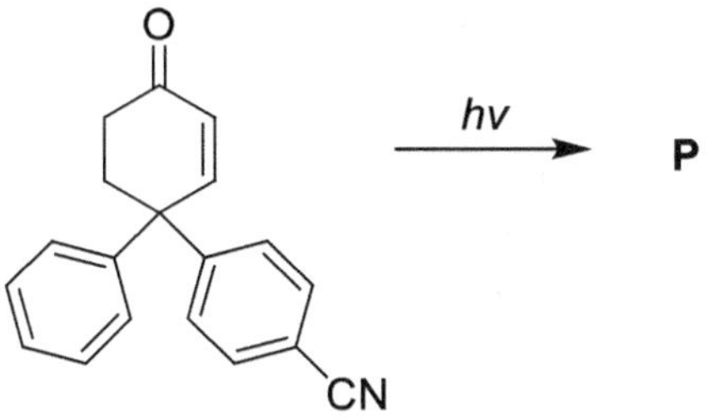

A.

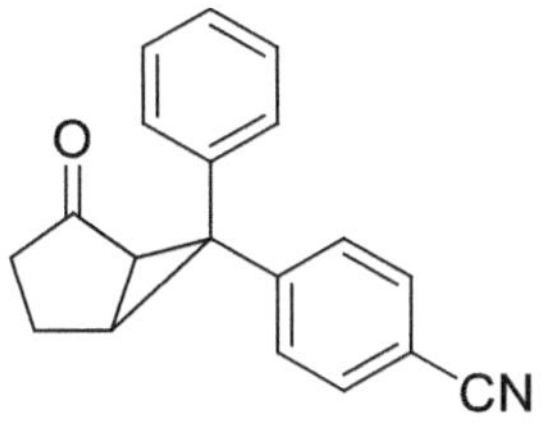

B.

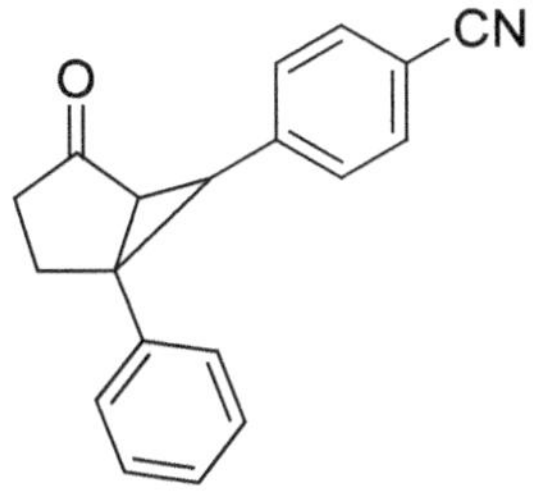

C.

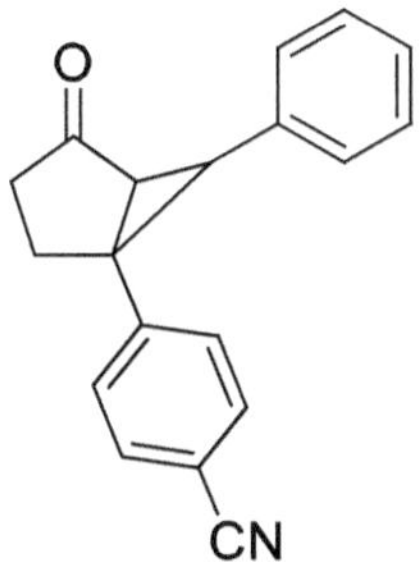

D.

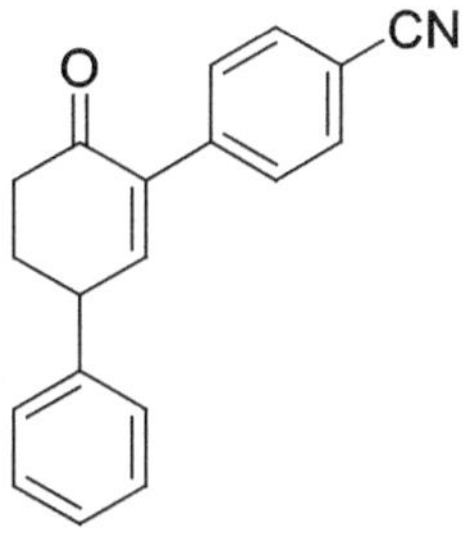

Answer: B. The major product **P** formed in the given photochemical Type B or Di-π-methane rearrangement is 4-(4-oxo-1-phenylbicyclo[3.1.0]hexan-6-yl)benzonitrile in which C4 position **R** can be aryl, vinyl, alkyl, etc. On the other hand, the product **Q** is formed in the case of rotationally constrained Michael enones *via* Lumiketone rearrangement (where, **R** is always an alkyl substituents).

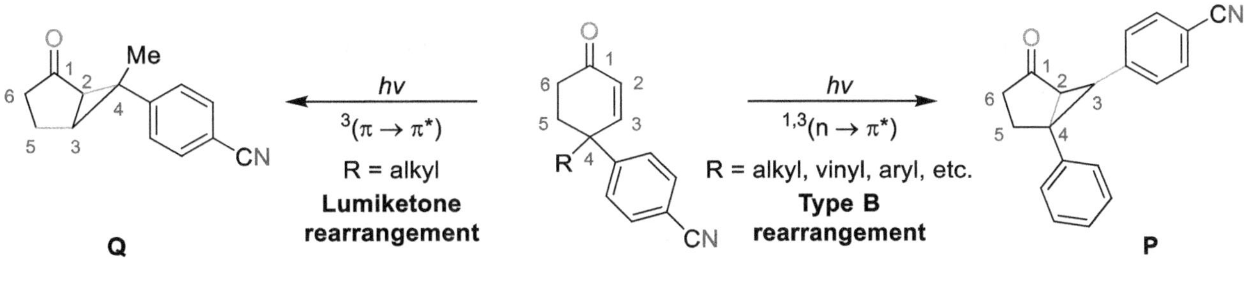

Type B (Di-π-methane) rearrangement of the given compound undergoes n $\rightarrow$ π* transition from S_0 to S_1 state. Further, the spin multiplicity changes from S_1 to T_1 state *via* the non-radiative intersystem crossing (ISC) process. In the next step, the carbon radical associated with double bond conjugation forms 1,4-diradical, followed by carbon radical stabilization by *p*-cyanophenyl group (*via* dative effect) and migration occurs from carbon C4 to C3. Finally, the 1,5-diradical derivative undergoes a radical recombination reaction producing 4-(4-oxo-1-phenylbicyclo[3.1.0]hexan-6-yl)benzonitrile as the major product.

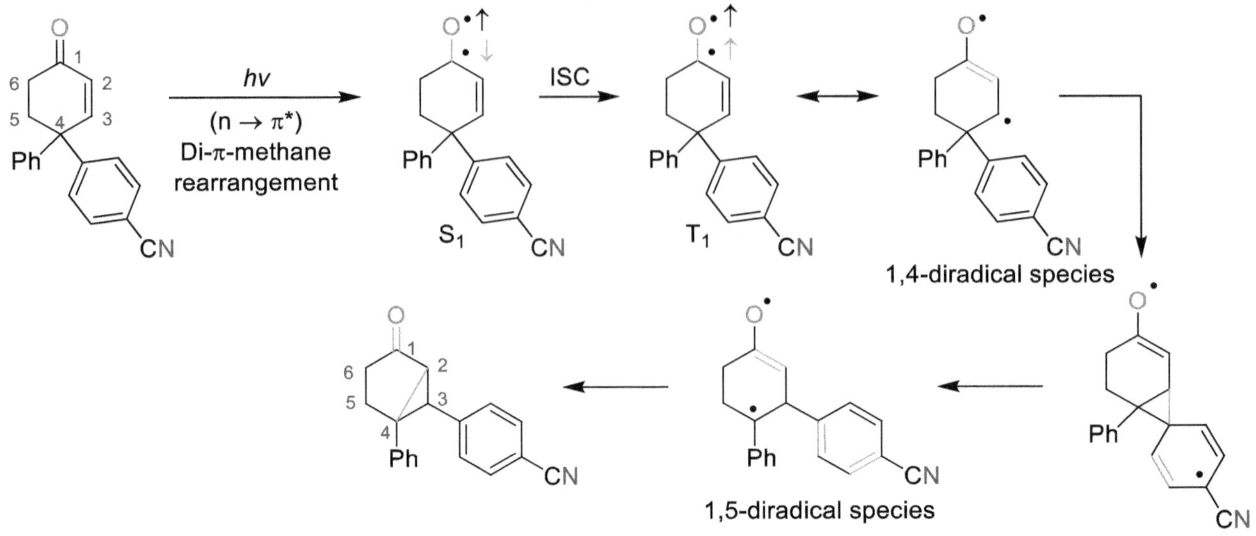

Zimmerman, H. E.; Rieke, R. D.; Scheffer, J. R. *J. Am. Chem. Soc.* **1967**, *89*, 2033-2047.

Reguero, M.; Bernardi, F.; Olivucci, M.; Robb, M. A. *J. Org. Chem.* **1997**, *62*, 6897-6902.

Question No-61: An organic compound having molecular formula $C_8H_{12}O_2$ exhibits the following peaks in IR and ^{1}H NMR spectra.

IR: 1720 cm^{-1}

^{1}H NMR: δ at 6.95 (1H, d, J = 8.5 Hz), 5.90 (1H, d, J = 8.5 Hz), 4.53 (1H, q, J = 6 Hz), 1.41 (3H, d, J = 6 Hz), 1.20 (3H, s), 1.15 (3H, s).

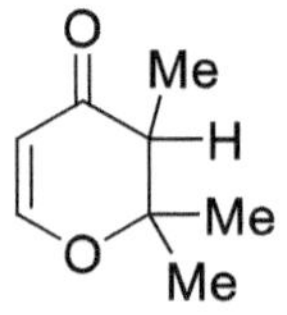

Answer: C. The given IR and ^{1}H NMR spectral data revealed that the compound should be 5,5,6-trimethyl-5,6-dihydro-2*H*-pyran-2-one.

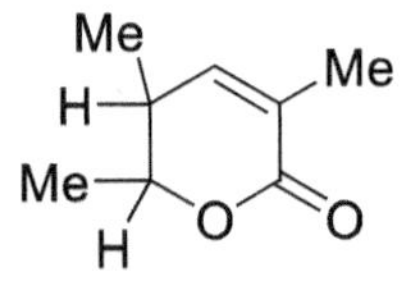

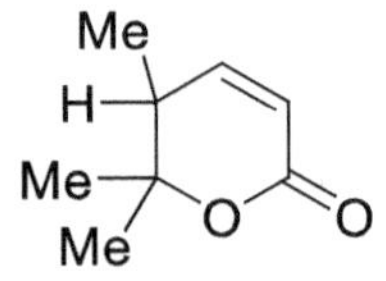

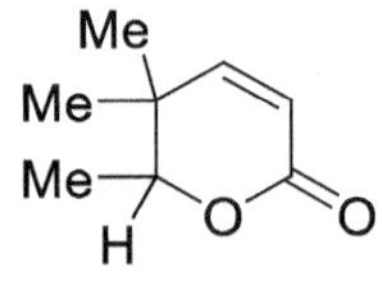

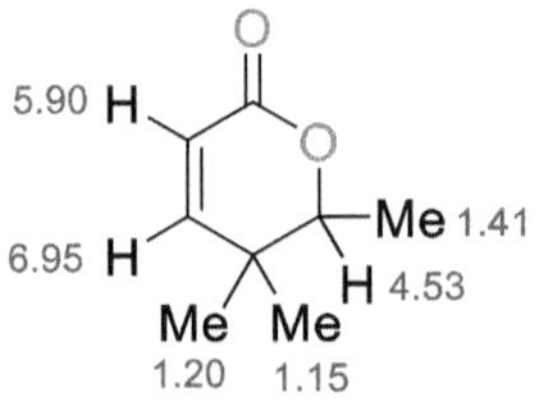

Questions 74 - 75 contain a Statement with a **Reason** and an **Assertion**. For each question, choose the correct answer from the following four choices

Question No-74: Statement: D-Glucose and D-mannose give the same phenylosazone

Reason: Osazone formation results in a loss of the stereocentre at C2 but does not affect other stereocenters

Assertion: D-Glucose and D-mannose are enantiomers

A. Both **Reason** and **Assertion** are correct

B. Both **Reason** and **Assertion** are wrong.

C. **Reason** is correct but **Assertion** is wrong

D. **Reason** is wrong but **Assertion** is correct

Answer: C. Reason is correct but **Assertion** is wrong because D-Glucose and D-mannose are diastereomers (belonging to the category of an epimer) to each other.

Question No-75: Statement: Nucleosides are stable in the dilute base but undergo hydrolysis in dilute acid. **Reason:** Nucleosides have an *N*-glycosidic linkage.

Assertion: *N*-Glycosidic linkage behaves like an *O*-glycosidic linkage which is rapidly hydrolyzed by aqueous acid but stable in aqueous base.

A. Both **Reason** and **Assertion** are correct

B. Both **Reason** and **Assertion** are wrong.

C. **Reason** is correct but **Assertion** is wrong

D. **Reason** is wrong but **Assertion** is correct

Answer: A. Both **Reason** and **Assertion** are correct. Adenine riboside (D-Adenosine) is a class of nucleosides that on mild acidic hydrolysis liberates adenine and ribose sugar.

Linked Answer Q. 81(a) and Q. 81(b)

Question No-81(a): As per Huckel theory, π-electron energy levels of cyclobutadiene are

A. $\alpha + 2\beta, \alpha + \beta, \alpha - \beta, \alpha + 2\beta$

B. $\alpha + 2\beta, \alpha - \beta, \alpha - \beta, \alpha - 2\beta$

C. $\alpha + 2\beta, \alpha, \alpha, \alpha - 2\beta$

D. $\alpha + \beta, \alpha - \beta, \alpha - \beta, \alpha - 2\beta,$

Answer: C. As per Huckel theory, π-electron energy levels of cyclobutadiene are $(\alpha + 2\beta, \alpha, \alpha, \alpha - 2\beta)$.

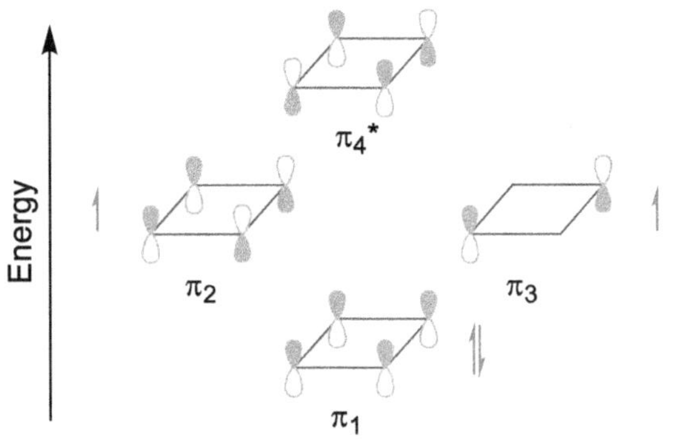

Fig (a). Molecular Orbital Diagram

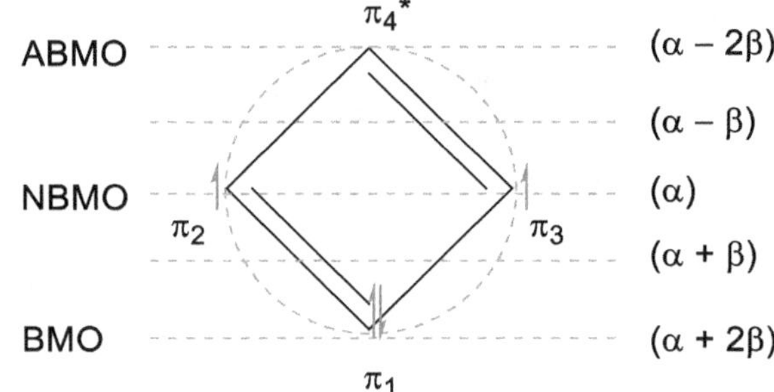

Fig (b). Frost Circle Diagram

Where, BMO = bonding molecular orbital, NBMO = nonbonding molecular orbital and ABMO = antibonding molecular orbital.

Note. The green dotted line in the molecular orbital diagram shows the passing of nodal planes.

Question No-81(b): Given that $\beta = -75$ kJ/mol,

A. paramagnetic and its lowest absorption energy is 150 kJ/mol

B. paramagnetic and its lowest absorption energy is 75 kJ/mol

C. diamagnetic and its lowest absorption energy is 150 kJ/mol

D. diamagnetic and its lowest absorption energy is 75 kJ/mol

Answer: A. From the above diagrams, it is clear that the cyclobutadiene molecule has two NBMOs which consist of two unpaired electrons thus, it is paramagnetic.

The energy of the system 2β [form $(\alpha + 2\beta)$] $= 2(-75$ kJ/mol$) = -150$ kJ/mol (negative sign shows stabilization energy).

Linked Answer Q. 84(a) and Q. 84(b)

Question No-84(a): The major product **P** of the following reaction is

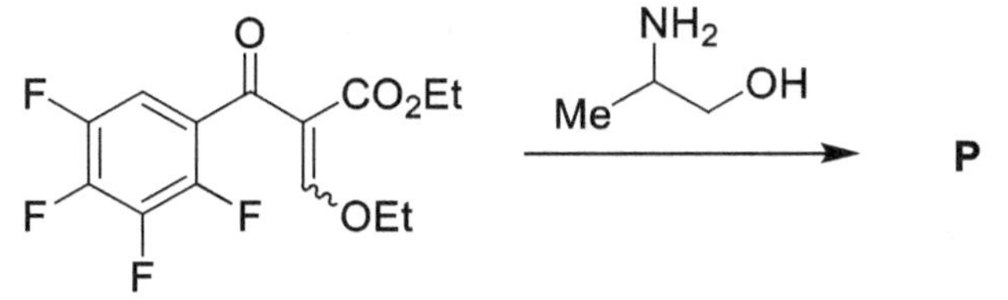

P

A.

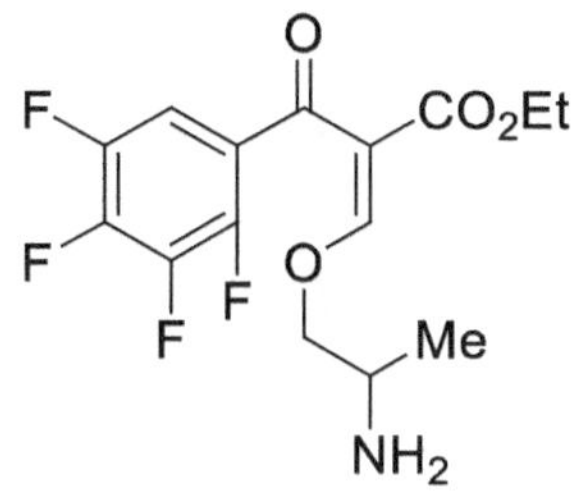

B.

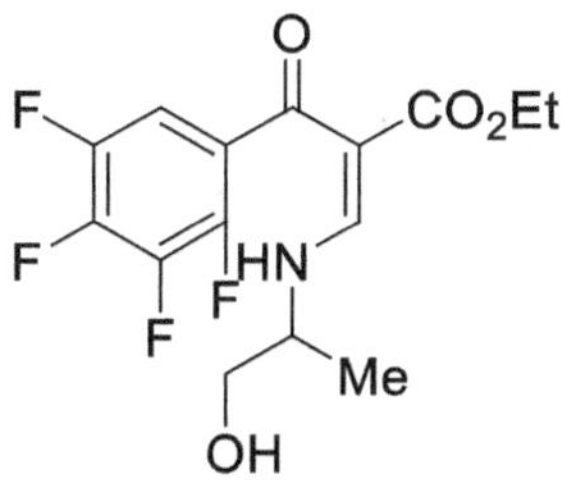

C.

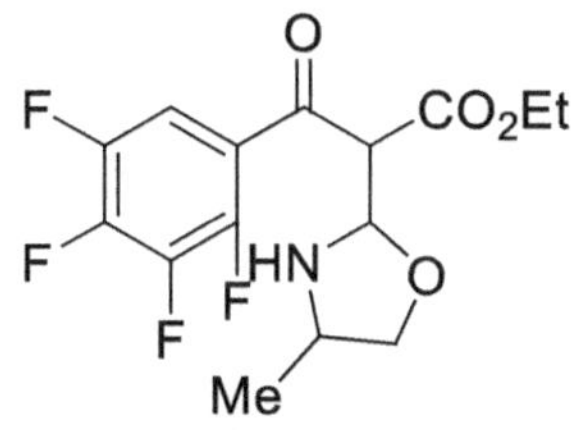

D.

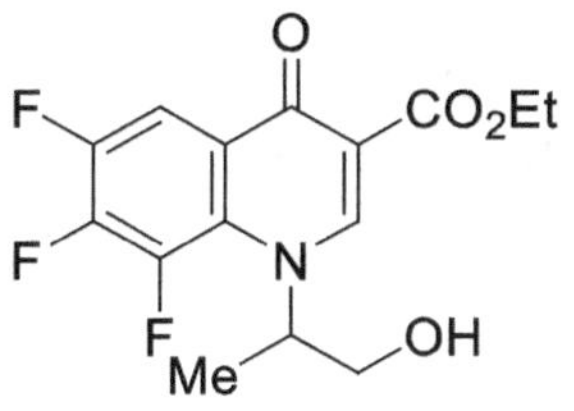

Answer: B. The major product **P** of the given reaction is shown below.

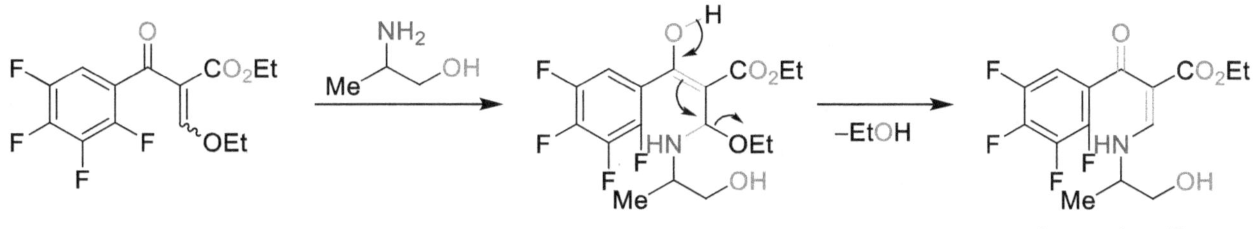

−EtOH

major product **P**

Question No-84(b): Major compound **Q** obtained on the reaction of **P** with NaH in DMF is

A.

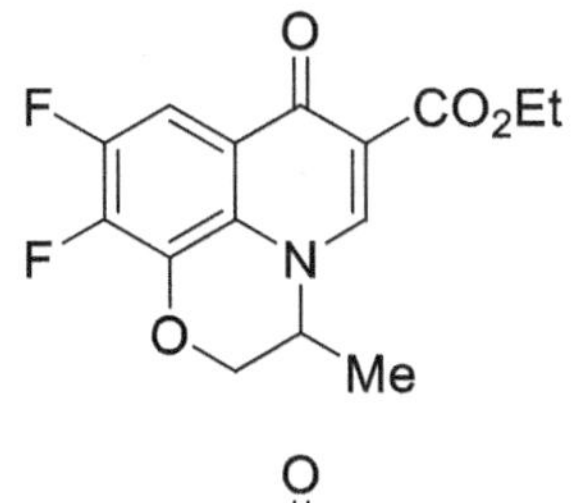

B.

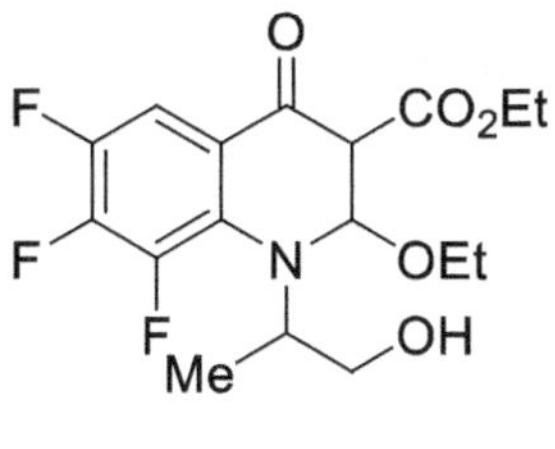

C.

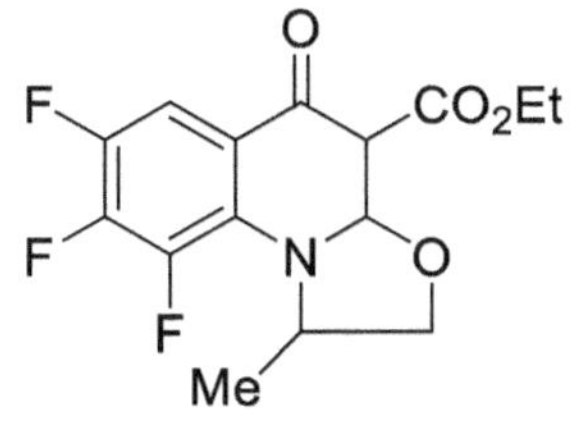

D.

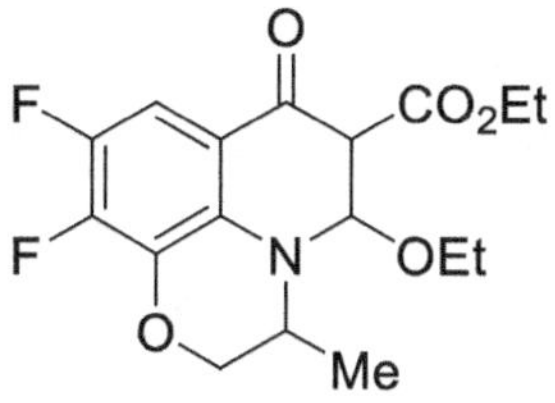

Answer: A. The major compound **Q** obtained on the reaction of **P** with NaH in DMF is shown below.

major product **P**

major product **Q**

Note. The given targeted product **Q** is used as a precursor for the synthesis of antibiotic Levofloxacin derivatives, and is widely used for the treatment of bacterial sinusitis, pneumonia, urinary tract infections, chronic prostatitis, etc.

Mittscher, L. A.; Sharma, P. N.; Chu, D. T. W.; Shen, L. L.; Pernet, A. G. *J. Med. Chem.* **1987**, *30*, 2283–2286.

Linked Answer Q. 85(a) and Q. 85(b)

Question No-85(a): In the following sequence of reactions, the major product **Q** is

$$\text{Fluorobenzene} \xrightarrow[\text{(ii) furan}]{\text{(i) NaNH}_2} P \xrightarrow[\text{(ii) H}^+]{\text{(i) H}_2, \text{Pd/C}} Q$$

A. **B.** **C.** **D.**

Answer: C. Fluorobenzene reacts with sodamide to give benzyne intermediate which undergoes [4+2]-cycloaddition reaction with furan leading to the product **P**. Next, the hydrogenation with H_2/Pd-C and the dehydration reaction furnishes product **Q**.

Question No-85(b): The major product on sulphonation of **Q** with H_2SO_4 at 160 °C is

A — HO_3S—(furan)—Ph

B — (naphthalene)—SO_3H

C — (naphthalene)—SO_3H

D — (furan)—(benzene)—SO_3H

Answer: C. The sulphonation of the prior obtained product **Q** with H_2SO_4 at 160 °C offers thermodynamically controlled product naphthalene-2-sulfonic acid.

kinetically
controlled product

SO_3, H_2SO_4
80 °C

sulphonation of **Q**

SO_3, H_2SO_4
160 °C

thermodynamically
controlled product

Question No-2: In the Huckel model for benzene, the π electronic transitions from the occupied to the unoccupied molecular orbitals do NOT occur at

A. 4β	B. 3β	C. 2β	D. 1β

Answer: C. The benzene molecule obeys the Huckel law of aromaticity by following $(4n + 2)\pi$-electrons and both the π-molecular orbitals (π-MOs) of benzene HOMO (π_2 and π_3) and LUMO (π_4^* and π_5^*) are doubly degenerate.

According to the Frost circles for benzene,

Energy of the system = [bonding electron(s) – antibonding electron(s)] – [n($\alpha + \beta$)] = [2(α - 2β) + 4(α - β)] – [6(α - β)] = [6α - 8β] – [6α - 6β)] = -2β.

Where n = total number of electron(s) and the negative sign indicates the stabilization energy of the system.

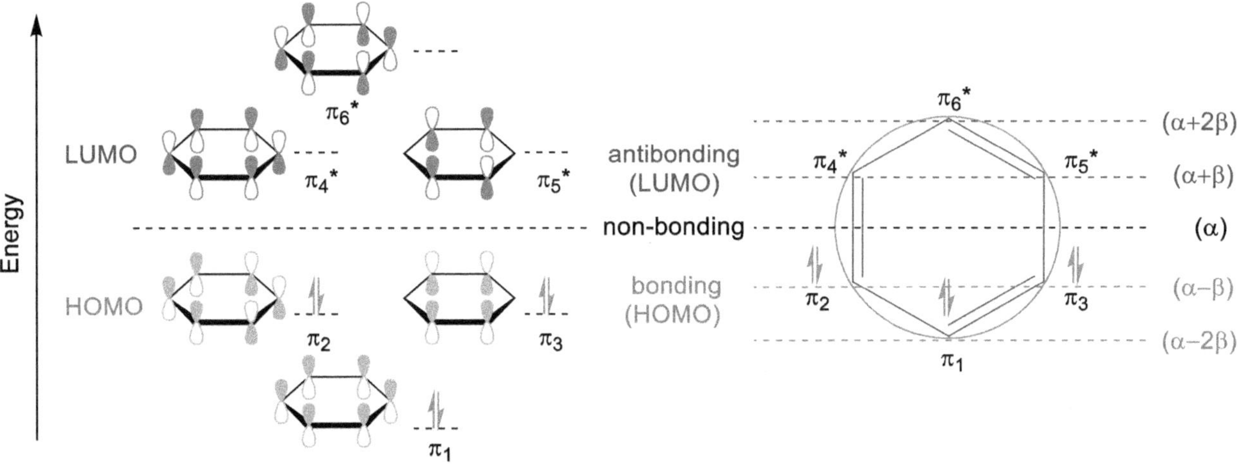

Thus, in the Huckel model for benzene, the π electronic transitions from the HOMO to LUMO <u>don't</u> occur at 2β.

Question No-13: The most stable conformation of the following compound is

C.

D.

Answer: C. The most stable conformation of the given compound is the conformer in which both the methyl groups are axial and the bulkier locking group *t*-butyl at the equatorial position.

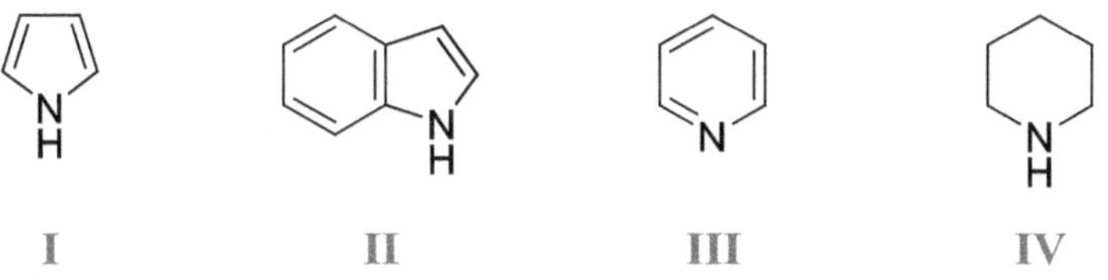

Energy of the **conformer** C_1 = 4 (1,3-diaxial interactions) = 4 × 0.9 kcal/mol = 3.6 kcal/mol.

Energy of the **conformer** C_2 = 2 (1,3-diaxial interactions) + equatorial dimethyl interaction = [(2 × 2.5) + (0.90)] kcal/mol = 5.9 kcal/mol.

Thus, the conformer C_1 is more stable than C_2 because it has 2.3 kcal/mol lower energy.

Question No-14: The correct order of the basicity of the following compound is

| I | II | III | IV |

Code

A. IV > III > II > I B. III > IV > I > II C. IV > III > I > II D. III > IV > II > I

Answer: A. The nitrogen atom of pipyridine is more basic than pyridine because it has less s-character (sp³-hybridization: 25%) in compression to pyridine (sp²-hybridization: 33.3%). Obviously, indole is less basic than pyridine as its lone pair electron is not available to get donated, and pyrrole is least basic because it is more aromatic than indole.

Thus, the correct order of the basicity of the given compound is **IV > III > II > I.**

Question No-15: Match the following compounds with their respective classes

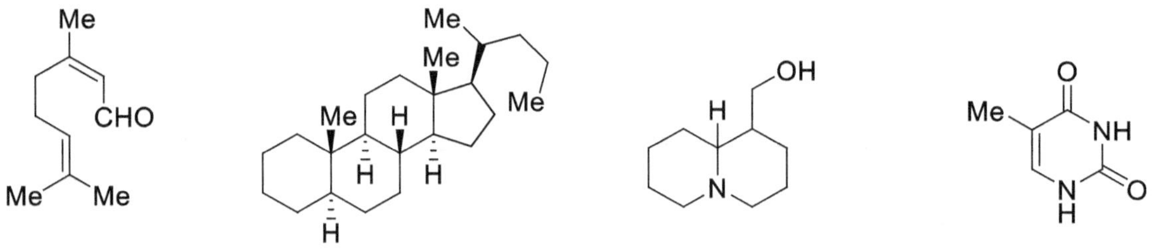

I II III IV

Code

A. I: steroid; II: terpenoid; III: alkaloid; IV: DNA base

B. I: terpenoid; II; steroid; III: alkaloid; IV: DNA base

C. I: terpenoid; II: steroid; III: DNA base; IV: alkaloid

D. I: steroid; II: terpenoid; III: DNA base; IV: alkaloid

Answer: B. The correct match of the given compounds with their respective classes is I: terpenoid; II; steroid; III: alkaloid; IV: DNA base.

Question No-16: Which of the following absorptions is shown by 1,3-butadiene in its UV absorption spectrum recorded in *n*-hexane (ε_{max} is the molar absorptivity)?

A. λ_{max} 217 nm (ε_{max} = 21,000) B. λ_{max} 214 nm (ε_{max} = 210)

C. λ_{max} 253 nm (ε_{max} = 50,000) D. λ_{max} 250 nm (ε_{max} = 500)

Answer: A. The absorptions of 1,3-butadiene in its UV absorption spectrum recorded in *n*-hexane at λ_{max} 217 nm (ε_{max} = 21,000).

Question No-17: Which of the following compounds is expected to show a sharp singlet for one of its protons at $\delta \geq 8$ ppm in ^{1}H NMR spectrum, given that this signal remains unaffected on shaking the solution thoroughly with D_2O?

A. MeCOOH B. MeCONHPh C. *n*-$C_6H_{13}C{\equiv}CH$ D. *n*-$C_6H_{13}CHO$

Answer: D. In ^{1}H NMR spectrum, the aldehyde peak at $\delta \geq 8$ ppm remains unaffected on shaking the sample solution in D_2O.

Note. Amide (-CONH-) and carboxylic acid (-CO_2H) undergo a proton exchange reaction with D_2O.

Question No-18: The most appropriate starting materials for one-step synthesis of the compound (I) are

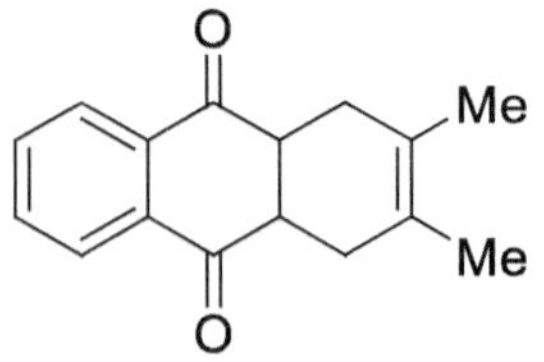

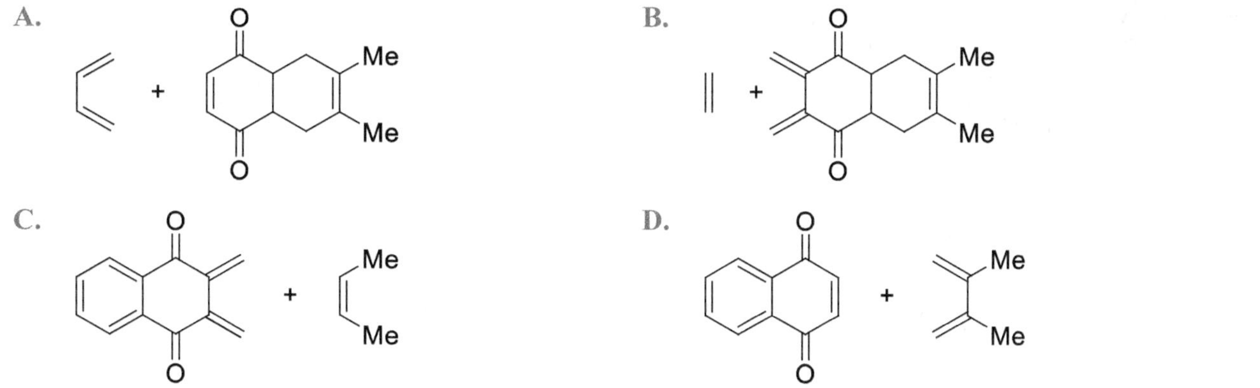

A.

B.

C.

D.

Answer: D. The most appropriate starting materials for one-step synthesis of the compound (I) are 1,4-naphthoquinone and 2,3-dimethylbuta-1,3-diene.

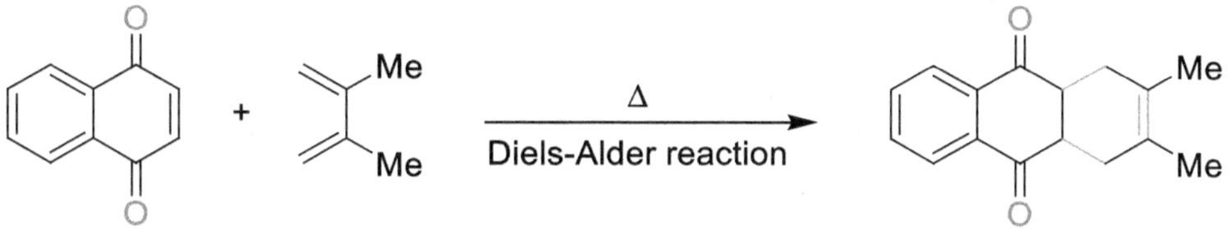

Diels-Alder reaction, Δ

Question No-19: Identify the major product **P** in the following reaction

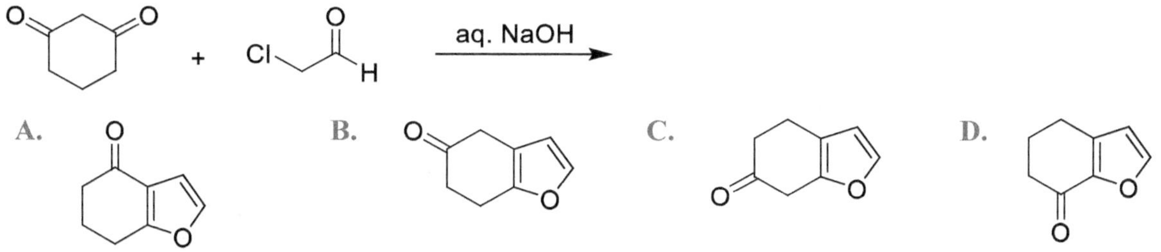

aq. NaOH

A.

B.

C.

D.

Answer: A. The given reaction is similar to the Feist–Benary synthesis of furan derivative. The major product **P** formed in the given reaction is 6,7-dihydrobenzofuran-4(5H)-one.

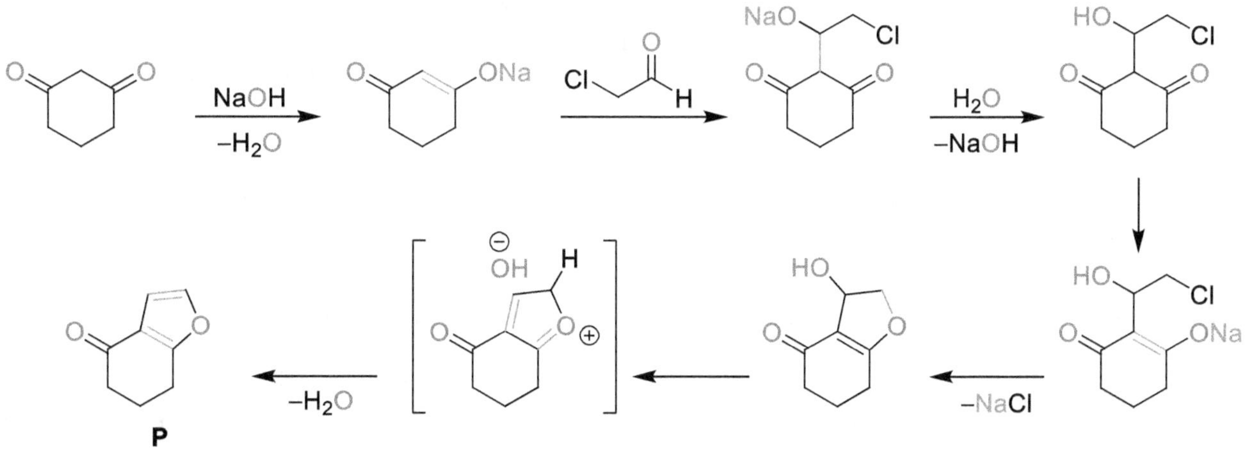

Question No-20: Which of the statement is CORRECT about the mechanism of the following reaction

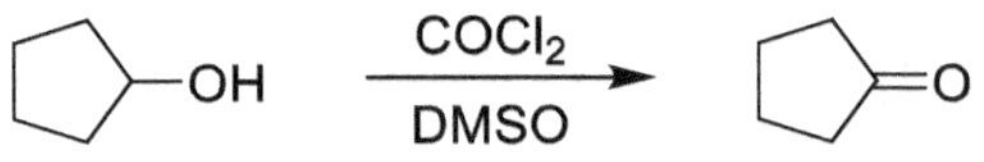

$$\text{cyclopentanol} \xrightarrow[\text{DMSO}]{\text{COCl}_2} \text{cyclopentanone}$$

Codes

A.

DMSO reacts with alcohol initially to give [cyclopentyl–O–S$^+$(Me)Me], which reacts with $(COCl)_2$.

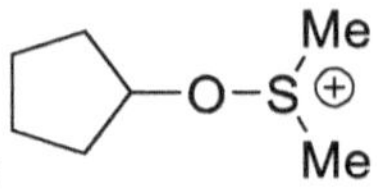

B.

$(COCl)_2$ reacts with the alcohol initially to give [cyclopentyl–Cl], which reacts with DMSO.

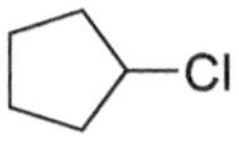

C.

DMSO reacts with $(COCl)_2$ initially to give [Cl—S$^+$(Me)Me], which reacts with the alcohol.

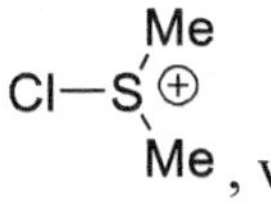

D.

$(COCl)_2$ reacts with DMSO initially to give [Cl—O—S$^+$(Me)Me], which reacts with the alcohol.

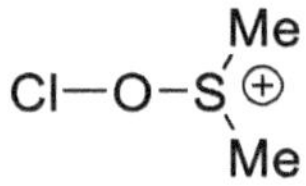

Answer: C. In Swern oxidation, dimethyl sulfoxide reacts initially with oxalyl chloride to give chlorodimethylsulfonium chloride, which further reacts with the alcohol in the presence of nitrogenous organic base furnishing oxidized product carbonyl derivative.

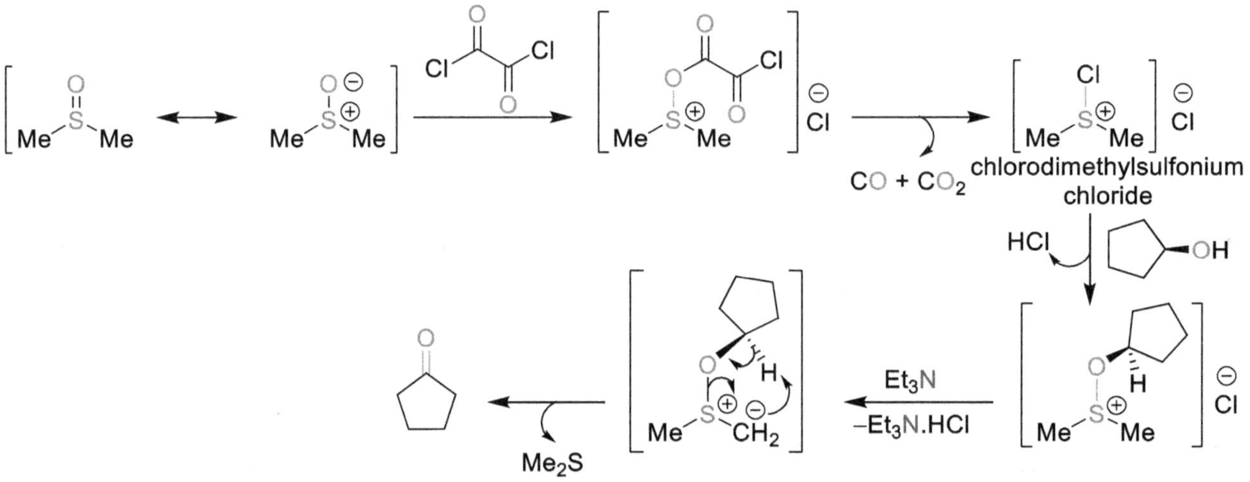

Note. The reaction of alcohol with chlorodimethylsulfonium chloride in the absence of base gives chlorocyclopentane *via* S_N2-reaction.

Question No-47: The metal ion that is expected to shift the C1-methylene group in heptanol from 2 to 10 ppm in ^{1}H NMR is

A.   Eu(III)   B.   Tl(III)   C.   Al(III)   D.   Sc(III)

*Answer: A.** The metal ion that is expected to shift the C1-methylene group in heptanol from 2 to 10 ppm in ^{1}H NMR is Eu(III).

Question No-48: When Al_4C_3 and Mg_2C_3 react with H_2O, then major products formed respectively, are

A. ethyne and ethane

B. methane and propyne

C. propane and propene

D. methane and propene

Answer: B. When Al_4C_3 and Mg_2C_3 react with H_2O, then major products are formed methane and propyne, respectively.

$$Al_4C_3 + 12H_2O \longrightarrow 4Al(OH)_3 + 3CH_4$$

$$Mg_2C_3 + 4H_2O \longrightarrow Mg(OH)_2 + Me\text{-}C\equiv CH$$

Question No-49: The arrangement of sulfur in zinc blende and wurtzite structures, respectively, are,

A. hexagonal close packing and cubic close packing

B. cubic close packing and hexagonal close packing

C. simple cubic packing in both the structures

D. hexagonal close packing in both the structures

Answer: B. The arrangement of sulfur in zinc blende and wurtzite structures are cubic close packing and hexagonal close packing, respectively.

Question No-54: In the proton decoupled ^{13}C and ^{31}P NMR spectra of $Me_3P=O$, the number of lines observed, respectively, are

A. two and one   B. one and two   C. three and one   D. two and two

Answer: D. In the proton decoupled ^{13}C and ^{31}P NMR spectra of $Me_3P=O$, the number of lines for each nuclei is two because the nuclear spin value of both isotopes i.e. ^{13}C and ^{31}P NMR is ½.

Note. In the case of trimethyl phosphine oxide ^{31}P exhibits two signals due to the presence of the three equivalents similar environment of carbons nuclei.

Question No-55: Among, RO^-, $AsMe_3$, ROR', CN^-, RCO_2^-, SCN^- the set of ligands with good π-acceptor nature are

A. RO^-, RCO_2^-, SCN^-

B. RO^-, RCO_2^-, $AsMe_3$

C. $AsMe_3$, CN^-, SCN^-

D. RO^-, ROR', RCO_2^-

Answer: C. Among these, the set of ligands with good π-acceptor nature are $AsMe_3$, CN^-, SCN^-.

Note. $AsMe_3$ also acts as a π-acceptor due to the presence of the vacant d-orbital.

Question No-56: Identify the correct stereochemical relationship amongst the hydrogen atoms H_a, H_b and H_c in the following molecule

A. H_a and H_b : enantiotopic

B. H_a and H_b : diastereotopic

C. H_a and H_c : enantiotopic

D. H_b and H_c : diastereotopic

Answer: B. Among these, the correct stereochemical relationship for the given molecule is that H_a and H_b as well as H_a and H_c are diastereotopic while H_b and H_c are enantiotopic protons.

Diastereotopic relationship between H_a and H_b

Diastereotopic relationship between H_a and H_c

Enantiotopic relationship between H_b and H_c

Question No-57: The configurations of the reactant and the product in the following reaction, respectively, are

A. R, R

B. R, S

C. S, R

D. S, S

Answer: D. The configurations of the reactant and the product in the given reaction are S and S, respectively. The reaction proceeds through S_N2-reaction (inversion of stereocenter), not *via* S_N1 because the carbocation will be destabilized by the electron-withdrawing group (ester).

$$D \overset{CO_2Me}{\underset{H}{\overset{|(S)}{-}\!\!-\!Br}} \quad \xrightarrow[\text{EtOH}]{\text{KCN}} \quad NC \overset{CO_2Me}{\underset{H}{\overset{|(S)}{-}\!\!-\!D}}$$

Question No-58: Match the reactions of some *p*-substituted benzene derivatives (a)–(d) given in **List I** with the Hammett's ρ-values (i)-(iv) in **List II** and identify the correct match

<table>
<tr><td colspan="2" align="center">List I</td><td colspan="2" align="center">List II</td></tr>
<tr><td>a.</td><td>$ArCH_2Cl \xrightarrow[70\ ^\circ C]{\text{aq. acetone}} ArCH_2OH + HCl$</td><td>i.</td><td>+8.50</td></tr>
<tr><td>b.</td><td>$ArCH_2-CO_2H \underset{25\ ^\circ C}{\overset{H_2O}{\rightleftharpoons}} ArCH_2-CO_2^- + H^+$</td><td>ii.</td><td>+1.00</td></tr>
<tr><td>c.</td><td>$Ar-Cl \xrightarrow[50\ ^\circ C]{\text{MeONa/MeOH}} Ar-OMe + Cl^-$</td><td>iii.</td><td>+0.49</td></tr>
<tr><td>d.</td><td>$Ar-CO_2H \underset{25\ ^\circ C}{\overset{H_2O}{\rightleftharpoons}} Ar-CO_2^- + H^+$</td><td>iv.</td><td>-1.88</td></tr>
</table>

Codes

A.	a-i, b-iv, c-iii, d-ii	B.	a-iv, b-i, c-ii, d-iii
C.	a-i, b-ii, c-iv, d-iii	D.	a-iv, b-iii, c-i, d-ii

Answer: D. The correct match of **List I** with **List II** is a-iv, b-iii, c-i, d-ii.

http://research.cm.utexas.edu/nbauld/unit4.htm

Question No-59: On heating with dilute sulfuric acid, naphthalene-1-sulfonic acid gives predominantly

A.	natphthalene	B.	naphthalene-2-sulfonic acid
C.	1-naphthol	D.	2-naphthol

Answer: B. On heating with dilute sulfuric acid, naphthalene-1-sulfonic acid (kinetically controlled product) gets converted into naphthalene-2-sulfonic acid (thermodynamically controlled product).

Question No-60: Predict the major product **P** in the following reaction

HNO$_2$ → **P**

A.

B.

C.

D.

Answer: A. Semipinacol rearrangement of the given compound in the presence of nitrous acid (HNO$_2$) produces major product 2,2-dimethylheptan-4-one **P**.

Question No-61: Select the correct classification in the following reaction, from the option I to IV given below,

I.   Conrotatory electrocyclic reaction

II.   Disrotatory electrocyclic reaction

III.   Valence isomerization

IV.   [$_x4_s + \pi2_a$] cycloaddition reaction

Codes

A.   I and III   B.   II and IV   C.   II and III   D.   I and IV

Answer: C. The correct statements for the given degenerate Cope rearrangement can undergo disrotatory electrocyclic reaction as well as valence isomerization.

Question No-62: Identify the major product **P** in the following reaction

$\dfrac{hv}{t\text{-BuOH}}$ → **P**

A. 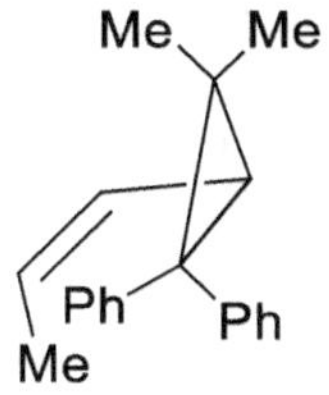   Me Me   B. 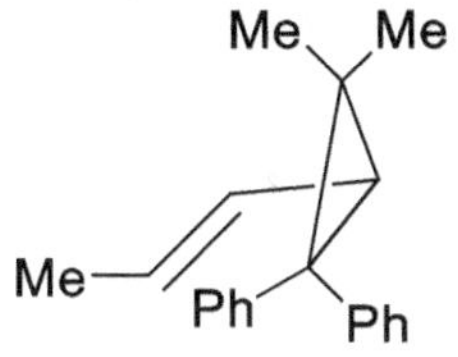   Me Me   C. 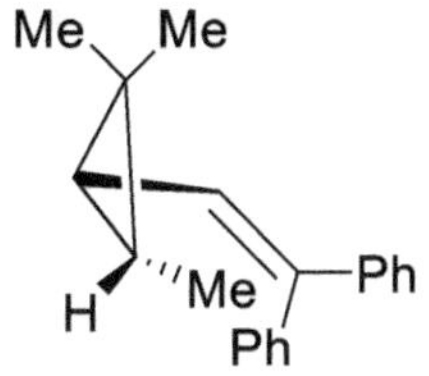   Me Me   D. 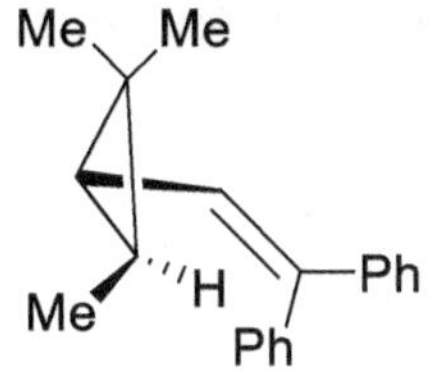   Me Me

Answer: A. The given reaction is an example of photochemical Di-π-methane rearrangement, in which the formed major product **P** is (Z)-(2,2-dimethyl-3-(prop-1-en-1-yl)cyclopropane-1,1-diyl)dibenzene.

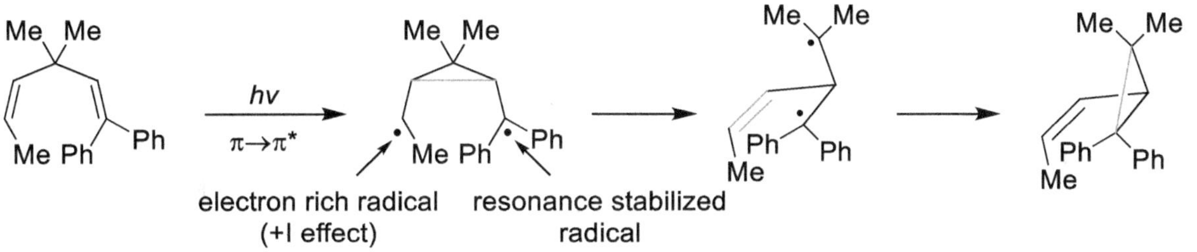

Question No-63: Identify the major products **P** and **Q** in the following reactions from the list of compounds I to IV.

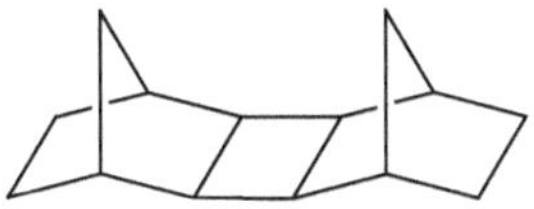

I 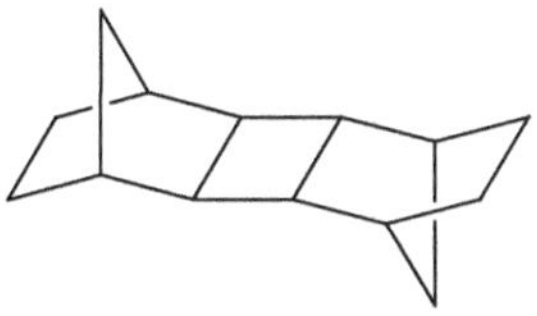   II 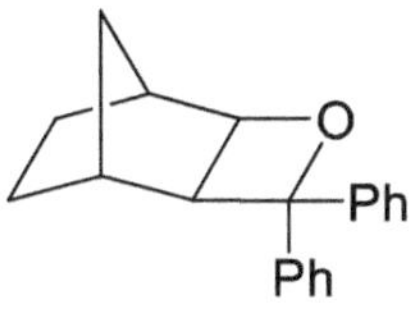   III 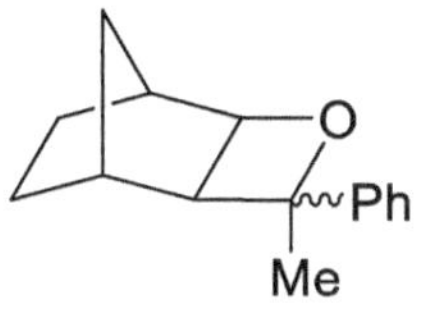   IV

Codes

A.   P : I and Q : II   B.   P : I and Q : III   C.   P : IV and Q : II   D.   P : IV and Q : III

Answer: B. The photochemical reaction of norbornene in the presence of sensitizer acetophenone gives norbornene dimer **P**. The photochemically excited acetophenone molecule transfers its energy to norbornene and comes back to the ground state (due to the large energy difference between the triplet state to the ground state; E_T = 74 kcal/mol). On the other hand, in presence of benzophenone produces oxetane derivative **Q** via the Paternò-Büchi reaction because it has less energy difference (E_T = 69 kcal/mol) than acetophenone.

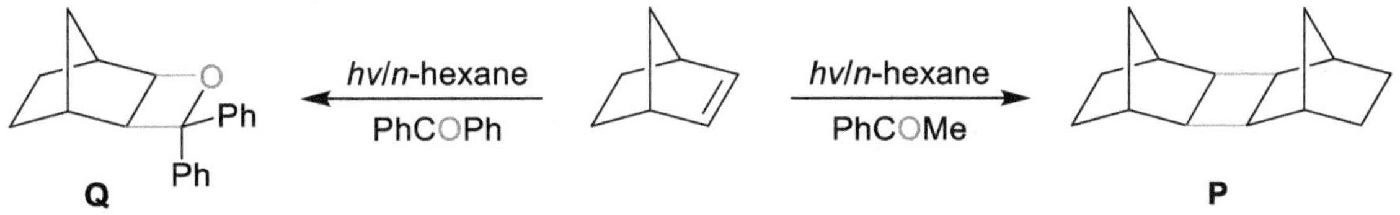

Question No-64: Identify the major product **P** in the following reaction,

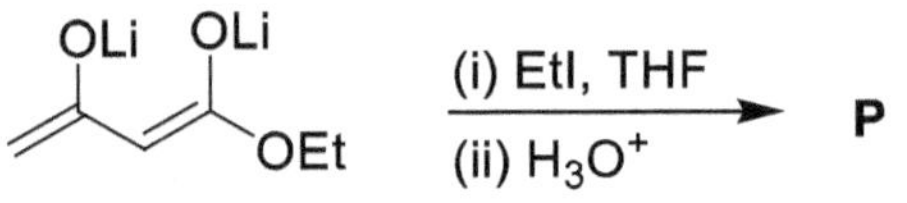

A. 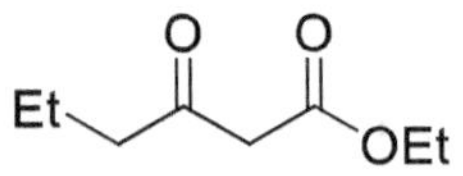 B. 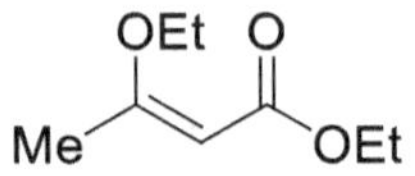 C. 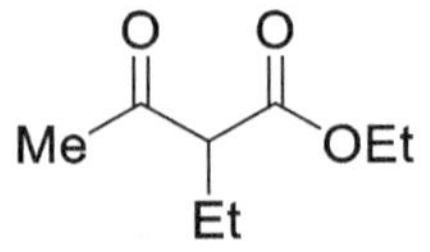 D. 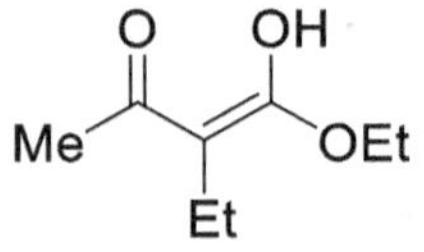

Answer: C. The thermodynamically controlled major product **P** formed in the given reaction is ethyl 2-ethyl-acetoacetate.

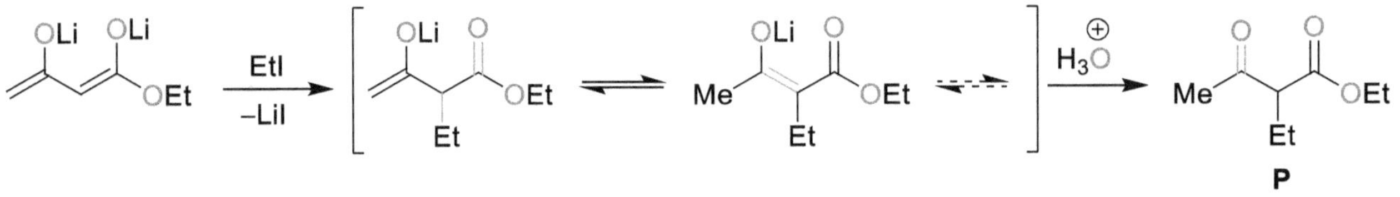

Question No-65: Identify the correct set of stereochemical relationships amongst the following monosaccharides I-IV

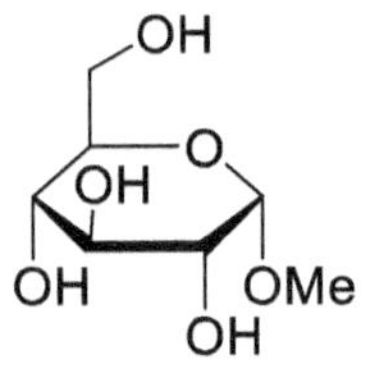
I

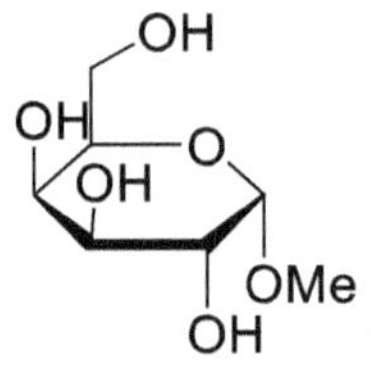
II

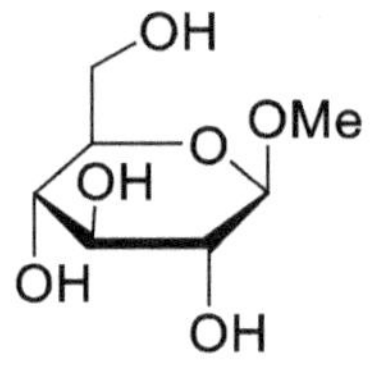
III

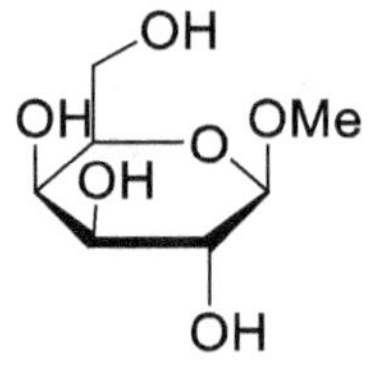
IV

Codes

A. I and II are anomers; III and IV are epimers
B. I and III are epimers; II and IV are anomers
C. I and II are epimers; III and IV are anomers
D. I and III are anomers; I and II are epimers

Answer: D. The correct stereochemical relationships amongst the given monosaccharides **I** to **IV**: I and III are anomers (stereochemistry difference at the acetal/ketal carbon), and I and II are epimers (stereochemistry difference at any one of the carbon).

Note. Anomers can also be considered as epimers but *vice-versa* is not true (thus option **B** is also true).

Question No-66: Select the correct pair of statements.

I. Complementary strands run antiparallel in a double-stranded DNA.
II. The triplet codons, represented by the genetic code, are expressed by ribonucleic acids.
III. t-RNA carries the genetic information to the site of DNA replication.
IV. A nucleoside contains ribose or deoxyribose and phosphate constituents only.

Codes

A.   I and II   B.   II and III   C.   III and IV   D.   I and IV

***Answer: A.** The correct pair of statements are: (i) complementary strands run antiparallel in a double-stranded DNA and (ii) triplet codons represented by the genetic code, are expressed by ribonucleic acids.

Question No-67: Match the compounds in **List-I** with the stretching frequencies (cm^{-1}) of the principal functional groups given in **List-II**.

	List-I		List-II
1.	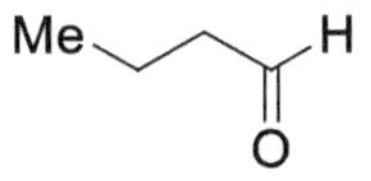 Me‒CH$_2$‒CHO	(i)	2240
2.	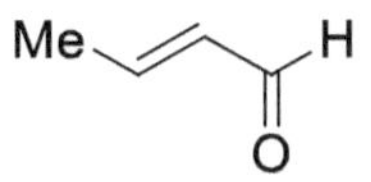 Me‒CH=CH‒CHO	(ii)	1795
3.	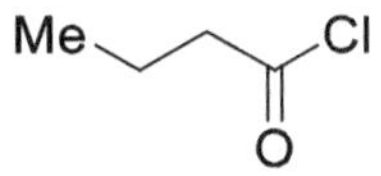 Me‒CH$_2$‒COCl	(iii)	1750
4.	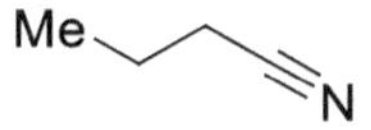 Me‒CH$_2$‒CH$_2$‒C≡N	(iv)	1725
		(v)	1695

Codes

A.   1-iii, 2-iv, 3-i, 4-v   B.   1-iii, 2-iv, 3-ii, 4-v   C.   1-iv, 2-v, 3-ii, 4-i   D.   1-iv, 2-iii, 3-v, 4-i

Answer: C. The correct match of List I with List II is: 1-iv, 2-v, 3-ii, 4-i.

Question No-68: Pick the major product **P** in the following reaction,

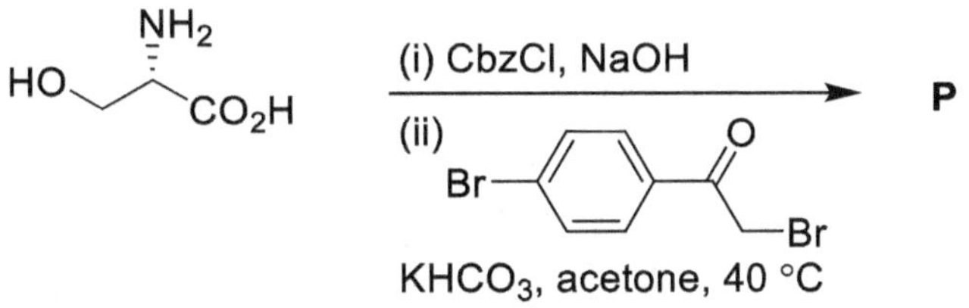

HO‒CH$_2$‒CH(NH$_2$)‒CO$_2$H

(i) CbzCl, NaOH
(ii) 4-bromophenacyl bromide (Br‒C$_6$H$_4$‒CO‒CH$_2$‒Br)
KHCO$_3$, acetone, 40 °C → **P**

[CbzCl is PhCH$_2$OCOCl]

A.   CbzO‒CH$_2$‒CH(NH$_2$)‒CO‒O‒C$_6$H$_4$‒CO‒CH$_2$‒Br

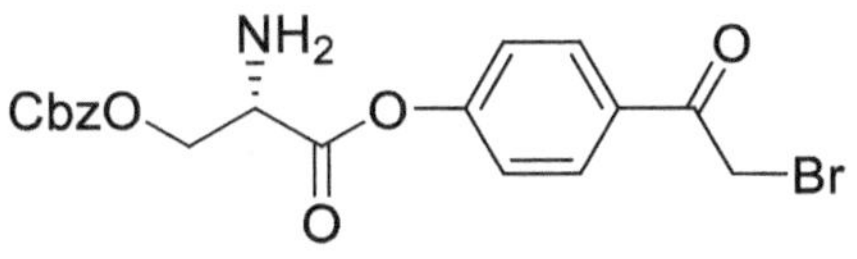

B.   CbzO‒CH$_2$‒CH(NH$_2$)‒CO‒O‒CH$_2$‒CO‒C$_6$H$_4$‒Br

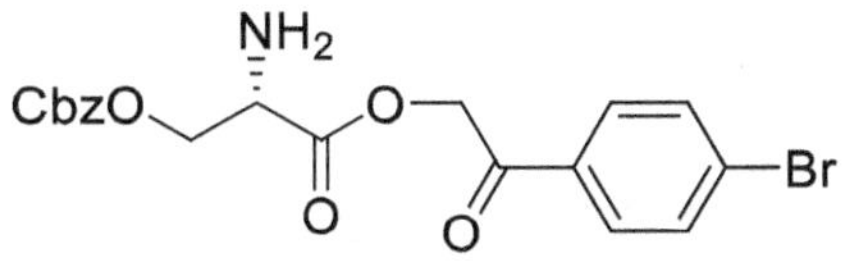

C.   HO‒CH$_2$‒CH(NHCbz)‒CO‒O‒C$_6$H$_4$‒CO‒CH$_2$‒Br

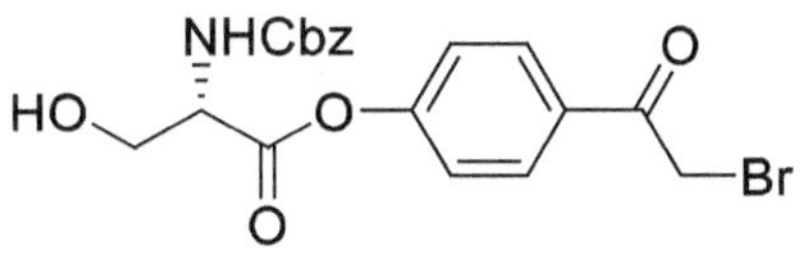

D.   HO‒CH$_2$‒CH(NHCbz)‒CO‒O‒CH$_2$‒CO‒C$_6$H$_4$‒Br

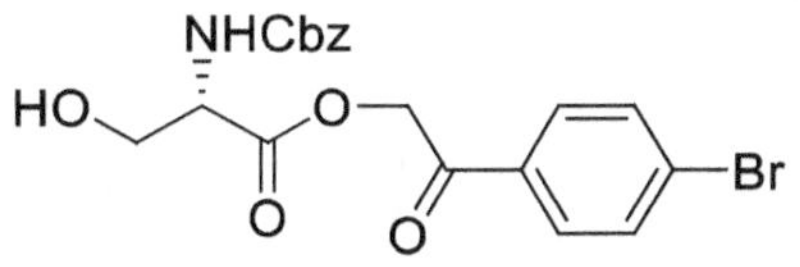

Answer: D. The benzyl chloroformate is a selective reagent for amines and it is resistant to strong acid. The chemoselective amine protection of serine followed by S$_N$2-reaction using 4-bromophenacyl bromide in basic media furnishes 2-(4-bromophenyl)-2-oxoethyl ((benzyloxy)carbonyl)-L-serinate **P** as the major product.

Question No-69: Pick the major product **P** in the following reaction,

A. B. C. D.

Answer: C. The major product **P** formed in the given reaction is 1-(1-vinylcyclohexyl)ethan-1-one.

Question No-70: Identify the major **P** in the following two-step reaction,

$$\text{(i) Cl}_3\text{COCl, Et}_2\text{O, rt}$$
$$\text{(ii) 90\% HNO}_3, -50\ °C$$

A

O_2N — pyrrole — CCl_3 (with C=O)

B

O_2N — pyrrole — CCl_3 (with C=O)

C

O_2N — pyrrole — CCl_3 (with C=O)

D

pyrrole — CCl_3 (with C=O), O_2N

Answer: B. Pyrrole reacts with trichloroacetyl chloride at room temperature and furnishes 2-acetylpyrrole, which on further reaction with nitric acid produces 2,2,2-trichloro-1-(4-nitro-1*H*-pyrrol-2-yl)ethan-1-one as the major product.

$$\text{pyrrole} \xrightarrow[\text{Et}_2\text{O, rt}]{\text{Cl}_3\text{COCl}} \text{2-(trichloroacetyl)pyrrole} \xrightarrow[-50\ °C]{90\%\ \text{HNO}_3} \mathbf{P}$$

Note. The reaction of pyrrole with *N*-acetylimidazole gives the major product *N*-acetylpyrrole.

Linked Answer Type Q.80 and Q.81

Question No-80: Identify the major product **P** in the following reaction,

$$\text{cyclopentadiene} \xrightarrow[\text{Et}_3\text{N/0–50 °C}]{\text{MeCH(Cl)COCl}} \mathbf{P}$$

A.   (bicyclic structure with C=O, Cl, Me)

B.   (bicyclic structure with C=O, Me, Cl)

C.   (bicyclo[3.2.0] structure with H, C=O, Cl, Me, H)

D.   (bicyclo[3.2.0] structure with H, C=O, Me, H, Cl)

Answer: C. The reaction of 2-chloropropanoyl chloride in the presence of triethyl amine produces ketene derivative which further undergoes thermal reaction with cyclopentadiene giving major product 7-chloro-7-methylbicyclo[3.2.0]hept-2-en-6-one **P**.

$$\text{Me–CHCl–COCl} \xrightarrow[-\text{Et}_3\text{N·HCl}]{\text{Et}_3\text{N}} \text{Me–CCl=C=O} \longrightarrow [\text{transition state}] \longrightarrow \mathbf{P}$$

Note. In a 3D view, the methyl group is larger than the chlorine group.

Question No-81: Product **P** of the above reaction transforms to a product **Q** on treatment with n-Bu$_3$SnH in the presence of AIBN in benzene solution. Identify **Q**

A.

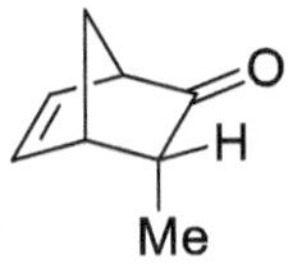

B.

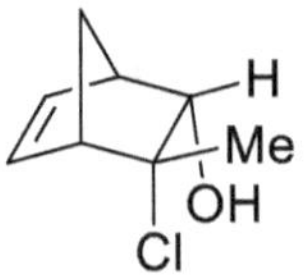

C.

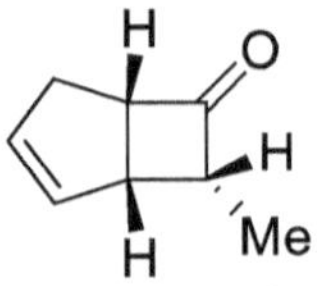

D.

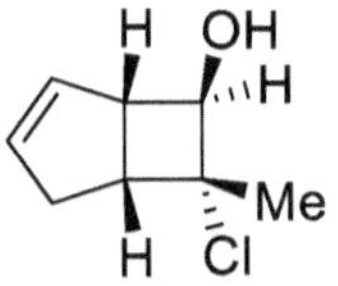

Answer: C. The reduction of **P** with n-Bu$_3$SnH in the presence of AIBN offers halogen-reduced product **Q** with retention of stereochemistry (w.r.t. chlorine) due to the steric hindrance from the concave side.

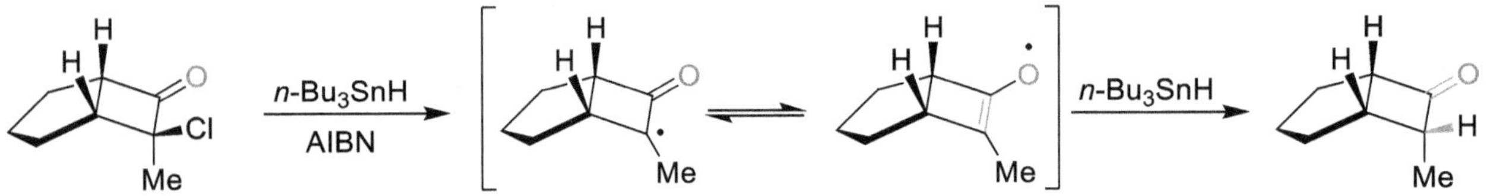

Linked Answer Type Q.82 and Q.83

Question No-82: In the following Wittig reaction, the structure of the major product **P** and the intermediate **[X]**, respectively, are

$$ArCHO \;+\; Ph_3P{=}CH{-}Et \xrightarrow[\text{inorganic salt}]{\substack{\text{benzene} \\ \text{free of}}} [X] \longrightarrow P$$

	P	[X]		P	[X]
A.	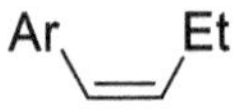	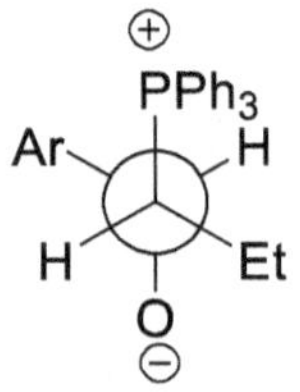	B.	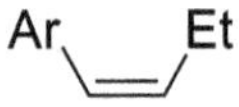	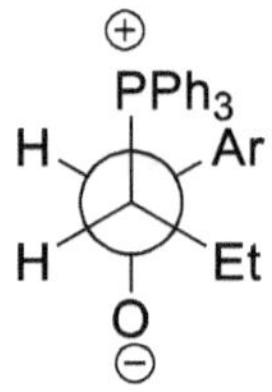
C.	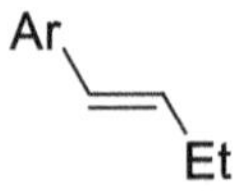	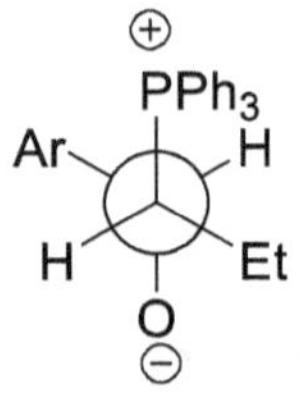	D.	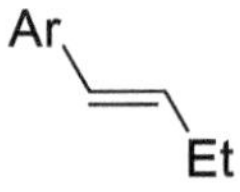	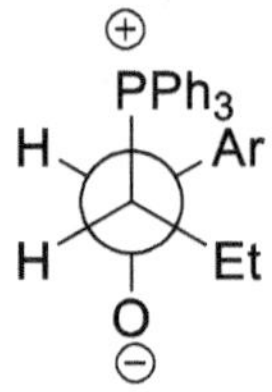

Answer: A. In the given Wittig reaction, the structure of the major product **P** and the intermediate **[X]** is shown below.

[X]

Note. The reaction of ketone/aldehyde with destabilized ylide having electron donating group offers *Z*-olefin whereas with stabilized ylide having electron withdrawing group produces *E*-olefin **Q**.

[Y]

Question No-83: Which of the following sets of characteristic NMR signals will be compatible with the structure of **P** in the above reaction? (Ar = Ph)

A. $\delta = 7.18$ (d, $J = 6$ Hz, 2H), 7.01 (d, $J = 6$ Hz, 2H), 6.41 (d, $J = 18$ Hz, 1H)

B. $\delta = 7.11$ (d, $J = 6$ Hz, 1H), 7.10 (s, 1H), 7.09 (t, $J = 5$ Hz, 1H), 6.94 (d, $J = 5$ Hz, 1H), 6.41 (d, $J = 17$ Hz, 1H)

C. $\delta = 7.18$ (d, $J = 6$ Hz, 2H), 7.01 (d, $J = 6$ Hz, 2H), 6.35 (d, $J = 9$ Hz, 1H)

D. $\delta = 7.44$ (2H, d, $J = 8.1$ Hz), 7.14-7.36 (3H, m), 6.37 (1H, d, $J = 11.7$ Hz), 5.66 (1H, dt, $J = 11.7$, 6.9 Hz), 2.25-2.34 (2H, m), 0.98 (3H, t, $J = 7.5$ Hz)

Answer: D. The correct spectral data of the (*Z*)-1-phenyl-1-butene is δ 7.44 (2H, d, $J = 8.1$ Hz), 7.14-7.36 (3H, m), 6.37 (1H, d, $J = 11.7$ Hz), 5.66 (1H, dt, $J = 11.7$, 6.9 Hz), 2.25-2.34 (2H, m), 0.98 (3H, t, $J = 7.5$ Hz) ppm.

Moussaoui, Y.; Saïd, K.; Salem, R. B. *Arkivoc* **2006**, (*xii*), 1-22.

Linked Answer Type Q.84 and Q.85

Question No-84: The products **P** and **Q** in the following sequence of reactions, respectively, are

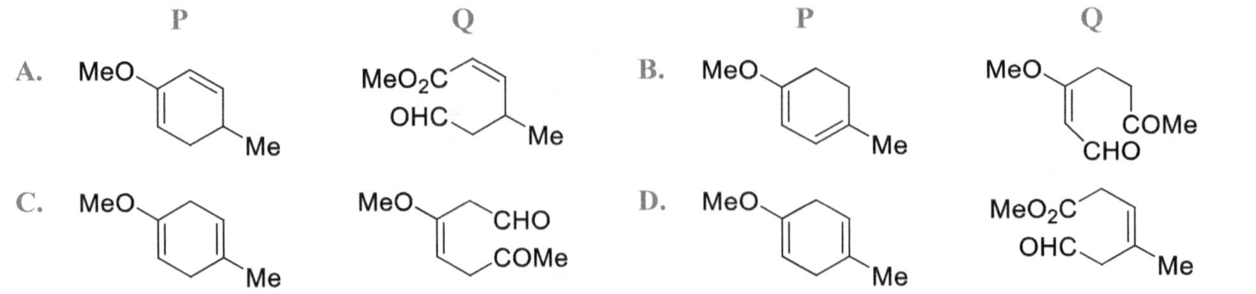

Answer: D. The product 1-methoxy-4-methylcyclohexa-1,4-diene **P** is obtained by the reduction of *p*-methyl anisole using the Birch reagent. Next, the reductive ozonolysis of the electron-rich double bond conjugated with the methoxy group gets converted into ester and aldehyde functionalities due to a strong +*R*-effect.

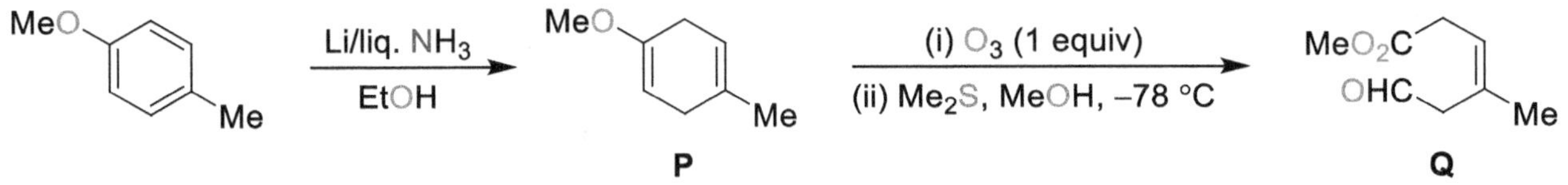

Note. It is perceived that the addition of 1,4-dihydrogen with aryl ring having electron-donating substituents occurs at the site of *ortho*-and *meta*-positions whereas with electron-donating substituents at the *ipso*- and *para*-position.

Question No-85: The reagent for selective reduction of the aldehyde group in **Q** obtained in the above reaction is

A. H_2, $(Ph_3P)_3RhCl$ B. $(Me_2CHCH_2)_2AlH$ C. $Na(AcO)_3BH$ D. $LiAlH_4$

Answer: C. The above product **Q** upon treating with a mild reducing reagent i.e. with sodium triacetoxyborohydride produces methyl (*Z*)-6-hydroxy-4-methylhex-3-enoate, whereas Wilkinson's catalyst furnishes the final product methyl 4-methylpent-3-enoate *via* decarbonylation process.

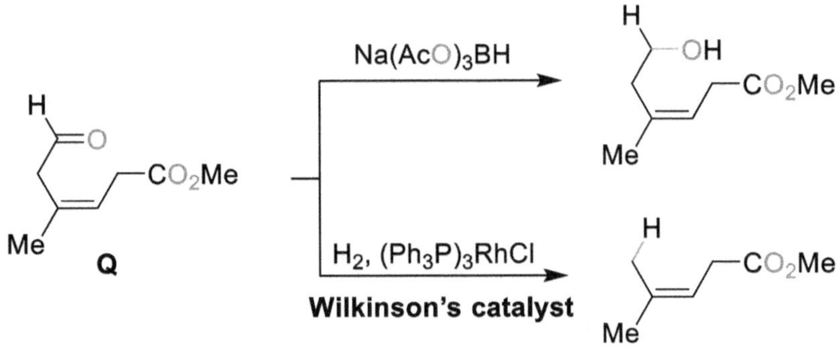

Question No-1: The rate of sulfonation of benzene can be significantly enhanced by the use of

- A. A mixture of HNO_3 and H_2SO_4
- B. conc. H_2SO_4
- C. A mixture of SO_3 and H_2SO_4
- D. SO_3

Answer: C. The rate of sulfonation of benzene can be significantly enhanced by the use of a mixture of SO_3 and H_2SO_4.

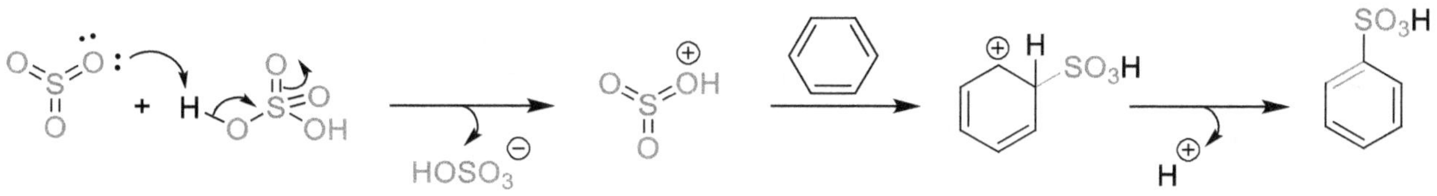

Question No-2: The reaction

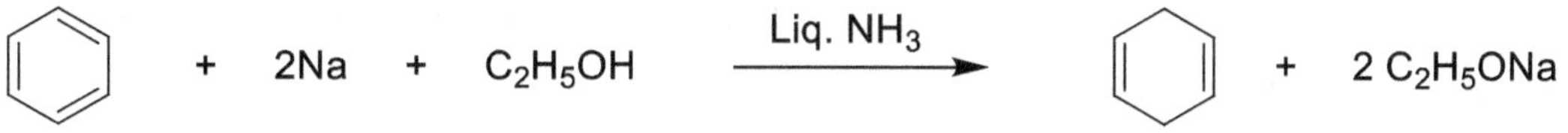

$$\text{benzene} + 2Na + C_2H_5OH \xrightarrow{\text{Liq. NH}_3} \text{cyclohexa-1,4-diene} + 2\,C_2H_5ONa$$

is an example of

- A. Birch reduction
- B. Clemmensen reduction
- C. Wolff-Kishner reduction
- D. Hydride reduction

Answer: A. Birch reduction of benzene using alkali metal in presence of alcoholic solvent gives cyclohexa-1,4-diene.

Question No-3: The major product [X] of the monobromination reaction is

$$\text{Me-cyclohexane} \xrightarrow{\text{NBS/}\Delta} \textbf{[X]}$$

- A. 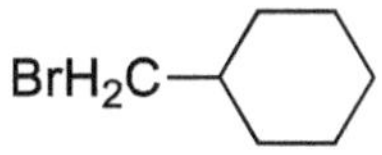 BrH_2C-cyclohexane
- B.  Me-cyclohexane-Br (para)
- C. 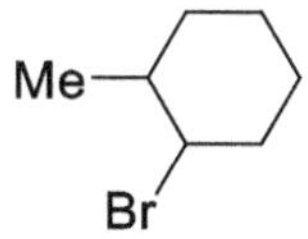 Me-cyclohexane with Br
- D. 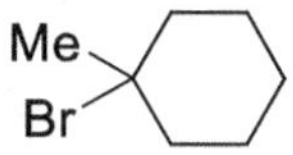 Me, Br on cyclohexane

Answer: D. The major product [X] of the monobromination reaction is 1-bromo-1-methylcyclohexane.

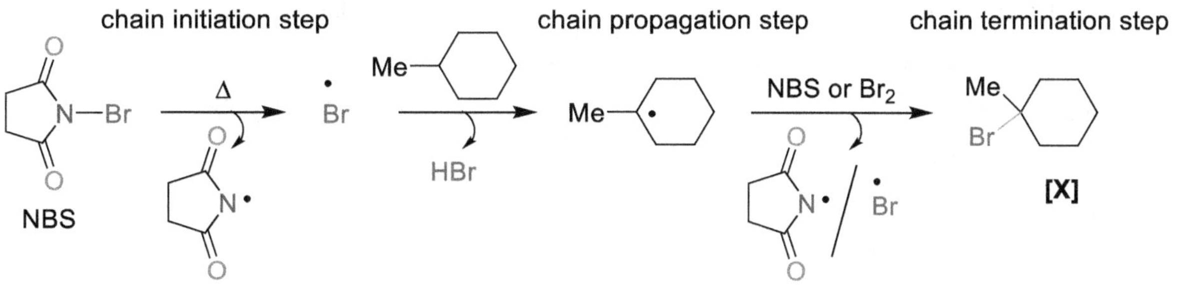

Note. In the propagation step, the succinimide radical with hydrobromic acid produces a limited amount of bromine that reacts with methylcyclohexane radical giving 1-bromo-1-methylcyclohexane.

Question No-4: Benzene can't be iodinated with I_2 directly. However, in presence of oxidants such as HNO_3, iodination is possible. The electrophile formed in this case is

A. $[I^+]$ B. $[I^\cdot]$ C. $\left[\begin{array}{c} {}^{-\delta}\ {}^{+\delta} \\ I\text{--}OH_2 \end{array}\right]^+$ D. $\left[\begin{array}{c} {}^{+\delta}\ {}^{-\delta} \\ I\text{--}OH_2 \end{array}\right]^+$

Answer: A. The oxidation of I_2 with HNO_3 in an acidic medium produces $[I^+]$ ion which easily undergoes electrophilic substitution reaction with benzene and produces iodobenzene.

$$I_2 \;+\; HNO_3 \;+\; H^{\oplus} \longrightarrow [\;:\!\overset{\oplus}{I}\!:\;] \longrightarrow \quad \xleftarrow{\;\times\;} \text{no reaction} \quad I_2 \;+$$

$$NO_2 + H_2O$$

Question No-5: Classify the following species as electrophiles (**E**) and nucleophiles (**N**) in routine organic synthesis

	SO_3	Cl^+	CH_3NH_2	H_3O^+	BH_3	CN^-

A. $E = SO_3, Cl^+, BH_3$; $N = CH_3NH_2, H_3O^+, CN^-$

B. $E = Cl^+, H_3O^+$; $N = SO_3, CH_3NH_2, BH_3, CN^-$

C. $E = Cl^+, H_3O^+, BH_3$; $N = SO_3, CH_3NH_2, H_3O^+, CN^-$

D. $E = SO_3, Cl^+, H_3O^+, BH_3$; $N = CH_3NH_2, CN^-$

Answer: D. The electrophiles and nucleophiles are as follows

Electrophiles (E)	**Nucleophiles (N)**
Electro = Electron and philes = loving species.	Nucleo = nucleus and philes = loving species.
Eg. SO_3, Cl^+, H_3O^+, BH_3	Eg. CH_3NH_2, CN^-

Question No-6: The major product obtained upon treatment of compound **X** with H_2SO_4 at 80 °C is

(X)

A.   B.   C.   D.

Answer: C. The thermal dehydration of the 2-methylhexan-2-ol in the presence of sulfuric acid gives 2-methylhex-2-ene.

Question No-30: The compounds **X** and **Y** in the following reaction are

$$P_4S_{10} \xrightarrow{\text{EtOH}} (X) \xrightarrow{Cl_2} (Y) \xrightarrow{p\text{-}O_2NC_6H_4ONa} \text{parathion}$$

A.   X = (Et)$_2$P(S)SH   ; Y = (Et)$_2$P(S)Cl

B.   X = (EtO)$_2$P(S)SH   ; Y = (EtO)$_2$P(S)Cl

C.   X = (EtO)$_2$PSH   ; Y = (EtO)$_2$PCl

D.   X = (Et)$_3$PO   ; Y = (Et)$_3$PCl

Answer: B. The compounds **X** and **Y** in the given reactions are O,O-diethyl-S-hydrogen phosphorodithioate and O,O-diethyl phosphorochloridothioate, respectively.

Fee, D. C.; Gard, D. R.; Yang, C. "Phosphorus Compounds". Kirk-Othmer Encyclopedia of Chemical Technology. John Wiley & Sons: New York, 2005. doi:10.1002/0471238961.16081519060505.a01.pub2. ISBN 978-0471238966.

Question No-38: The catalyst used in the conversion of ethylene to acetaldehyde using Wacker process is

A. $HCo(CO)_8$ B. $[PdCl_4]^{2-}$ C. V_2O_5 D. $TiCl_4$ in the presence of $Al(C_2H_5)_3$

Answer: B. The catalyst used in the conversion of ethylene to acetaldehyde using the Wacker process is $[PdCl_4]^{2-}$ in combination with the reagents system $CuCl_2/H_2O/O_2$ in DMF.

Question No-55: Match the structure in **List** I with their correct names given in **List II**

	List I		**List II**
a.	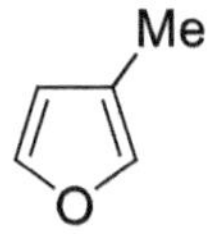	(i)	2-methyl furan
b.		(ii)	Imidazole
c.	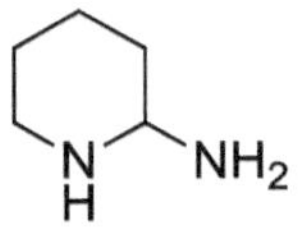	(iii)	5-hydroxybenzothiazole
d.	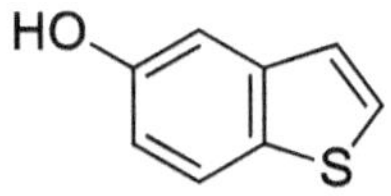	(iv)	2-amino pipyridine
e.	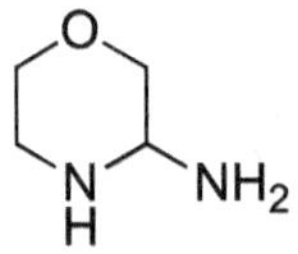	(v)	2-amino morpholine
		(vi)	2-amino azine
		(vii)	3-methyl furan
		(viii)	4-hydroxybenzothiazole

Codes

A. a-vii, b-ii, c-vi, d-iii, e-iv

B. a-vii, b-ii, c-vi, d-viii, e-iv

C. a-vii, b-ii, c-iv, d-iii, e-v

D. a-i, b-ii, c-vi, d-iii, e-iv

Answer: C. The correct match of **List I** with **List II** is a-vii, b-ii, c-iv, d-iii, e-v.

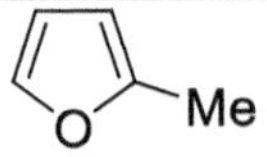

2-methyl furan

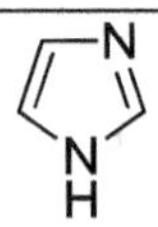

Imidazole

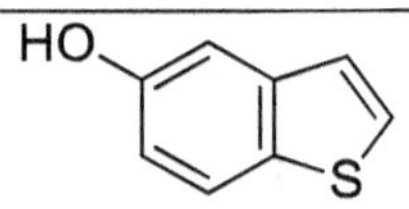

5-hydroxybenzothiazole

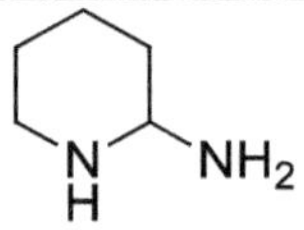

2-amino pipyridine

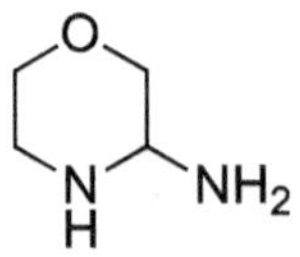

2-amino morpholine

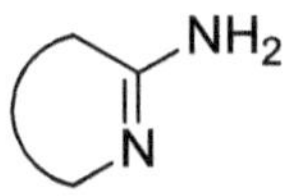

2-amino azine

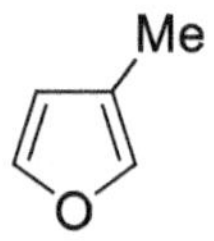

3-methyl furan

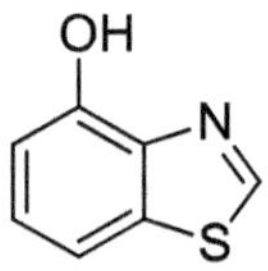

4-hydroxybenzothiazole

Question No-56: The result of the reduction of either (R) or (S)-2-methylcyclohexanone, in separate reactions, using LiAlH$_4$ is that the reduction of

A.   the R enantiomer is stereoselective

B.   the R enantiomer is stereospecific

C.   the S enantiomer is stereospecific

D.   both R and S enantiomer is stereoselective

Answer: D. The result of the reduction of either (R) or (S)-2-methylcyclohexanone, is stereoselective.

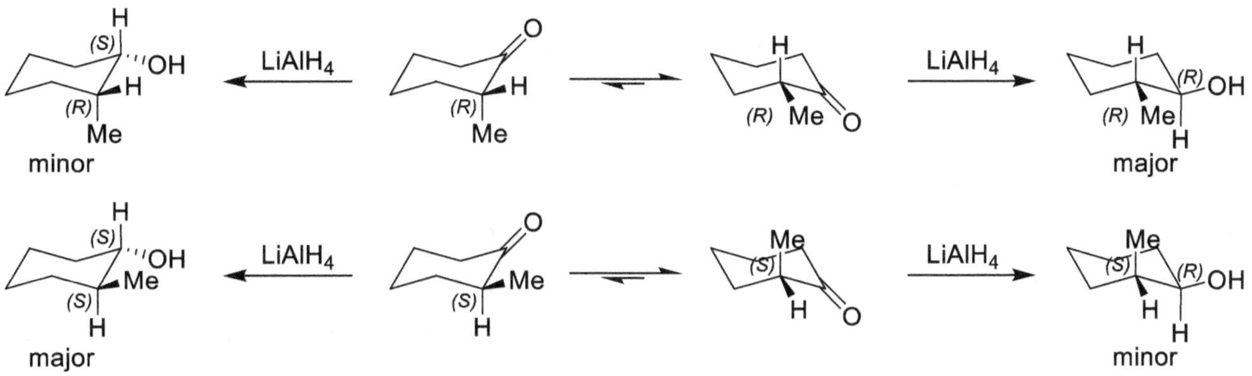

Question No-57: The increasing order of basicity among the following is

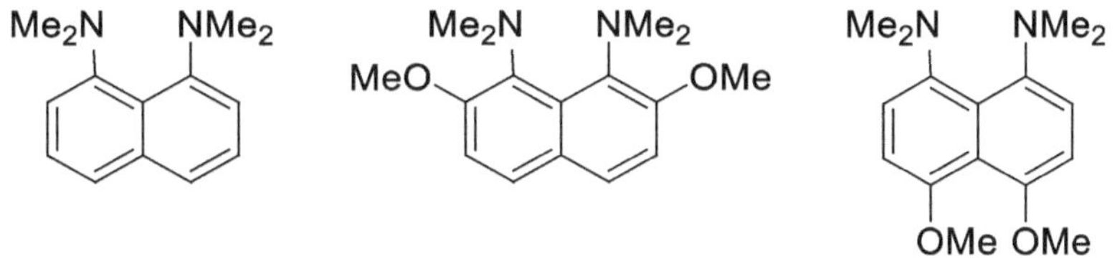

(X)   (Y)   (Z)

A. $Y < X < Z$ B. $Y < Z < X$ C. $X < Z < Y$ D. $X < Y < Z$

Answer: C. The increasing order of basicity of the given compound is $X < Z < Y$.

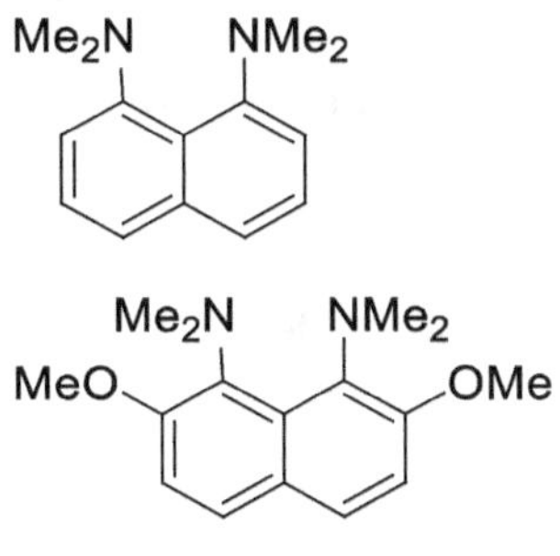

Compound '**X**' is the least basic than other derivatives because the lone pair electron of the nitrogen atom can be easily delocalized in the ring, that's why decreases the basicity.

Compound '**Y**' is the most basic in nature than other derivative, because the lone pair electron of Nitrogen atom can't easily delocalized in the ring due to steric crowding, and results in increases of basicity.

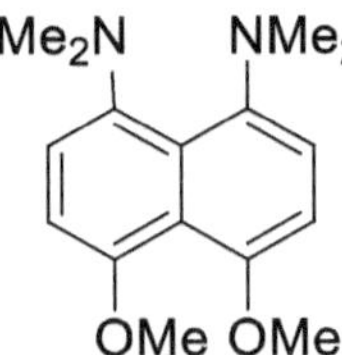

Compound 'Z' is more basic than **X** because the lone pair electrons of nitrogen can easily be delocalized in the ring, but the presence of –OMe group restricts the complete delocalization. As a result, it is less basic than '**Y**'.

Question No-58: In the reaction

$$\text{Et}^{\prime\prime\prime\prime}\overset{\text{Me}}{\underset{\text{Pro}}{\underset{(S)}{|}}}\text{Br} \xrightarrow{\text{OH}^- \text{ (aq)}}$$

If the concentration of both is doubled, then the rate of the reaction will

A.   Remain unchanged

B.   Quadruple

C.   Reduce to one fourth

D.   Double

Answer: B. If the concentration of both is doubled, then the rate of the reaction shall also be quadruple (second order reaction).

Question No-59: Match the structure in the **List I** with the coupling constant [^{1}H, J (Hz)] given in **List II**

List I		List II	
a.	Br—CH=CH—Cl (H, H cis)	(i)	~1 Hz
b.	Br—CH=CH—Cl (Br/H, H/Cl)	(ii)	~10 Hz
c.	Br—CH=CH—Cl (Br/H, Cl/H)	(iii)	~15 Hz

Code

A.   a-i, b-ii, c-iii   B.   a-ii, b-iii, c-i   C.   a-iii, b-ii, c-i   D.   a-iii, b-i, c-ii

Answer: B. The correct match of List I with List II is a-ii, b-iii, c-i.

Br—CH=CH—Cl (H, H)	Br—CH=CH—H (H, Cl)	Br—CH=CH—H (Cl, H)
~10 Hz	~15 Hz	~1 Hz

Question No-60: Phenol on reaction with formaldehyde and dimethyl amine mainly gives

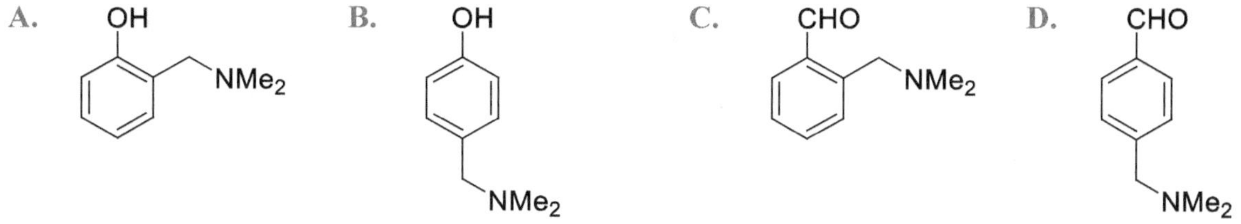

A.   [structure: OH with CH₂NMe₂ ortho]

B.   [structure: OH para CH₂NMe₂]

C.   [structure: CHO with CH₂NMe₂ ortho]

D.   [structure: CHO para CH₂NMe₂]

Answer: A. The given above reaction is an example of the Mannich reaction. At first, formaldehyde reacts with the secondary amine to form an iminium hydroxide derivative. Further, it reacts with phenol to give 2-((dimethylamino)methyl)benzaldehyde as the major product.

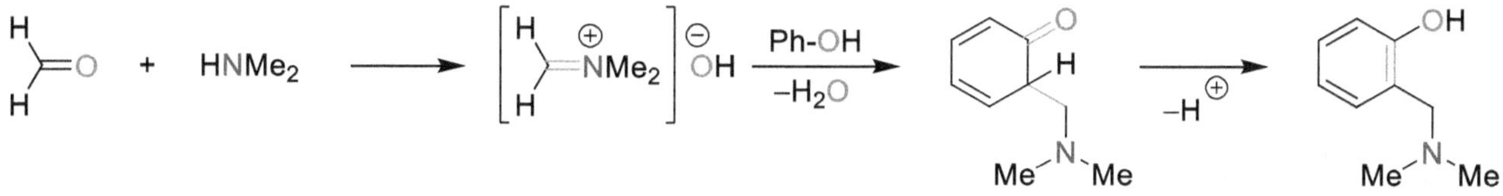

Question No-61: The mono protonation of adenine **X** in acidic solution

(X)

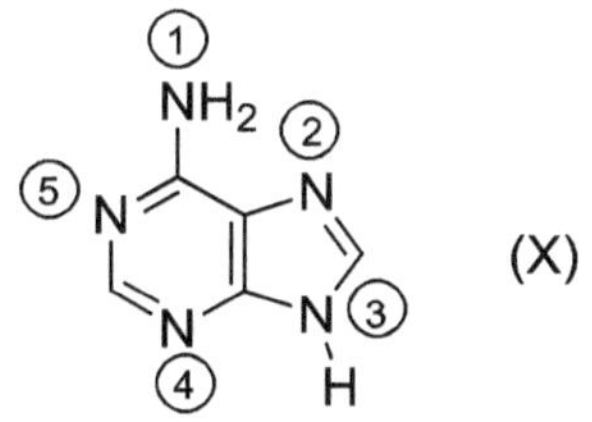

mainly occurs at

A.   position 1   B.   position 2   C.   position 3   D.   either position 4 or 5

Answer: D. The mono protonation of adenine **X** in acidic solution preferentially occurred at either position 4 or 5.

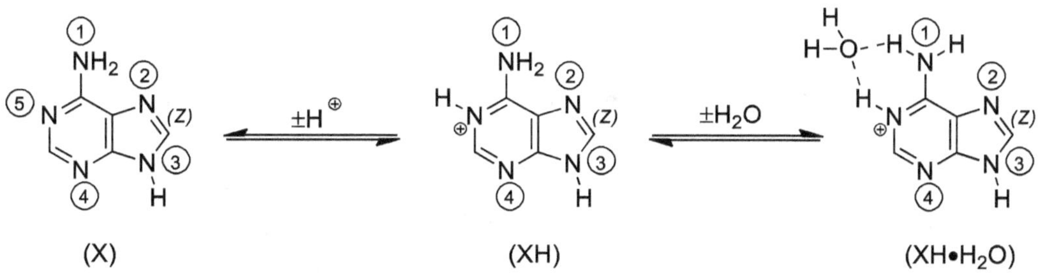

(X)   (XH)   (XH•H₂O)

Next, monoprotonated adenine in acidic solution preferentially second-time protonation occurred at position 2.

(XH•H$_2$O) (XH$_2$•H$_2$O) (XH$_2$•2H$_2$O)

Wincel, H. *J Am Soc Mass Spectrom* **2009**, *20*, 1900.

Question No-62: In the following reaction

$$H_2C=N_2 \xrightarrow[\text{benzophenone}]{hv} (X) \xrightarrow{\text{cis-2-butene}} (Y)$$

(**X**) and (**Y**) are respectively

A. ^{1}:CH$_2$ and *cis*-1,2-dimethylcyclopropane

B. ^{3}:CH$_2$ and *cis*-1,2-dimethylcyclopropane

C. ^{1}:CH$_2$ and a mixture of cis-/trans-1,2-dimethylcyclopropane

D. ^{3}:CH$_2$ and a mixture of *cis-/trans*-1,2-dimethylcyclopropane

Answer: D. The photochemical irradiation of diazomethane forms singlet carbene which gets converted into triplet carbene in the presence of sensitizer benzophenone. Next, this triplet carbene undergoes electrophilic [2+1]-cycloaddition with *cis*-2-butene in a step-wise manner (non-concerted pathway) producing a mixture of *cis-/trans*-1,2-dimethylcyclopropane (due to single carbon-carbon bond ration can occur in case of the zwitterionic form).

Question No-63: The major product obtained upon treating with a mixture of

and

with strongly acidic solution of H_2SO_4 is

A. H_2N—⟨ ⟩—⟨ ⟩—NH_2 and H_2N—⟨ ⟩(Me)—⟨ ⟩—NH_2(Me)

B. H_2N—⟨ ⟩—⟨ ⟩(Me)—NH_2 and H_2N—⟨ ⟩—⟨ ⟩—NH_2(Me)

C. (Me)H_2N—⟨ ⟩—⟨ ⟩—NH_2 and (Me)(NH_2)⟨ ⟩—⟨ ⟩—NH_2

D. H_2N—⟨ ⟩—⟨ ⟩(Me)(H_2N) and H_2N—⟨ ⟩—⟨ ⟩—Me(H_2N)

Answer: A. Benzidine rearrangement of a mixture of 1,2-diphenylhydrazine and 1,2-di-*o*-tolylhydrazine under thermal conditions *via* stereospecific intramolecular concerted [5,5]-sigmatropic shift in the presence of H_2SO_4 or H*Cl* produces [1,1'-biphenyl]-4,4'-diamine (benzidine) and 3,3'-dimethyl-[1,1'-biphenyl]-4,4'-diamine as the major products.

Note. Benzidine rearrangement is stereospecific and doesn't gives intermolecular cross-products. Some other sigmatropically intramolecular self-rearranged products are also observed, like [3,3]-shift as benzidine, [3,5]-shift as diphenyline, [3,3]/[1,5]-shift as *o-/p*-semidine.

Question No-64: Match the observed principal observations in the visible spectrum shown **List I** with the bond that shows this observation in **List II**.

	List I		List II
a.	$\sigma - \sigma^*$	(i)	C-C
b.	$n - \sigma^*$	(ii)	C-O
c.	$n - \pi^*$	(iii)	C=O
d.	$\pi - \pi^*$	(iv)	C=C

Codes

A. a-i, b-ii, c-iii, d-iv B. a-i, b-iii, c-ii, d-iv C. a-ii, b-i, c-iv, d-iii D. a-iv, b-ii, c-iii, d-i

Answer: A. The correct matches of **List I** with **List II** is a-i, b-ii, c-iii, d-iv. Possibilities of the transition in the given compounds are as follows

C-C	C-O	C=O	C=C
$\sigma - \sigma^*$	$\sigma - \sigma^*$ and $n - \sigma^*$	$\sigma - \sigma^*$, $n - \sigma^*$ and $n - \pi^*$	$\sigma - \sigma^*$, $n - \sigma^*$, $n - \pi^*$ and $\pi - \pi^*$

Question No-65: Among the isomers of $C_{10}H_{14}$ shown,

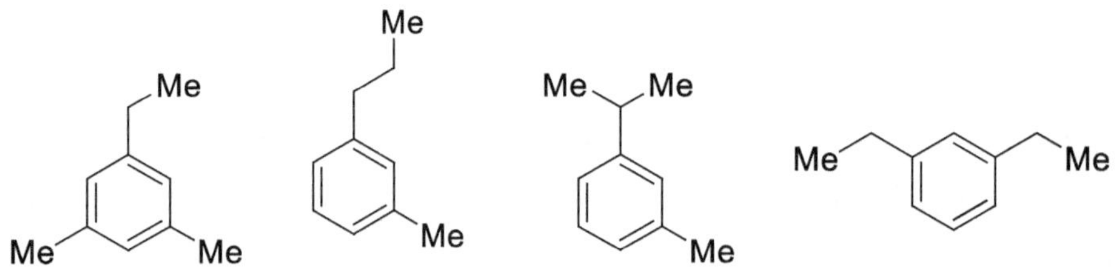

The isomer that can be identified uniquely by mass spectrometry alone is

A. W B. X C. Y D. Z

Answer: C. Among these, *m*-cymene **Y** can be identified uniquely by mass spectrometry.

Compound W; R = R' = Me
Compound Z; R = H R' = Et

m/z: 134.1096

m/z: 105.0699

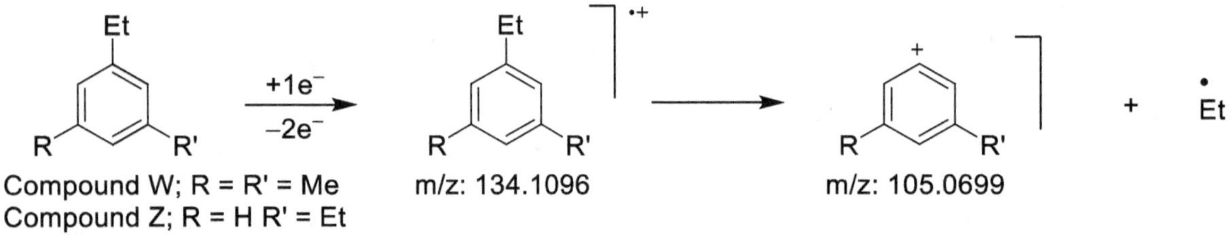

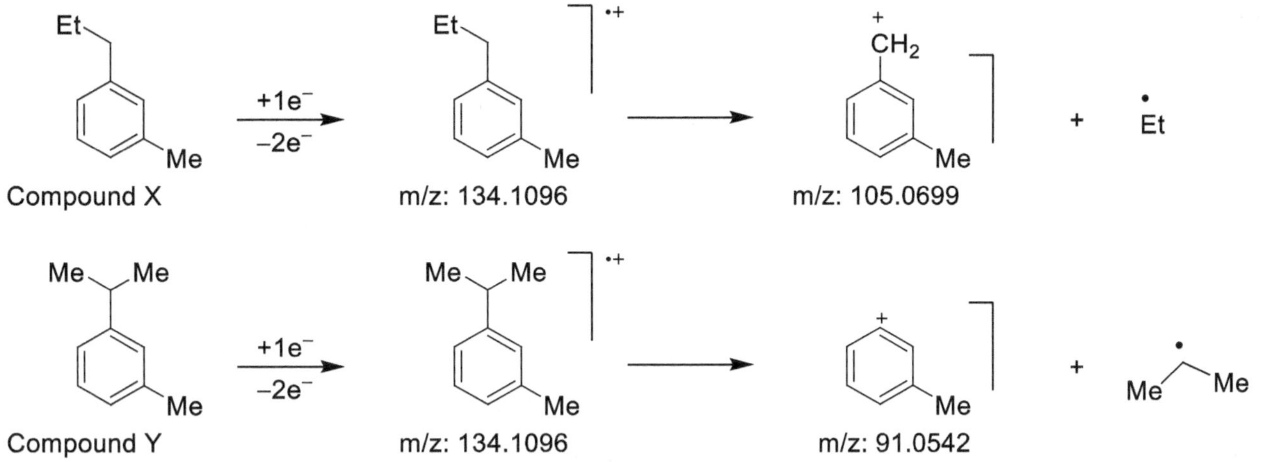

Question No-66: The direction of the rotation of the following thermal electrocyclic ring closure

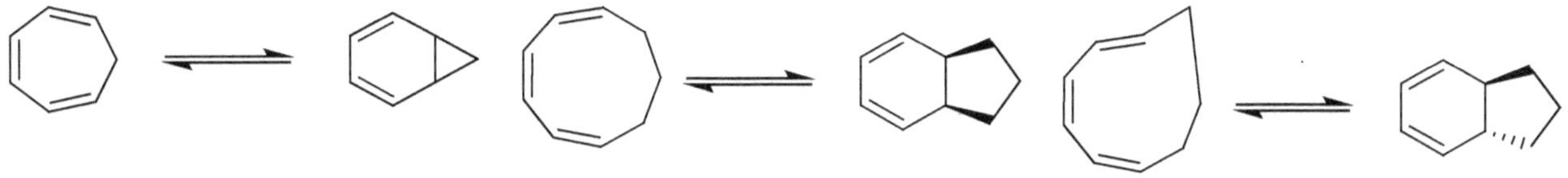

respectively, is

A. Disrotatory, disrotatory, disrotatory
B. Conrotatory, conrotatory, conrotatory
C. Disrotatory, disrotatory, conrotatory
D. Disrotatory, conrotatory, disrotatory

Answer: C. The direction of the rotation of the given thermal electrocyclic ring closure is disrotatory, disrotatory, and conrotatory, respectively.

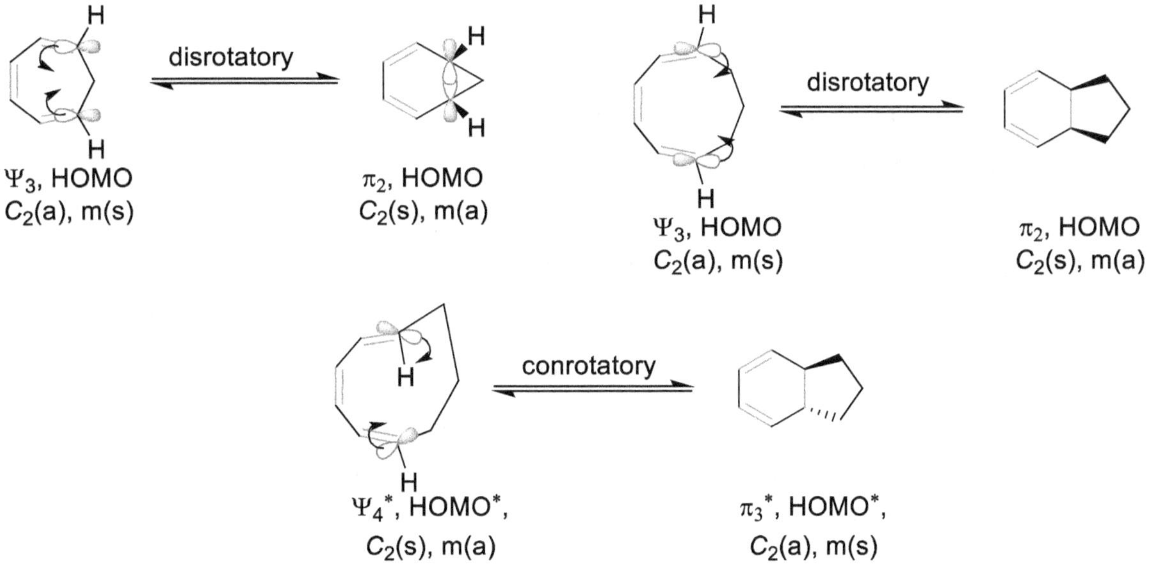

Question No-67: The molecule(s) that exist as *meso* structure(s)

K   L   M

is/are

A. Only M   B. Both K and L   C. Only L   D. Only K

Answer: B. The (1*R*,3*S*)-1,3-dimethylcyclohexane **K** and (1*R*,2*S*)-1,2-dimethylcyclohexane **L** are *meso*-compounds as they have mirror plane of symmetry (optically inactive).

K (optically inactive)   **L** (optically inactive)   **M** (optically active)

Question No-68: The stereochemical description for atoms labeled H_a and H_b in the structures

X   Y   Z

respectively are

A. X = homotopic, Y = enantiotopic and Z = diastereotopic

B. X = enantiotopic, Y = homotopic and Z = diastereotopic

C. X = diastereotopic, Y = homotopic, and Z = enantiotopic

D. X = homotopic, Y = diastereotopic and Z = enantiotopic

Answer: C. The given compound **X** is diastereotopic because it already has a fixed chiral center throughout our the marked proton exchange process. In the case of compound **Y**, both the protons are in a similar environment due to the presence of two methyl groups at the same carbon. Whereas compound **Z** has enantiotopic protons because on exchanging the marked protons sequentially offer two isomers (enantiomers).

$H_b \to$ **Br** $H_a \to$ **Br**   X = diastereotopic

$$H_b \rightarrow Br \qquad H_a \rightarrow Br$$

Ha—C(Br)(Me)(Me)	Ha,Hb—C(Me)(Me)	Br,Hb—C(Me)(Me)

Y = homotopic

Z = enantiotopic

Question No-69: Treatment of the pentapeptide Gly-Arg-Phe-Ala-Ala in separate experiments, with the enzymes Trypsin, Chymotrypsin, and Carboxypeptidase A respectively, gives

A.   Gly-Arg + Phe-Ala-Ala; Gly-Arg-Phe + Ala-Ala; Gly-Arg-Phe-Ala + Ala

B.   Gly-Arg-Phe + Ala-Ala; Gly-Arg-Phe + Ala-Ala; Gly-Arg-Phe-Ala + Ala

C.   Gly-Arg + Phe-Ala-Ala; Gly-Arg-Phe- Ala + Ala; Gly-Arg-Phe + Ala-Ala

D.   Gly-Arg + Phe-Ala-Ala; Gly-Arg-Phe + Ala-Ala; Gly + Arg-Phe-Ala + Ala

Answer: A. The correct sequence for the given statement will be Gly-Arg + Phe-Ala-Ala; Gly-Arg-Phe + Ala-Ala; Gly-Arg-Phe-Ala + Ala, which is summarized below.

Trypsin identifies the basic amino acid in the polypeptide chain which hydrolyses the peptide linkage at the carboxyl side of arginine (Arg) and lysine (Lys) (exception: histidine; due to its basic nature).

Chymotrypsin identifies the aromatic amino acid in the polypeptide chain which hydrolyses the peptide linkage at the carboxyl side of phenylalanine (Phe), tyrosine (Tyr) and tryptophan (Trp).

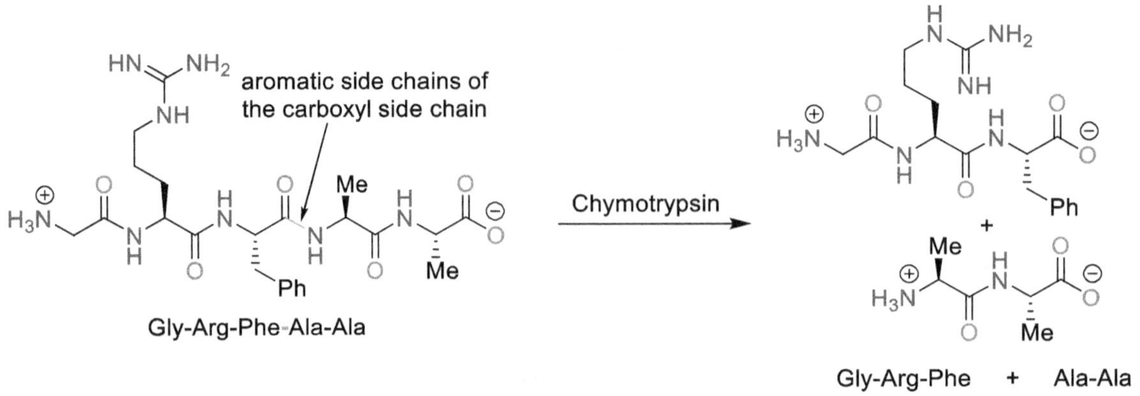

Carboxypeptidase enzyme sequentially hydrolyzed the peptide linkage from the *C*-terminus of the polypeptide chain until the –COOH group is blocked. The rate of hydrolysis of the polypeptide can be different for the different amino acids.

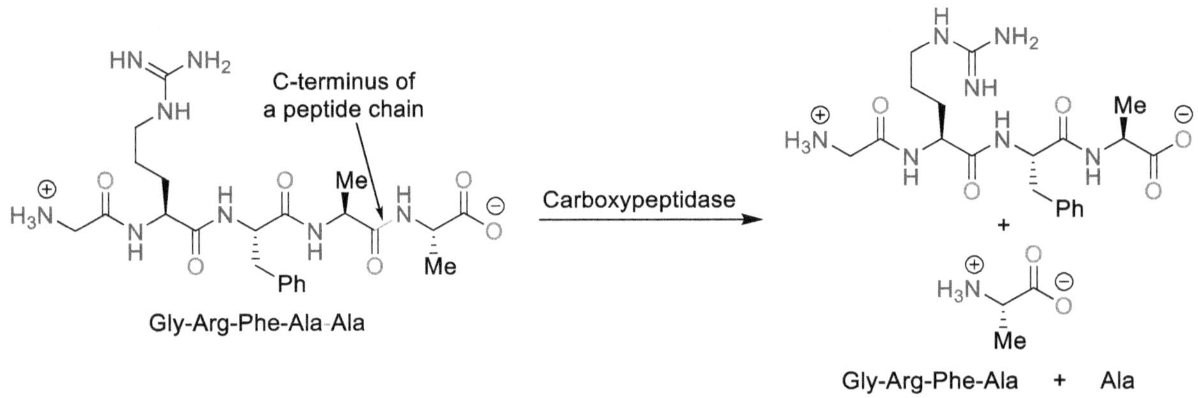

Aminopeptidase enzyme sequentially hydrolyzed the peptide linkage, from the *N*-terminus of the polypeptide chain at the carboxyl side, until the –NH_2 group is blocked. The rate of hydrolysis of the aminopeptidase enzyme is faster than the carboxypeptidase enzyme. Thus, it can't be used as partial hydrolysis of the polypeptide chain.

Thermolysin identifies the hydrophobic amino acid residues in the polypeptide chain which hydrolyzed peptide linkage at the side of phenylalanine (Phe), tryptophan and also leucine (Leu).

Question No-70: Hordenine (**X**), an alkaloid, undergoes Hoffman degradation to give compound (**Y**).

$$HO{-}\langle C_6H_4\rangle{-}CH_2CH_2NMe_2$$

(X)

(**Y**) on treatment with alkaline permanganate gives (**Z**). **Y** and **Z** respectively, are

A. OH (4-vinylphenol) and OH with CO_2H (4-hydroxybenzoic acid)

B. OMe with CO_2H and OMe (4-methoxystyrene)

C. OMe (4-methoxystyrene) and OMe with CH_2CO_2H

D. OMe (4-methoxystyrene) and OMe with CO_2H

Answer: A. Hordenine (**X**) undergoes Hoffman degradation to give 4-vinylphenol (**Y**) which on further treatment with alkaline permanganate produces 4-hydroxybenzoic acid (**Z**).

Question No-74 - 75: Reactivity of aryl amines towards electrophilic aromatic substitution is much higher than that of aliphatic amines. Hence differential reactivity of the amino group is desirable in many reactions.

Question No-74: The compound which is reacting with aniline, will **NOT** form an acetanilide?

A.   B.   C.   D.

Answer: B. All the given reagents can be employed for the transformation of aniline to acetanilide (exception: with acetaldehyde; forms imine derivative).

Question No-75: Aniline can be distinguished from methylamine by its reaction with

A. p-toluene sulphonyl chloride/KOH   B.   (i) $NaNO_2$/HCl, 0−5 °C (ii) alkaline β-naphthol

C.   Sn/HCl D.   acetyl chloride

Answer: B. Among these, the diazotization reaction is one of the best choice to distinguish between aniline and methylamine.

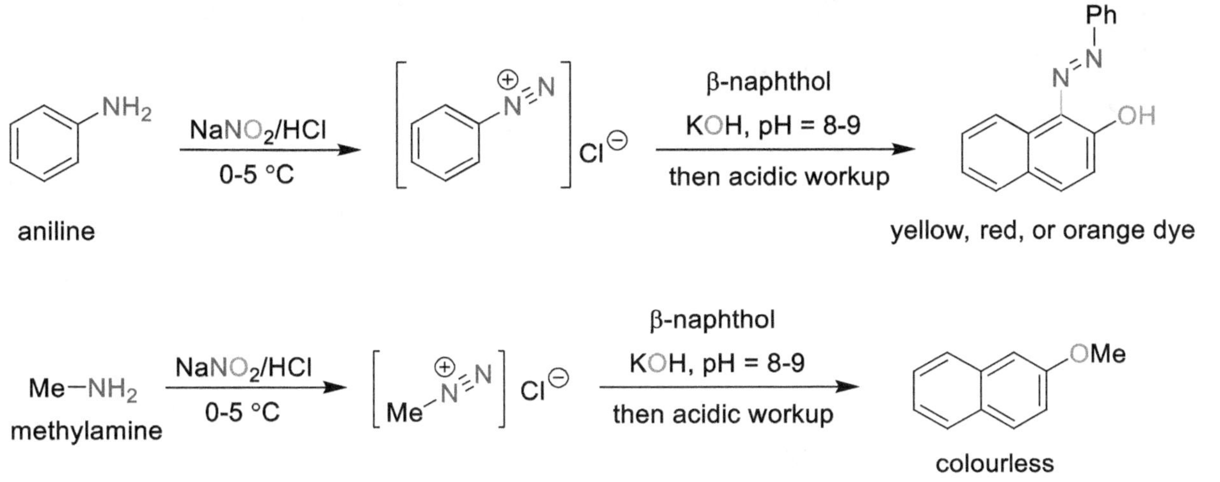

Note. Hinsberg's reagent is used for the detection of the primary and secondary amine, which is based on their solubility. While tertiary amine shall not be able to react in the first step itself due to the absence of proton.

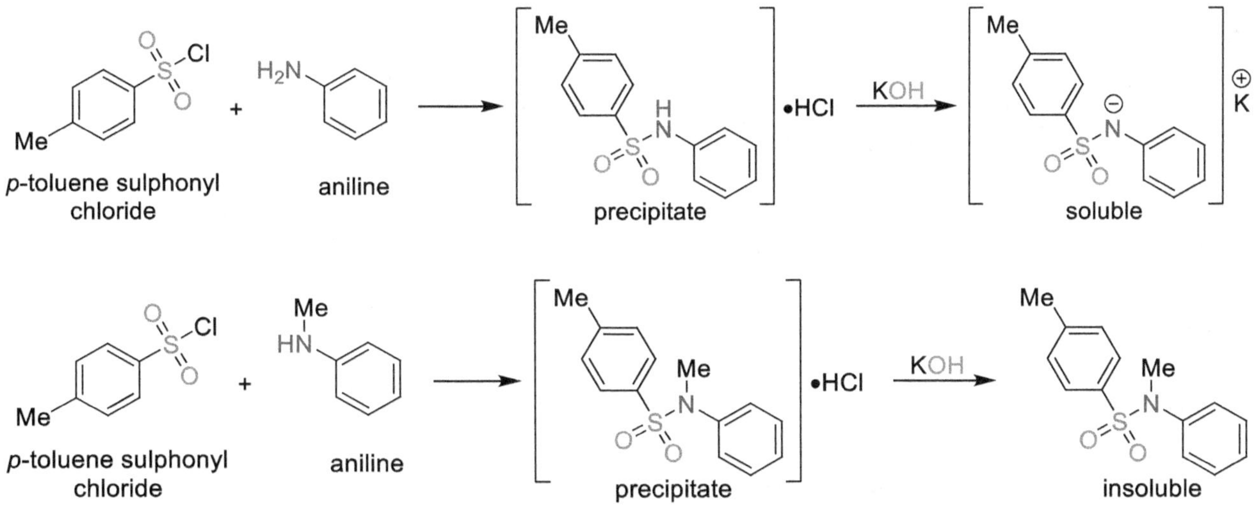

Linked Answer Question No-76 & 77

Question No-76: In the reaction

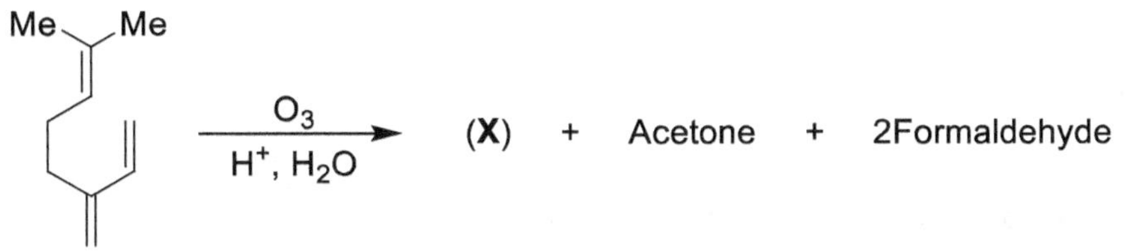

$$\text{(X)} \;+\; \text{Acetone} \;+\; 2\,\text{Formaldehyde}$$

Compound (**X**) is

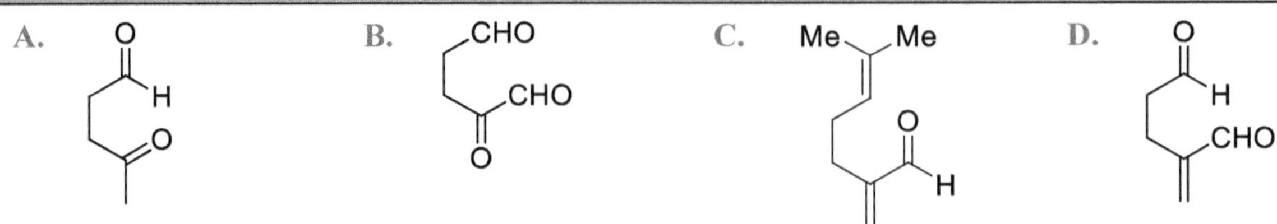

Answer: B. Ozonolysis of the given compound myrcene gives 2-oxopentanedial **X** along with acetone and formaldehyde.

Question No-77: Oxidation of (**X**) with chromic acid chiefly gives

Answer: A. The oxidation of 2-oxopentanedial **X** using chromic acid chiefly gives succinic acid as a major product.

myrcene → O_3 then H^+, H_2O, $-[Me_2CO + 2HCHO]$ → 2-oxopentanedial **X** → chromic acid → succinic acid

Linked Answer Question No-78 & 79

Question No-78: In the reaction

$$AMP \xrightarrow[175\ ^\circ C]{aq.\ NH_3} (X) + H_3PO_4$$

Compound (**X**) is

  A. Adenine   B. Xanthine   C. 2,6-diaminopurine   D. adenosine

***Answer: D.** The reaction of AMP with ammonia can give adenosine.

Question No-79: Compound **X** on treatment with conc. HC*l* gives

  A. Uric acid   B. Adenine   C. Hypoxanthine   D. Guanine

***Answer: B.** Compound **X** on treatment with conc. HC*l* gives adenine.

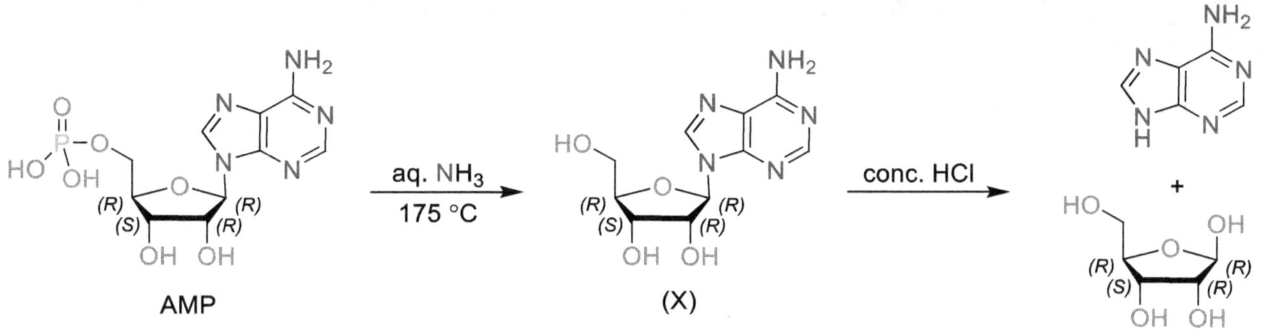

AMP $\xrightarrow[\text{175 °C}]{\text{aq. NH}_3}$ (X) $\xrightarrow{\text{conc. HCl}}$

Question No-7: The compound that is **NOT** aromatic is

A. 
B. 
C. 
D. 

Answer: B. Huckel rule of Aromaticity. According to this rule, the molecule should be conjugated, planner, sp^2 hybridized (all the ring carbon), and should have a resonance stabilized transition state along with $(4n+2)\pi$ electron system. Among the given compounds except for compound **B** all three are aromatic. The compound B obeys $(4n)\pi$ electron rule instead of $(4n + 2)\pi$ electron, thus it is antiaromatic.

Question No-8: The order of the stability for the cyclic olefins is

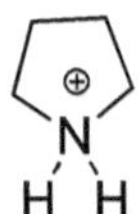
I

II

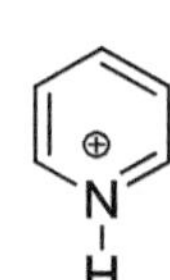
III

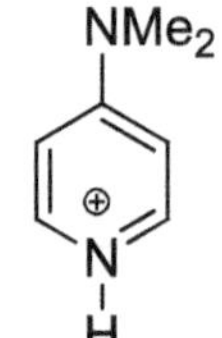
IV

Code

A. I < II < III < IV   B. II < III < IV < I   C. II < III < I < IV   D. IV < II < I < III

Answer: C. Usually, the less strained system is more stable than all. In the given examples compound **IV** is more stable than **I** due to less strain.

Hence, the correct order of the stability for the cyclic olefins is **II < III < I < IV**.

Note. According to Bredt's rule, the double bond at the bridge carbon in the polycyclic (bicyclic, tricyclic, etc.) molecule is not stable due to the improper overlap of the p-orbitals during sp^2-hybridization (loses planarity) and ring strains. Although, compound **III** is relatively more stable than **II** due to its large ring size.

Question No-9: The most acidic species is

A.

B.

C.

D. NMe$_2$

Answer: B. Among these, the pyrrolium cation is antiaromatic and highly acidic because this after losing its proton becomes more stable by obeying the Huckel rule of aromaticity.

Question No-10: The major product of the following reaction is

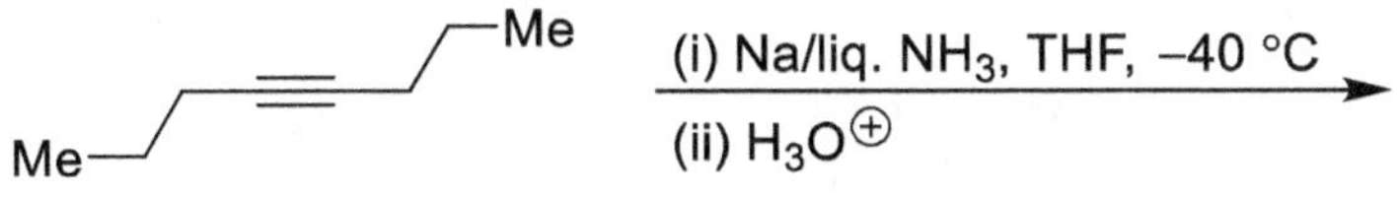

(i) Na/liq. NH$_3$, THF, $-40\,°C$
(ii) H$_3$O$^\oplus$

A.

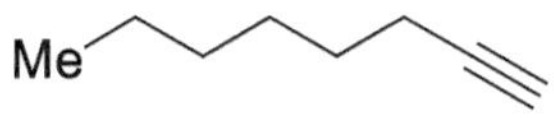

B.

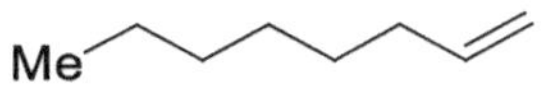

C.

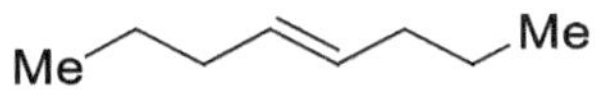

D.

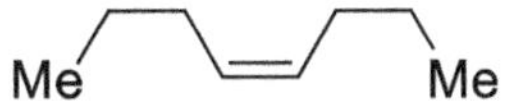

Answer: C. The stereospecific reduction of 4-octyne into *trans*-4-octene using alkali metal in liquid ammonia is known as Birch reduction.

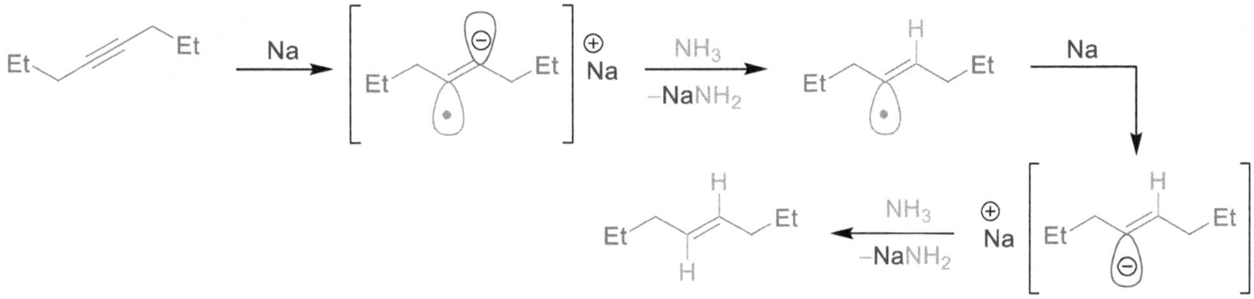

Question No-11: In the carbylamine reaction **R-X** is converted to **R-Y** *via* the intermediate **Z**. **R-X**, **R-Y** and **Z** respectively are

A.   R-NH$_2$, R-NC, carbene

B.   R-NH$_2$, R-NC, nitrene

C.   R-NC, R-NH$_2$, carbene

D.   R-OH, R-NC, nitrene

Answer: A. In the carbylamine reaction, **R-X** is R-NH$_2$ which gets converted to **R-Y** as R-NC *via* carbene intermediate **Z**. The complete reaction shown below.

$$Cl_3CH \quad + \quad NaOH \longrightarrow \quad :CCl_2 \,(\text{intermediate } Z) \quad + \quad NaCl \quad + \quad H_2O$$

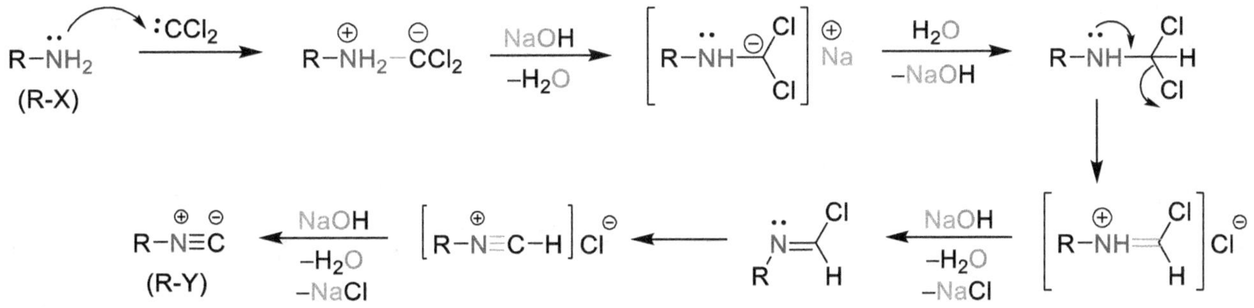

Question No-12: The compound that is **NOT** oxidized by KMnO₄ is

A.

B.

C.

D.

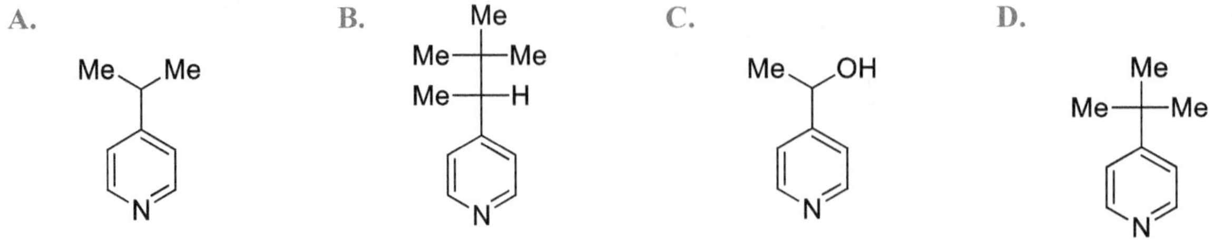

Answer: D. The compound that is NOT oxidized by KMnO₄ is *tert*-butylpyridine due lack of α-hydrogen(s) at benzylic carbon(s).

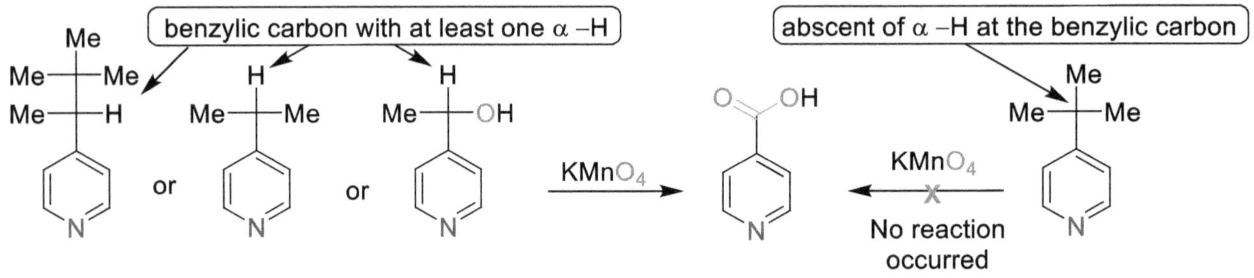

Question No-13: Cyanogen bromide (CNBr) specifically hydrolyses the peptide bond formed by the C-side of

A. methionine   B. glycine   C. proline   D. serine

Answer: A. Cyanogen bromide (CNBr) specifically hydrolyses the peptide bond formed by the C-side of methionine.

For example: The hydrolysis of Phy-Gly-Met-Gly using cyanogen bromide is shown below.

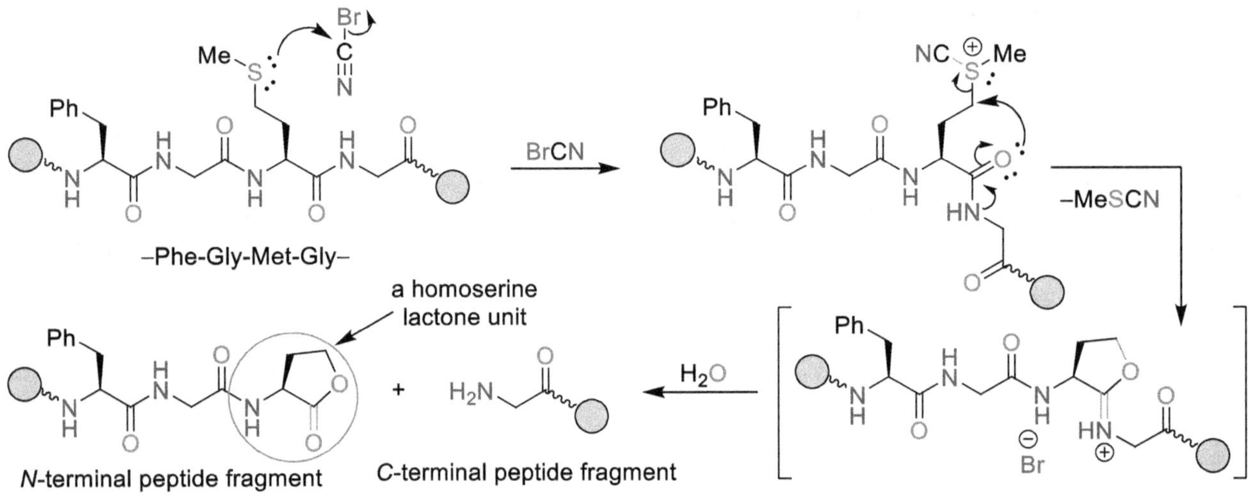

Note. Edman degradation and Sanger reagents react with the *N*-terminus of the polypeptide chain while in this example cyanogen bromide reacts from the *C*-terminus of the polypeptide chain.

https://www2.chemistry.msu.edu/faculty/reusch/virttxtjml/protein2.htm

Question No-14: The Hammett reaction constant ρ is based on

  A.   the rate of alkaline hydrolysis of substituted ethyl benzoates

  B.   the dissociation constants of substituted acetic acid

  C.   the dissociation constants of substituted benzoic acid

  D.   the dissociation constants of substituted phenols

Answer: C. The Hammett reaction constant ρ is based on the dissociation constants of substituted benzoic acid.

Question No-37: Match the entries **a-d** with their corresponding structure **p-s**.

a	bridge system	p
b	atropisomeric system	q
c	spiro system	r
d	fused system	s

Codes

  A.   a-s; b-r; c-q; d-p

  B.   a-p; b-s; c-q; d-r

  C.   a-q; b-p; c-s; d-r

  D.   a-s; b-r; c-p; d-q

Answer: D. Match the entries **a-d** with their corresponding structure **p-s** is a-s; b-r; c-p; d-q.

Question No-38: The reaction between **X** and **Y** to give **Z** proceeds *via*

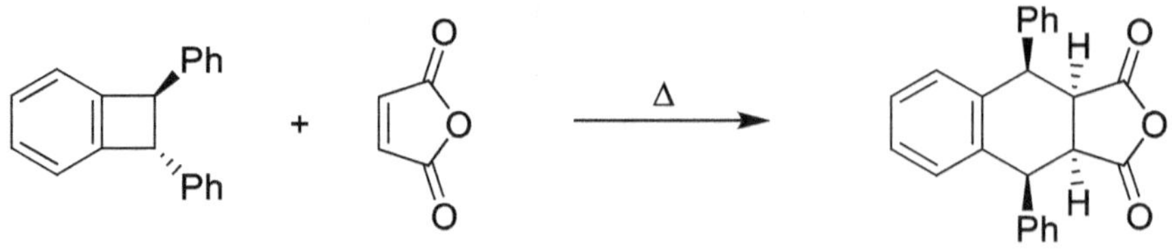

X   **Y**   **Z**

A. 4π-conrotatory opening of **X** followed by *endo* Diels-Alder cycloaddition

B. 4π-disrotatory opening of **X** followed by *endo* Diels-Alder cycloaddition

C. 4π-conrotatory opening of **X** followed by *exo* Diels-Alder cycloaddition

D. 4π-disrotatory opening of **X** followed by *exo* Diels-Alder cycloaddition

Answer: A. The reaction between **X** and **Y** to give **Z** proceeds *via* a thermal 4π-electron conrotatory opening of **X** followed by *endo*-Diels-Alder cycloaddition.

X   **Z**

Ψ_2, HOMO, C_2(a), m(s) Ψ_2, HOMO, C_2(a), m(s)

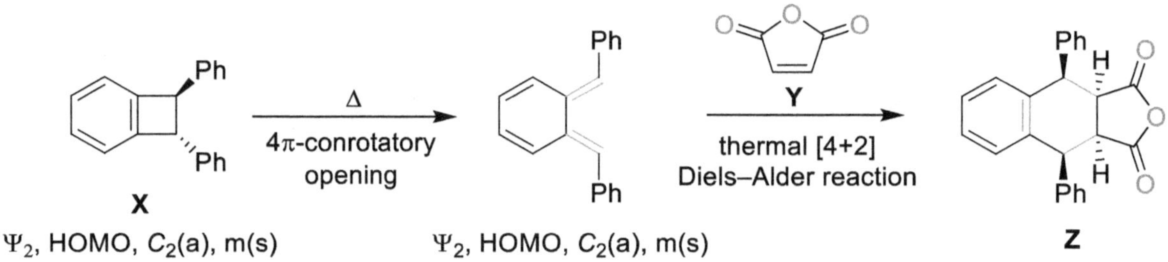

Question No-39: The major products P_1 and P_2 respectively, in the following reaction sequence are

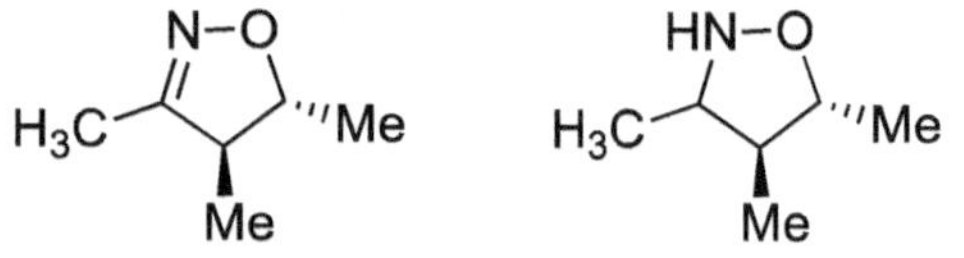

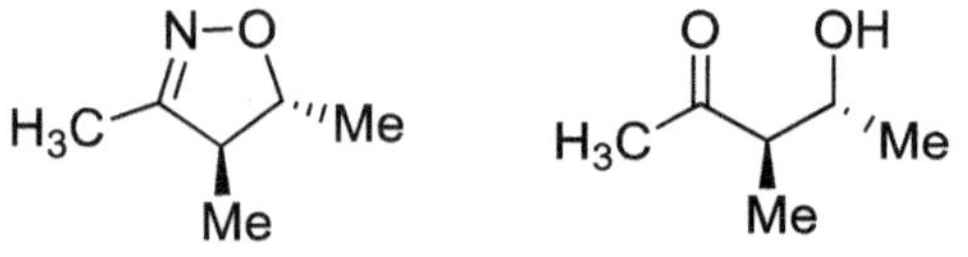

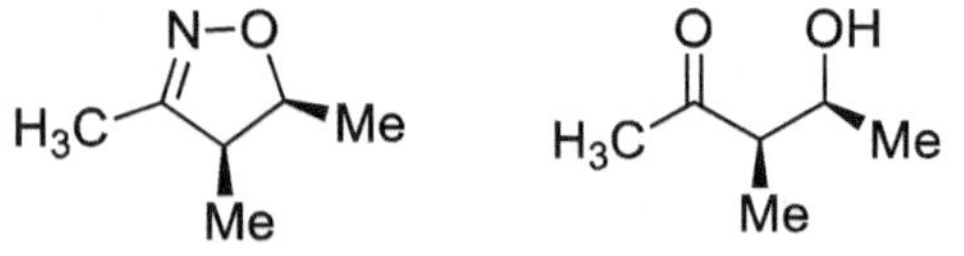

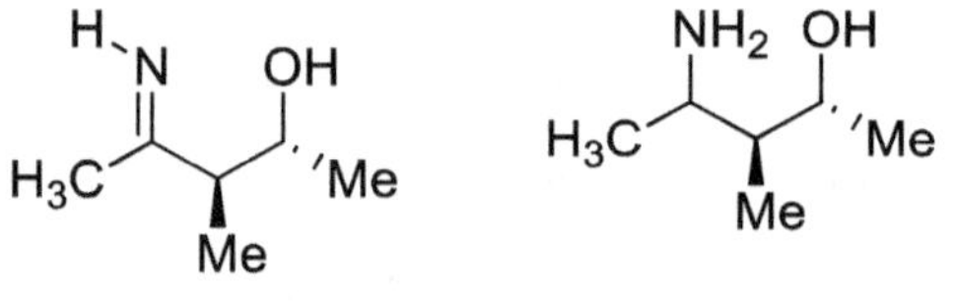

Answer: B. The thermal [3+2]-cycloaddition of acetonitrile-*N*-oxide with *cis*-butene gives *cis*-trimethyl 4,5-dihydroisoxazole P_1, which on further reduction with Rainey Ni in the presence of hydrogen gas produces stereoselective *anti*-aldol type molecule P_2.

Clayden, J.; Greeves, N.; Warren, S. Pericyclic Reactions 1: Cycloadditions. In *Organic Chemistry*, 2nd Ed.; Oxford University Press, 2012; pp 902-903.

Question No-40: The product **Y** and **Z** are formed, respectively, form **X** *via*

A. *hv*, conrotatory opening and Δ, disrotatory opening

B. *hv*, disrotatory opening and Δ, conrotatory opening

C. Δ, conrotatory opening and *hv*, disrotatory opening

D. Δ, disrotatory opening and *hv*, conrotatory opening

Answer: A. The photochemical conrotatory electrocyclic ring opening of **X** gives product **Y** whereas the thermal electrocyclic disrotatory ring opening produces product **Z** as the major product.

Y		**X***		**X**		**Z**
	conrotatory opening anticlockwise each ('C') C_2 symmetric ring opening		*hv*		disrotatory opening m symmetric ring opening	
Ψ_4*, HOMO*		π_3*, HOMO*		π_2, HOMO		Ψ_3, HOMO
C_2(s), m(a)		C_2(a), m(s)		C_2(s), m(a)		C_2(a), m(s)

Question No-41: *o*-bromophenol is readily prepared from phenol using the following conditions

A   i) Ac_2O; ii) Br_2; iii) HCl/H_2O, Δ

B   i) H_2SO_4, 100 °C; ii) Br_2; iii) H_3O^+, 100 °C

C   *N*-Bromosuccinimide, dibenzoyl peroxide, $CCl_4/Δ$

D $Br_2/FeBr_3$

Answer: B. Among these, *o*-bromophenol is readily prepared from phenol using the given conditions i) H_2SO_4, 100 °C, ii) Br_2 and iii) H_3O^+, 100 °C.

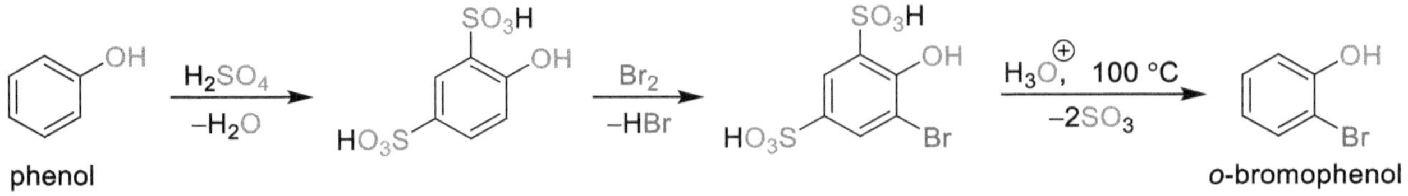

phenol

o-bromophenol

Clayden, J.; Greeves, N.; Warren, S. Pericyclic Reactions 1: Cycloadditions. In *Organic Chemistry*, 2nd Ed.; Oxford University Press, 2012; p 565.

Question No-42: The major product of the following reaction is

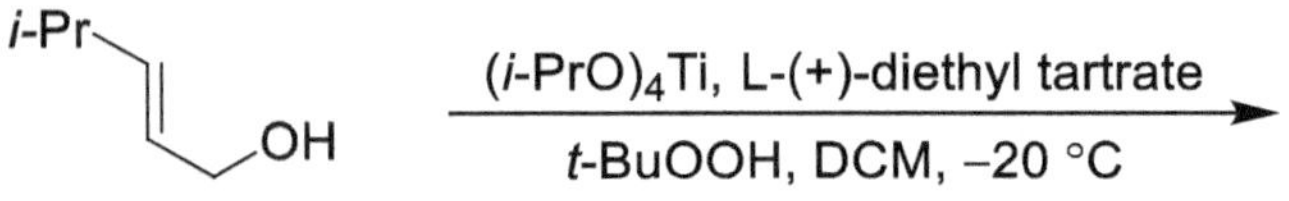

A.

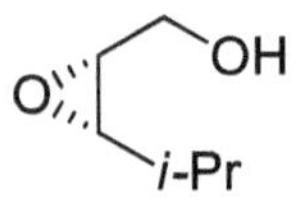

B.

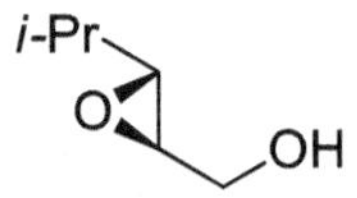

C.

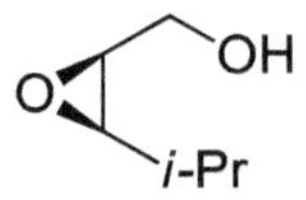

D.

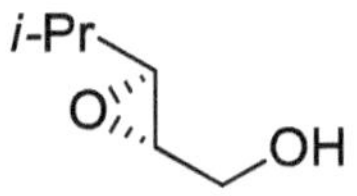

Answer: D. The major product formed in the give asymmetric Sharpless epoxidation is ((2*S*,3*S*)-3-isopropyloxiran-2-yl)methanol.

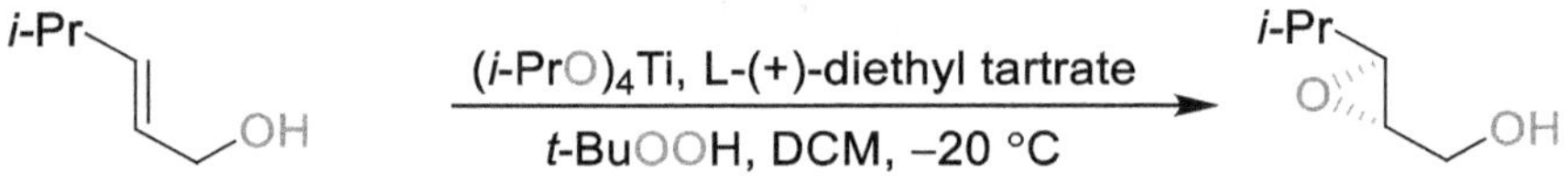

Remember. When substituted allyl alcohol derivative consists of methyl carbinol group on right-hand side then the epoxide ring shall be delivered from the bottom of the plane on using (+)-DET in Sharpless reaction condition.

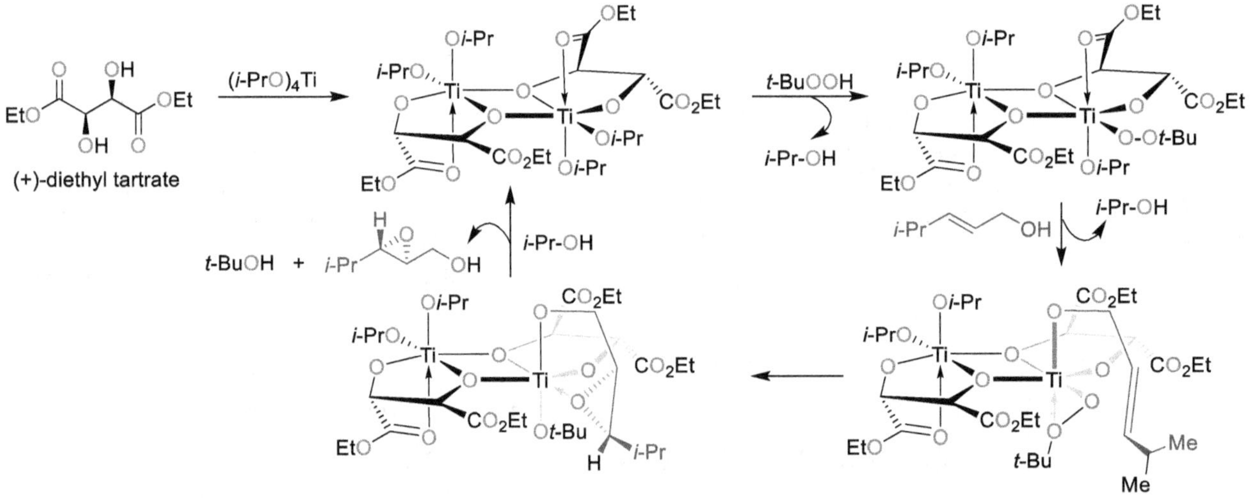

Note. In the given above reaction, the opposite major enantioselectivity will be achieved with (-)-DET.

Question No-43: The photochemical reaction of 2-methylpropene with HF gives 2-fluoro-2-methylpropane and 1-fluoro-2-methylpropane in 14:86 ratio. The corresponding ratio of the bromo product in the above reaction using HBr is most likely to be

A.   14 : 86   B.   50 : 50   C.   1 : 9   D.   99 : 1

***Answer: A.** The photochemical reaction of propene and HF is proceeding through a free radical mechanism. The addition of fluorine radical takes place at the terminal end of the double bond due to the formation of a tertiary radical intermediate which further picks a proton from the HF and offers a major anti-Markovnikov product i.e. 1-fluoro-2-methylpropane (84%). Similarly, the corresponding ratio of the bromo product in the given reaction using HBr is most likely to be the same due to the parallel mechanistic path.

Note. The direct addition of F_2 to the C=C is not feasible. The cleavage of F-F bond required a high amount of energy and then releases also which can break the C=C.

Question No-44: The major product **P** of the following reaction is

A.

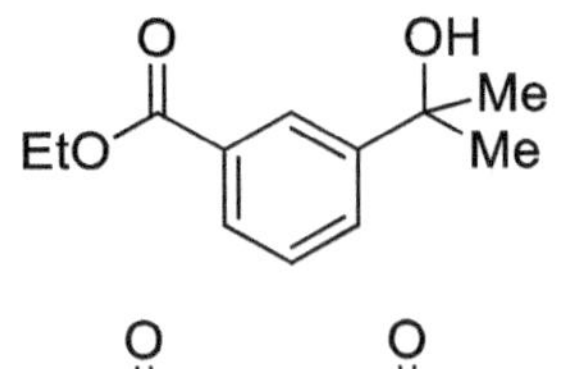

B.

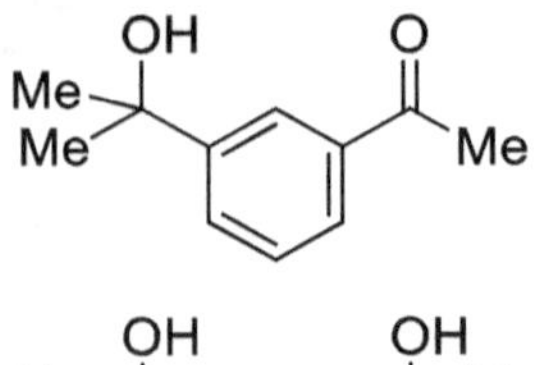

C.

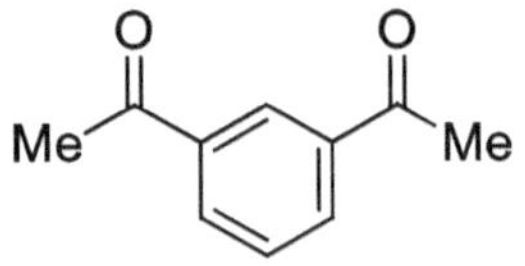

D.

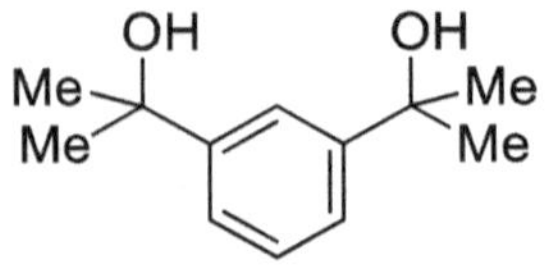

Answer: B. The chemoselective reaction of carbonyl of ketone is more reactive than ester. In order to reverse the selectively of the given reaction, functionalization of the more reacting group in the form of the least reacting group is done at first. Here, the carbonyl of ketone has been protected using the 1,3-diol derivative which gives the least reacting group 1,3-dioxane. Furthermore, the generated first step product has been treated with an excess of Grignard reagent and subsequent hydrolysis offers major product 1-(3-(2-hydroxypropan-2-yl)phenyl)ethan-1-one.

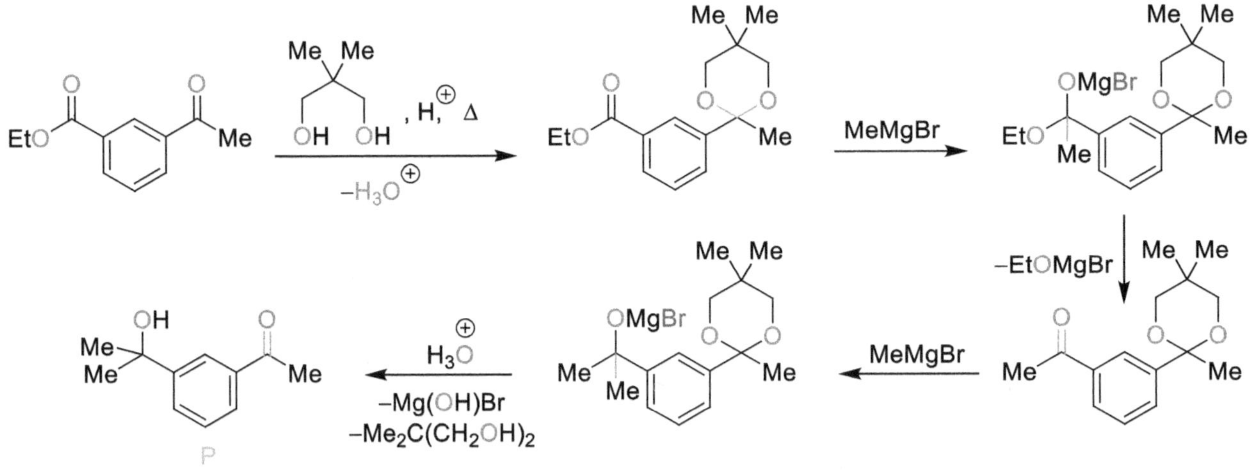

Question No-45: The reagent **X** in the following reaction is

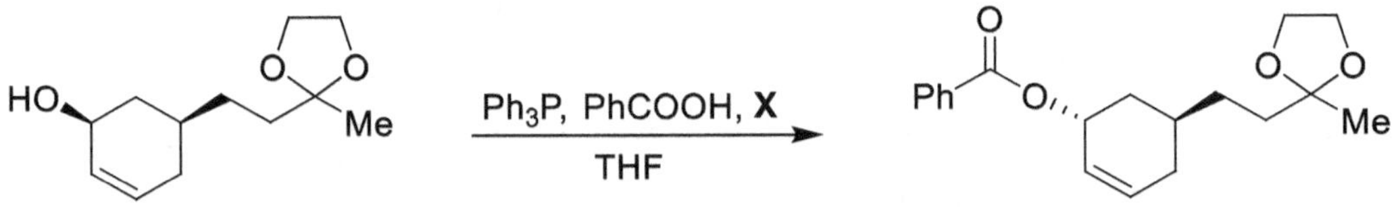

A.   HOOCN=NCOOH

B.   EtOOC-HC=CH-COOEt

C.   EtOOC-N=N-COOEt

D. 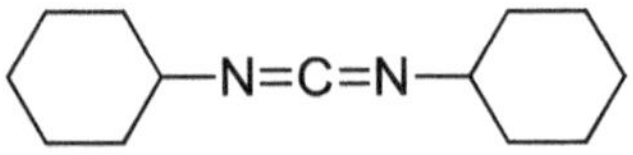

Answer: C. The given reaction is an example of the Mitsunobu reaction and the mechanism of the reaction is shown below.

Similarly, the conjugate attack of benzoate on the C=C furnishes S_N2' products.

Note. The formation of an equal amount of both S_N2 (direct attack-inversion) and S_N2' products (conjugate attack-retention) products take place due to the lack of a specific regioselective approach.

Hughes, D. L. *Org. Prep. Proced. Int.* **1996**, *28*, 127-164.

Question No-46: The major product of the following reaction is

i) Hg(OAc)$_2$, H$_2$O, THF

ii) NaBH$_4$, OH,$^{\ominus}$ heat

A.

B.

C.

D.

Answer: D. The regioselective Markovnikov's electrophilic addition of mercuric acetate on the C=C in aqueous media is known as oxymercuration reaction, which further undergoes demercuration reaction and the saponification reaction (first order reaction) using sodium borohydride in the basic media furnishing final product 5-methylhexane-1,5-diol.

Question No-47: The major product of the following reaction is

$$\text{(cyclopropane-fused cyclohexene with } CO_2Me) \xrightarrow[\text{AcOH, rt}]{H_2, PtO_2 \text{ (cat.)}}$$

A. (Me, Me substituted cyclohexene with CO_2Me)

B. (Me, Me substituted cyclohexane with CH_2OH)

C. (Me, Me substituted cyclohexane with CO_2Me)

D. (Me substituted cyclohexene with CO_2Me)

Answer: C. The major product of the given reaction is methyl 3,3-dimethylcyclohexane-1-carboxylate.

$$\text{(cyclopropane-fused cyclohexene with } CO_2Me) \xrightarrow[\text{AcOH, rt}]{H_2, PtO_2 \text{ (cat.)}} \text{(Me, Me substituted cyclohexane with } CO_2Me)$$

Question No-48: In the following compound, the hydroxy group that is most readily methylated with CH_2N_2 is

A. p

B. q

C. r

D. s

Answer: B. In the given compound, the hydroxy group **q** is highly acidic and most readily methylated with CH_2N_2 due to strong conjugation with the carbonyl of ester.

$$\text{(ascorbic acid with labeled OH groups q, p, r, s)} \xrightarrow{CH_2N_2 \text{ (1 equiv)}} [\text{(enolate intermediate)} + Me\text{–}N_2] \longrightarrow \text{(methylated product MeO at q)}$$

Question No-49: The most appropriate sequence of reactions for carrying out the following transformations is

A. (i) O_3/H_2O_2; (ii) excess $SOCl_2$/pyridine; (iii) excess NH_3; (iv) $LiAlH_4$

B. (i) O_3/Me_2S; (ii) excess $SOCl_2$/pyridine; (iii) $LiAlH_4$; (iv) excess NH_3

C. (i) O_3/H_2O_2; (ii) excess $SOCl_2$/pyridine; (iii) $LiAlH_4$; (iv) excess NH_3

D. (i) O_3/Me_2S; (ii) excess $SOCl_2$/pyridine; (iii) excess NH_3; (iv) $LiAlH_4$

Answer: A. The most appropriate sequence of reactions for carrying out the given transformations is (i) O_3/H_2O_2; (ii) excess $SOCl_2$/pyridine; (iii) excess NH_3; and (iv) $LiAlH_4$.

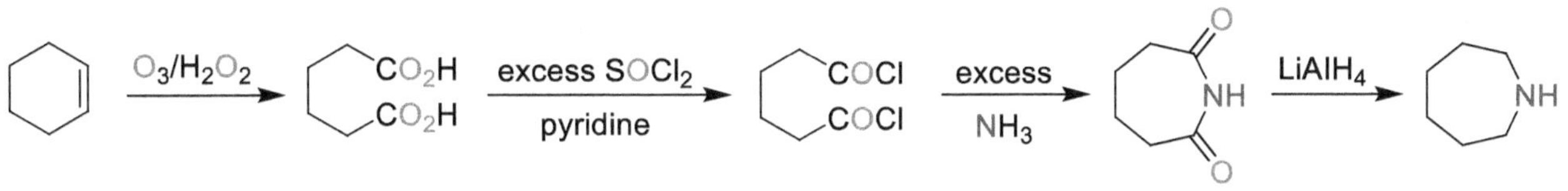

Question No-50: The number of optically active stereoisomers possible for 1,3-cyclohexanediol in its chair conformation is

A. 4 B. 3 C. 2 D. 1

Answer: C. The number of optically active stereoisomers possible for 1,3-cyclohexanediol in its chair conformation is two (*cis*-isomers having *R,R* and *S,S* configurations).

(a) *cis*-1,3-cyclohexanediol is optically inactive due to the presence of a plane of symmetry.

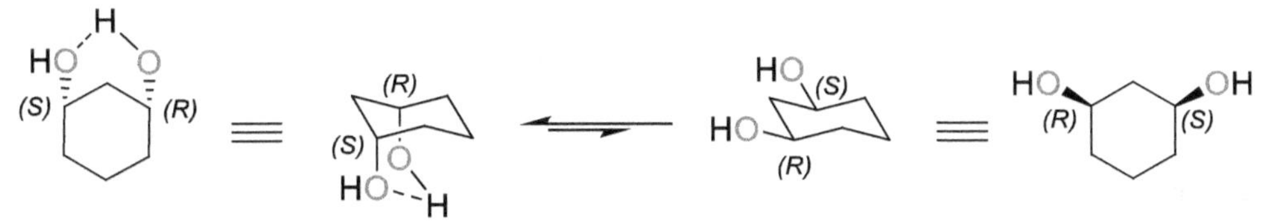

(b) *cis*-1,3-cyclohexanediol is an optically active isomer due to the absence of a plane of symmetry.

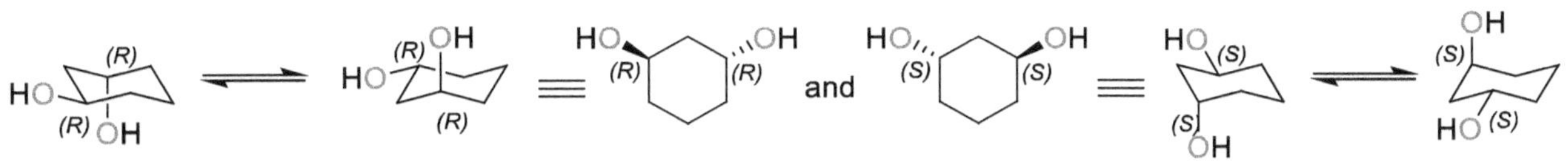

Question No-51: The major product of the following reaction is

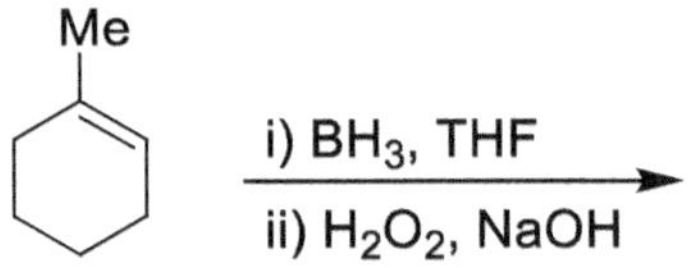

A.
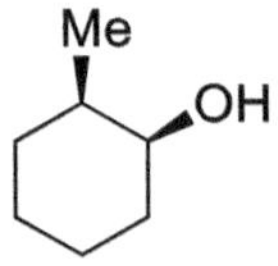

B.
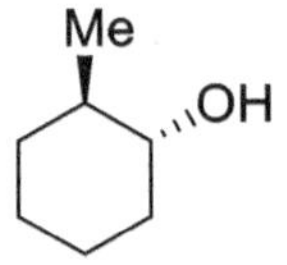

C.
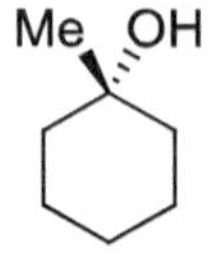

D.
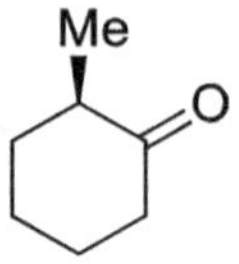

Answer: B. The major product of the given methyl cyclohexene with borane and then acidic hydrolysis offered *trans*-methyl cyclohexanol as the final product.

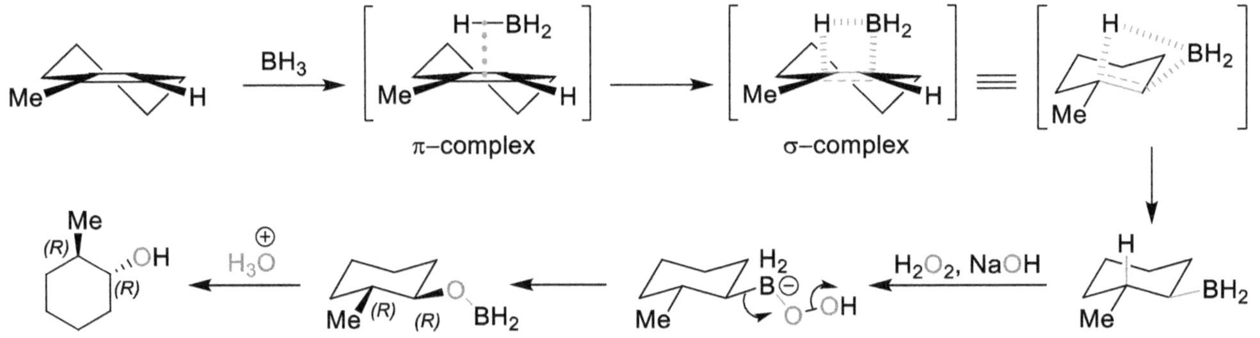

Question No-52: In the following reaction,

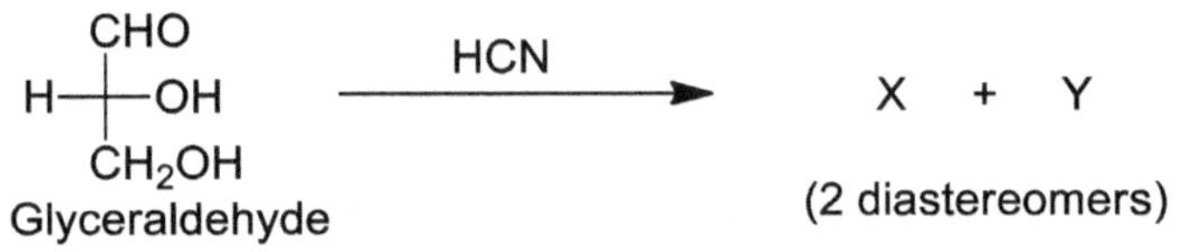

The absolute configuration of the chiral centers in **X** and **Y** are

A. 2*S*, 3*R* and 2*R*, 3*R*
B. 2*S*, 3*R* and 2*R*, 3*S*
C. 2*S*, 3*S* and 2*R*, 3*R*
D. 2*S*, 3*R* and 2*S*, 3*R*

Answer: A. The absolute configuration of the chiral centers in **X** and **Y** are 2*S*, 3*R* and 2*R*, 3*R*, respectively.

X = (2S,3R)-2,3,4-trihydroxybutanenitrile

Glyceraldehyde

Y = (2R,3R)-2,3,4-trihydroxybutanenitrile

Question No-53: The IR stretching frequencies (cm^{-1}) for the compound **X** are as follows: 3300-3500 (s, br); 3000 (m); 2225 (s); 1680 (s).

X

The correct assignment of the absorption bands is

A. $\bar{v}_{(OH)}$ = 3300-3500; $\bar{v}_{(CH)}$ = 3000; $\bar{v}_{(CN)}$ = 2225; $\bar{v}_{(CO)}$ = 1680

B. $\bar{v}_{(OH)}$ = 3000; $\bar{v}_{(CH)}$ = 3300-3500; $\bar{v}_{(CN)}$ = 2225; $\bar{v}_{(CO)}$ = 1680

C. $\bar{v}_{(OH)}$ = 3300-3500; $\bar{v}_{(CH)}$ = 3000; $\bar{v}_{(CN)}$ = 1680; $\bar{v}_{(CO)}$ = 2225

D. $\bar{v}_{(OH)}$ = 3000; $\bar{v}_{(CH)}$ = 3300-3500; $\bar{v}_{(CN)}$ = 1680; $\bar{v}_{(CO)}$ = 2225

Answer: A. The IR stretching frequencies (cm^{-1}) for the given compound **X** will be $\bar{v}_{(OH)}$ = 3300-3500; $\bar{v}_{(CH)}$ = 3000; $\bar{v}_{(CN)}$ = 2225; $\bar{v}_{(CO)}$ = 1680.

Linked Answer Question No-76 & 77

In reaction,

$$(Ph_3P)_3RhCl \xrightarrow{\text{MeCN}} X + Y$$

Question No-76: compound **X** is

A. $Ph_3P\text{-}\underset{\underset{H_3C\equiv\equiv N}{|}}{\overset{\overset{PPh_3}{|}}{Rh}}\text{-}Cl$

B. $Ph_3P\text{-}\underset{\underset{N\equiv C\text{-}CH_3}{|}}{\overset{\overset{PPh_3}{|}}{Rh}}\text{-}PPh_3$

C. $Ph_3P\text{-}\underset{\underset{H_3C\equiv\equiv N}{|}}{\overset{\overset{Cl}{|}}{Rh}}\text{-}PPh_3$

D. $Ph_3P\text{-}\underset{\underset{N\equiv C\text{-}CH_3}{|}}{\overset{\overset{Cl}{|}}{Rh}}\text{-}PPh_3$

Answer: D. The compound chloridotris(triphenylphosphine)rhodium(I) is commonly known as Wilkinson's catalyst which binds with the nitrogen lone pair donor atom of acetonitrile to form complex **X**, as shown below.

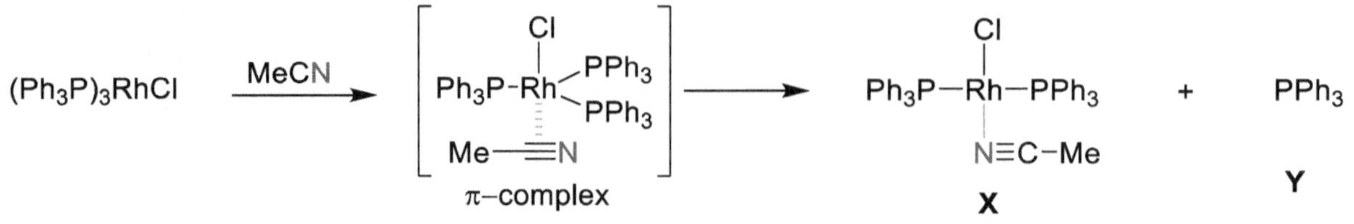
(Ph3P)3RhCl
MeCN
π–complex
X
Y

Palacios, L.; Giuseppe, A. D.; Castarlenas, R.; Lahoz, F. J.; Pérez-Torrentea, J. J.; Oroa, L. A. *Dalton Trans.* **2015**, *44*, 5777

Question No-77: Rh $(PPh_3)_3Cl$ reacts very fast with a gaseous mixture of H_2 and C_2H_4 to immediately gives **Z**. The structure of **Z** is

A. Me–Me

B. 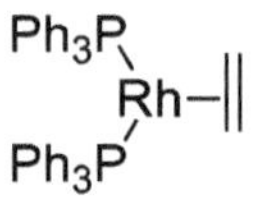

C. $(Ph_3P)_2RhCl(\eta^2–C_2H_5)$

D. 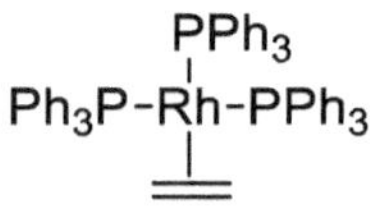

Answer: A. Wilkinson's catalyst reacts very fast with a gaseous mixture of H_2 and C_2H_4 which gives ethane **Z** as the final product of the reaction.

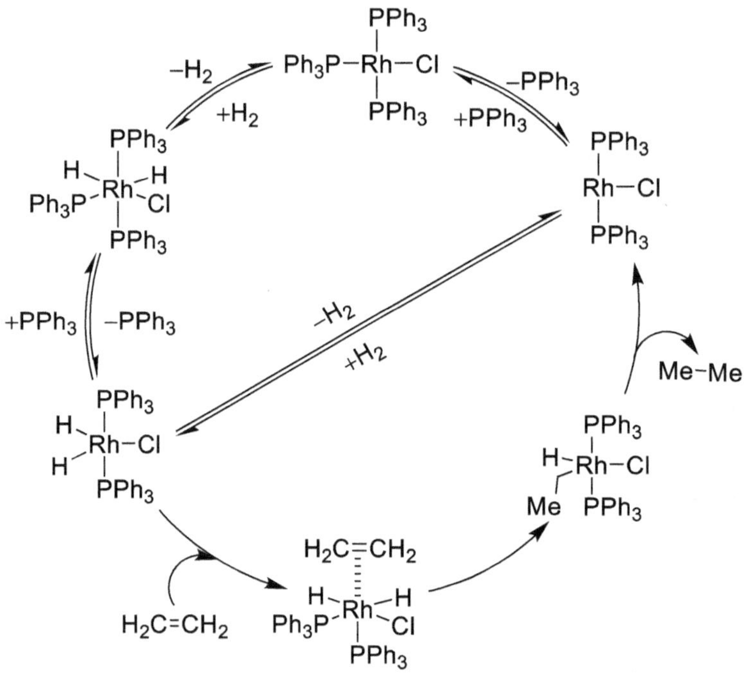
–H2
+H2
–PPh3
+PPh3
Me–Me
H2C=CH2

Cotton, S. A. Rhodium and Iridium. In *Chemistry of Precious Metals*; Blackie Academic & Professional, 1997; p 96.

Linked Answer Question No-80 & 81

For butyrophenone (PhCOCH$_2$CH$_2$Me),

Question No-80: The most probable fragmentation observed in the electron impact ionization (1:1) mass spectrometry is

A. [PhCOMe]$^{\bullet+}$ + H$_2$C=CH$_2$

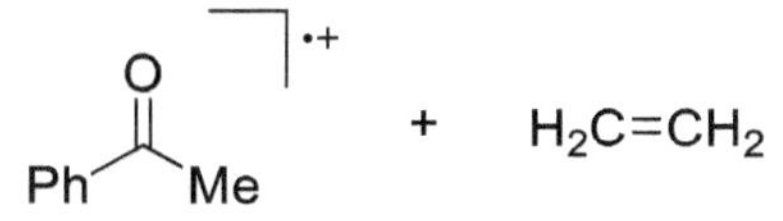

B. [PhCOMe]$^{\bullet-}$ + H$_2$C=CH$_2$

C. [PhCOCH$_2$Me]$^+$ + $^\bullet$CH$_3$

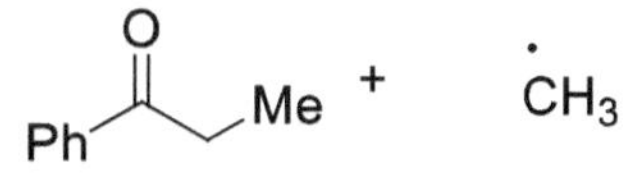

D. [PhCHO] + H$_2$C=CHMe

Answer: A. The most probable fragmentation observed in the electron impact ionization (1:1) mass spectrometry *via* McLafferty rearrangement is acetophenone radical cation and ethylene.

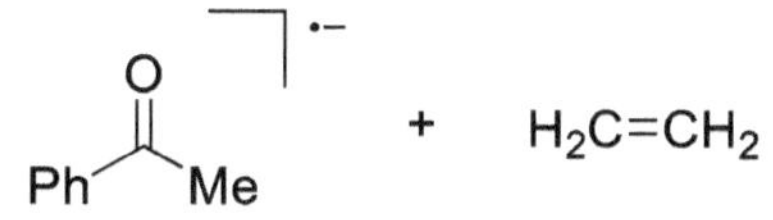

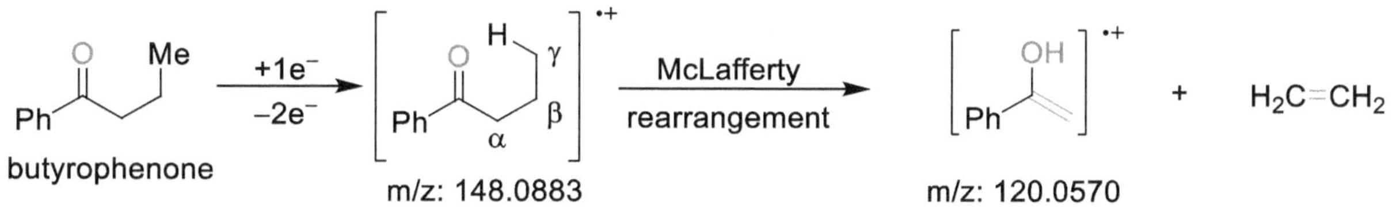

butyrophenone
m/z: 148.0883

$\xrightarrow{\text{McLafferty rearrangement}}$

m/z: 120.0570 + H$_2$C=CH$_2$

Question No-81: Photoirradiation leads to the following set of products

A. [PhCHO] + H$_2$C=CHMe

B. benzene + [OHC–CH$_2$CH$_2$–Me]

C. [PhCOMe] + Me–Me

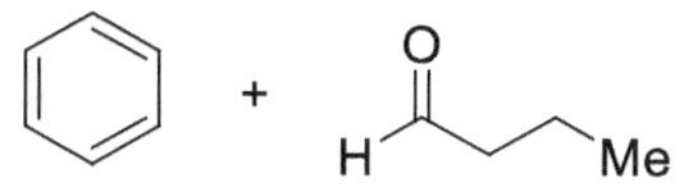

D. [Ph(OH)cyclobutane] + [PhCOMe] + H$_2$C=CH$_2$

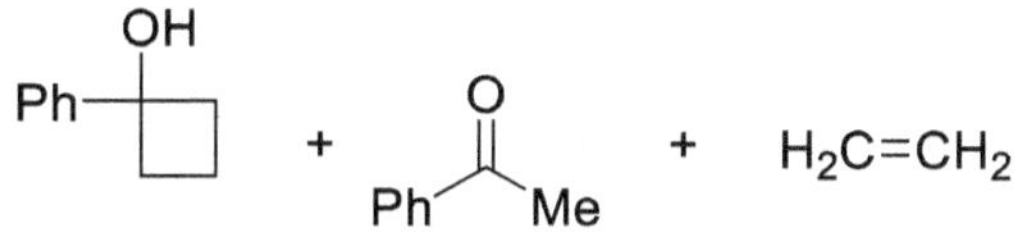

Answer: D. Photoirradiation of butyrophenone forms both singlet as well as triplet diradical intermediates which undergo γ-hydrogen abstraction. The singlet diradical intermediate gives α,β-bond cleaved acetophenone and ethylene *via* Norrish type II fragmentation reaction, whereas the triplet diradical intermediate after cyclization produces a four-membered cyclic Norrish-Yang product.

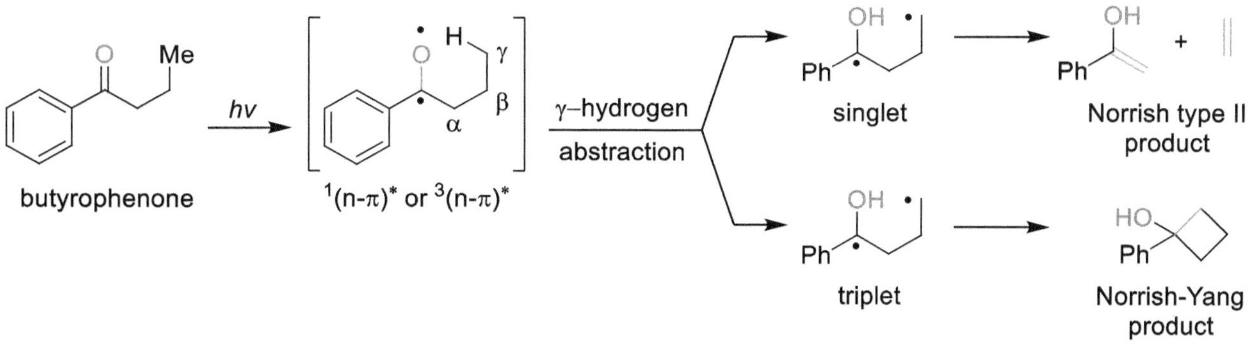

butyrophenone $\xrightarrow{hv}$ ^{1}(n-π)* or ^{3}(n-π)* $\xrightarrow[\text{abstraction}]{\gamma-\text{hydrogen}}$ singlet → Norrish type II product

triplet → Norrish-Yang product

Chiba, S.; Chen, H. *Org. Biomol. Chem.* **2014**, *12*, 4051.

Linked Answer Question No-82 & 83

In the following reaction,

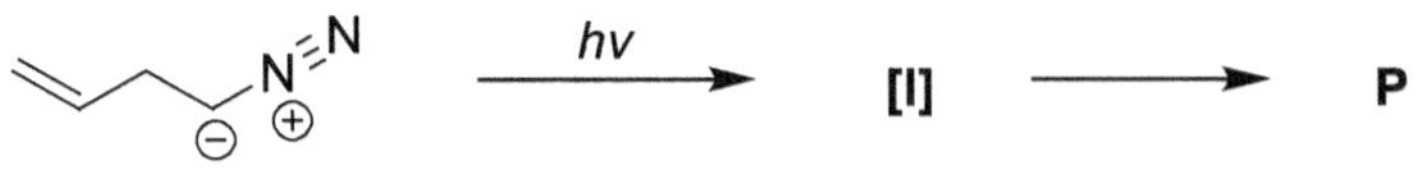

$$\text{allyl–}N{=}N \xrightarrow{hv} [\mathbf{I}] \longrightarrow \mathbf{P}$$

Question No-82: The reactive intermediate [**I**] and the product **P** are

A.

Carbene and

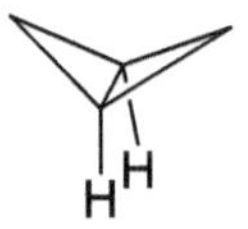

B.

radical and

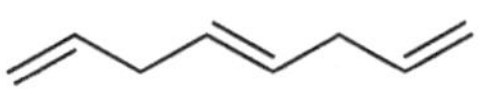

C.

Carbene and

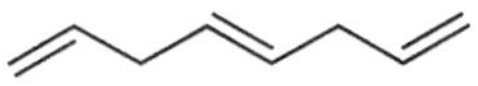

D.

radical and

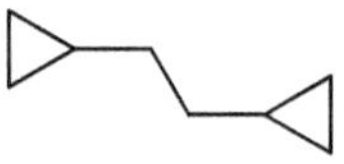

Answer: A. The reactive intermediate **I** and the product **P** are carbene and *cis*-bicyclo[1.1.0]butane, respectively.

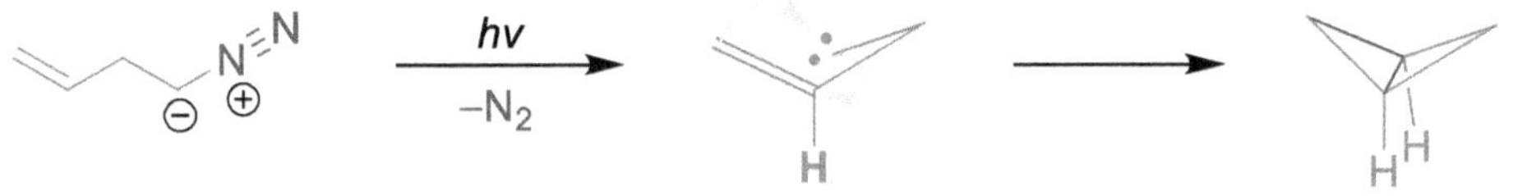

[I] = carbene intermediate   P

Question No-83: The product **P** shows 'm' and 'n' number of signals in ^{1}H NMR and ^{13}C NMR spectra respectively. The values of m' and 'n' are

A.   m = 3 and n = 2   B.   m = 2 and n = 3   C.   m = 2 and n = 2   D.   m = 4 and n = 3

Answer: A. Form the given above statement, the values of m' and 'n' are three and two, respectively.

^{1}H NMR

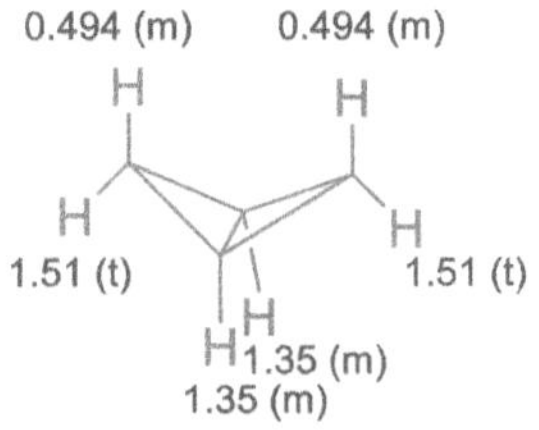

0.494 (m)   0.494 (m)

H   H

H   H

1.51 (t)   1.51 (t)

H
H 1.35 (m)
1.35 (m)

m = 3

^{13}C NMR

H   H

6.1   -5.7   6.1

H   H

-5.7

H
H H

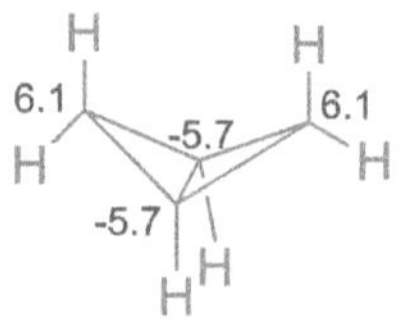

n = 2

Kelly,C. B.; Colthart, A. M.; Constant, B. D.; Corning, S. R.; Dubois, L. N. E.; Genovese, J. T.; Radziewicz, L J.; Sletten, E. M.; Whitaker, K. R.; Tilley, L. J. *Org. Lett.* **2011**, *13*, 1646.

Question No-8: For the compound

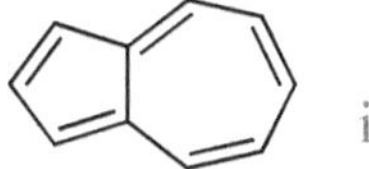

the stereochemical notations are

A.   2*Z*, 4*R*   B.   2*Z*, 4*S*   C.   2*E*, 4*R*   D.   2*E*, 4*S*

Answer: D. The IUPAC name of the given compound is (4*S*,2*E*)-4-hydroxy-2,5-dimethylhex-2-enoic acid.

Question No-9: The compound is

A.   Aromatic and has a high dipole moment   B.   Aromatic and has no dipole moment

C.   Non-aromatic and has a high dipole moment   D.   Non-aromatic and has no dipole moment

Answer: A. Azulene is a non-benzenoid aromatic compound and it has a large dipole moment and very high resonance energy.

Question No-10: In the reaction

the major product **X** is

A.

B.

C. [structure: 4-oxo-4-(p-tolyl)butanoic acid, Me on para position of benzene ring, OH]

D. [structure: bicyclic naphthalenedione with Me substituent, two C=O groups]

Answer: C. The given reaction is an example of Friedel-Crafts acylation reaction, in which toluene reacts with succinic anhydride in the presence of the excess of anhydrous $AlCl_3$ catalyst furnishing major product 4-oxo-4-(p-tolyl)butanoic acid [**X**].

[reaction mechanism scheme showing succinic anhydride + excess anhyd $AlCl_3$ → acylium intermediate, reaction with toluene (Me), through intermediates with Cl_3Al, $-AlCl_3$, yielding product [**X**]]

Question No-11: In the reaction

[structure: allyl phenyl ether with * = ^{13}C labelled carbon] $\xrightarrow{\Delta}$ [**X**] + [**Y**]

(* = ^{13}C labelled carbon)

the major products **X** and **Y** are

	X	**Y**		**X**	**Y**
A.	[ortho-allyl phenol, * at terminal vinylic carbon] and	[para-allyl phenol, * at terminal carbon]	**B.**	[ortho-allyl phenol, * at benzylic carbon] and	[para-allyl phenol, * at benzylic carbon]
C.	[ortho-allyl phenol, * at benzylic carbon] and	[para-allyl phenol, * at terminal carbon]	**D.**	[ortho-allyl phenol, * at terminal carbon] and	[para-allyl phenol, * at benzylic carbon]

Answer: B. The thermal [3,3]-sigmatropic Claisen rearrangement of the given labeled allyl phenyl ether produces *ortho*-allyl phenol [**X**] and *para*-allyl phenol [**Y**]. As it can be seen from the mechanism that the products [**X**] have labeled carbon at the terminal position (at the vinylic carbon) whereas in [**Y**] at the benzylic position (due to double [3,3]-sigmatropic shift).

Question No-12: In the reaction

Ph—CO—CH₂CH₂CH₂—CHO →[Ph₃P=CHCOOEt] **[X]**

the major product **[X]** is

A.

B.

C.

D.

Answer: C. The Wittig olefination reaction of the given compound with stabilized ylide furnishes ethyl (*E*)-7-oxo-7-phenylhept-2-enoate **[X]** as the major product.

aldehyde is less hindered and
more reactive than ketones

stabilized ylide

X = *E*-selective olefin

−Ph₃PO

Question No-13: The most suitable reagent combination to bring out the following transformation

is

A.   PhCOCl and pyridine

B.   DCC and PhCOOH

C.   PhBr, CO and Pd(PPh₃)₄

D.   EtOOC-N=N-COOEt, PPh₃ and PhCOOH

Answer: D. The most suitable reagent combination to bring out the given transformation is diethyl azodicarboxylate (DEAD), triphenylphosphine and benzoic acid. This reaction is an example of the Mitsunobu reaction.

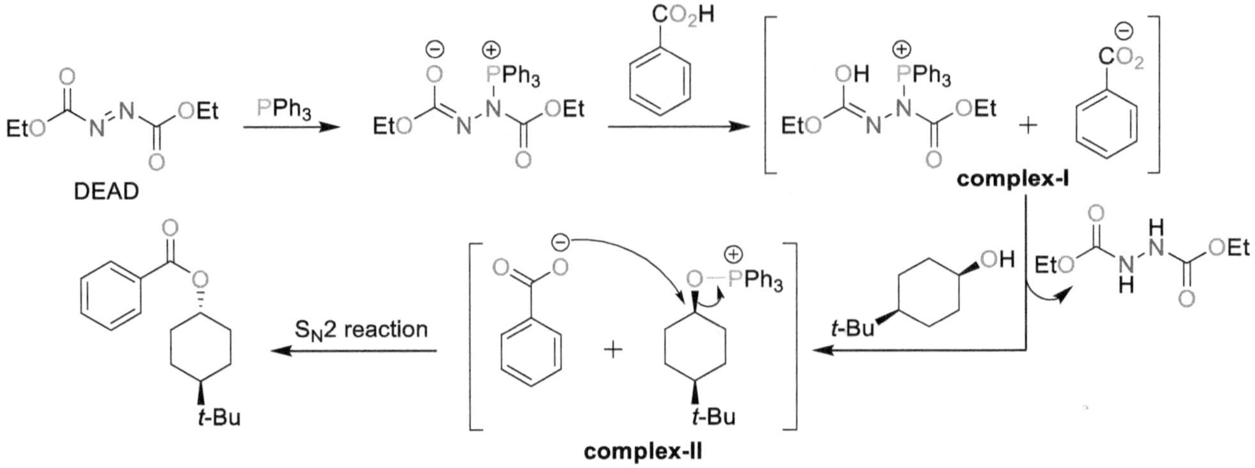

Note. Mitsunobu reaction is widely employed for the inversion of the stereochemistry at the reacting center.

Question No-14: In the two steps reaction sequence

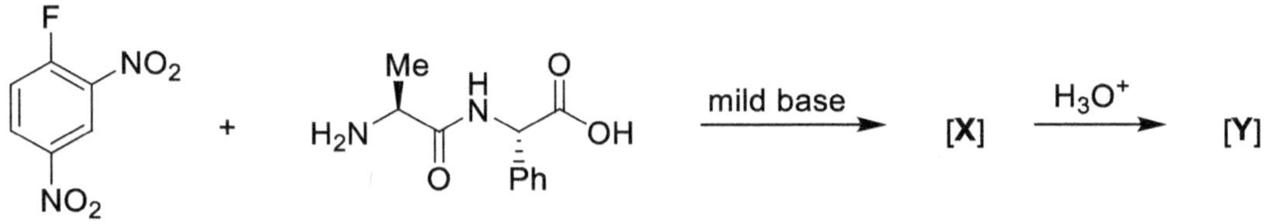

the major product **Y** is

A.

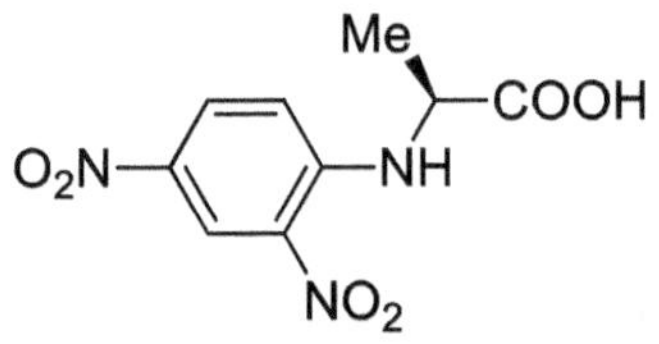

B.

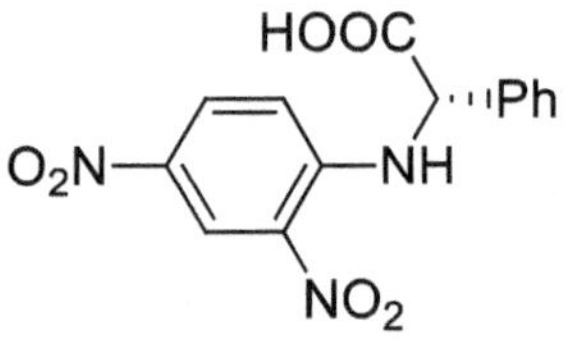

C.

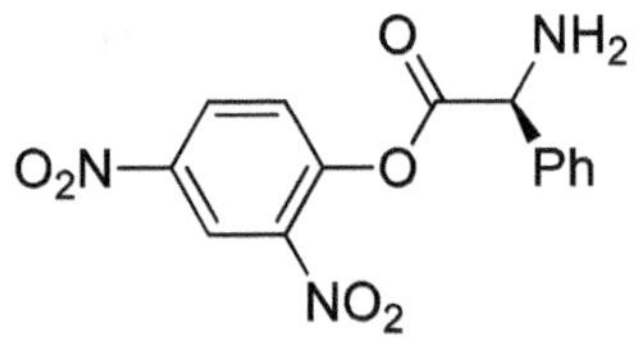

D.

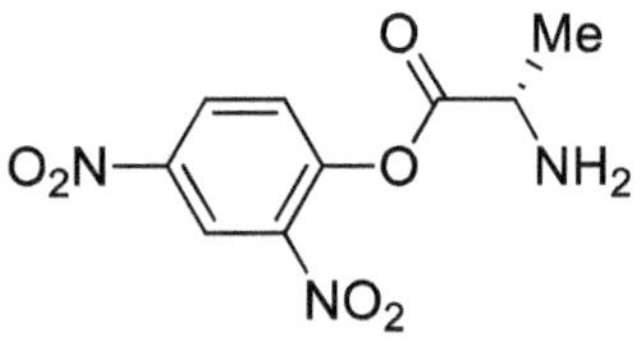

Answer: A. The aromatic nucleophilic substitution reaction of the given dipeptide with Sanger reagent (1-fluoro-2,4-dinitrobenzene) followed by acidic hydrolysis offers (2,4-dinitrophenyl)-L-alanine as the major product.

Question No-23: In the reaction

$$Ph_3P \xrightarrow{\text{MeI}} [X] \xrightarrow{n\text{-BuLi}} [Y]$$

The compounds **X** and **Y**, respectively, are

A. $[Ph_3P(Me)I]$; $Ph_3P=CH-CH_2-CH_2-CH_3$

B. $[Ph_3P(Me)I]$; $Ph_3P=CH_2$

C. $[Ph_3P(Me)_2]$; $Ph_3P=CH_2$

D. $[Ph_3P(Me)][I]$; $Ph_3P\text{–cyclopentyl}$

Answer: B. The compounds **X** and **Y** are methyl triphenylphosphonium iodide and methylene triphenyl-λ^5-phosphane, respectively. This is commonly known as Wittig ylide and is used for the olefination reaction.

$$Ph_3P \xrightarrow{\text{MeI}} \overset{\oplus}{Ph_3P}-Me\;\overset{\ominus}{I} \xrightarrow[-[n\text{-BuLi} + \text{LiI}]]{n\text{-BuLi}} \left[\overset{\oplus}{Ph_3P}-\overset{\ominus}{CH_2} \longleftrightarrow Ph_3P=CH_2 \right]$$
$$\qquad\qquad\qquad [X] \qquad\qquad\qquad\qquad\qquad\qquad\qquad [Y]$$

Question No-24: The ^{1}H NMR spectrum of HD consists of a

A. singlet   B. $1:1$ doublet   C. $1:1:1$ triplet   D. $1:2:1$ triplet

Answer: C. The ^{1}H NMR spectrum of H-D consists of a triplet peak with an intensity ratio of $1:1:1$ (according to $2nI + 1$, proton-coupled with D; for D the values of $n = 1$ and the $I = 1$ thus $2 \times 1 \times 1 + 1 = 3$).

Chen, J. Y.-C.; Marti, A. A.; Turro, N. J.; Komatsu, K.; Murata, Y.; Lawler, R. G. *J. Phys. Chem. B* **2010**, *114*, 14689.

Question No-30: In the reaction sequence

$$\text{(cyclooctatetraene)} + \text{(maleic anhydride)} \xrightarrow{\Delta} [X] \xrightarrow{\Delta} [Y]$$

X and **Y**, respectively, are

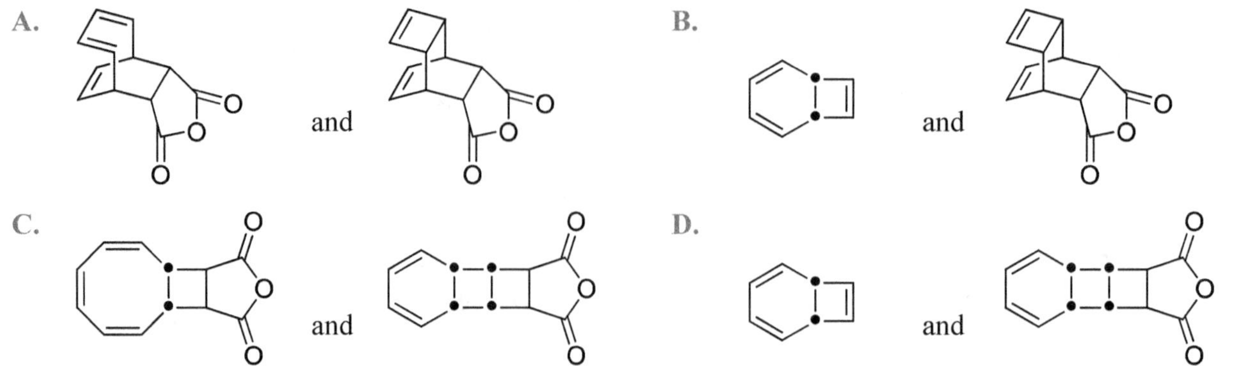

A. and
B. and
C. and
D. and

Answer: A. In the first step, the non-planar tub shape non-aromatic cyclooctatetraene (COT) molecule undergoes [4+2]-cycloaddition reaction (Diels-Alder reaction) yields product **[X]**. In the second step, the **[X]** molecules are converted into **[Y]** molecules *via* thermal electrocyclic 4π-electron ring closure reaction.

$$+ \xrightarrow[\text{[4+2]-cycloaddition reaction}]{\Delta} \textbf{[X]} \xrightarrow[\substack{\text{4π-electron} \\ \text{ring closure} \\ \text{reaction}}]{\Delta} \textbf{[Y]}$$

Question No-31: The major product **[X]** (based on the preferred conformation) in the reaction is

$$\xrightarrow{\text{KH}} \textbf{[X]}$$

(Ts = *p*-toluenesulfonyl)

A.   **B.**   **C.**   **D.**

Answer: B. The major product **[X]** based on the preferred conformation in the given above reaction is (*E*)-cyclodec-5-en-1-one

$$\equiv \xrightarrow{\text{KH}} \xrightarrow[\text{reaction}]{\text{fragmentation}} \equiv$$

Carruthers, W.; Coldham, I. Formation of Carbon-Carbon Double Bonds. In *Modern Method of Organic Synthesis*, 4th Ed.; Cambridge University Press, 2004; p 119.

Question No-32: In the reaction

$$[\mathbf{X}] \xleftarrow[\text{H}^+]{\text{PhCHO}} \text{D-glucose} \xrightarrow[\text{H}^+]{\text{acetone}} [\mathbf{Y}]$$

the major products **X** and **Y**, respectively, are

A.

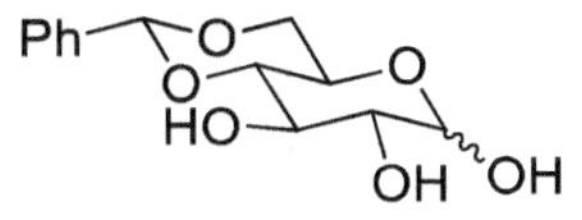

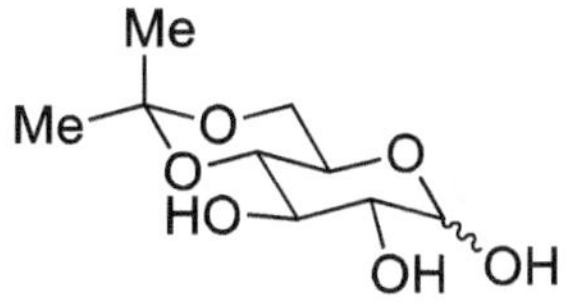

B.

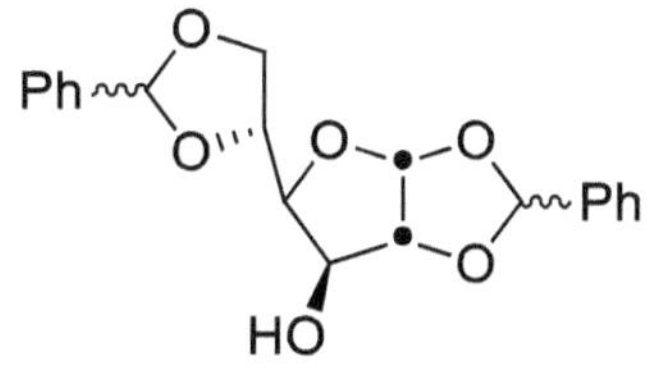

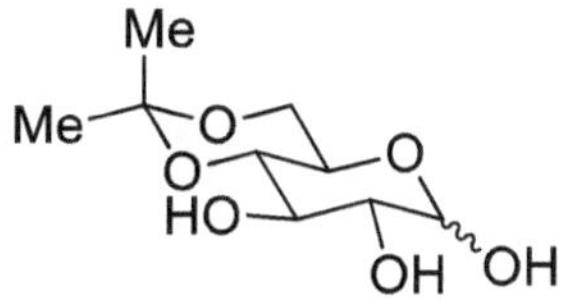

C.

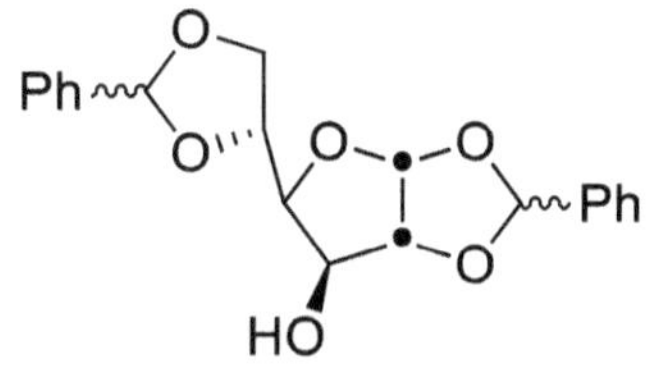

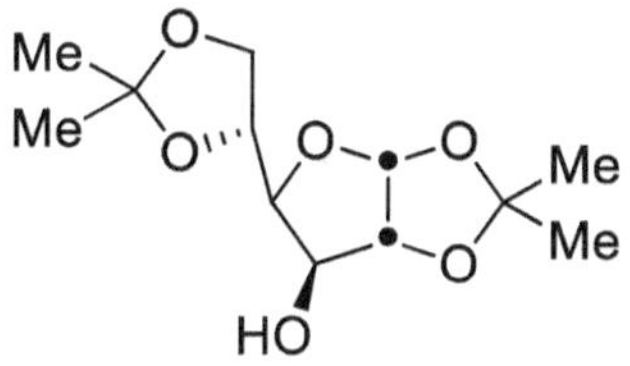

D.

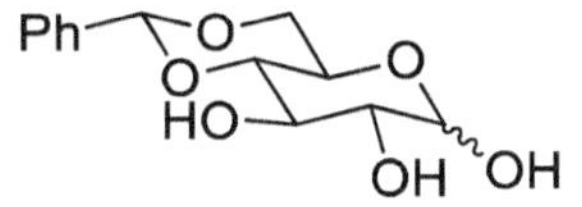

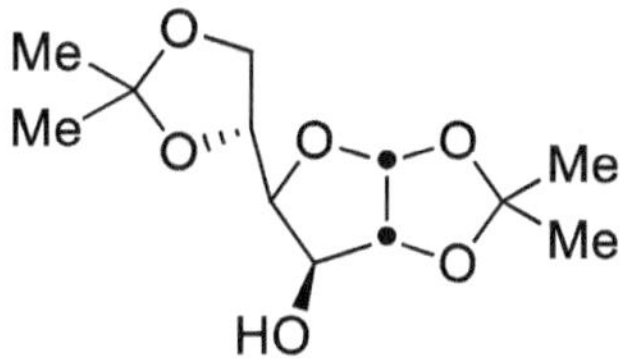

Answer: D. The reaction of D-Glucose with benzaldehyde in dil. acidic medium produces six-membered ring in which the phenyl group exists at the equatorial position due to less 1,3-diaxial interactions.

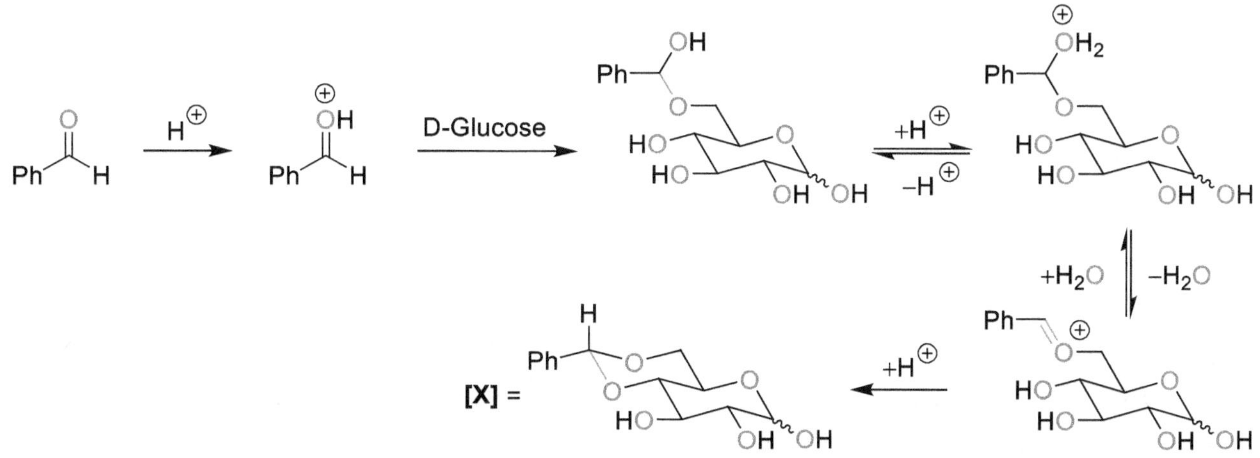

On the other hand, the reaction of D-Glucose and acetone in dilute acidic conditions furnishes diacetonide derivative with a five-membered ring derivative.

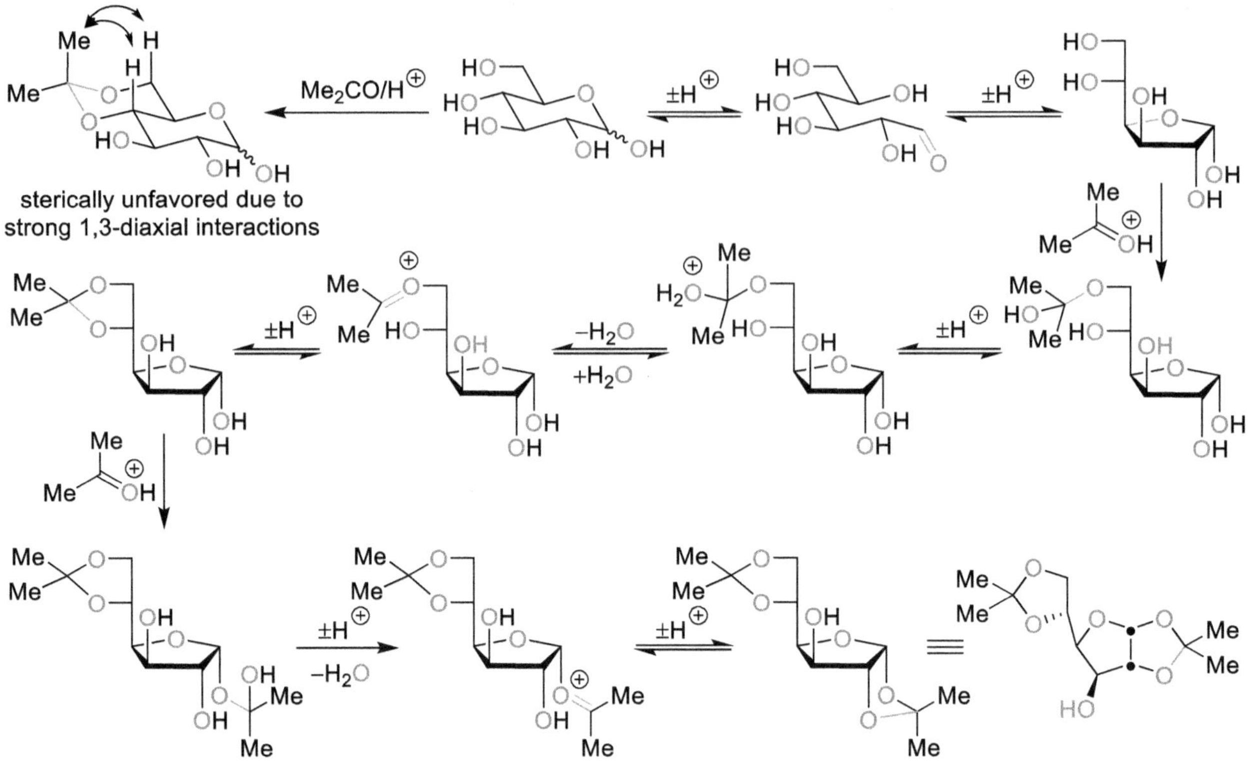

sterically unfavored due to
strong 1,3-diaxial interactions

Note. The formation of a six-membered cyclic ring with acetone is sterically unfavored due to strong 1,3-diaxial interactions by the axial methyl group.

Clayden, J.; Greeves, N.; Warren, S. Organic Chemistry of Life. In *Organic Chemistry*, 2nd Ed.; Oxford University Press, 2012; p 1144.

Question No-33: In the reaction

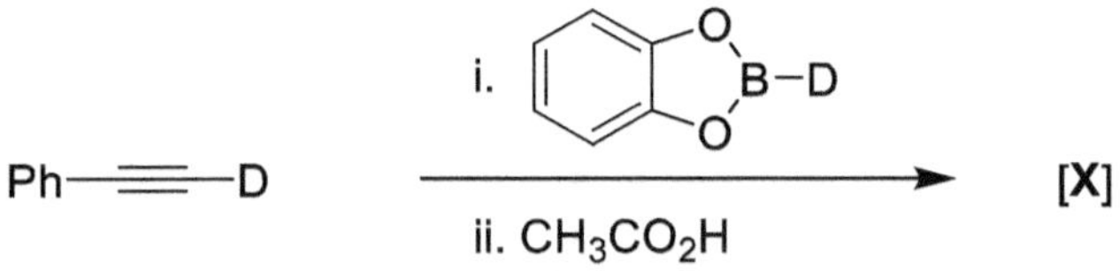

$$Ph—\!\!\!\equiv\!\!\!—D \xrightarrow[\text{ii. } CH_3CO_2H]{\text{i. catecholborane B–D}} [X]$$

the major product **X** is

A. (D, D; Ph, H) B. (H, D; Ph, D) C. (D, H; Ph, D) D. (D, D; Ph, D)

Answer: C. The regioselective *syn*-addition of deuterated catecholborane on the triple bond of (ethynyl-*d*)benzene followed by treatment with acetic acid (any other nucleophilic proton donor) offered anti-Markovnikov's selective *cis*-styrene-d_2 as the major product.

Question No-34: Reaction of *m*-methylanisole with lithium in liquid ammonia and *t*-butyl alcohol at -33 °C generates compound **X** as the major product. Treatment of compound **X** with dilute sulphuric acid produces compound **Y** as the major product. The compounds **X** and **Y**, respectively, are

A.   and

B.   and

C.   and

D.   and

Answer: D. The Birch reduction of the *meta*-methylanisole followed by acidic hydrolysis offered the major product 3-methyl cyclohexenone.

Question No-35: The number of signals that appear in the broad-band decoupled ^{13}C NMR spectrum of *ortho*-, *meta*- and *para*-dichlorobenzenes, respectively, are

A.   3, 4 and 2   B.   3, 3 and 2   C.   4, 4 and 2   D.   3, 4 and 4

Answer: A. The number of signals that appears in the broad-band decoupled ^{13}C NMR spectrum are shown below

ortho-dichlorobenzene

(3 signal)

meta-dichlorobenzene

(4 signal)

para-dichlorobenzene

(2 signal)

Question No-36: In the reaction sequence

$$[X] \xrightarrow[\text{90\%}]{\text{NH}_2\text{OH}} [Y] \xrightarrow[\text{70\%}]{\text{H}_2\text{SO}_4} [Z]$$

the structure of the major product **Z** and the overall yield for its formation from the ketone **X**, are

A. and 80%

B. and 63%

C. and 63%

D. and 80%

Answer: B. The major product **Z** is a caprolactam derivative and the given reaction is known as Beckmann rearrangement.

$$[X] \xrightarrow{\text{NH}_2\text{OH}} [Y] \xrightarrow{\text{H}_2\text{SO}_4} \cdots \xrightarrow[\text{-H}_2\text{O}]{} \cdots \xrightarrow[\text{-H}^{\oplus}]{\text{H}_2\text{O}} [Z]$$

The overall yield of the Caprolactam derivative $= \left(\dfrac{90}{100} \text{ of } [Y] \times \dfrac{70}{100} \text{ of } [Z]\right) \times 100 = \textbf{63\%}.$

Question No-37: In the reaction sequence

$$\xrightarrow[\substack{\text{ii) LDA, -50 °C} \\ \text{MeI}}]{\substack{\text{i) LDA, -50 °C} \\ \text{PhSeBr}}} [X] \xrightarrow{\text{H}_2\text{O}_2,\ 50\ °\text{C}} [Y]$$

the major products **[X]** and **[Y]**, respectively, are

A. and

B. and

C.

D.

and

Answer: A. The fused bicyclic lactam derivative having an umbrella shape is when made to react with phenylselenyl bromide/diphenyl diselenide, the phenylselenyl group approaches from the convex side (not from the concave side due to steric and electronic crowding). Further treatment with LDA and methyl iodide leads to methylation from the convex side [**X**]. Next, the oxidation of [**X**] using hydrogen peroxide under heating conditions goes to pericyclic *syn*-elimination (Ei-reaction) to offer product [**Y**].

Note. The bridged hydrogen is *trans* to the phenylselenoxide group thus it abstracts proton only from the methyl group.

Carruthers, W.; Coldham, I. Formation of Carbon-Carbon Double Bonds. In *Modern Method of Organic Synthesis*, 4th Ed.; Cambridge University Press, 2004; p 117.

Question No-38: In the reaction sequence

$$\text{(cyclohexanone with allyl group)} \xrightarrow[\substack{O_2, H_2O \\ DMF}]{PdCl_2, CuCl} [\text{X}] \xrightarrow{H_2SO_4} [\text{Y}]$$

the major products **X** and **Y**, respectively, are

A. ... and ...

B. ... and ...

C. ... and ...

D. ... and ...

Answer: D. The regioselective oxidative transformation of the terminal double bond to corresponding 1,4-diketone derivative **X** can be achieved with the Wacker process.

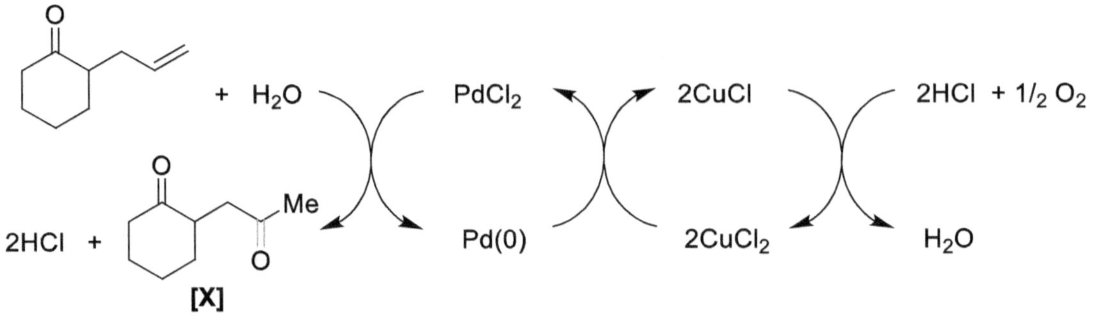

Next, the reaction of **X** in acidic media yields furan derivative product **Y** *via* Paal-Knorr furan synthesis.

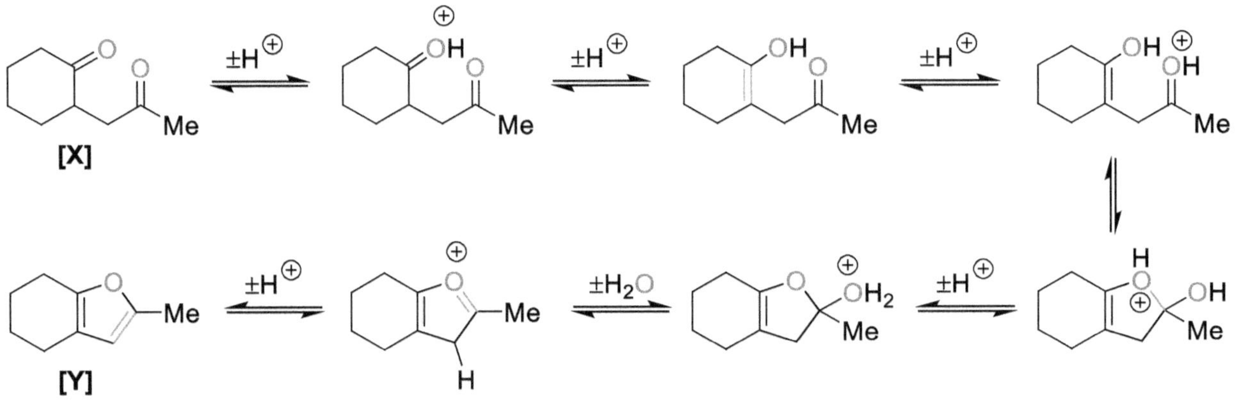

Tsuji, J. *Synthesis* **1984**, 369-384.

Amarnath, V.; Amarnath, K. *J. Org. Chem.* **1995**, *60*, 301–307.

Question No-39: In the reaction sequence

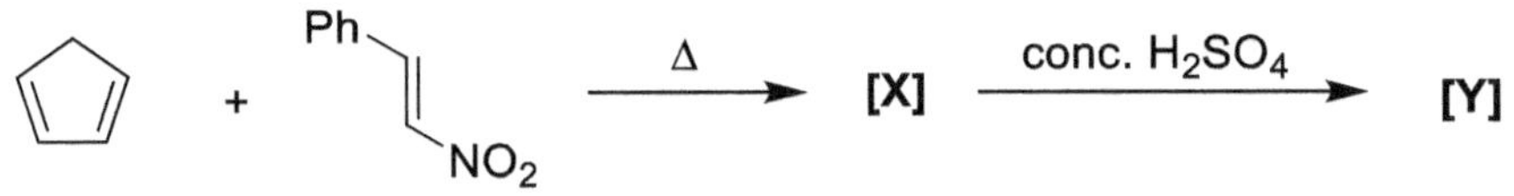

the major products **X** and **Y**, respectively, are

A.

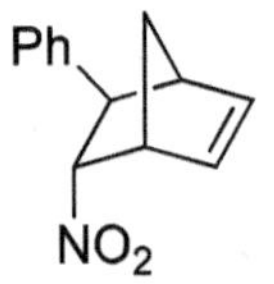

and

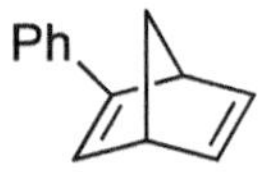

B.

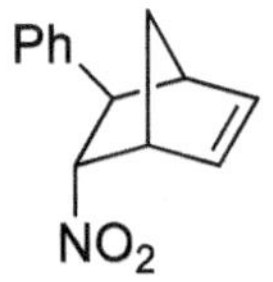

and

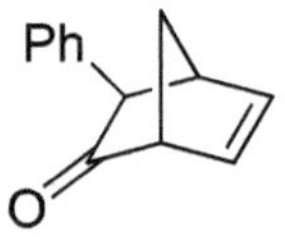

C.

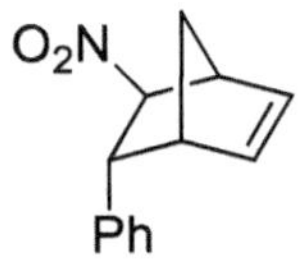

and

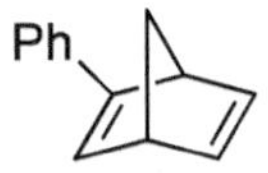

D.

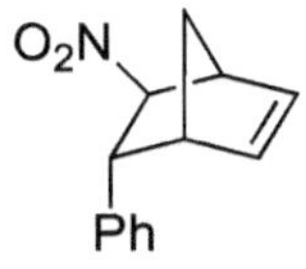

and

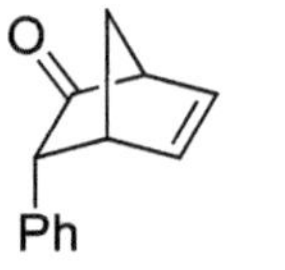

Answer: B. The [4+2]-cycloaddition reaction of cyclopentadiene with β-nitrostyrene produces major product **X** with endo-selectivity (secondary orbital interaction) which on further oxidative transformation using Nef oxidation furnishes carbonyl derivative **Y** as the end product.

Question No-40: In the photochemical reaction

The formation of the compound **X** can be inferred by the disappearance of the ^{1}H NMR signal at [^{1}H NMR spectrum of the starting material: δ 9.7 (1H, s), 7.8 (1H, d, $J = 8.0$ Hz), 7.1-6.8 (2H, m), 3.9 (3H, s), 2.5 (3H, s) ppm]

A. δ 9.7 ppm   B. δ 7.8 ppm   C. δ 3.9 ppm   D. δ 2.5 ppm

Answer: A. Formation of the 1-(4-methoxy-2-methylphenyl)ethane-2,2-d_2-1,2-diol-d_2 **X** can be inferred by the disappearance of the ^{1}H NMR signal at 9.7 (aldehyde peak).

Common Data for Questions 53 and 54

An organic compound **X** ($C_9H_{10}O$) exhibited the following spectral data.

IR: 1680 cm^{-1}

^{1}**H NMR:** δ 7.8 (2H, d, $J = 7.5$ Hz), 7.2 (2H, d, $J = 7.5$ Hz), 2.7 (3H, s) and 2.4 (3H, s).

Compound **X** on treatment with *m*-chloroperbenzoic acid produces two isomeric compounds **Y** (major) and **Z** (minor).

Question No-53: Compounds **Y** and **Z**, respectively, are

Y · Z · Y · Z

A ... and ...

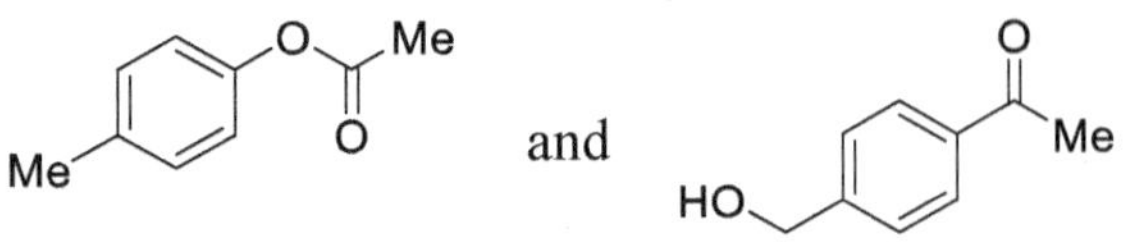

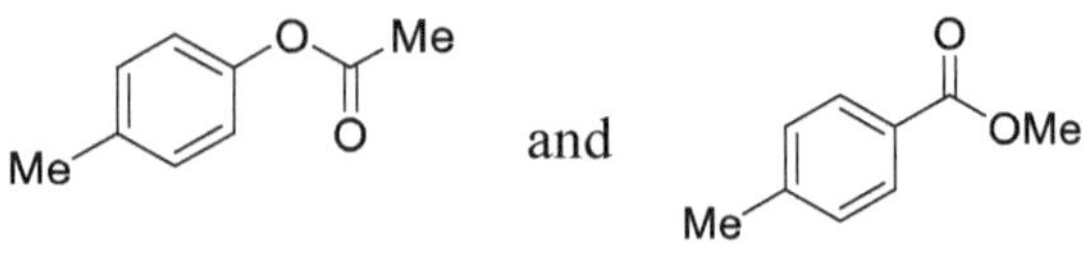

B ... and ...

C ... and ...

D ... and ...

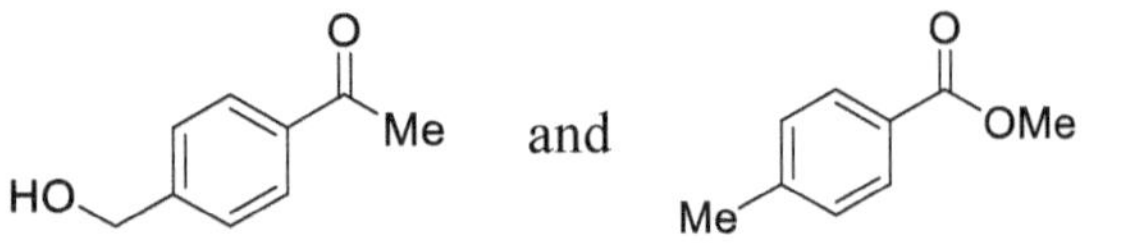

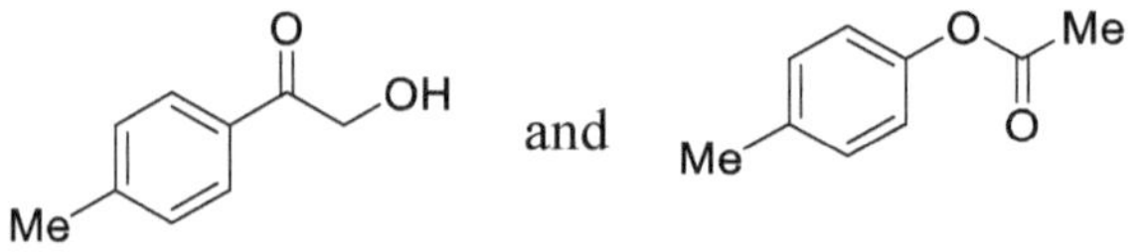

Answer: B. Methyl 4-tolyl ketone **X** on treatment with *m*-chloroperbenzoic acid (*m*-CPBA) produces two isomeric compounds 4-tolyl acetate **Y** (major) and methyl 4-methylbenzoate **Z** (minor).

Question No-54: Compounds **Y** and **Z** can be differentiated by carrying out basic hydrolysis, because

  A.   **Y** produces 4-methylphenol and **Z** is unaffected

  B.   **Y** produces 4-methylphenol and **Z** produces 4-methylbenzoic acid

  C.   **Y** is unaffected and **Z** produces 4-methylbenzoic acid

  D.   **Y** is unaffected and **Z** produces 4-methylphenol

Answer: B. Baeyer–Villiger oxidation of the compound **X** on treatment with *m*-chloroperbenzoic acid produces two isomeric compounds **Y** (major) and **Z** (minor) which are shown below.

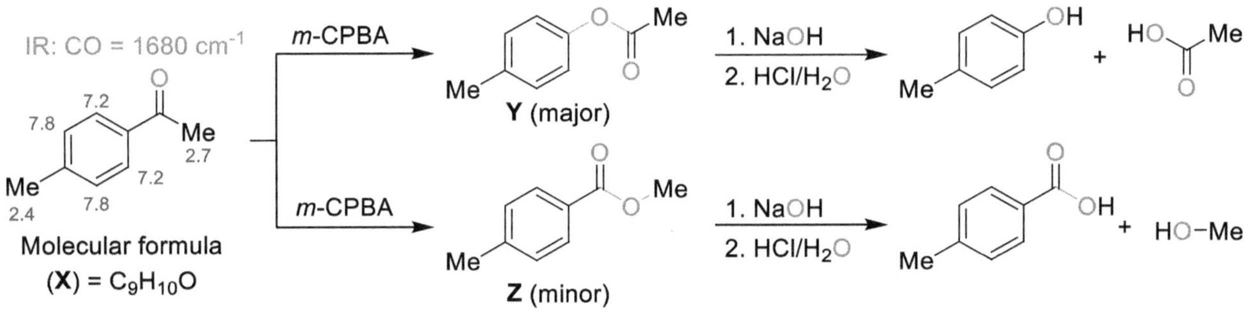

Question No-9: The absolute configurations for compounds, **X** and **Y** respectively are

[Structures of compound **X** (biphenyl with Et, Me, HO, H substituents) and compound **Y** (allene with Me, H, Br, H substituents)]

X   Y

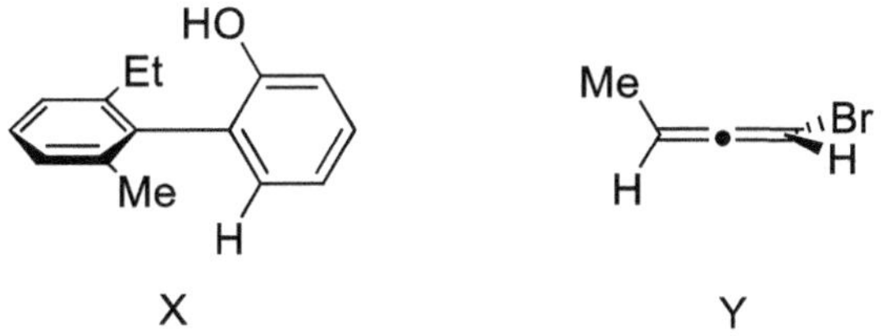

A. *R, S*   B. *S, R*   C. *R, R*   D. *S, S*

Answer: B. The absolute configurations for compounds, **X** and **Y** respectively are *S* and *R*.

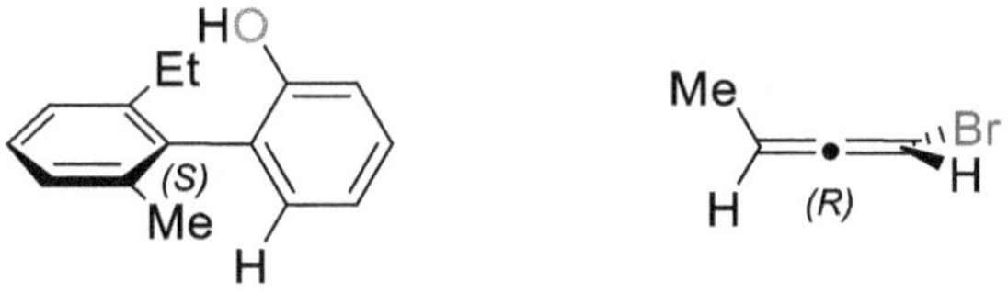

[Structures showing compound X labeled (S) and compound Y labeled (R)]

Question No-10: In the reaction,

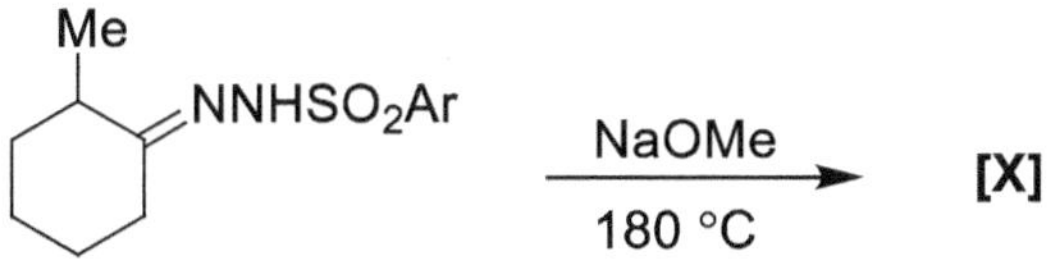

[Structure: 2-methylcyclohexanone tosylhydrazone with NNHSO$_2$Ar] $\xrightarrow[\text{180 °C}]{\text{NaOMe}}$ **[X]**

the major product [**X**] is

A. 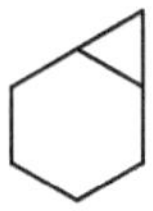 [bicyclo structure] B. 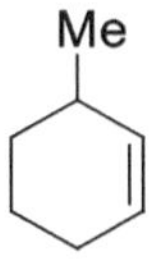 Me [3-methylcyclohexene] C. 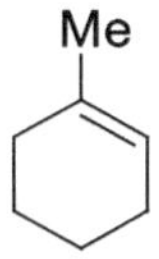 Me [1-methylcyclohexene] D. 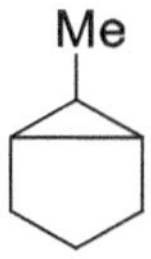 Me [bicyclic structure]

Answer: B. The given reaction is an example of Bamford-Stevens rearrangement which regioselectively offers the major product 3-methylcyclohexene. The mechanism of this reaction is proceeding through the carbene intermediate.

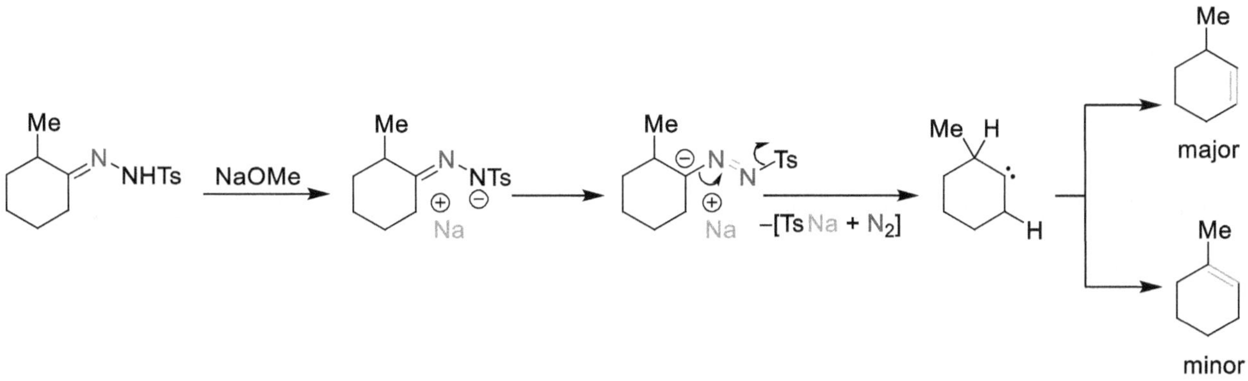

[Mechanism scheme showing the Bamford-Stevens rearrangement with NaOMe, intermediates, loss of $[\text{TsNa} + \text{N}_2]$, and carbene intermediate leading to major (3-methylcyclohexene) and minor (1-methylcyclohexene) products]

Note. When the given above reaction is treated with an excess of BuLi instead of alkoxide base then it is known as the Shapiro reaction.

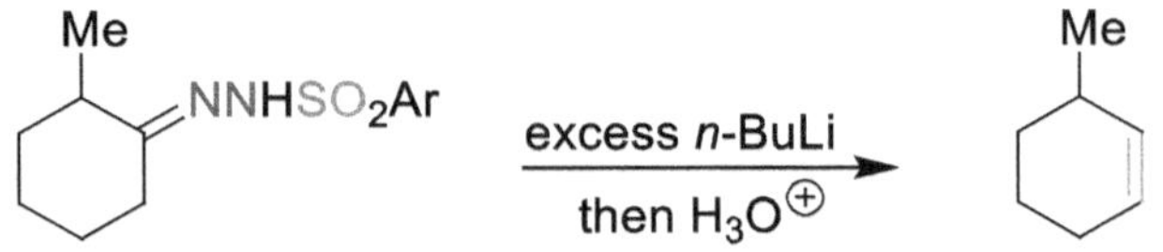

Question No-11: Among the following, a pair of resolvable configurational enantiomers is given by

A. *cis*-1,2-dimethylcyclohexane

B. *cis*-1,3-dimethylcyclohexane

C. *cis*-1,4-dimethylcyclohexane

D. *trans*-1,3-dimethylcyclohexane

Answer: D. Among these, a pair of resolvable configurational enantiomers is given by *trans*-1,3-dimethylcyclohexane. Whereas both *cis*-1,2-dimethylcyclohexane and *cis*-1,3-dimethylcyclohexane molecules have a plane of symmetry, thus their net optical rotation shall be zero.

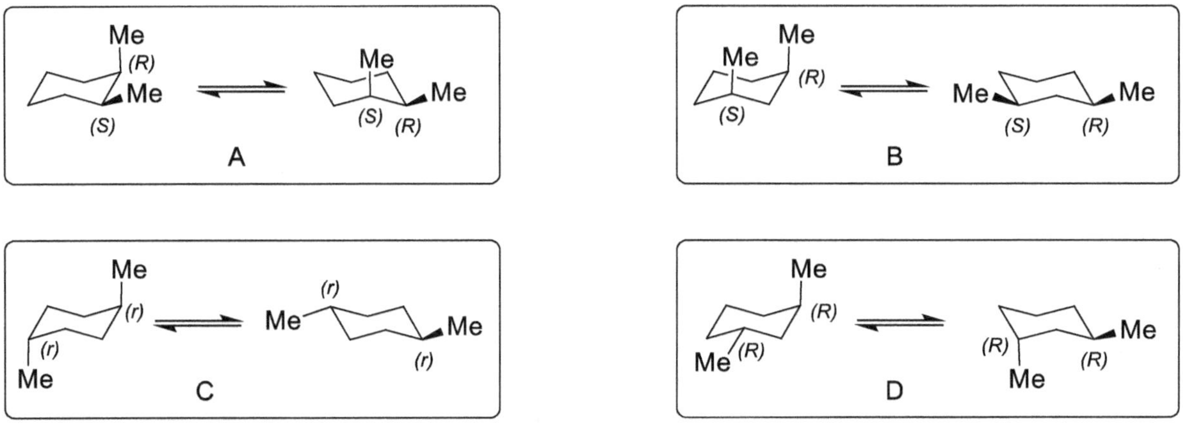

Question No-12: In the reaction

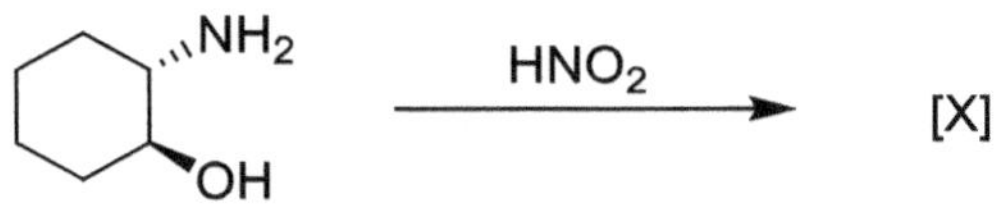

the major product [**X**] is

A. 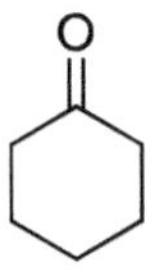   B. 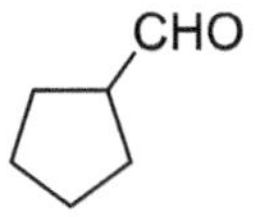   C. 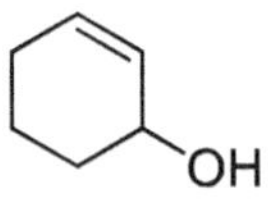   D.

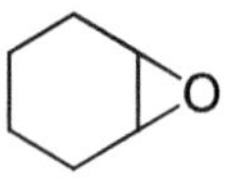

Answer: B. Semipinacol rearrangement of the given reaction offer cyclopentyl carboxaldehyde as the major product.

Question No-13: The decreasing order of isoelectric point for the following α-amino acids is

Lysine	Alanine	Glutamic acid
I	**II**	**III**

Code

A. I > II > III   B. II > I > III   C. III > I > II   D. I > III > II

Answer: A. The decreasing order of isoelectric point (pI) for the given α-amino acids is I > II > III.

AAs	Gly	Ala	*Val	*Leu	*Ile	*Phe	Pro	Ser	*Thr	Tyr
pI			6.0			5.5	6.3	5.7	5.6	5.7
AAs	Cys	*Met	Asn	Gln	*Trp	Asp	Glu	*Lys	*Arg	*His
pI	5.0	5.7	5.4	5.7	5.9	2.8	3.2	9.7	10.8	7.6

Note. Astric (*) symbolizes the essential amino acids (Arg and His are semi-essential amino acids)

Wade, L. G. Amino Acids, Peptides, and Proteins. In *Organic Chemistry*, 8th Ed.; Pearson Edu. Inc., 2013; pp 1157–1159.

Question No-14: The decreasing order of the reactively of the following compounds towards electrophiles is

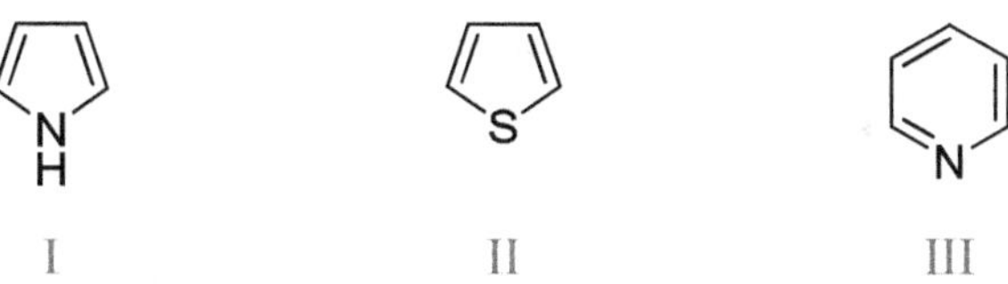

I	II	III

Code

A. II > I > III   B. II > III > I   C. III > I > II   D. I > II > III

Answer: D. Among these pyridine is more aromatic and has high resonance energy thus making it to reacts poorly with electrophiles whereas pyrrole is less aromatic and becomes more reactive (due to the participation of nitrogen lone pair of electrons in delocalization). Thus, the decreasing order of reactivity of the given compounds towards electrophiles is I > II > III.

Question No-15: In the reaction

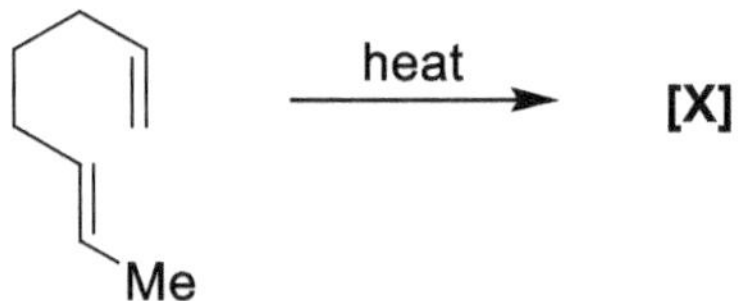

the major product [**X**] is

A.  B. C. Me D.

Answer: A. The Ene/Group-transfer reaction of the given compound gives a major product vicinal *cis*-methyl vinyl cyclopentane.

Question No-16: The decreasing order of acidity of the marked H of the following molecules is

I II III

Code

A. I > II > III B. III > I > II C. III > II > I D. II > I > III

Answer: C. Among these, 9-phenyl-9*H*-fluorene has a more acidic proton and strongly resonance stabilized the diphenylmethane. Thus, the decreasing order of acidity of the marked H of the given molecules is III > II > I.

Question No-17: The decreasing order of nucleophilicity for the following anions is

$$CH_3CO_2^-, CH_3O^-, C_6H_5O^-, NO_3^-$$

A. $CH_3CO_2^- > CH_3O^- > C_6H_5O^- > NO_3^-$

B. $CH_3O^- > NO_3^- > C_6H_5O^- > CH_3CO_2^-$

C. $CH_3O^- > C_6H_5O^- > CH_3CO_2^- > NO_3^-$

D. $C_6H_5O^- > CH_3O^- > NO_3^- > CH_3CO_2^-$

Answer: C. Among all, the nucleophilicity of nitrate is poor due to more resonating structures. Thus, the decreasing order of nucleophilicity for the give anions is $CH_3O^- > C_6H_5O^- > CH_3CO_2^- > NO_3^-$.

Question No-34: In the reaction

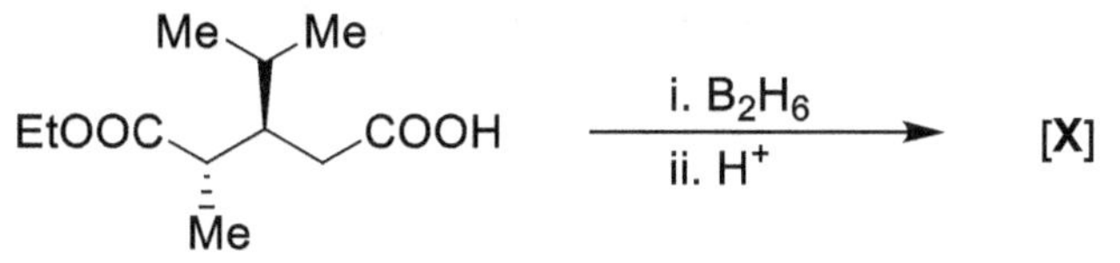

the major product [**X**] is

A. 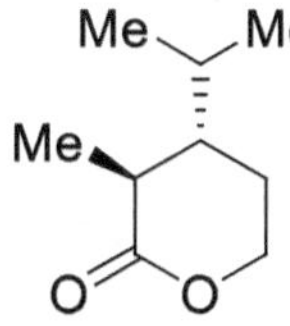 B. 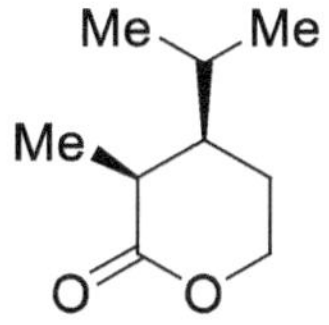 C. 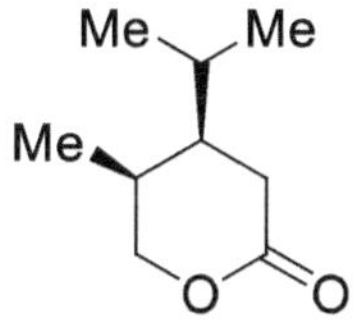 D.

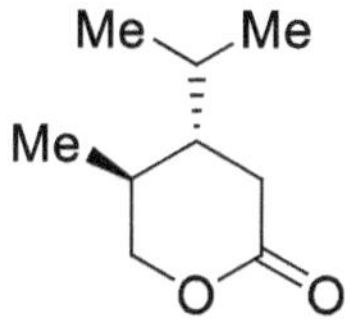

Answer: B. The chemoselective reduction of carbonyl of acid in the presence of ester with diborane gives a corresponding alcohol derivative, which undergoes a cyclization reaction in acidic media and produces a cyclic-lactone derivative as the major product.

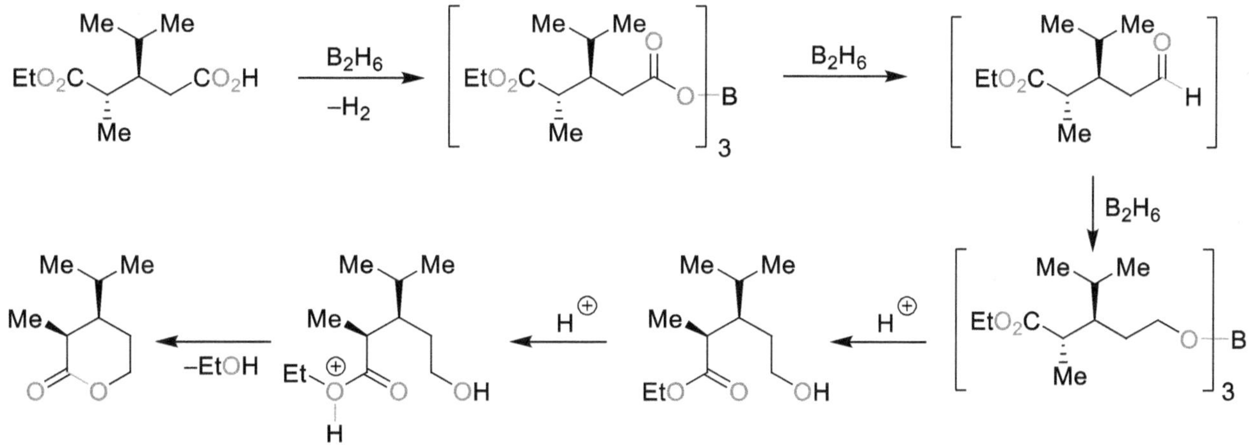

Clayden, J.; Greeves, N.; Warren, S. Chemoselectivity and Protecting Groups. In *Organic Chemistry*, 2nd Ed.; Oxford University Press, 2012; pp 531-532.

Question No-35: In the reaction

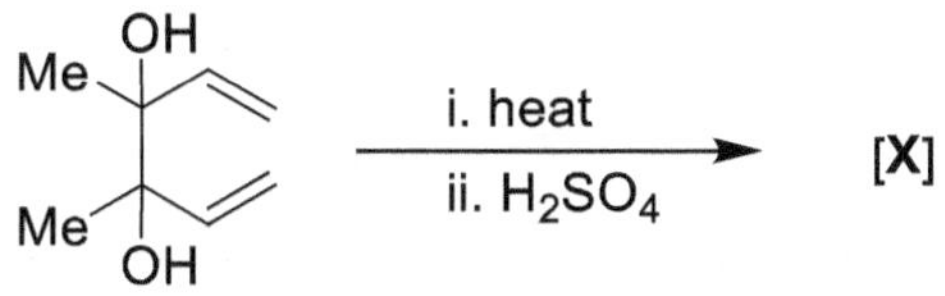

the major product [**X**] is

A. 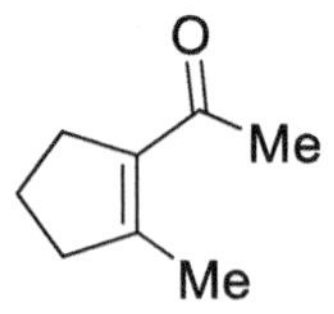 B. 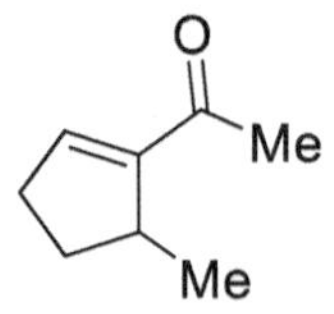 C. 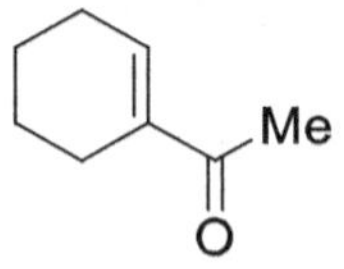 D.

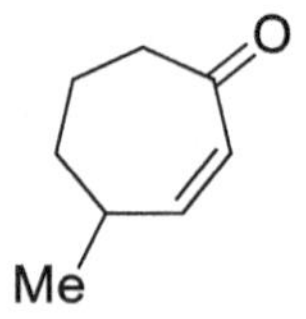

Answer: A. The [3,3]-sigmatropic shift followed by the thermodynamically controlled aldol condensation in acidic media offers a major product 1-(2-methylcyclopent-1-en-1-yl)ethan-1-one.

Cope rearrangement

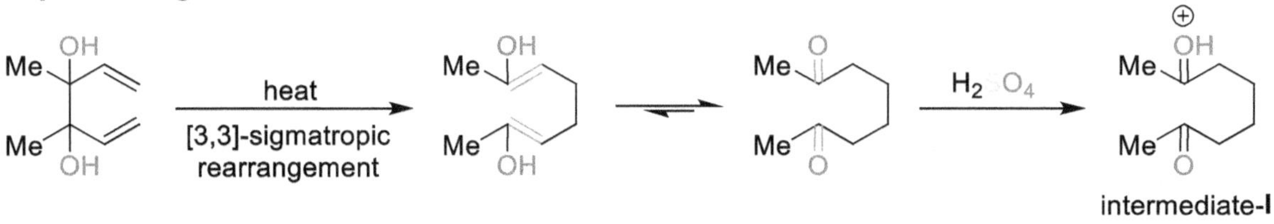

heat
[3,3]-sigmatropic
rearrangement

H_2O_4

intermediate-I

Aldol condensation

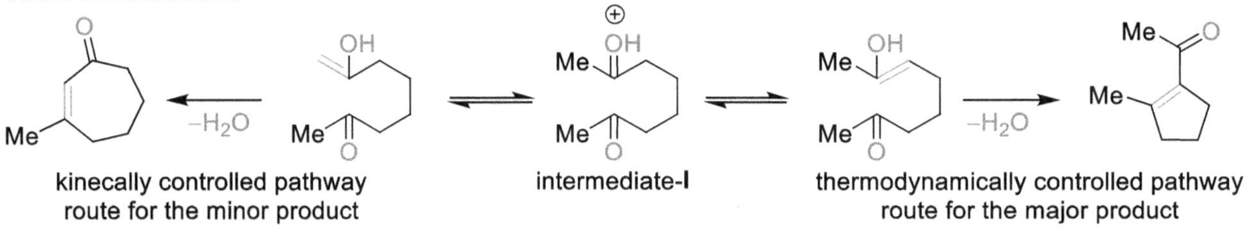

$-H_2O$

kinecally controlled pathway
route for the minor product

intermediate-I

$-H_2O$

thermodynamically controlled pathway
route for the major product

Note. Generally, acid-catalyzed reactions are proceeding in a thermodynamically controlled manner.

Question No-36: In the following reaction sequence

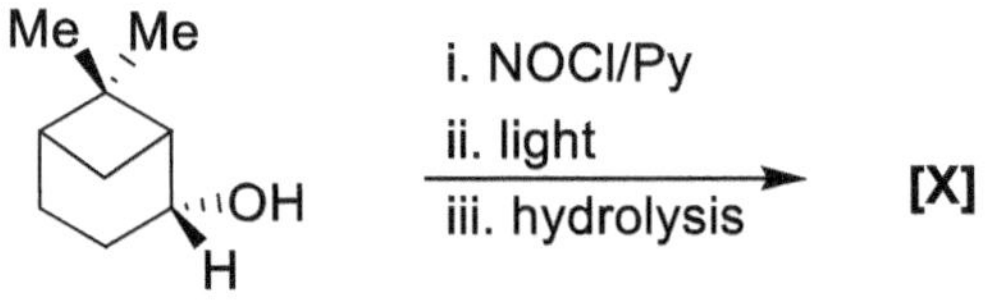

i. NOCl/Py
ii. light
iii. hydrolysis

[X]

the major product **[X]** is

A. 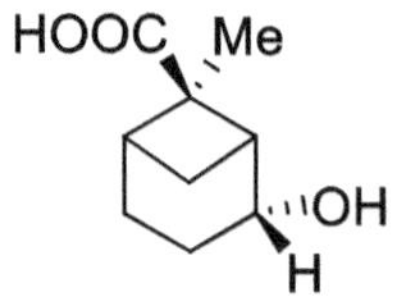 HOOC, Me B. 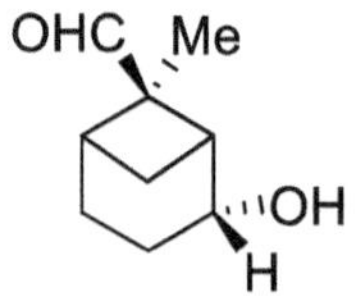 OHC, Me C. 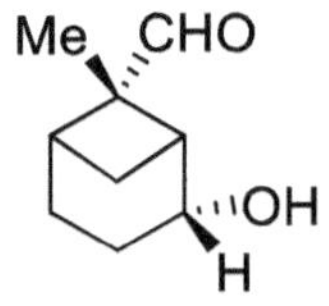 Me, CHO D. 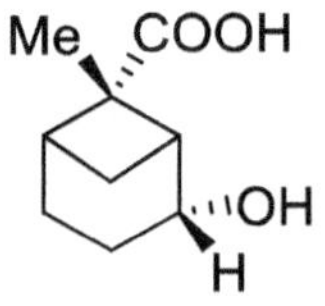 Me, COOH

Answer: C. Borton reaction is an excellent reaction for the chemoselective transformation of *syn*-oriented inactive δ-carbon to give the corresponding carbonyl derivative. In the given reaction sequence, alcohol derivative gets converted into corresponding alkyl nitrite with the help of nitrosyl chloride in combination with pyridine, which on further photochemical irradiation produces δ-nitroso alcohol derivative. Furthermore, the obtained δ-nitroso alcohol derivative on acidic hydrolysis furnishing major product δ-hydroxy alkanal derivative (also equilibrating into hemiacetal form).

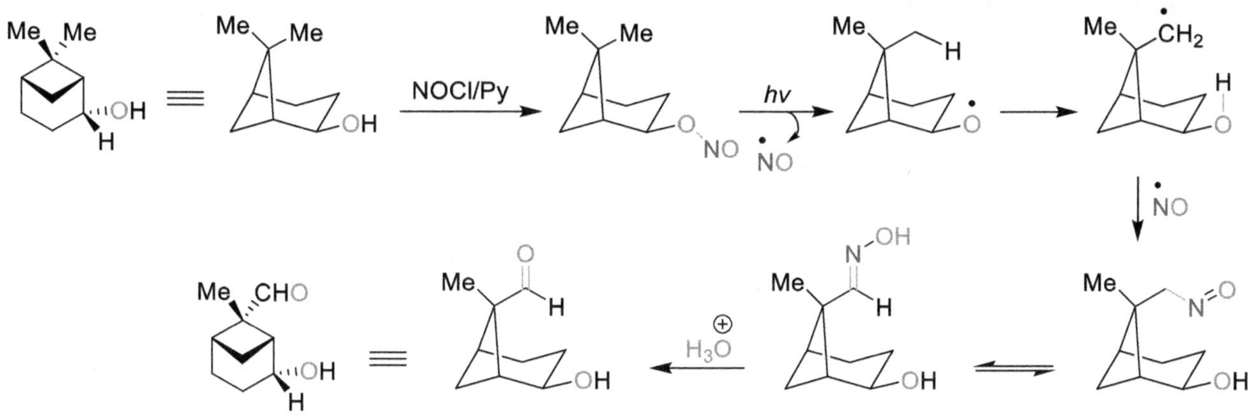

Carruthers, W.; Coldham, I. Radical and Carbene Chemistry. In *Modern Method of Organic Synthesis*, 4th Ed.; Cambridge University Press, 2004; pp 276-277.

Question No-37: In the reactions

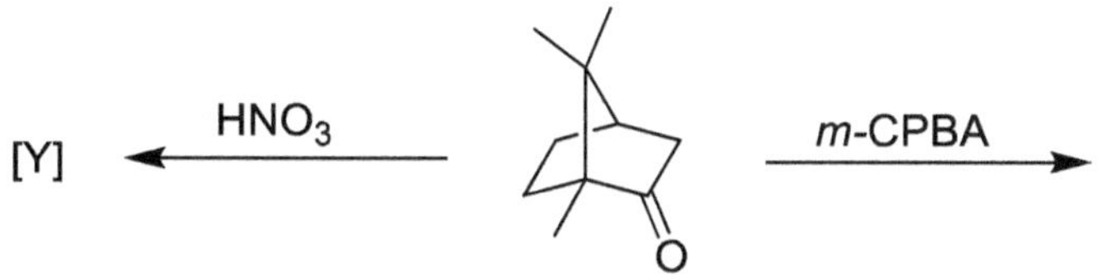

the major products, [**X**] and [**Y**], respectively, are

A.

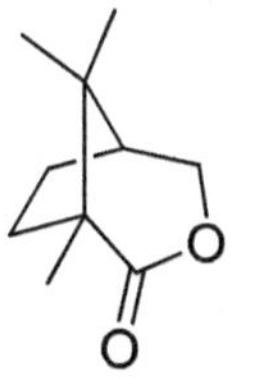

and

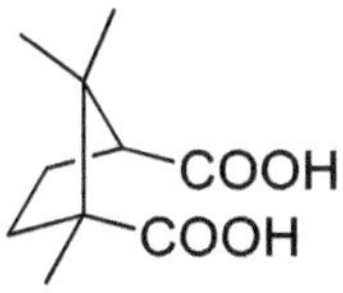

B.

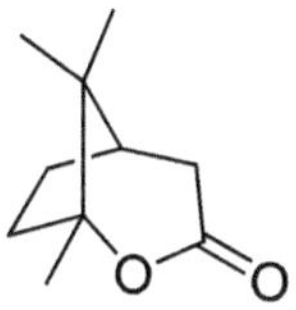

and

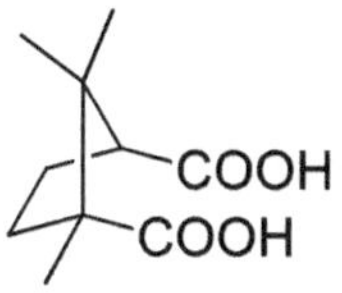

C.

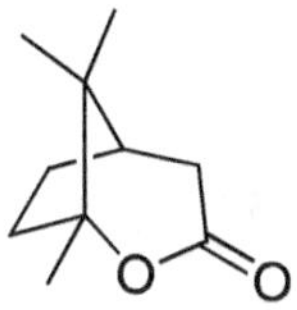

and

D.

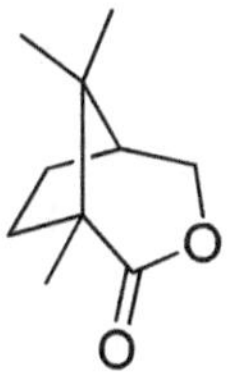

and

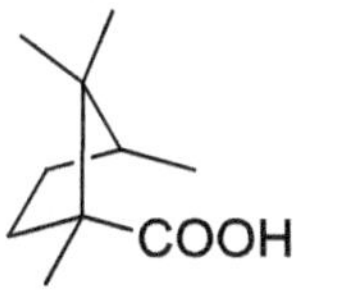

Answer: B. In Baeyer-Villiger rearrangement product is influenced by the migratory aptitude and steric effect. In the given reaction, the *endo*-attack of *m*-CPBA gives a preferred transition state due to the high migratory aptitude of bridgehead quaternary carbon (boat conformer) yielding a major product. Whereas the migration of methylene group offers a minor product with chair conformer. The *exo*-attack of *m*-CPBA is hindered by the methyl groups, thus the possibility of the formation of this transition state is less favored. The chair conformer of the *exo*-attack of *m*-CPBA gives a major product due to relief of steric and also supported by migratory aptitude.

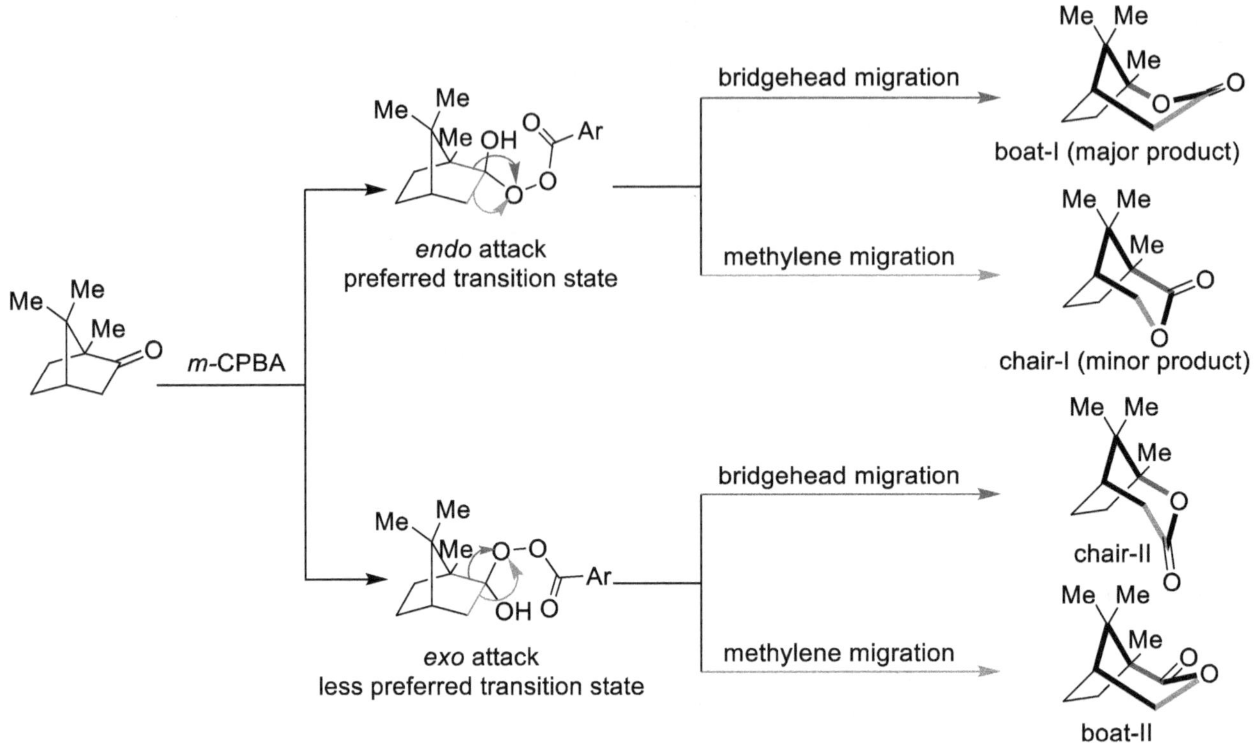

Also, the formation major product of takes place *via* conformer chair-II due to the migration of bridgehead quaternary carbon which gives a similar type of Criegee intermediate in both the mode attack.

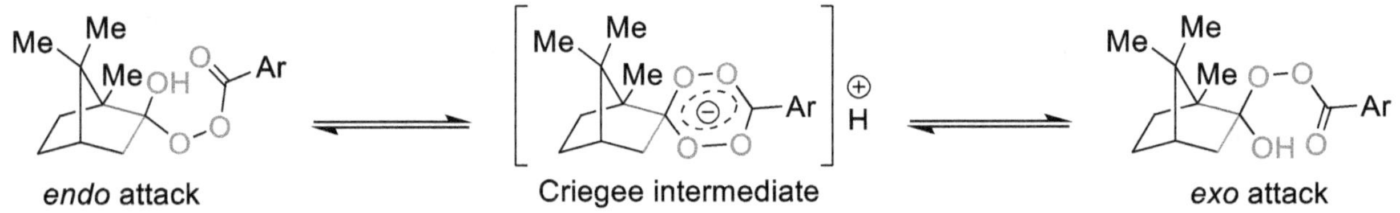

Nitric acid oxidizes camphor to the corresponding dicarboxylic acid derivative which is shown below.

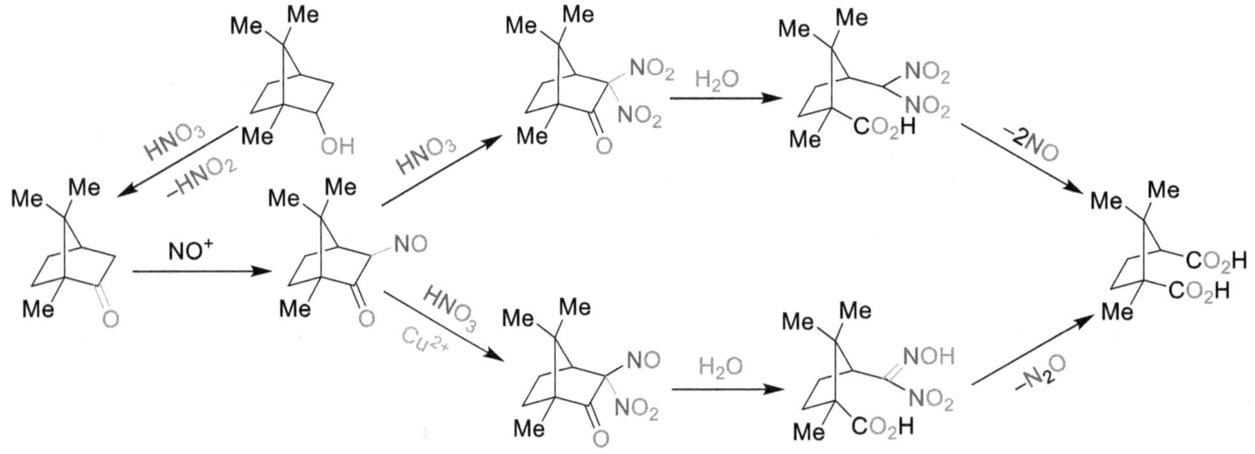

Note. On displacing the position of a bridgehead methyl group then the Baeyer-Villiger oxidation product proceeds through the migration of methylene carbon and offers an exclusively single product than the prior example while oxidation using nitric acid gives the same product.

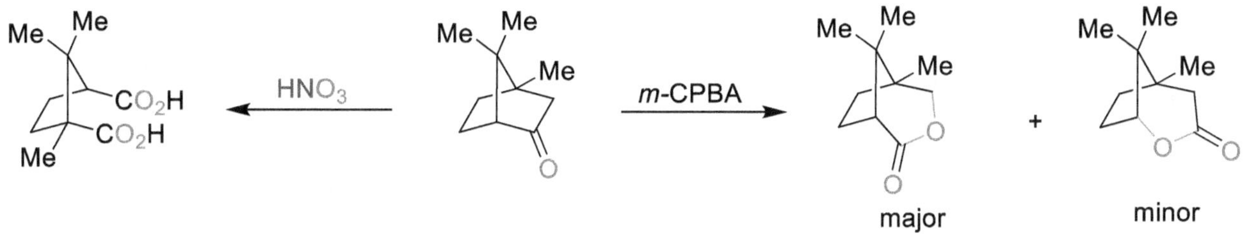

Renz, M.; Meunier, B. *Eur. J. Org. Chem.* **1999**, 737.

Question No-38: In the reactions

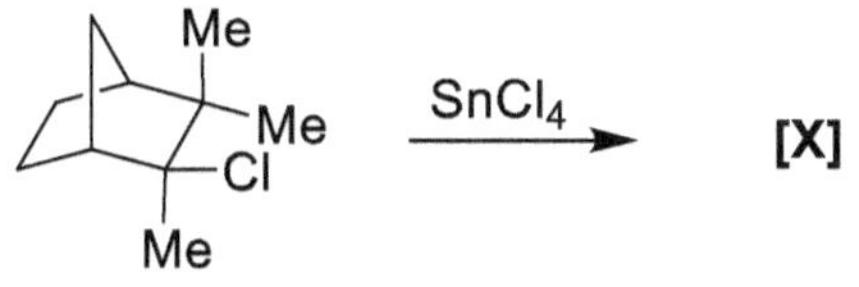

the major product [**X**] is

Answer: A. The major product formed in the given above reaction *via* Wagner-Meerwein rearrangement is isobornyl chloride [**X**].

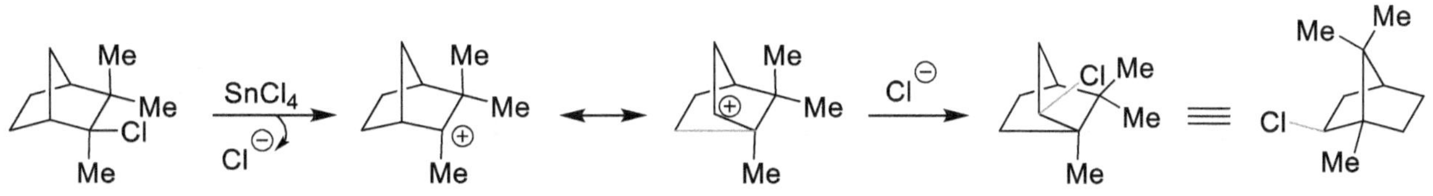

Question No-39: In the reactions

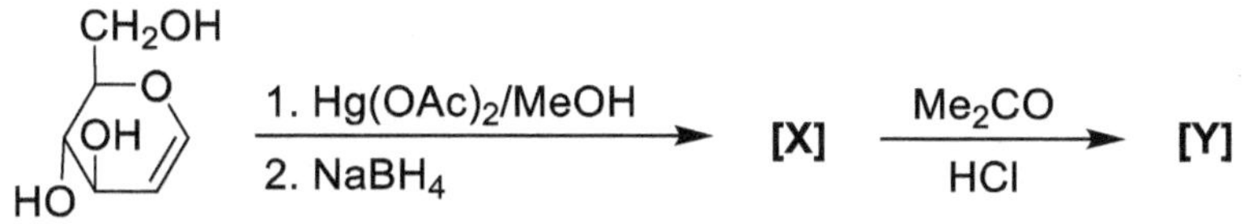

the major products, [**X**] and [**Y**], respectively, are

A. HO, HO, HO, MeO — and — O, O, HO, MeO

B. HO, HO, HO, MeO — and — O, O, HO, MeO

C. HO, HO, HO, OMe — and — O, O, HO, OMe

D. HO, HO, HO, OMe — and — O, O, HO, OMe

Answer: D. The mercuration reaction of dihydropyran derivative with mercuric acetate in the presence of nucleophilic polar protic methanol followed by demercuration using sodium borohydride produces non-reducible sugar [**X**] i.e. methyl D-2-deoxyglucoside. The final product [**Y**] is obtained on the treatment of [**X**] with acetone in presence of hydrochloric acid.

$$CH_2OH \xrightarrow{Hg(OAc)_2} CH_2OH \xrightarrow{MeOH} CH_2OH \xrightarrow{NaBH_4} CH_2OH$$

$$\xleftarrow{\pm H^{\oplus}} \xleftarrow[HCl]{Me_2C=O}$$

Common Data for Questions 50 and 51

An organic compound [**X**] ($C_{12}H_{16}O_3$) exhibits the following spectral data

IR: 1720 cm^{-1}

^{1}H NMR: δ 2.35 (s, 6H), 3.10 (s, 3H), 3.83 (t, 2H), 4.42 (t, 2H), 7.07 (s, 1H). 7.58 (s, 2H)

The compound [**X**] with an excess of MeMgBr gives a 1:1 mixture of compounds [**Y**] and [**Z**]. The compound [**Z**] exhibit, the following ^{1}H NMR data: δ 2.0 (bs. 1H), 3.30 (s, 3H), 3.56 (t. 2H), 3.70 (t, 2H)

Question No-50: The compound [**X**] is

A. MeO—\—O—C(=O)—Ar(Me, Me)

B. MeO—\—O—C(=O)—Ar(Me, Me)

C. 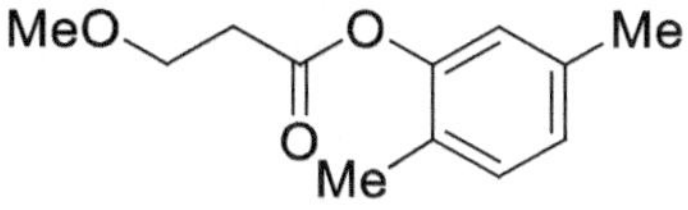 MeO~~O~~C(=O)O-aryl(Me, Me)

D. 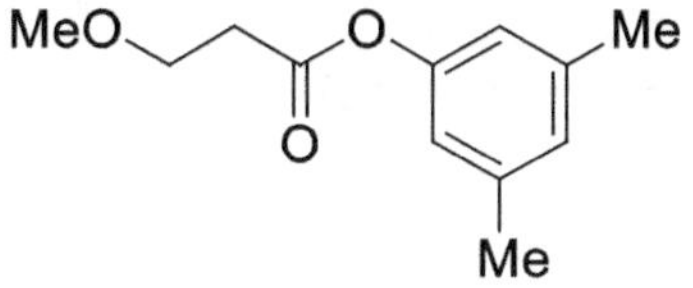 MeO~~O~~C(=O)O-aryl(Me, Me)

Answer: B. The given data reveals that compound [X] is methoxyethyl benzoate.

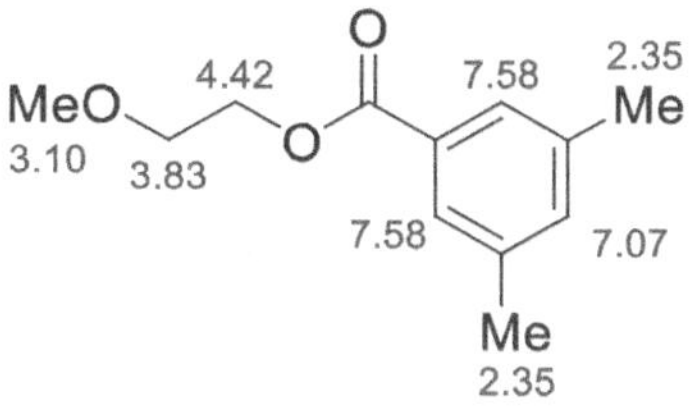

Question No-51: The compound [Y] is

A. 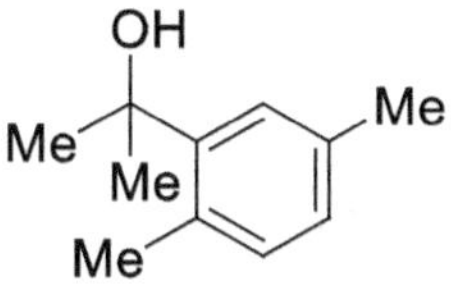 2-(2,5-dimethylphenyl)propan-2-ol and MeO~~OH

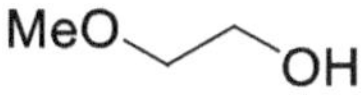

B. 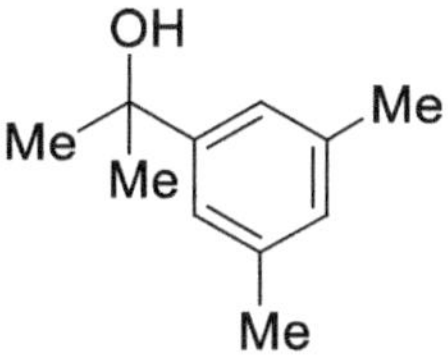 2-(3,5-dimethylphenyl)propan-2-ol and MeO~~OH

C. 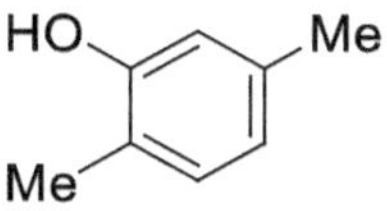 HO-aryl and MeO-C(Me)(Me)-OH

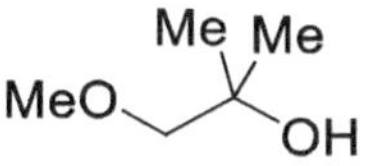

D. 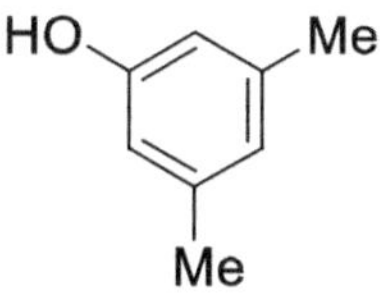 HO-aryl and MeO-C(Me)(Me)-OH

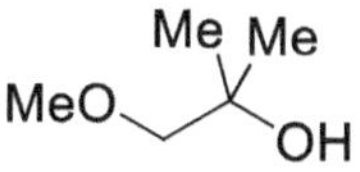

Answer: B. From the above-given statement, methoxyethyl benzoate in the presence of an excess methyl magnesium bromide gives major products having a 1:1 ratio of [Y] and [Z] are 2-(3,5-dimethylphenyl)propan-2-ol and 2-methoxyethanol, respectively.

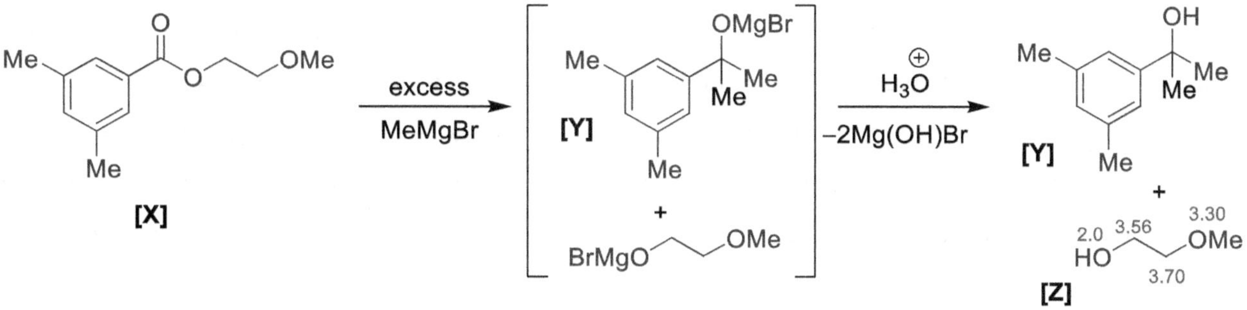

Statement for linked Questions 52 and 53

In the reaction sequence

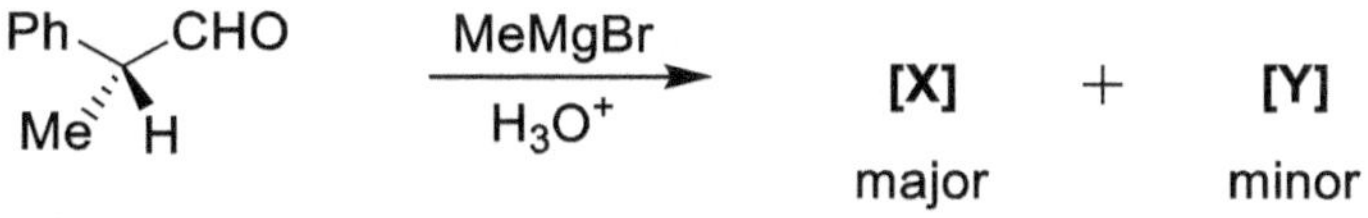

Ph-CH(Me)(H)-CHO →(MeMgBr, H₃O⁺)→ [X] + [Y]
                                        major   minor

[X] → [Z]
  1. TsCl/py
  2. NaOEt/EtOH

Question No-52: The compound [X] is

A.
Ph
H—Me
Me—H
OH

B.
Ph
Me—H
H—Me
OH

C.
Ph
Me—H
Me—H
OH

D.
Me
Ph—H
HO—H
Me

Answer: C. The reaction of 2-phenyl propanal with Grignard reagent gives diastereoselective major product [X] and minor product [Y]. The formation of these products can be visualized by the non-chelate Felkin-Anh model. In this model, the major product [X] is obtained when the larger substituent is perpendicular and the smaller group is away from the carbonyl group (favored conformer).

Note. The formation of major and minor products can also be explained by Cram's rule. In Cram's model, the larger substituents are eclipsed by the substituents of the carbonyl group, i.e. antiparallel to the carbonyl group. Although in both the models' nucleophile attacks at the side of a smaller group give a major product whereas the attack at the side of a medium group gives a minor product. In the case of Cram's model, the formation of products always ends up with the least stable eclipsed conformer but, the Felkin-Anh model gives staggered conformer.

Clayden, J.; Greeves, N.; Warren, S. Diastereoselectivity. In *Organic Chemistry*, 2ⁿᵈ Ed.; Oxford University Press, 2012; pp 858-865.

Question No-53: The compound [**Z**] is

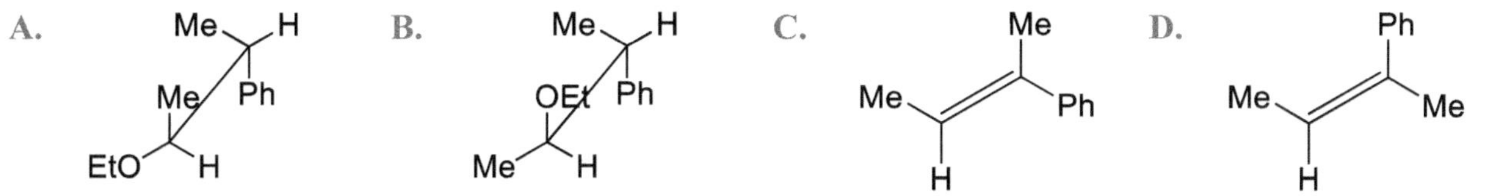

A.

B.

C.

D.

Answer: C. The tosylation of the product [**X**] using tosyl chloride in the presence of pyridine followed by the treatment with sodium ethoxide base gives the major product [**Z**].

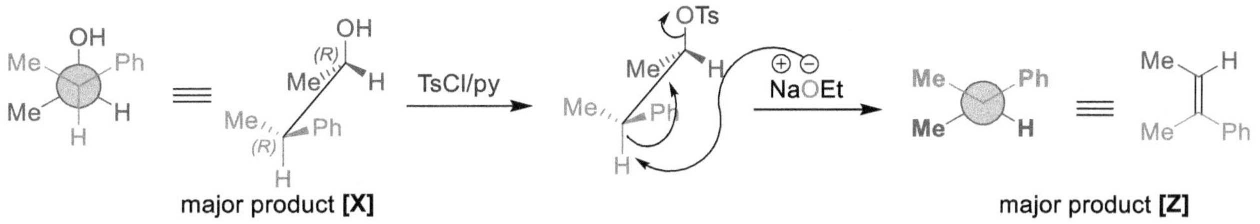

major product [X]   TsCl/py   NaOEt   major product [Z]

Carruthers, W.; Coldham, I. Formation of Carbon-Carbon Double Bonds. In *Modern Method of Organic Synthesis*, 4ᵗʰ Ed.; Cambridge University Press, 2004; pp 105-111.

Question No-9: In the following reaction

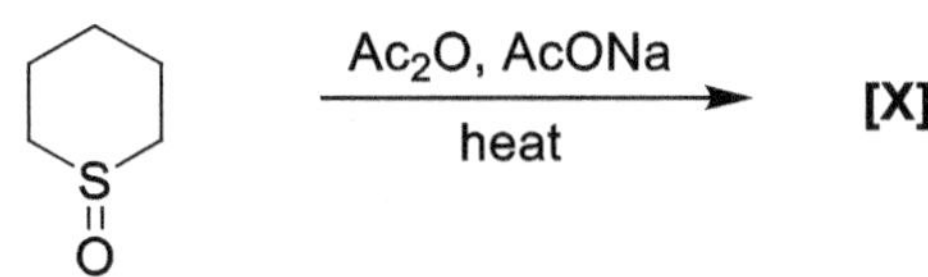

the major product [X] is

A.   B.   C.   D.

Answer: B. The rearrangement of the sulfoxide derivative to corresponding α-acetoxy thioether in the presence of acetic anhydride is known as Pummerer rearrangement.

Bur, S. K. *Chem. Rev.* **2004**, *104*, 2401.

Question No-10: In the following reaction sequence

i) NH$_2$OH.HCl

ii) ArSO$_2$Cl, Py

iii) heat

iv) H$_2$O

[X]

the major product [X] is

A.

B.

C.

D.

Answer: A. The given sequence of reagents helps the transformation of an acetyl group into a corresponding amide derivative *via* Beckmann rearrangement.

Question No-11: The diene which undergoes Diels-Alder reaction with maleic anhydride is

A.

B.

C.

D.

Answer: A. The diene which undergoes Diels-Alder reaction with maleic anhydride is 1-vinylcyclohex-1-ene due to the flexible orientation of the vinylic and cyclohexyl C-C single bond (*cis-* and *trans*-isomers).

Diels-Alder reaction

Question No-12: The sequence of an mRNA molecule produced from a DNA template strand with the composition 5'-AGCTACACT-3' is

A. 5'-AGUGUAGCU-3'

B. 5'-UCGAUGUGA-3'

C. 5'-AGTGTAGCT-3'

D. 5'-TCGATGTGA-3'

Answer: B. The strand of mRNA (AUGC base pair) and DNA (ATGC base pair) are complementary to each other. If, the sequence of an mRNA molecule produced from a DNA template strand with the composition 5'-AGCTACACT-3' is then the mRNA strand will be 3'-UCGAUGUGA-5'

Composition strand of the given DNA	5'-AGCTACACT-3'
Complementary strand mRNA	3'-UCGAUGUGA-5'

Question No-13: In the following reaction

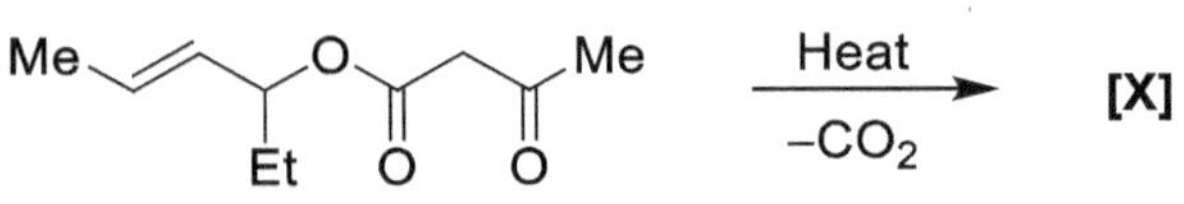

the major product **[X]** is

A. 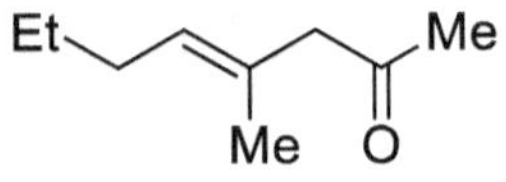 B.

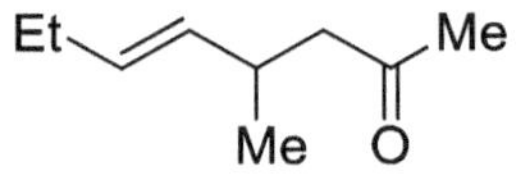

C. 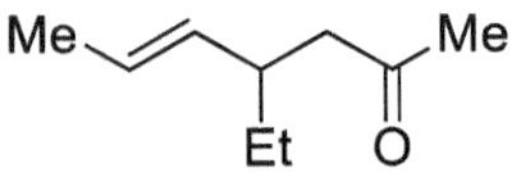 D.

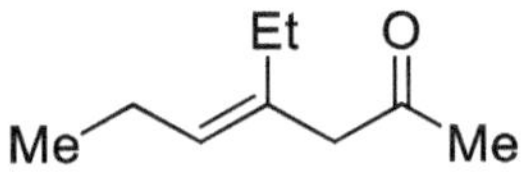

Answer: B. The given above starting material is tautomerized into the corresponding enolic form which undergoes [3,3]-sigmatropic shift *via* Claisen rearrangement. Further, the obtained rearranged product is converted into ketone derived by loss of carbon dioxide *via* retro-Ene reaction.

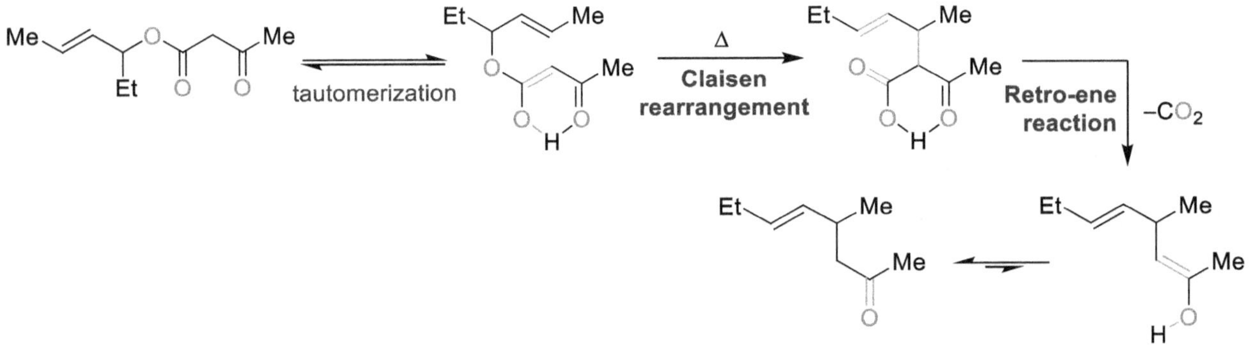

Note. The retro-Ene reaction is also a kind of Ei- reaction.

Question No-14: The structure of the dipeptide Ala-Pro derived from the natural amino acids is

A. 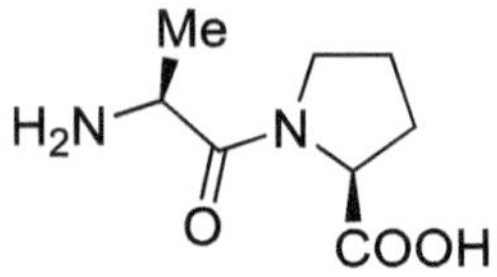 B.

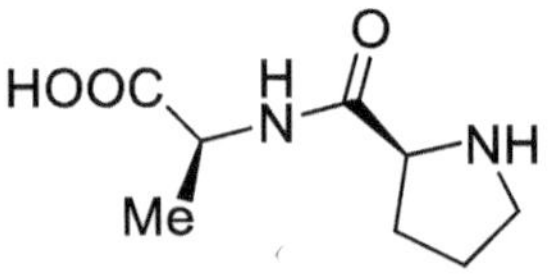

C.

D.

Answer: A. All the naturally occurring amino acids are L-amino acid except glycine (achiral). Based on retrosynthesis analysis, the structure of the dipeptide Ala-Pro derived from the natural amino acids is shown below.

L-alanine   L-Proline

Note. Similarly, the hydrolysis of the given dipeptide also can be done.

Question No-15: In the following reaction

$$\text{i) } n\text{-BuLi (2 equiv)}$$
$$-78\ ^\circ C \text{ to } 0\ ^\circ C$$
$$\text{ii) DMF} \longrightarrow [\mathbf{X}]$$

the major product [**X**] is

A.   **B.**   **C.**   **D.**

Answer: C. The decomposition of tosyl hydrazone derivative in the presence of excess butyl lithium gives vinyl lithium derivative which reacts with dimethylformamide (DMF) and yields a corresponding conjugated aldehyde derivative. This reaction is known as the Shapiro reaction.

Question No-16: In the following reaction

$$\text{[structure]} \xrightarrow{\text{H}^+} \text{[X]}$$

the major product **[X]** is

A.

B.

C.

D.

Answer: A. Dienone-phenol rearrangement of the given compound in acidic media offers a major product 4,8-dimethyl-5,6,7,8-tetrahydronaphthalen-2-ol **[X]**.

$$\text{[structure]} \xrightarrow{\text{H}^{\oplus}} \text{[structure]} \longrightarrow \text{[structure]} \xrightarrow[\text{shift}]{\text{1,2-methyl}} \text{[structure]}$$

$$\xleftarrow{-\text{H}^{\oplus}} \text{[structure]}$$

Question No-34: In the following reaction

$$\text{[structure]} \quad + \quad \text{PhCHO} \xrightarrow[\text{DMF}]{\text{NaCN (cat.)}} \text{[X]}$$

the major product **[X]** is

A.

B.

C.

D.

Answer: D. The benzoylation of 2-cyclohexenone at the positon-3 in a conjugate manner of benzaldehyde (umpolung synthon) using a catalytic amount of sodium cyanide furnishes major product 3-benzoylcyclohexan-1-one. The mechanism of the reaction is moreover similar to the Benzoin condensation.

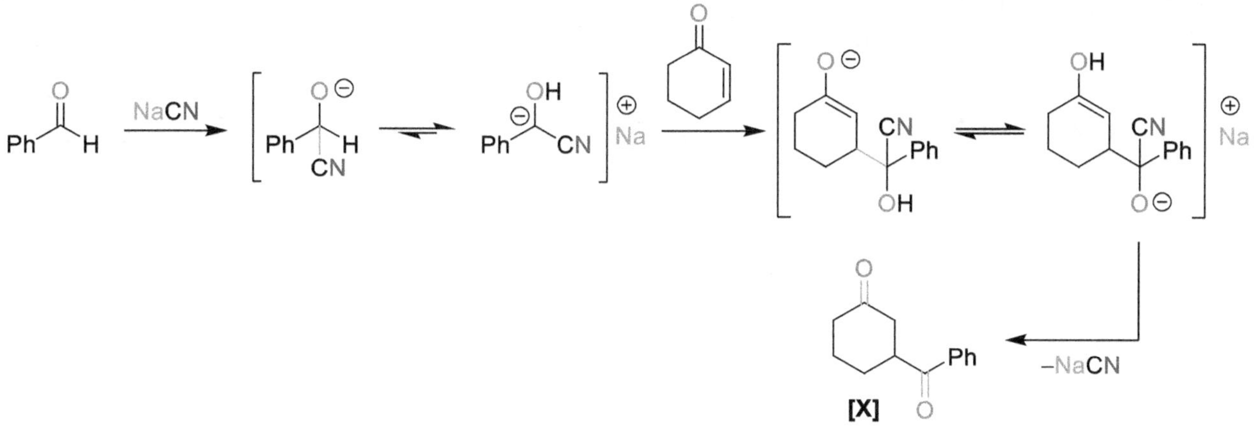

Brimacombe, J. S.; Zahur-ul-Haque, Murray, A. W. *Tetrahedron Lett.* **1974**, *47*, 4087.

Stetter, H.; Kuhlmann, H.; Lorenz, G. *Org. Synth.* **1979**, *59*, 53.

Question No-35: In the following reaction

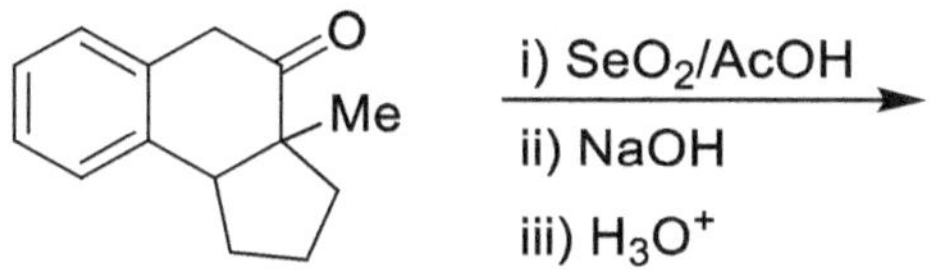

the major product **[X]** is

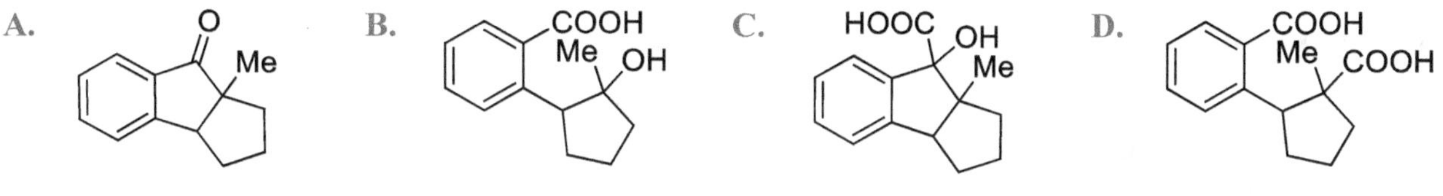

Answer: C. Benzylic oxidation using selenium dioxide is known as Riley oxidation. Here, in the reaction oxidation of the given compound with selenium dioxide offers a diketone derivative. Further, the obtained diketone with no α-hydrogen in the presence of sodium hydroxide (followed by hydrolysis) undergoes Benzilic acid rearrangement leading to *α*-hydroxycarboxylic acid derivative as the final product.

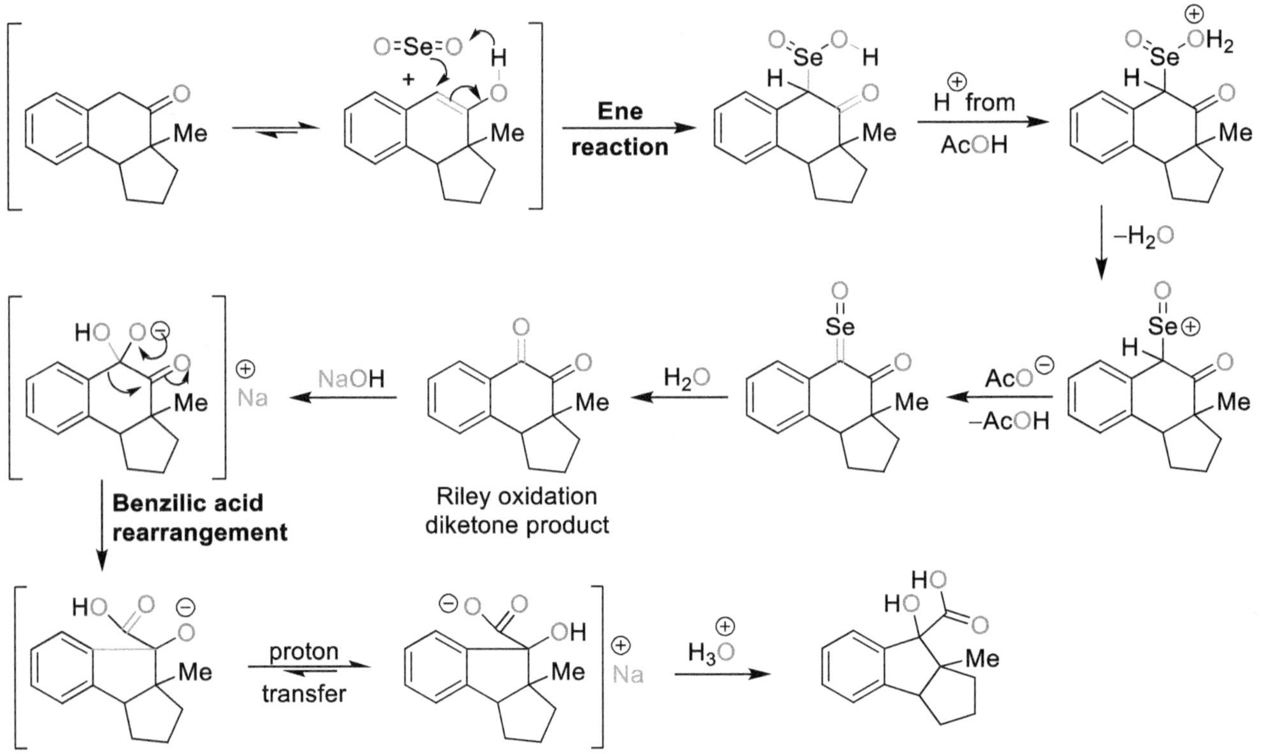

Corey, E. J.; Schaefer, J. P. *J. Am. Chem. Soc.* **1960**, *82*, 917.

Question No-36: In the following reaction

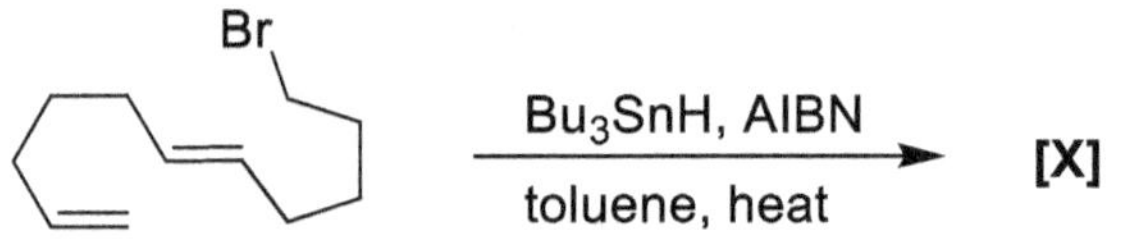

$$\text{(Br-substituted diene)} \xrightarrow[\text{toluene, heat}]{\text{Bu}_3\text{SnH, AIBN}} \text{[X]}$$

the major product **[X]** is

A. 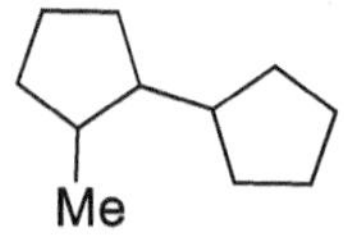 B. 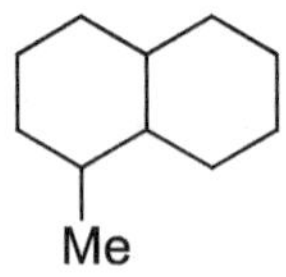 C. 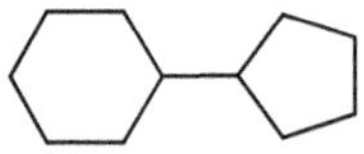 D.

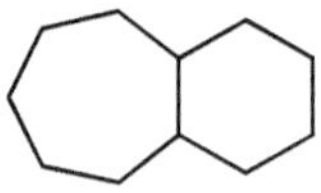

Me   Me

Answer: A. The reduction of the given compound with tributyltin hydride (TBTH) in the presence of catalytic mol% of azobisisobutyronitrile (AIBN) gives kinetically controlled major product 2-methyl-1,1'-bi(cyclopentane). The mechanism of the reaction follows a free radical path.

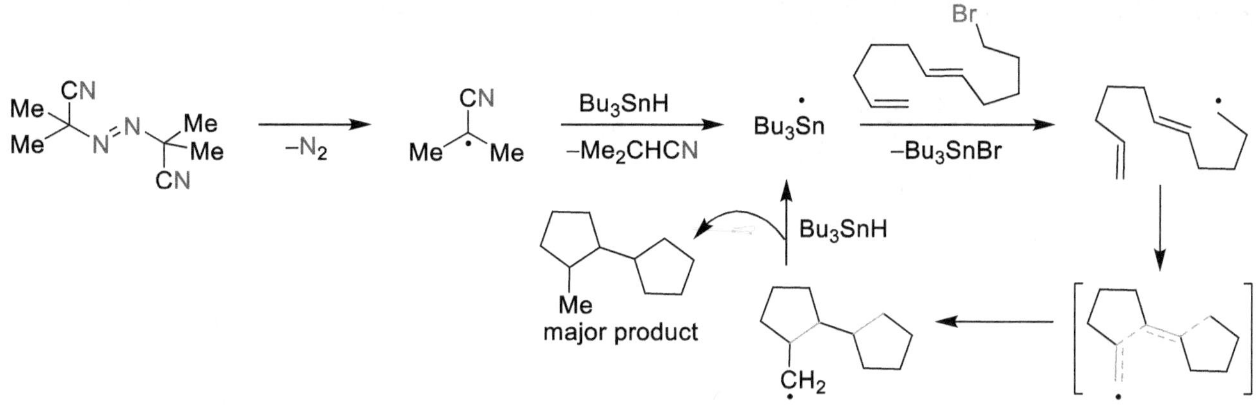

Question No-37: The most appropriate sequence of reactions for carrying out the following conversion is

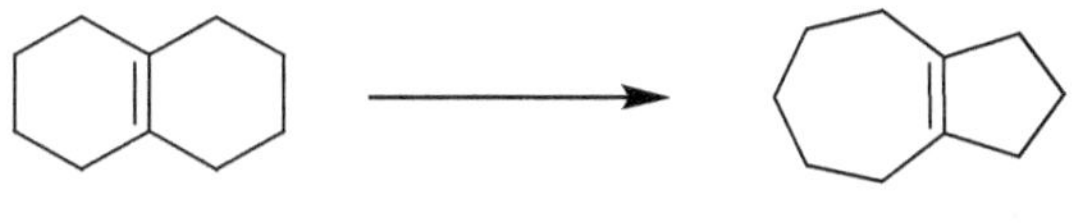

A.   (i) Peracid; (ii) H⁺; (iii) Zn/dil. HC*l*

B.   (i) Alkaline KMnO$_4$; (ii) NaIO$_4$; (iii) N$_2$H$_4$/KOH

C.   (i) Alkaline KMnO$_4$; (ii) H⁺; (iii) Zn/dil. HCl

D.   (i) O$_3$/Me$_2$S; (ii) NaOEt; (iii) N$_2$H$_4$/KOH

Answer: D. The given transformation can be done using the following sequence of the named reactions such as (i) Reductive ozonolysis, (ii) Aldol condensation, and (iii) Wolff-Kishner reduction.

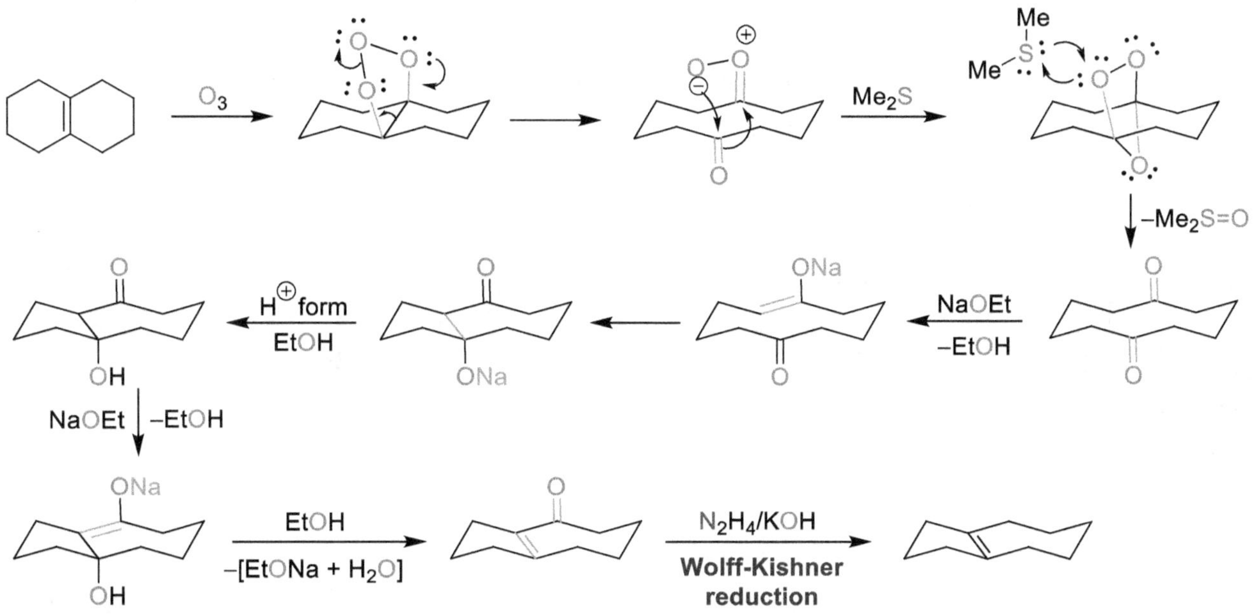

Question No-38: In the following reaction sequence

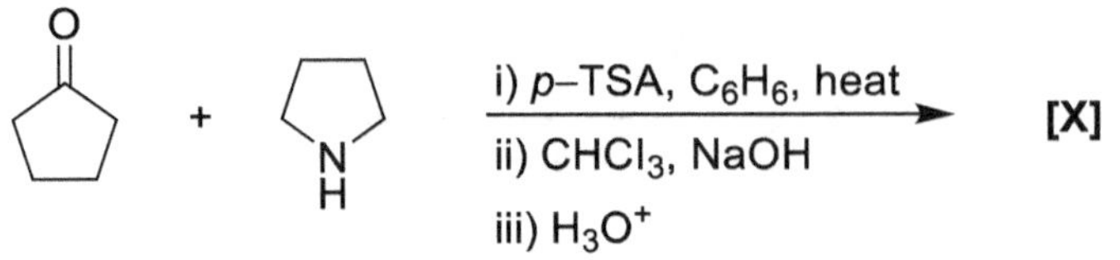

i) p–TSA, C_6H_6, heat
ii) $CHCl_3$, NaOH
iii) H_3O^+

[X]

the major product **[X]** is

A.

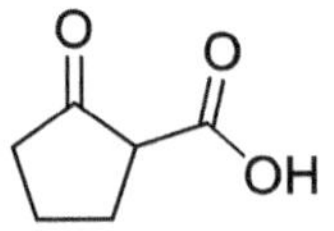

B.

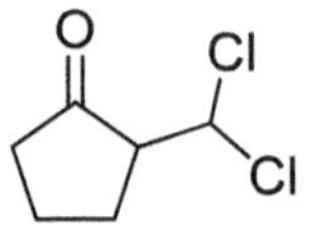

C.

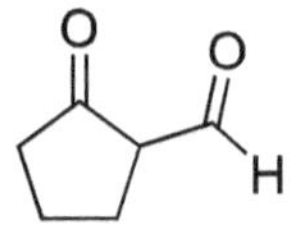

D.

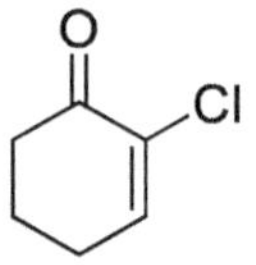

Answer: D. The major product formed in the given reaction *via* the type of Ciamician-Dennstedt rearrangement is 2-chloro-2-cyclohexenone.

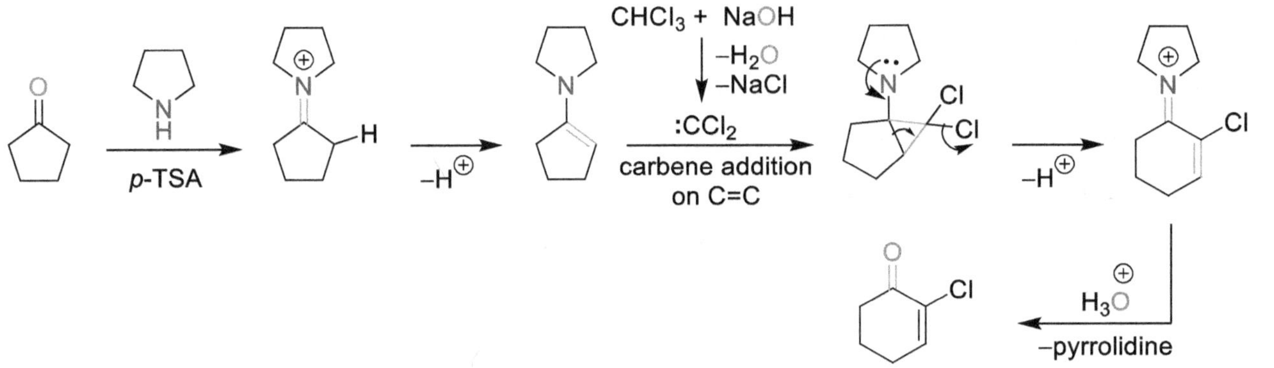

Note. Pyrrole reacts with singlet dichlorocarbene in the presence of aqueous polar solvents gives 2-oxocyclopentane-1-carbaldehyde *via* Reimer-Tiemann reaction.

Question No-39: In the following conversion

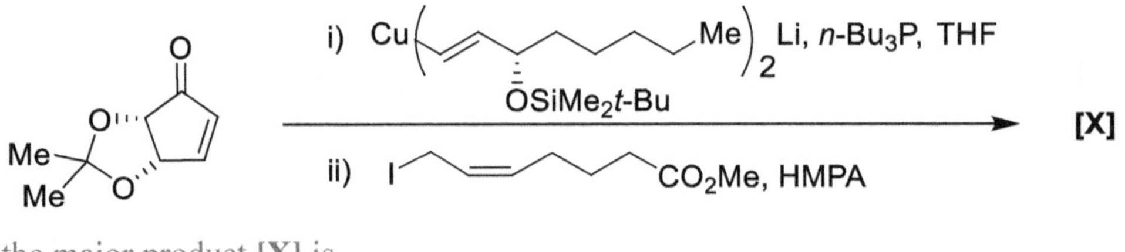

i) $Cu\left(\underset{\overset{|}{OSiMe_2t\text{-}Bu}}{\text{}}Me\right)_2$Li, n-Bu$_3$P, THF

ii) $I\underset{}{\overset{}{\text{}}}CO_2Me$, HMPA

[X]

the major product **[X]** is

A.

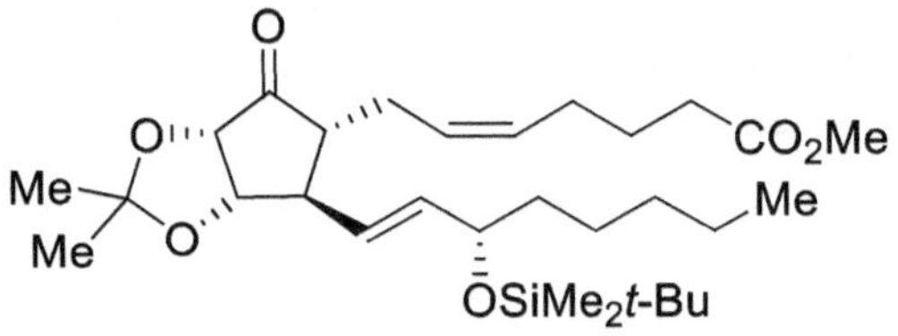

B.

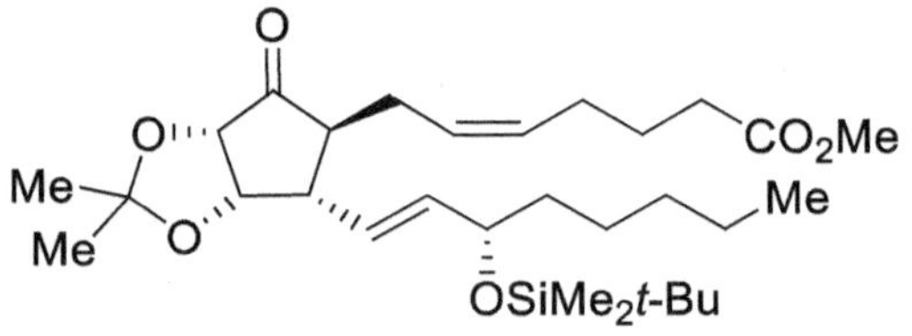

C.

D.

Answer: A. The major product formed in the given reaction using Gillman reagent followed by direct substitution of iodide in alkyl iodide derivative by lithium-enolate is shown below.

[X]

Krause, N. Modern Organocopper Chemistry. Wiley-VCH, 2002.

Question No-40: In the following reaction

$$\xrightarrow[\text{ii) Raney Ni}]{\text{i) } t\text{-BuOK}} \quad \textbf{[X]}$$

EtOH

the major product **[X]** is

A.

B.

C.

D.

Answer: B. Generally, the conjugate addition is performed by the zwitterionic species sulfonium ylide due to its soft nature of nucleophilicity. The given compound has intramolecularly *in situ* generated sulfonium ylide which undergoes Michael addition and is later converted into cyclopropane *via* attack of enolate ion. The mechanism of the reaction is shown below.

Matthews, R. S.; Meteyer, T. E. *Chem. Commun.* **1971**, 1576.

Question No-41: In the reaction

Optically pure (+)-*trans*-2-acetoxycyclohexyl tosylate $\xrightarrow[\Delta]{\text{HOAc, KOAc}}$ **[X]**

the major product **[X]** is

- A. racemic *trans*-1,2-cyclohexanediol diacetate
- B. optically active *trans*-1,2-cyclohexanediol diacetate
- C. racemic *cis*-1,2-cyclohexanediol diacetate
- D. optically active *cis*-1,2-cyclohexanediol diacetate

Answer: A. The reaction of optically pure (+)-*trans*-2-acetoxycyclohexyl tosylate with potassium acetate in acetic acid furnishes racemic *trans*-1,2-cyclohexanediol diacetate. The formation of the racemic product takes place due to the anchimeric assistance shown by the axial acetoxy group.

Clayden, J.; Greeves, N.; Warren, S. Participation, Rearrangement, and Fragmentation. In *Organic Chemistry*, 2nd Ed.; Oxford University Press, 2012; pp 932-933.

Statement for Linked Answer Questions 54 and 55

A ketone on treatment with bromine in methanol gives the corresponding monobromo compound [**X**] having molecular formula C_5H_9BrO. The compound [**X**] when treated with NaOMe in MeOH produces [**Y**] as the major product. The spectral data for compound [**X**] are

^{1}H NMR: δ 1.17 (*d*, 6H), 3.02 (*m*, 1H), 4.10 (*s*, 2H);

^{13}C NMR: δ 17, 37, 39 and 210.

Question No-54: The compound [**X**] is

A. 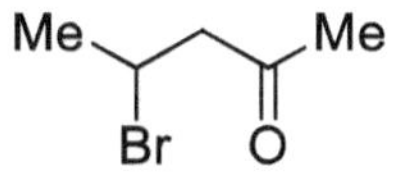   B. 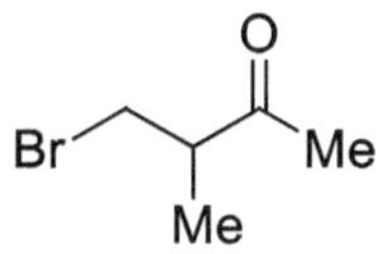   C. 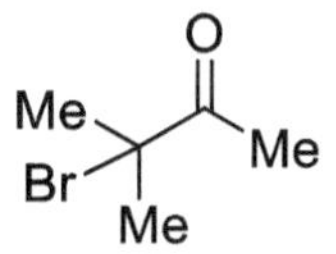   D.

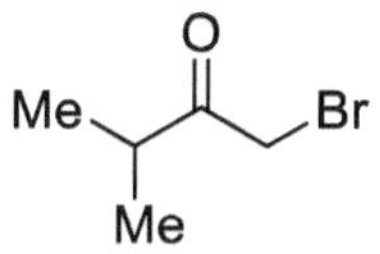

Answer: D. The given statement and spectroscopic data reveal that compound [**X**] is bromomethyl isopropyl ketone.

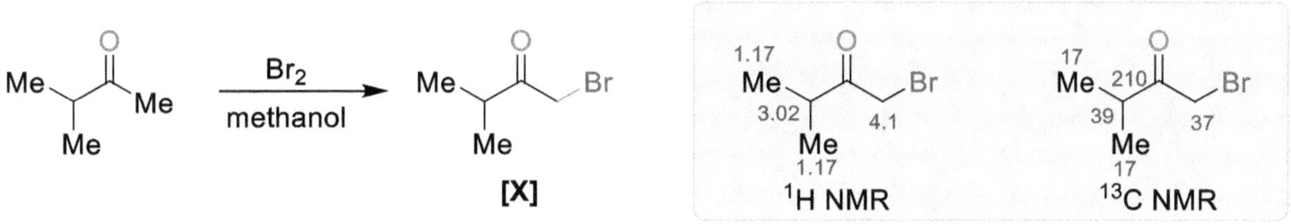

Question No-55: The major product [**Y**] is

A. 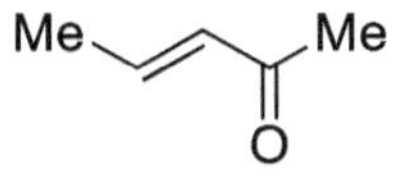   B. 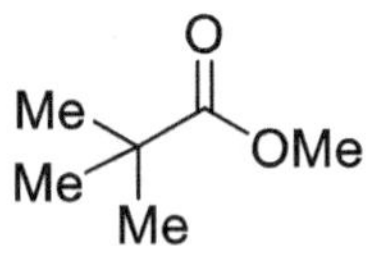   C. 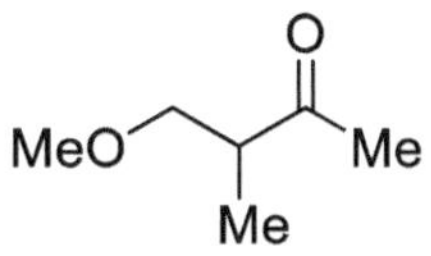   D.

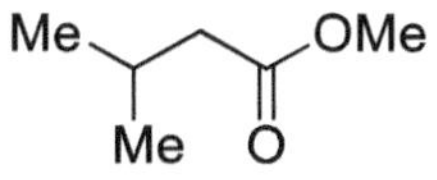

Answer: B. The compound [**X**] when treated with NaOMe in MeOH produces methyl neopentanoate [**Y**] as the major product. The given reaction is an example of Favoraskii rearrangement. During the reaction mechanism, a three-membered cyclic intermediate is formed which can adopt either path-a or path-b. Here, the formation of the primary carbon anion is more stable and gives a major product. Whereas, path-b is adopted by the molecule having aryl group(s) instead of alkyl substituent(s).

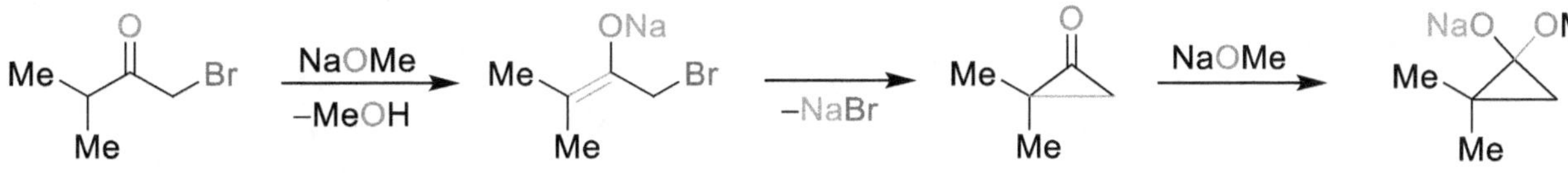

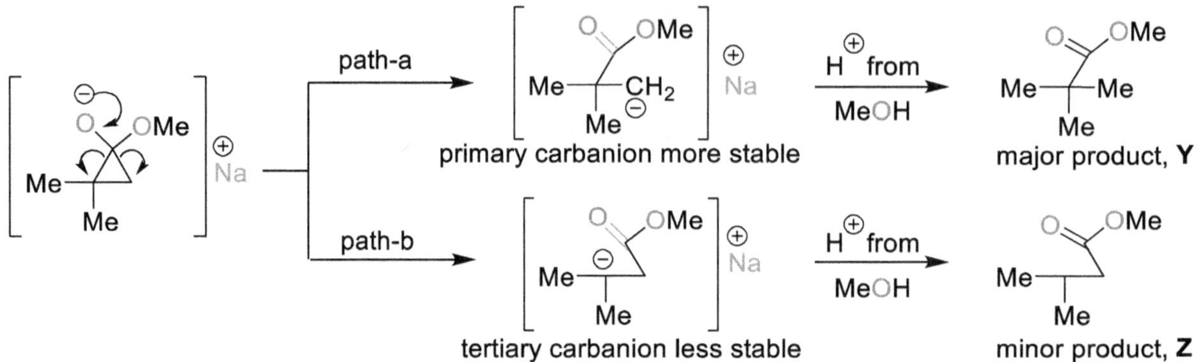
path-a
path-b
primary carbanion more stable
tertiary carbanion less stable
H⁺ from
MeOH
H⁺ from
MeOH
major product, Y
minor product, Z

Question No-1: In the proton decoupled ^{13}C NMR spectrum of 7-norbornanone, the number of signals obtained is

A. 7   B. 3   C. 4   D. 5

Answer: B. The number of signals obtained in the proton decoupled ^{13}C NMR spectrum of 7-norbornanone is three.

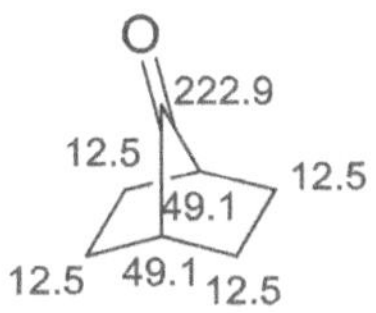

Question No-2: Identify the most probable product in the given reaction

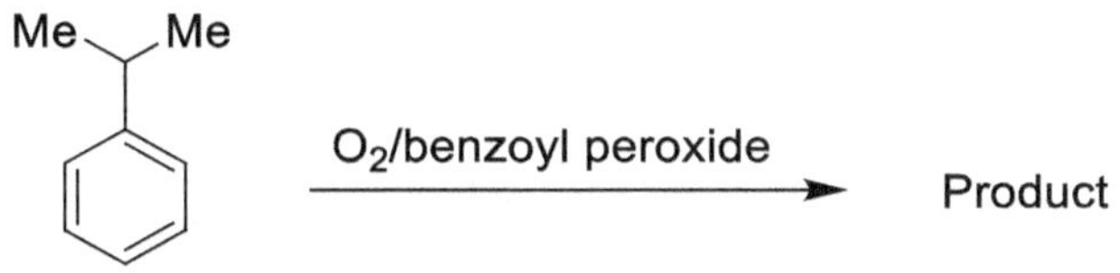

O$_2$/benzoyl peroxide ⟶ Product

A. 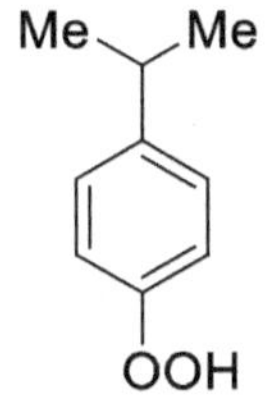   B. 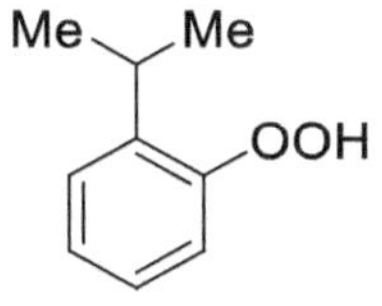   C. 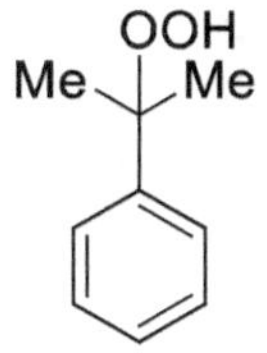   D.

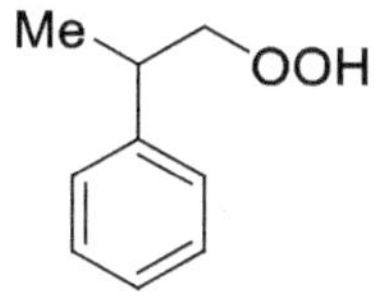

Answer: C. The thermal or photochemical hemolytic cleavage of benzoyl peroxide produces a radical intermediate that abstracts a benzylic proton from the cumene. Next, this radical reacts with an oxygen molecule and undergoes a proton exchange reaction with another cumene in a radical manner to furnish the major product cumene hydroperoxide (CHP).

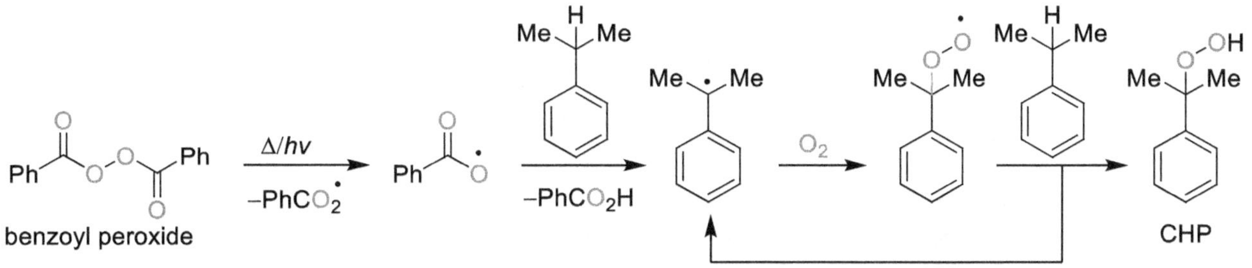

Furthermore, the reaction of CHP in an acidic environment produces phenol and acetone as the end product. This reaction is largely employed for the synthesis of phenol on an industrial scale.

Question No-3: In the cyclization reaction given below, the most probable product formed is

$$HO\text{-}CH_2\text{-}CHBr\text{-}CH_2\text{-}OH \xrightarrow{\text{NaH}} \text{Product}$$

A. B. C. D.

Answer: C. In the cyclization reaction given above, the major product is (R)-2-(oxiran-2-yl)ethan-1-ol. Among these, the three-membered ring system is more facile and stable than the four-membered ring due to the presence of a banana bond in the former one.

$$\xrightarrow[-2H_2]{\text{NaH (excess)}}$$

3-*exo-tet*-cyclization then acidic workup → major

4-*exo-tet*-cyclization then acidic workup → minor

Question No-7: Shown below is a Hammett plot obtained for the reaction

$$Ar\text{-}COCl \xrightarrow{H_2O} Ar\text{-}COOH$$

The change in slope of the plot indicates that

A.   the reaction does not follow a linear free energy relationship

B.   electrons are being withdrawn from the transition state in the mechanism

C.   electrons are being donated to the transition state in the mechanism

D.   the mechanism of the reaction is changing

Answer: D. The change in the given slope of the plot indicates that the mechanism of the reaction is changing.

Question No-8: The ratio of relative intensities of the two molecular ion peaks of methyl bromide (CH_3Br) in the mass spectrum is

A. $M^+ : (M+2)^+ = 1:3$ B. $M^+ : (M+2)^+ = 3:1$ C. $M^+ : (M+2)^+ = 1:1$ D. $M^+ : (M+2)^+ = 1:2$

Answer: C. The ratio of relative intensities of the two molecular ion peaks of methyl bromide (CH_3Br) in the mass spectrum is $[M]^+ : [M + 2]^+ = 1:1$. It is due to the presence of two types of approximately equal amount of isotopic abundances of bromine i.e. ^{79}Br (50.68%) and ^{81}Br (49.32%).

Question No-9: A disaccharide that will not give Benedict's test and will not form osazone is

A.   maltose   B.   lactose   C.   cellobiose   D.   sucrose

Answer: D. Sucrose will not give Benedict's test [deep blue color: $Cu(citrate)_2^{2-}$] and will not form osazone.

Note. Benedict's solution is a mixture of $CuSO_4.5H_2O$, Na_2CO_3 and sodium citrate. It is used for the detection of reducing sugar in a sample. This solution oxidizes the aldehyde group to corresponding carboxylic acid and the solution turns into red color due to the formation of cuprous oxide (Cu_2O).

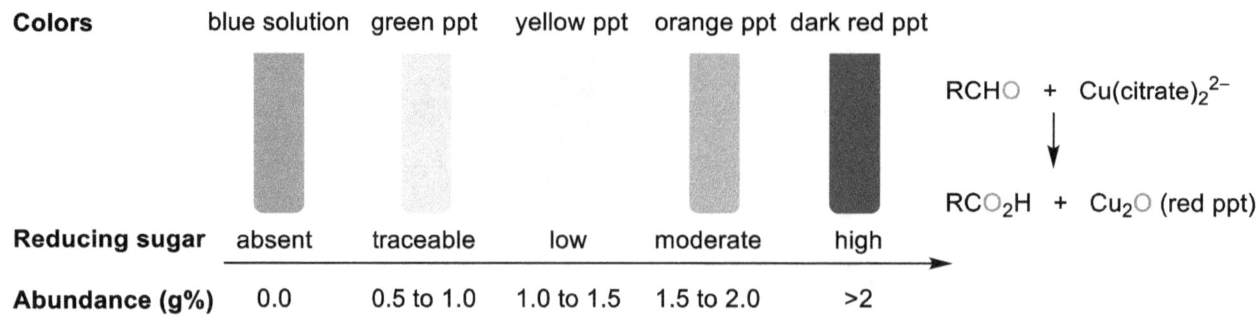

A detail of this is available in this book, GATE-2015, Question Answer No-20.

Question No-13: The bond that gives the most intense band in the infrared spectrum for its stretching vibration is

A. C—H   B. N—H   C. O—H   D. S—H

Answer: C. Among these, —OH is more electronegative and more polar, thus intensity is much higher than all.

$$\text{Intensity} \propto \text{Polarity of the compound}$$

Question No-19: Among the following substituted silanes, the one that give cross-linked silicone polymer upon hydrolysis is

A. $(CH_3)_4Si$ B. CH_3SiCl_3 C. $(CH_3)_2SiCl_2$ D. $(CH_3)_3SiCl$

Answer: B. Methyltrichlorosilane can give cross-linked silicone polymer upon hydrolysis.

Question No-26: From a carboxymethyl-cellulose column at pH 6.0, arginine, valine and glutamic acid will elute in the order

A. arginine, valine, glutamic acid   B. arginine, glutamic acid, valine

C. glutamic acid, arginine, valine   D. glutamic acid, valine, arginine

Answer: D. From a carboxymethyl-cellulose column at pH 6.0 (acidic environment); arginine, valine and glutamic acid will elute in the order: glutamic acid > valine > arginine. In the case of acidic amino acid, no interaction takes place in the column thereby making it move faster than others and *vice versa*.

Question No-33: Identify the product from the following reaction

(**9-BBN** = 9-Borabicyclo[3.3.1]nonane)

A **B** **C** **D**

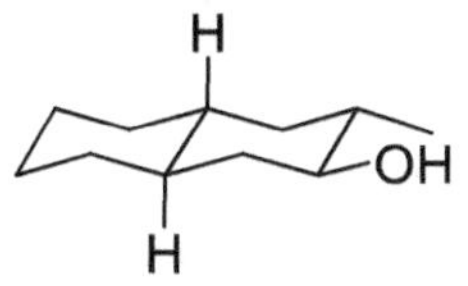

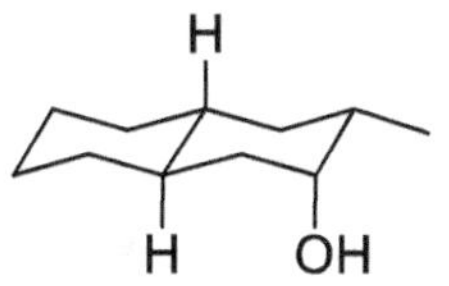

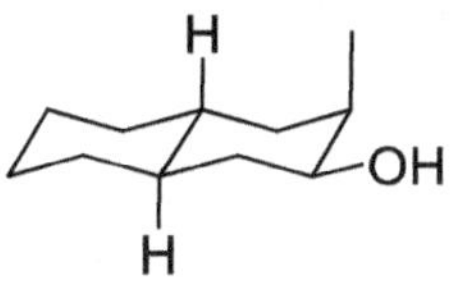

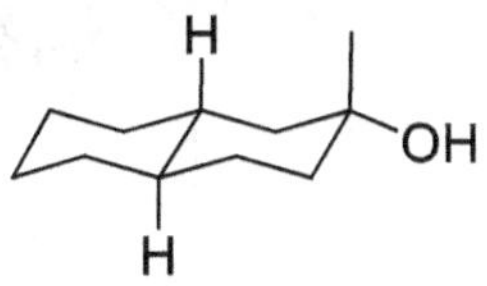

Answer: A. At first, the regioselective addition of 9-BBN on the double bond of the given compound takes place and then the oxidation using hydrogen peroxide in the presence of sodium hydroxide yields the corresponding perhydronaphthol product.

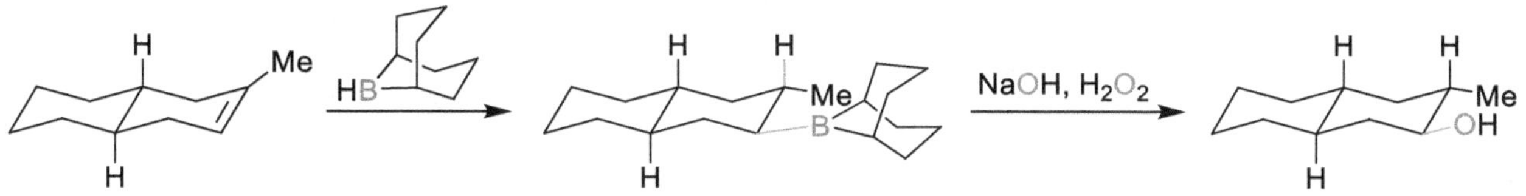

Question No-34: The product from the following reaction is

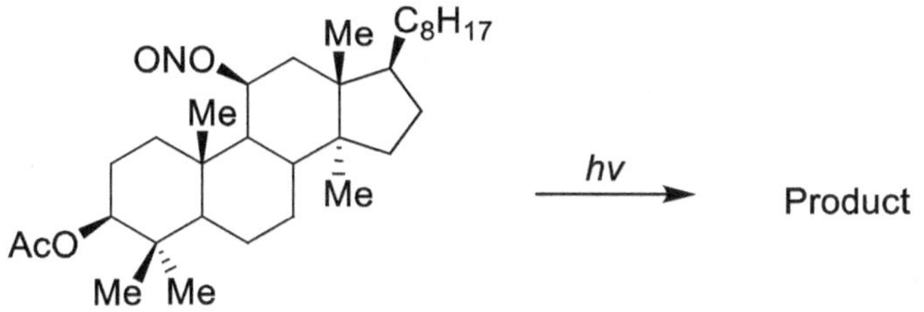

hv → Product

A.

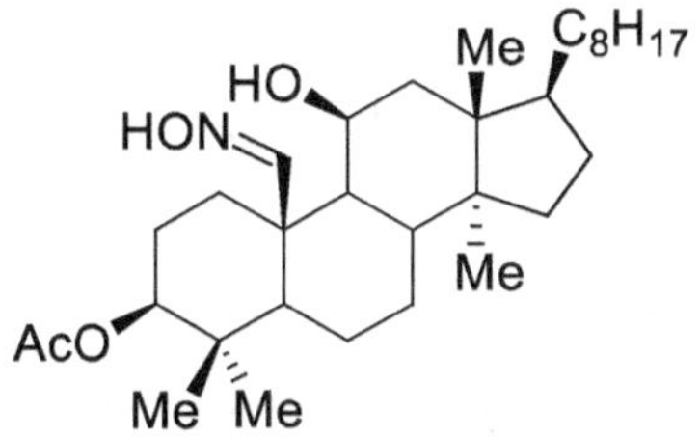

B.

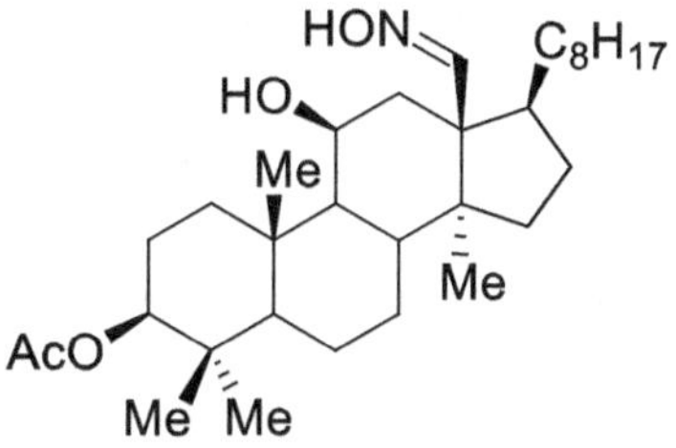

C.

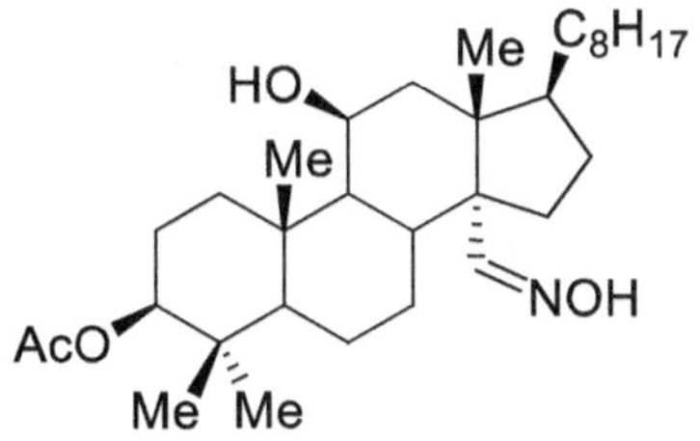

D.

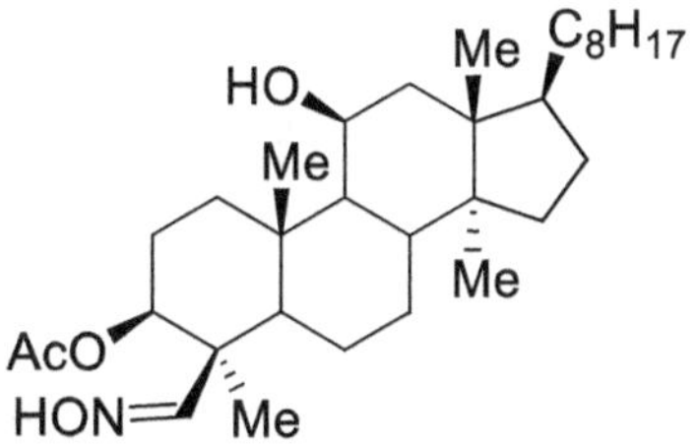

Answer: A, B and D. The photochemical hemolytic cleavage of the given nitrite derivative undergoes δ-functionalization of the inactive *syn*-oriented carbon which has at least one δ-hydrogen. During the reaction, alkoxy radical abstracts δ-hydrogen via the formation of the six-membered cyclic transition state and later the nitroso radicals combine with the radical of δ-carbon to form the corresponding nitroso alcohol derivative. This reaction is known as the Barton reaction or Barton nitrite ester reaction.

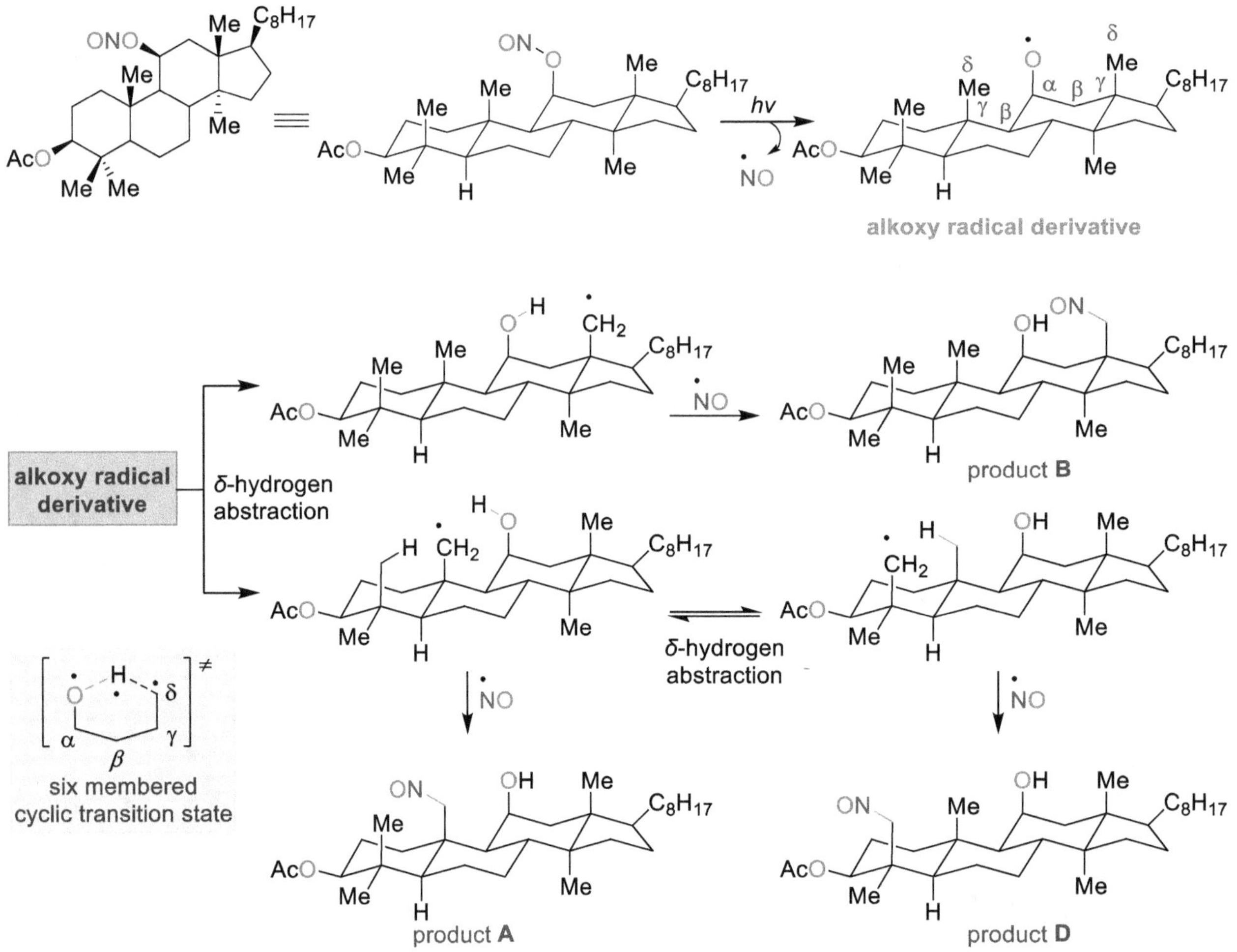

alkoxy radical derivative

alkoxy radical derivative — δ-hydrogen abstraction

$$\left[\begin{array}{c} \overset{\bullet}{O} \cdots H \cdots \overset{\bullet}{\delta} \\ \alpha \qquad \gamma \\ \beta \end{array}\right]^{\ddagger}$$

six membered cyclic transition state

product **B**

δ-hydrogen abstraction

product **A**

product **D**

Note. The formation of the given product **C** may not be possible due to the opposite orientation of the methyl and alkoxy radical intermediate which cannot form a six-membered cyclic transition state.

Singh, J.; Singh, J. Photochemistry and Pericyclic Reactions. In *Photo Substitution Reactions at sp³ Hybrid Carbon Having at Least One Hydrogen*, 3rd Ed.; New Academic Science, 2012; pp 301-306.

Question No-35: The acid-catalyzed cyclization of 5-ketodecan-1,9-diol is given below

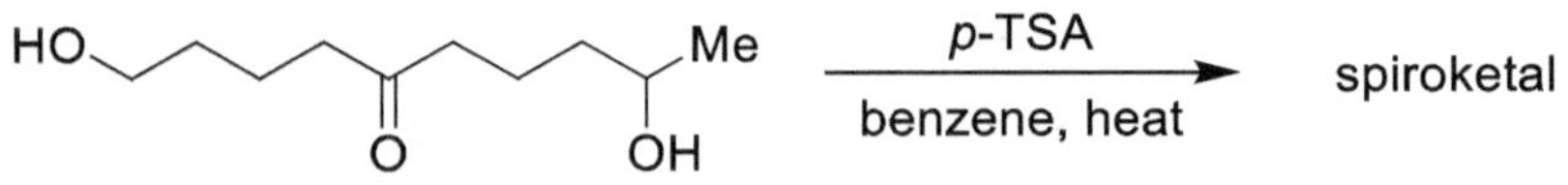

$$\text{HO} \diagdown\diagup\diagdown\diagup\diagdown\diagup \text{Me} \quad \xrightarrow[\text{benzene, heat}]{p\text{-TSA}} \quad \text{spiroketal}$$

the most predominant spiroketal is

A. 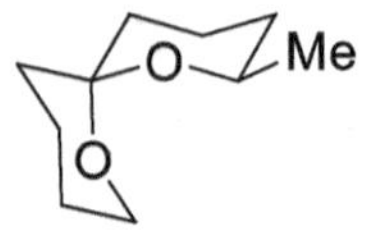   **B.** 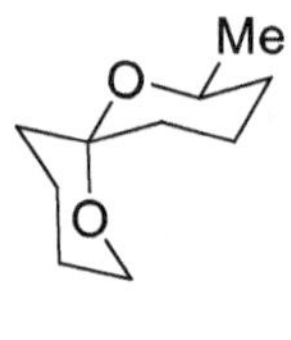   **C.**    **D.**

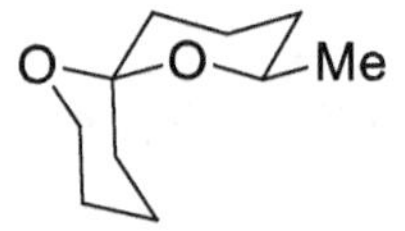

Answer: A. The mechanism of the reaction of the given spiroketal derivative is shown below.

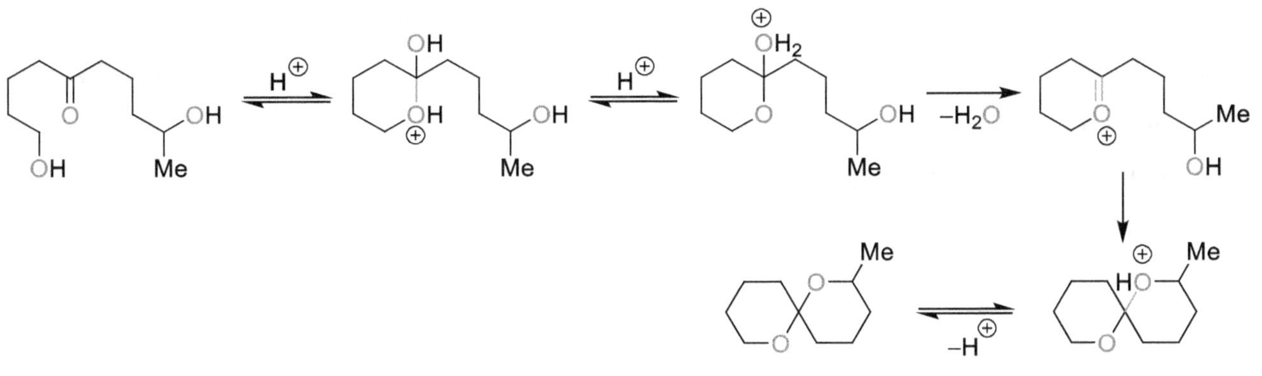

Among these, the most predominant spiroketal is conformer **A** as it is stabilized by two anomeric effects (axial lone pair of the green and pink lobe in **A**) which gives extra stability and it exists in equilibrium.

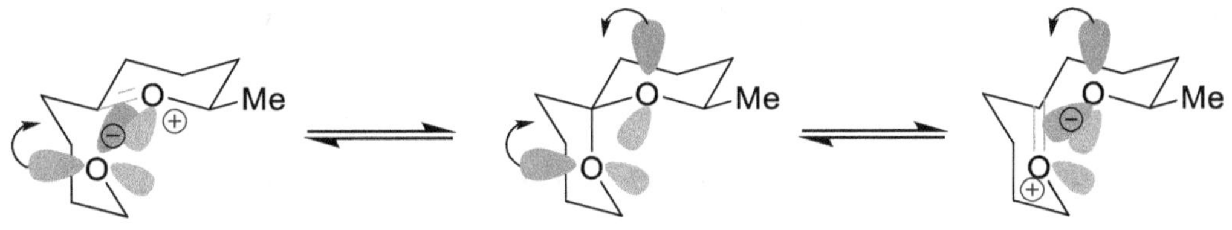

A'   **A**   **A"**

Both the spiroketals **B** and **D** have one anomeric effect and have equal stability (axial lone pair of the green orbital in conformer **B** and pink orbital in conformer **D**).

B   **B'**   **D**   **D'**

Conformational stability of spiroketal. The conformer **A** benefited due to two stereoelectronic effects and the energy of the conformer is lowered by $2 \times (-1.4 \text{ kcal/mol}) = -2.8 \text{ kcal/mol}$ and has four 1,3-diaxial interactions $4 \times (0.4 \text{ kcal/mol}) = 1.6 \text{ kcal/mol}$.

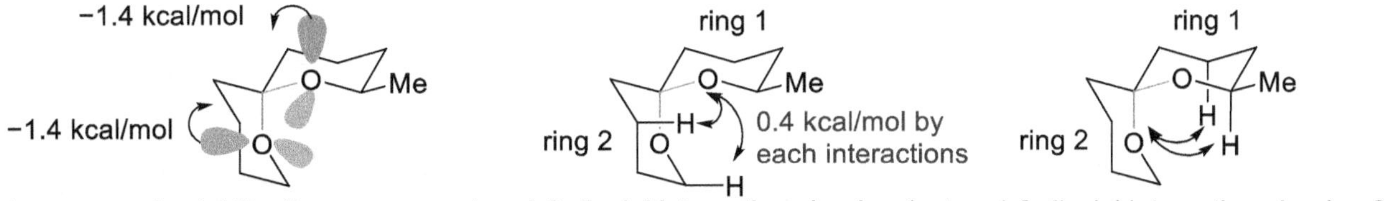

-1.4 kcal/mol

-1.4 kcal/mol

two anomeric stabilizationenergy
$2(-1.4 \text{ kcal/mol}) = -2.8 \text{ kcal/mol}$

ring 1

ring 2

0.4 kcal/mol by each interactions

two 1,3-diaxial interactions by ring 1
$2(0.4 \text{ kcal/mol}) = 0.8 \text{ kcal/mol}$

ring 1

ring 2

two 1,3-diaxial interactions by ring 2
$2(0.4 \text{ kcal/mol}) = 0.8 \text{ kcal/mol}$

Hence, the energy of the conformer **A** = −2.8 kcal/mol + 1.6 kcal/mol = **−1.2 kcal/mol**.

The conformers both **B** and **D** are benefited by one anomeric effect and the energy of the conformer is lowered by 1 × (−1.4 kcal/mol) = −1.4 kcal/mol. Herein, conformers **B** is destabilized by two diaxial gauche butane interactions due to the axial methylene (1.8 kcal/mol) and two diaxial interactions by axial oxygen (0.8 kcal/mol). Similarly, the energy of the conformer **D** can also be calculated as such.

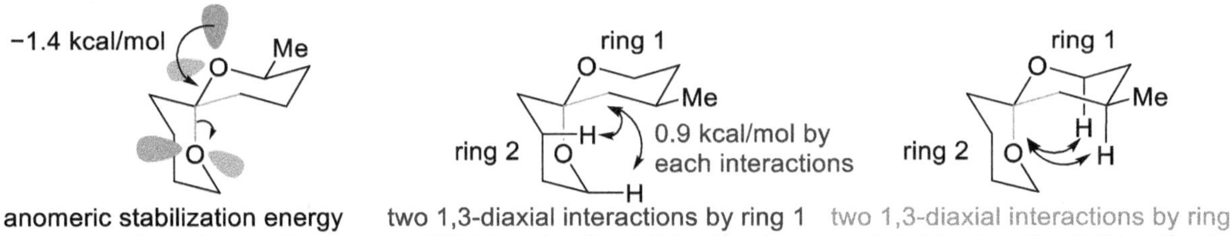

So, the energy of the conformer **B** = (−1.4 kcal/mol) + (1.8 + 0.8) kcal/mol = **1.2 kcal/mol**.

The conformer **C** does not exhibit any anomeric effects but it is destabilized by four 1,3-diaxial gauche butane interactions due to the axial methylenes being 4 × 0.9 kcal/mol = 3.6 kcal/mol.

Thus, the correct decreasing order of the stabilities of the given spiroketal conformers is **A > B = D > C**.

Yadav, V. K. Steric and Stereoelectronic Control of Organic Molecular Structures and Organic Reactions. In *Steric and Stereoelectronic Effects in Organic Chemistry*. 1st Ed.; Springer Nature, 2016; p 12.

Question No-38: In the reaction

the product formed is

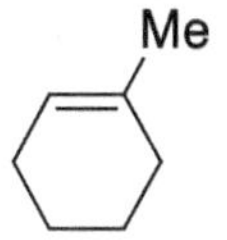

Answer: A. The thermodynamically controlled major product formed in the given Aldol condensation is 1-acetyl cyclopentene and the kinetically controlled offered minor product is 2-cycloheptenone.

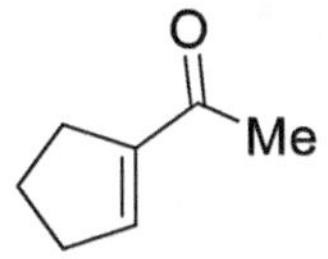

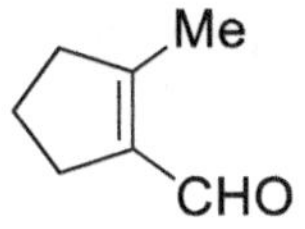

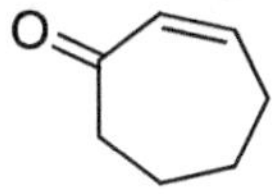

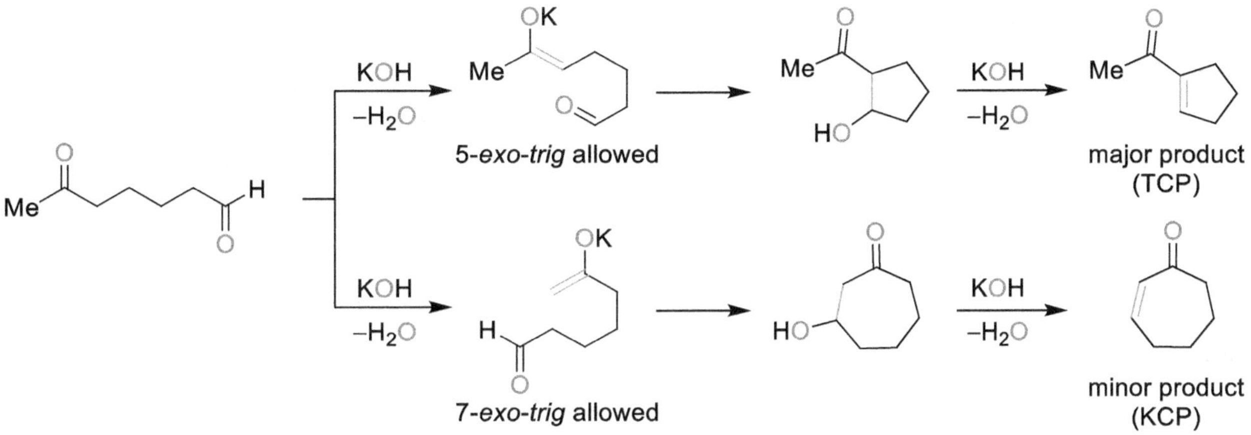

Note. The less hindered base KOH, NaOH, NaH and CaH_2, etc. gives thermodynamically controlled more substituted Aldol condensation product while highly hindered base LDA, LiHMDS, *t*-BuOK, etc. offered kinetically controlled product.

Gilmore, K.; Alabugin, I. V. *Chem. Rev.* **2011**, *111*, 6513.

Question No-39: In the reaction given below, identify the product

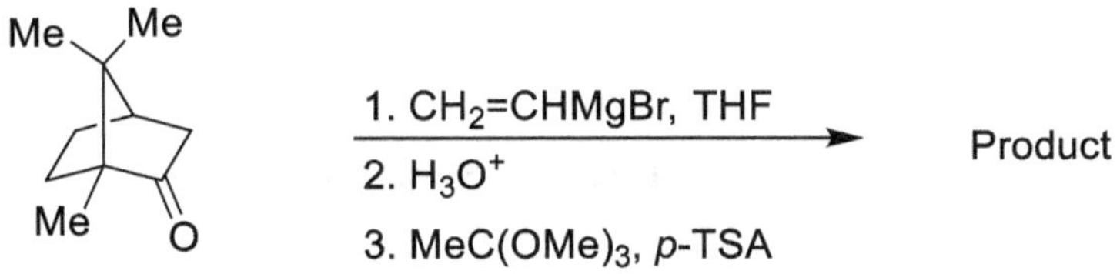

Me, Me

1. CH_2=CHMgBr, THF
2. H_3O^+
3. $MeC(OMe)_3$, *p*-TSA

Product

A.

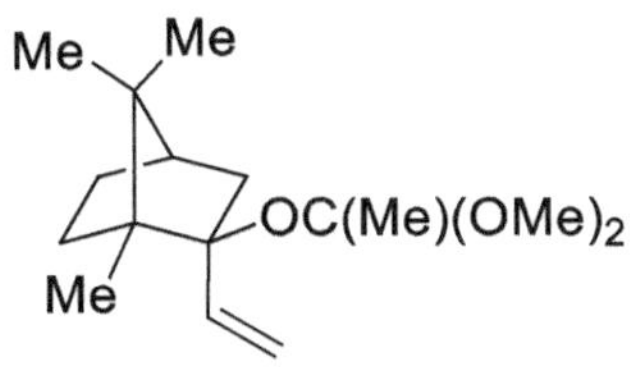

Me, Me

OC(Me)(OMe)₂

Me

B.

Me, Me

Me

O

OMe

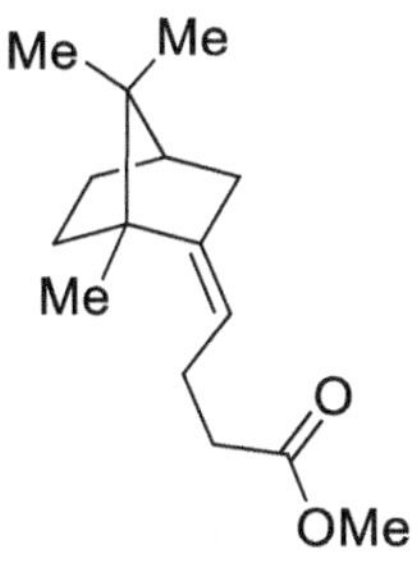

C.

Me Me

Me O OMe

D.

Me Me

Me OC(Me)(OMe)$_2$

Answer: All. All the products can form in the given reaction. The modified Grignard reagent i.e. vinyl magnesium bromide with (+)-camphor gives the following both the major and minor products.

Me Me → $CH_2=CHMgBr$ → Me Me OH (major) + Me Me OH (minor)

$MeO \overset{\oplus}{\underset{Me}{\diagup}} OMe$ $\xleftarrow[\text{−MeOH}]{\text{H}^+ \text{ from } p\text{-TSA}}$ $MeO \underset{Me}{\diagup} OMe$ OMe

The reaction of the major product with the oxonium ion gives corresponding intermediate **A** which further converts into product **C**.

Me Me OH + $MeO \overset{\oplus}{\underset{Me}{\diagup}} OMe$ ⇌ Me Me OMe O OMe **A** $\xrightarrow[\text{−MeOH}]{\pm H^{\oplus}}$ Me Me O OMe H

↕ $\pm H^{\oplus}$

Me Me O OMe **C** $\xleftarrow[\text{sigmatropic shift}]{[3,3]}$ Me Me O OMe

Simultaneously, the minor product also reacts with the oxonium ion to furnish product **B** proceeding through the formation of intermediate product **D**.

Common Data for Questions 48 and 49: Consider the reaction sequence shown below

$$\text{(starting material)} \xrightarrow[\text{2. TsCl, pyridine}]{\text{1. X}} \text{(OTs, OH intermediate)} \xrightarrow{t\text{-BuOK}/t\text{-BuOH}} \text{Product}$$

TsCl = p-toluenesulfonyl chloride

Question No-48: The oxidant **X** used in step 1 is

A. CrO_3

B. OsO_4

C. $NaIO_4$

D. m-CPBA followed by NaOH

Answer: B. The oxidant **X** used in step 1 is OsO_4.

Question No-49: The product is

A. B. C. D.

Answer: D. The vicinal hydroxyl tolylsulfonate derivative in the presence of potassium *tert*-butoxide gives ketone derivative *via* Semipinacole rearrangement.

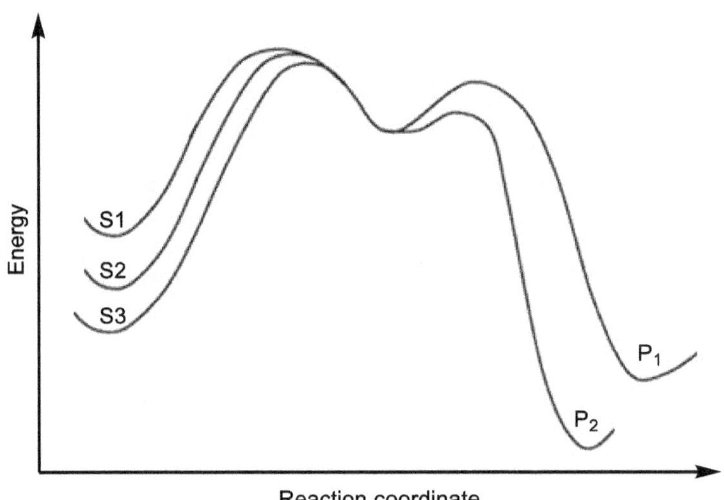

Common Data for Questions 50 and 51: Consider the E1 reaction of *tert*-amyl halides from the energy profile given below.

Question No-50: In the above reaction, X = C*l*, Br or I. Based on the graph, identify the alkyl halides (R-X) as S1, S2 and S3

A. S1 = R-C*l*, S2 = R-Br and S3 = R-I

B. S1 = R-I, S2 = R-Br and S3 = R-C*l*

C. S1 = R-C*l*, S2 = R-I and S3 = R-Br

D. S1 = R-I, S2 = R-C*l* and S3 = R-Br

Answer: B. Among all the alkyl halides, the C-C*l* bond is stronger than C-I bond due to its smaller size and more electronegativity. As a result, the C-C*l* bond is shorter and less reactive (high bond dissociation energy i.e. more stable with low energy).

Thus, the correct match of the R-X as S1, S2 and S3 in the graph; S1 = R-I, S2 = R-Br and S3 = R-C*l*.

Question No-51: Identify product P₁ and its yield relative to P₂

A. P₁ is M and is the major product

B. P₁ is N and is the minor product

C. P₁ is N and is the major product

D. P₁ is M and is the minor product

Answer: D. In the given energy profile diagram, all the E1 reactions take place through the formation of a carbocation intermediate which loses proton from the more substituted β-carbon to give a more substituted olefin *via* Saytzeff elimination (also known as Zaitsev elimination) as the major product (**P₂** is **N**), whereas the formation of a less substituted olefin takes place *via* Hofmann elimination as the minor product (**P₁** is **M**).

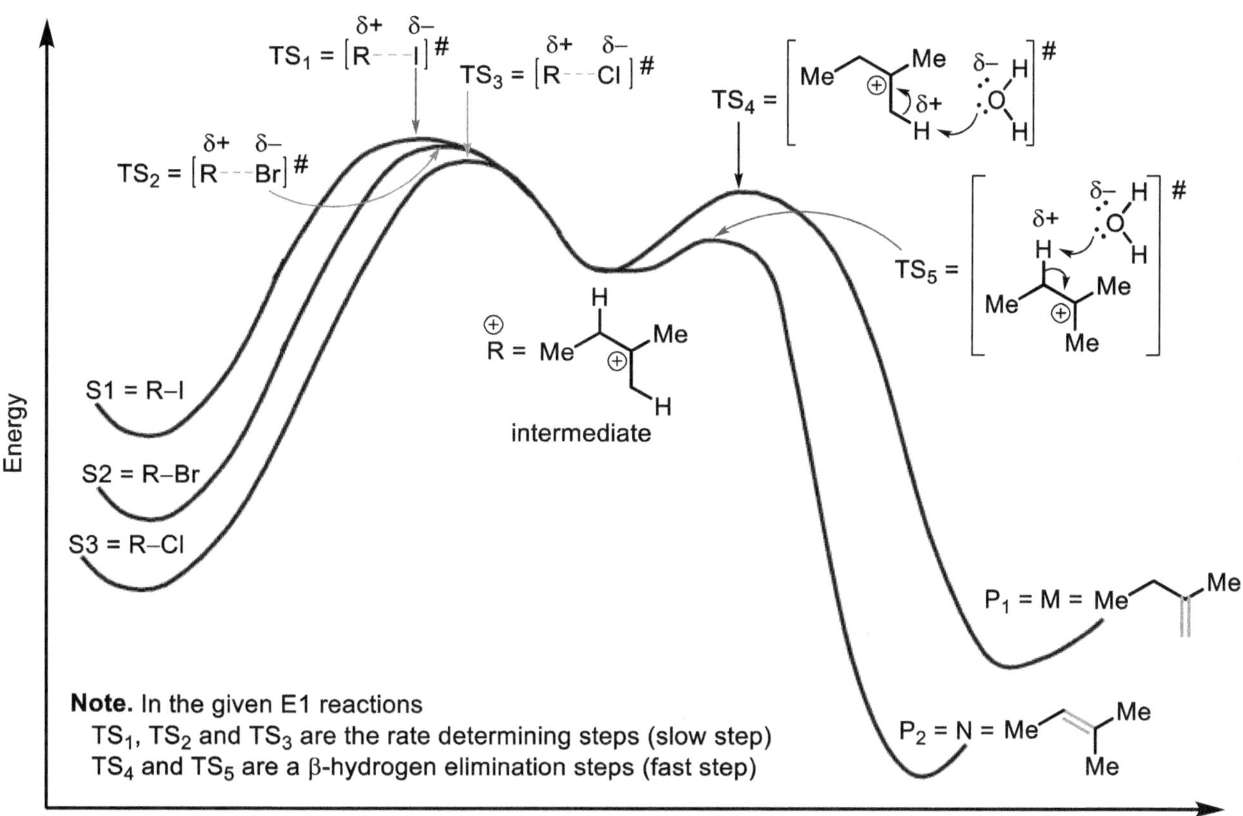

Question No-1: The point group symmetry of $CH_2=C=CH_2$ is

A. D_2h B. C_2h C. C_2v D. D_2d

Answer: D. The point group symmetry of $CH_2=C=CH_2$ is D_2d. An odd number of symmetrical carbon (same group) has three C_2(s) like Td structure, which consists of a C_2 principle axis and $2\sigma d$ with a $2C_2$ subsidiary axis. Thus, the point group symmetry D_2d.

Question No-17: The maximum number of stereoisomers possible for the compound given below is

Answer: 4. The maximum number of stereoisomers possible for the compound given below is four.

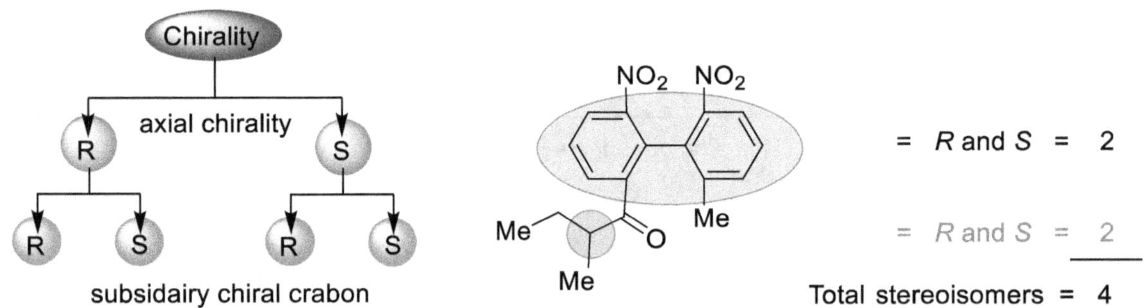

Question No-18: The correct sequence of the amino acids present in the tripeptide given below is

A. Val-Ser-Thr   B. Val-Thr-Ser   C. Leu-Ser-Thr   D. Leu-Thr-Ser

Answer: A. The correct sequence of the amino acids present in the given tripeptide is Val-Ser-Thr.

Val-Ser-Thr   valine   serine   threonine

Question No-19: Among the compounds given in options A-D, the one that can be used as a *formyl anion equivalent* (in the presence of a strong base) is

A. Ethylene   B. Nitroethane   C. 1,3-dithiane   D. 1,4-dithiane

Answer: C. The reaction of 1,3-dithiane with alkyl/aryl halide followed by hydrolysis using Hg^{2+}/H_2O is known as the Corey-Seebach reaction, in which 1,3-dithiane acts as a formyl anion equivalent.

Note. The reaction of the nitromethane with alkyl/aryl halide followed by an alkylation reaction gives a higher substituted compound. Herein, nitromethane can also act as a formyl anion equivalent.

Question No-20: The major product formed in the reaction given below is

1. Me_2CuLi, Et_2O
2. H_3O^+

A.   B.   C.   D.

Answer: D. The Gillman reagent is a soft nucleophile that is well known for the Michael adduct product. In the given reaction scheme the major product is (3R,5R)-3-(*tert*-butyl)-5-methylcyclohexan-1-one.

Question No-21: The major product formed in the reaction given below is

$$\text{phthalimide} \xrightarrow[\text{2. } H_3O^+]{\text{1. NaOH, } Br_2}$$

A. 2-aminobenzoic acid (NH_2, CO_2H)

B. (Br, $CONH_2$)

C. (CO_2H, $CONH_2$)

D. (phthalic anhydride)

Answer: A. The major product formed in the given Hofmann bromide reaction is anthranilic acid.

phthalimide $\xrightarrow[-H_2O]{\text{NaOH}}$ (NNa) $\xrightarrow[-NaBr]{Br_2}$ (N–Br) $\xrightarrow[-H_2O]{\text{2NaOH}}$ (CO_2Na, Na) $\xrightarrow{-NaBr}$ isocyanate derivative ($N{=}C{=}O$, CO_2Na) $\xrightarrow{H_2O}$ carbamic acid derivative (NH, CO_2Na) $\xrightarrow[-[CO_2 + H_2O]]{\text{NaOH}}$ ($NHNa$, CO_2Na) $\xrightarrow[-2[NaOH + H_2O]]{2H_3O^{\oplus}}$ anthranilic acid (NH_2, CO_2H)

Question No-22: The pericyclic reaction given below is an example of

A.   [1,3]-sigmatropic shift

B.   [1,5]-sigmatropic shift

C.   [3,5]-sigmatropic shift

D.   [3,3]-sigmatropic shift

Answer: D. The pericyclic reaction given above is an example of [3,3]-sigmatropic shift (Cope rearrangement).

Question No-23: The major product formed in the reaction of quinoline with potassium amide (KNH_2) in liquid ammonia is

A. [structure] B. [structure] C. [structure] D. [structure]

Answer: B. The given reaction is an example of the Chichibabin reaction, which is widely employed for the amination purpose as shown below.

Question No-24: The number of signals that appear in the proton decoupled ^{13}C NMR spectrum of benzonitrile (C_7H_5N) is _________

Answer: 5. The number of peaks that appeared in the proton decoupled ^{13}C NMR spectrum of PhCN is five.

Question No-25: Among the compounds given in options A-D, the one that exhibits a sharp band at around 3300 cm^{-1} in the IR spectrum is

A. 1,2-butadiene   B. 1,3-butadiene   C. 1-butyne   D. 2-butyne

Answer: C. Among these, 1-butyne exhibits a sharp band at around 3300 cm^{-1} in the IR spectrum.

Question No-26: In the metathesis reaction given below, 4.32 g of compound **X** was treated with 822 mg of catalyst **Y** to yield 2.63 g of product **Z**. The mol% of the catalyst **Y** used in this reaction is _________

[Atomic weights of Ru = 101; P = 31; Cl = 35.5]

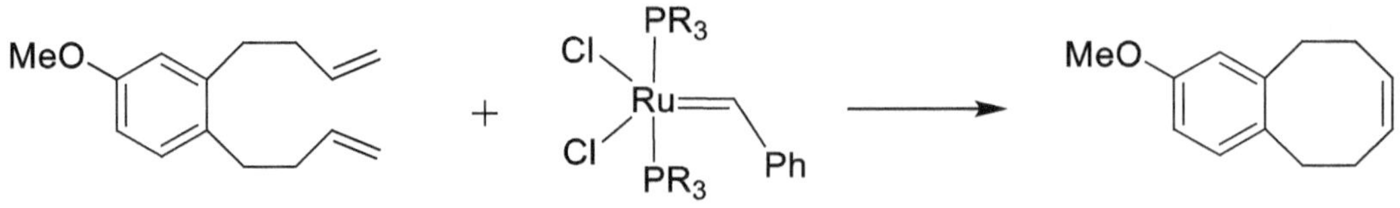

X + Y → Z

(R = cyclohexyl)

Answer: 4.9 to 5.1. The molecular weights of **X** ($C_{15}H_{20}O$) and **Y** ($C_{43}H_{72}Cl_2P_2Ru$) are 216 g/mol and 822 g/mol, respectively.

The mol of **X** = 4.32g/216 g/mol = 0.02 mol

The mol of **Y** = 0.822g/822 g/mol = 0.001 mol

The mol% of the catalyst **Y** is used = (0.001 mol of **Y**/0.02 mol of **X**) × 100 = **5 mol%.**

Question No-27: An organic compound **Q** exhibited the following spectral data:

IR: 1760 cm^{-1}

^{1}H NMR δ (ppm): 7.2 (1H, d, J = 16.0 Hz), 5.1 (1H, m), 2.1 (3 H, s), 1.8 (3H, d, J = 7.0 Hz)

^{13}C NMR δ (ppm): 170 (carbonyl carbon).

Compound **Q** is

A. 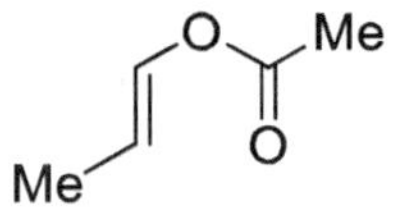 B. 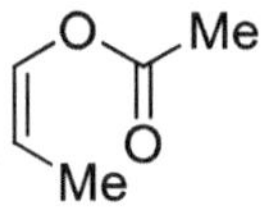 C. 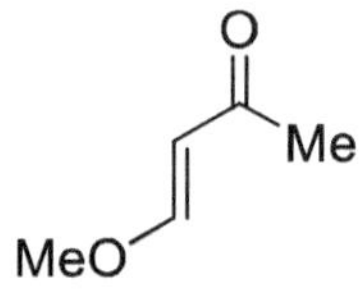 D.

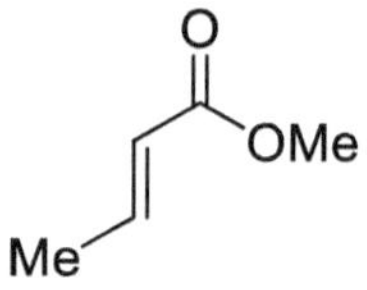

Answer: A. The given spectroscopic data analysis reveals that the compound is (*E*)-acetyl 1-propenyl ether.

^{1}H NMR (δ in ppm)	**^{13}C NMR (δ in ppm)**	**IR spectrum**
		1760 cm^{-1}

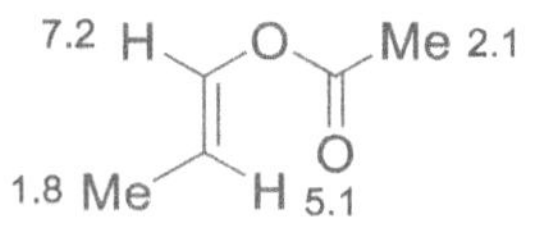

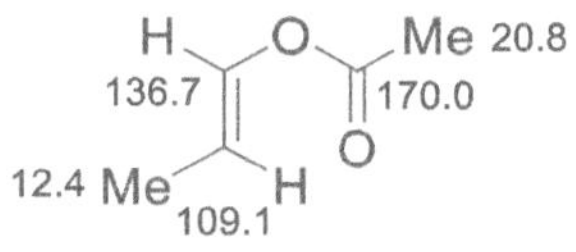

Question No-28: The major product formed in the Beckmann rearrangement of the compound given below is

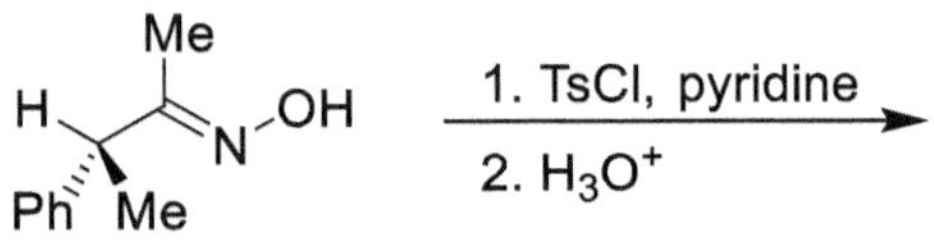

1. TsCl, pyridine
2. H_3O^+

A.

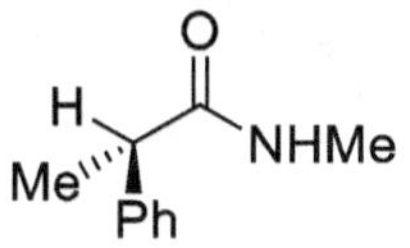

B.

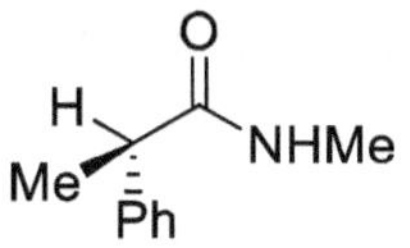

C.

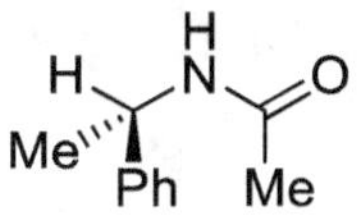

D.

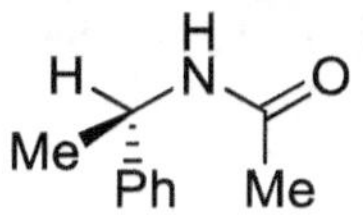

Answer: D. The major product formed in the given Beckmann rearrangement is (R)-N-(1-phenylethyl)acetamide which proceeds through a concerted mechanism of rearrangement. The concerted mechanism is suggested because the stereochemistry of the chiral carbon is not changing.

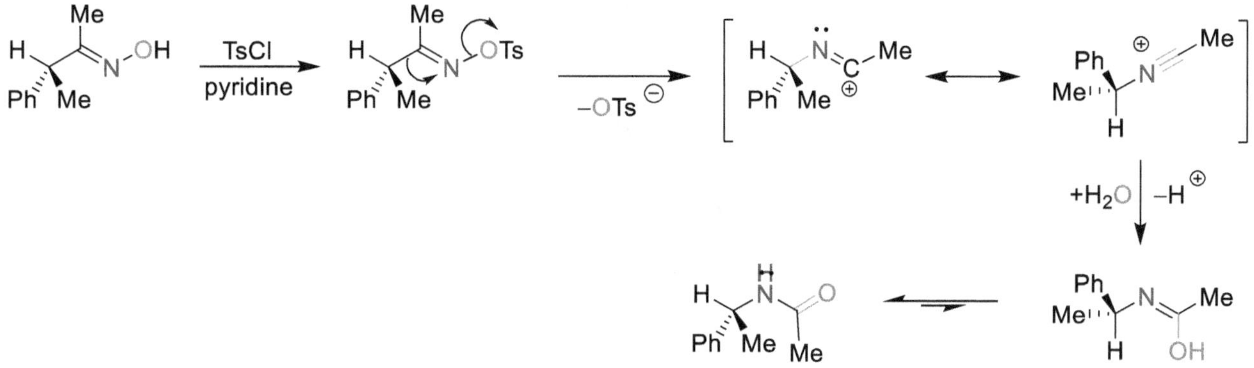

Pi, H.; Dong, J.; An, N.; Du, W.; Deng, W. *Tetrahedron* **2009**, *65*, 7790.

Question No-29: The major product formed in the reaction given below is

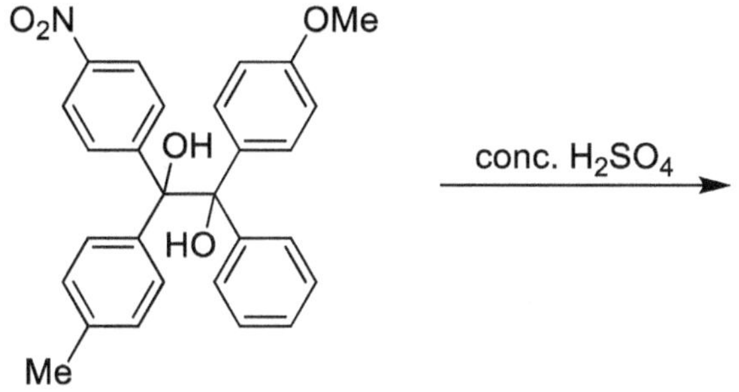

conc. H_2SO_4

A.

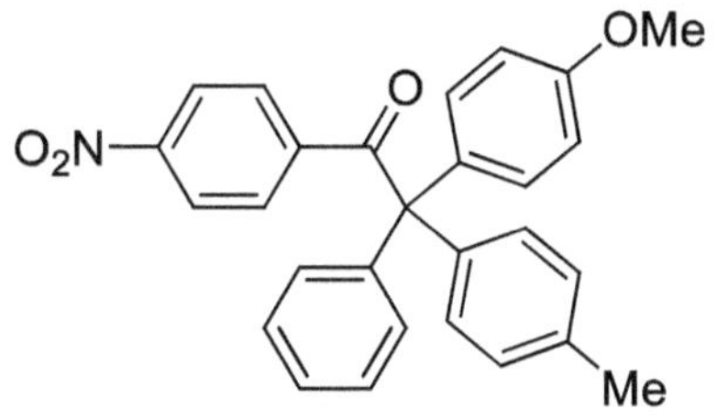

B.

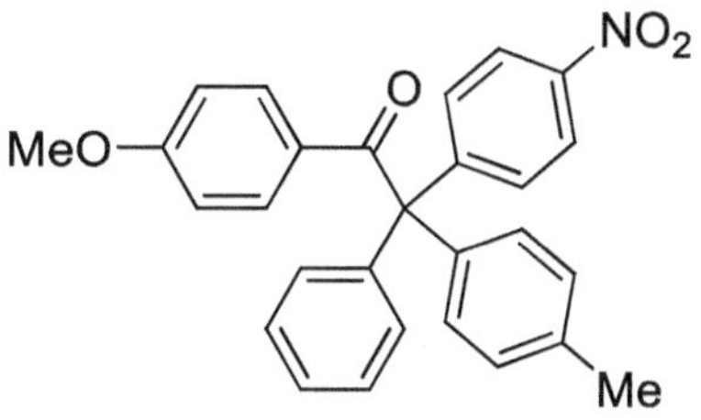

C.

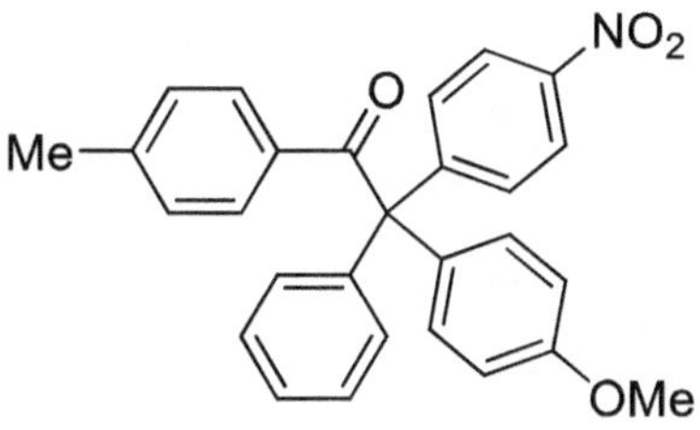

D.

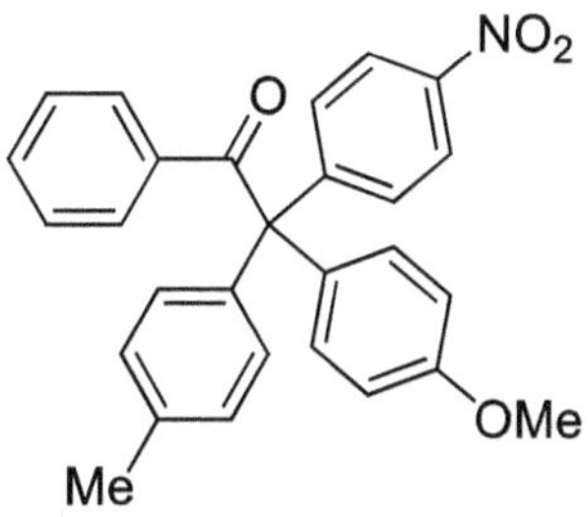

Answer: A. Pinacol-pinacolone of the given reaction is proceeding through a stable carbocation intermediate which is further rearranged into the product 2-(4-methoxyphenyl)-1-(4-nitrophenyl)-2-phenyl-2-(*p*-tolyl)ethan-1-one due to the migration of tolyl group.

Question No-30: The major product formed in the reaction given below is

A.

B.

C.

D.

Answer: D. The major product formed in the reaction given above reaction is decahydronaphthalen-2-ol proceeding through ring enlargement. This reaction is known as Tiffeneau–Demjanov rearrangement.

Question No-31: The major product(s) formed in the reaction sequence given below is(are)

A.

and

B.

and

C.

D.

Answer: A. In the given reaction, the first step involves the synthesis of the Grignard reagent which reacts with benzaldehyde producing a vicinal hydroxyl silane derivative. Next, the Peterson elimination of the vicinal hydroxyl silane derivative in acidic media gives a mixture of both *cis-* and *trans-*olefins.

Note. In an acidic medium, *trans*-elimination takes place due to parallel interaction between bond pair electron of $\sigma_{C\text{-}Si}$ orbital with the anti-bonding orbital of $\sigma^*_{C\text{-}O}$ orbital.

Peterson, D. J. *J. Org. Chem.* **1968**, *33*, 780.

Question No-32: Match the compounds in column **I** with the photochemical reactions that they can undergo given in column **II**

<table>
<tr><td colspan="2" align="center">column I</td><td align="center">column II</td></tr>
<tr><td>i.</td><td>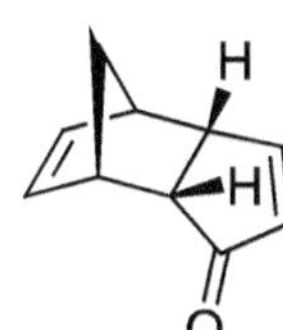</td><td>(p)   Oxa-di-π-methane rearrangement</td></tr>
<tr><td></td><td></td><td>(q)   Paterno-Buchi reaction</td></tr>
<tr><td>ii.</td><td></td><td>(r)   Intramolecular [2+2]-cycloaddition</td></tr>
<tr><td>iii.</td><td>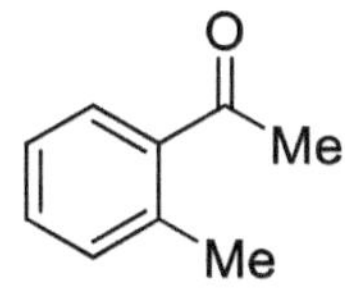</td><td>(s)   Photoenolization</td></tr>
</table>

A. (i)-(q); (ii)-(s); (iii)-(p)   B. (i)-(r); (ii)-(p); (iii)-(s)

C. (i)-(p); (ii)-(r); (iii)-(q)   D. (i)-(r); (ii)-(q); (iii)-(s)

Answer: B. The correct match of **Column I** with **Column II** is (i)-(r); (ii)-(p); (iii)-(s).

An intramolecular photochemical [2+2]-cycloaddition of the given below

Oxa-di-π-methane rearrangement in the presence of sensitizer (acetone) produces a tricyclic compound while its absence produces conjugated cyclohexadiene and ketene

Photoenolization of the 2-methyl acetophenone in the presence of light gives corresponding enols as shown below.

Klunder, A. J. H.; Huizinga, W. B.; Hulshof, A. J. M.; Zwanenburg, B. *Tetrahedron Lett.* **1986**, *27*, 2543.

Givens, R. S.; Oettle, W. F.; Coffin, R. L.; Carlson, R. G. *J. Am. Chem. Soc.* **1971**, *93*, 3957.

Wintgens, V.; Netto-Ferreira, J. C.; Scaiano, J. C. *Photochem. Photobiol. Sci.* **2002**, *1*, 184.

Common Data for Questions 48 and 49:

N,N-Dimethylformamide (DMF) gives different patterns of signals for the methyl protons when its ^{1}H NMR spectrum is recorded at different temperatures.

Question No-48: Match the patterns of the NMR signals given in column **I** with temperatures given in column **II**.

	Column I		Column II
i.	Two singlets, for three protons each, at δ 2.87 and 2.97 ppm	(x)	25 °C
ii.	One sharp singlet for six protons at δ 2.92 ppm	(y)	120 °C
iii.	One broad signal for six protons	(z)	150 °C

Codes

A. (i)-(x); (ii)-(y); (iii)-(z)   B. (i)-(x); (ii)-(z); (iii)-(y)

C. (i)-(z); (ii)-(x); (iii)-(y)   D. (i)-(z); (ii)-(y); (iii)-(x)

Answer: B. The correct match of Column I with Column II is (i)-(x); (ii)-(z); (iii)-(y).

Question No-49: Based on the above data, the calculated difference in the frequencies of the two methyl singlets, if the spectrum is recorded on a 300 MHz spectrometer is __________ Hz.

Answer: 30. The calculated difference in the frequencies of the two methyl singlets at 25 °C is (δ 2.97 - 2.87) ppm = 0.1 ppm.

If the spectrum is recorded at 300 MHz spectrometer = 300 MHz × 0.1 ppm = 30 Hz.

Linked Answer Questions 52 and 53

Question No-52: The major product **X** formed in the reaction given below is

2,2-dimethoxypropane
p-toluenesulfonic acid
(catalytic)

A.

B.

C.

D.

Answer: C. The reaction of Conduritol with 2,2-dimethoxypropne in the presence of p-TSA forms acetonide derivative **X** with the vicinal *syn*-diols as shown below.

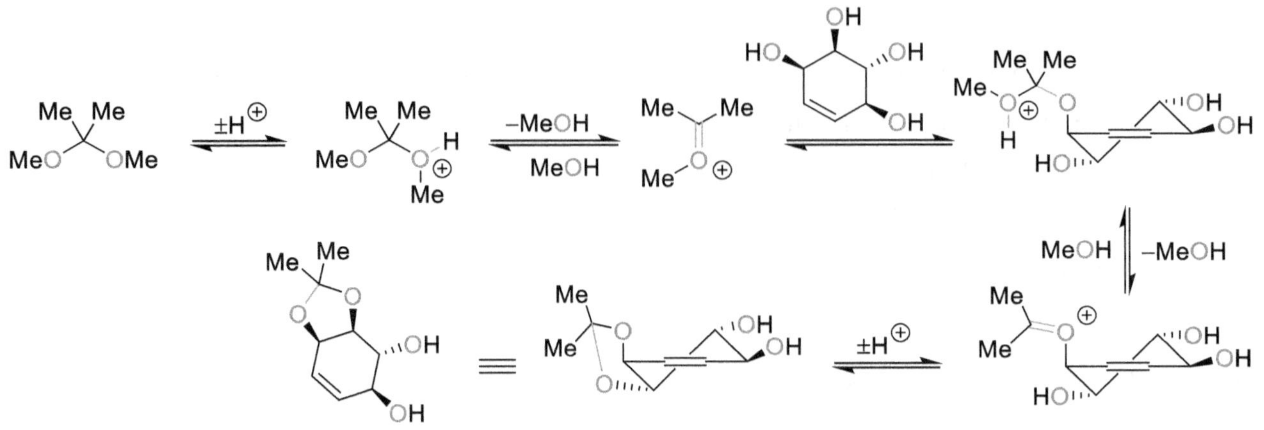

Note. If the reaction is not moisture sensitive then instead of 2,2-dimethoxypropne, directly acetone can be employed for the same.

Question No-53: Oxidation of the product **X**, obtained in the above reaction with active manganese dioxide followed by acidic hydrolysis gives

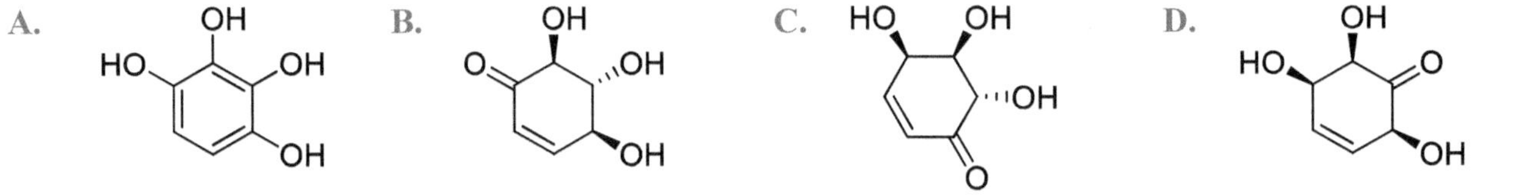

Answer: C. The chemoselective allylic oxidation of Conduritol diacetonide **X** with manganese dioxide followed by acidic hydrolysis produces (4*R*,5*R*,6*S*)-4,5,6-trihydroxycyclohex-2-en-1-one as the major product.

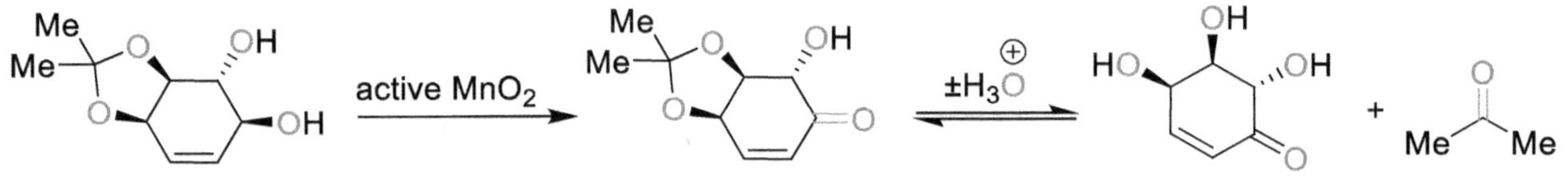

Question No-3: The number of IR active vibrational normal modes of CO_2 is

Answer: 3. Carbon dioxide is a linear molecule. Thus, the total number of vibrational normal modes is calculated by $(3N - 5) = 4$. Where $N = 3$ (2 oxygen + 1 carbon) number of the atoms in the CO_2 molecule.

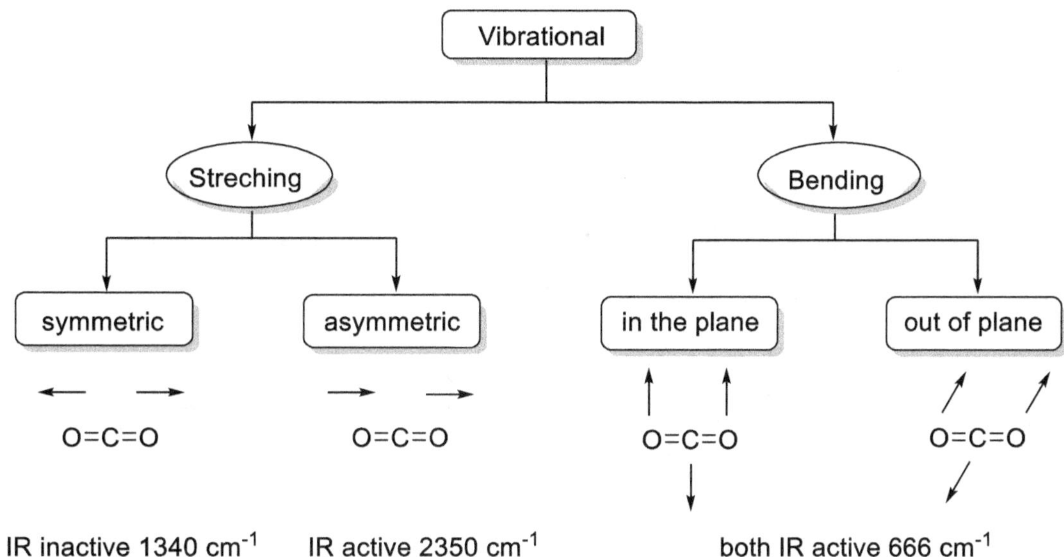

Question No-4: The number of C_2 axes in CCl_4 is

Answer: 3. There are three σ_d planes present in CCl_4, which is equivalent to the C_2 axis in Td (tetrahedral) compound.

Question No-17: The major product of the following reaction is

Answer: C. The reaction of D-glucose with dimethyl sulfate in basic media offers pentamethyl D-glucose which further on acidic hydrolysis produces selective demethylated product at the anomeric carbon.

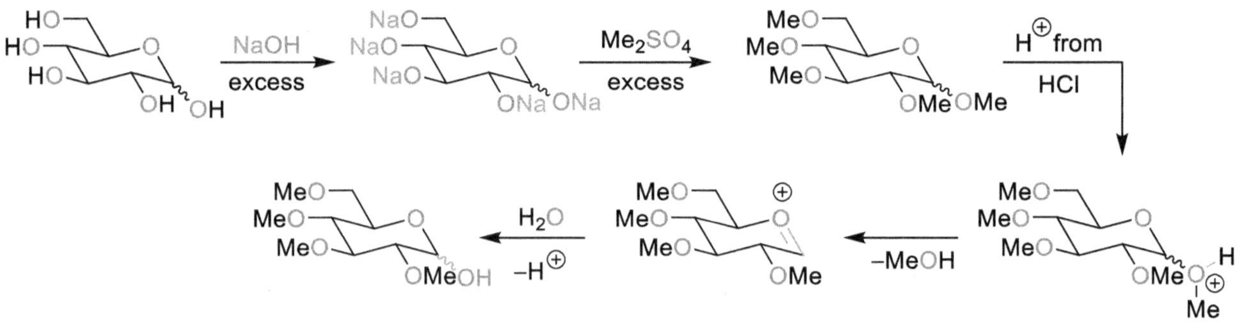

Note. The open structure of the D-glucose (0.02%) in acidic media is equilibrating into mutarotation products; (i) α-D-glucose (36%) and (ii) β-D-glucose (64%).

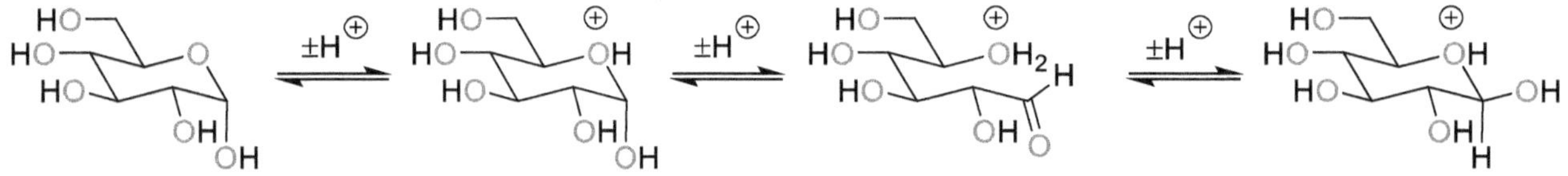

α-D-glucose (36%)   D-glucose (0.02%)   β-D-glucose (64%)

Question No-18: Amongst the following, the structure of guanosine is

A.

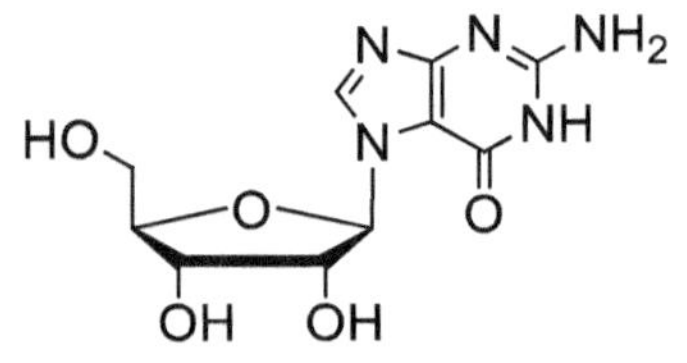

B.

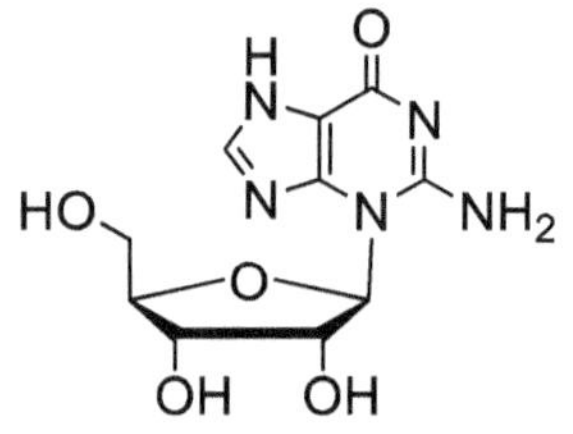

C.

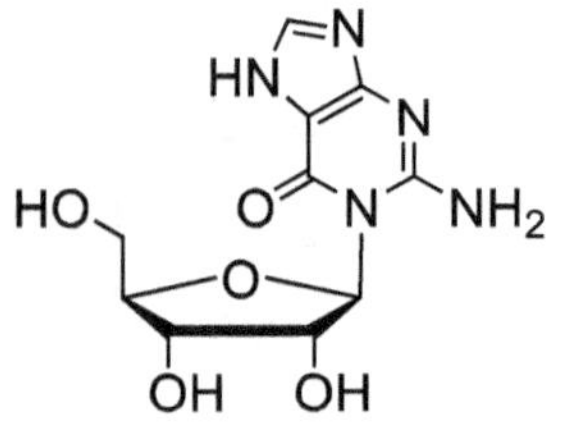

D.

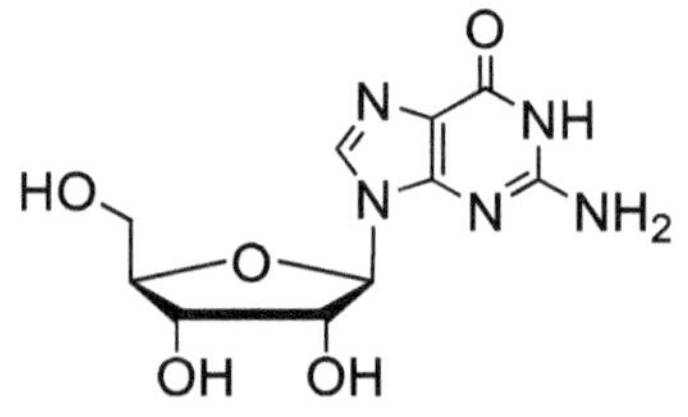

Answer: D. Amongst these, the structure of guanosine is compound **D** in which a five-membered purine ring of the C9-position is joined with ribose sugar.

Question No-19: The correct order of IR stretching frequency of the C=C in the following olefins is

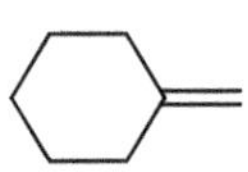

I 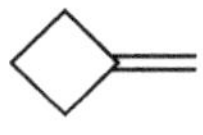   II 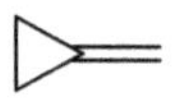   III

A. I > II > III   B. II > III > I   C. III > II > I   D. III > I > II

Answer: C. The correct order of IR stretching frequency of the given exocyclic C=C having molecules depends on their high values of ring strain (force constant, k) and molecular mass (reduced mass, μ).

As we know that the IR stretching frequency $(v) = (1/2\pi c)\,(k/\mu)^{1/2}\,cm^{-1}$

Thus the order of IR stretching frequency = III > II > I.

Question No-20: The correct order of the rate of solvolysis for the following chlorides in acetic acid is

I	II	III

A.   II > I > III   B.   III > II > I   C.   III > I > II   D.   I > III > II

Answer: B. The rate of solvolysis in a polar solvent is more common. In compound III the formation of bicyclic oxonium ion intermediate to the product *via* neighboring group participation (NGP) is faster than in compound II due to ring strain. In case of compound I, it undergoes normal S_N2-reaction thus it exhibits a poor rate of solvolysis.

The correct order of the rate of solvolysis for the given chlorides in AcOH = III > II > I.

Question No-21: Formation of the product in the following photochemical reaction involves

A.   Di-π-methane rearrangement   B.   Paterno-Buchi reaction

C.   [2,3]-Sigmatropic rearrangement   D.   Norrish type I reaction

Answer: A. Formation of the product in the given photochemical reaction involves Di-π-methane rearrangement.

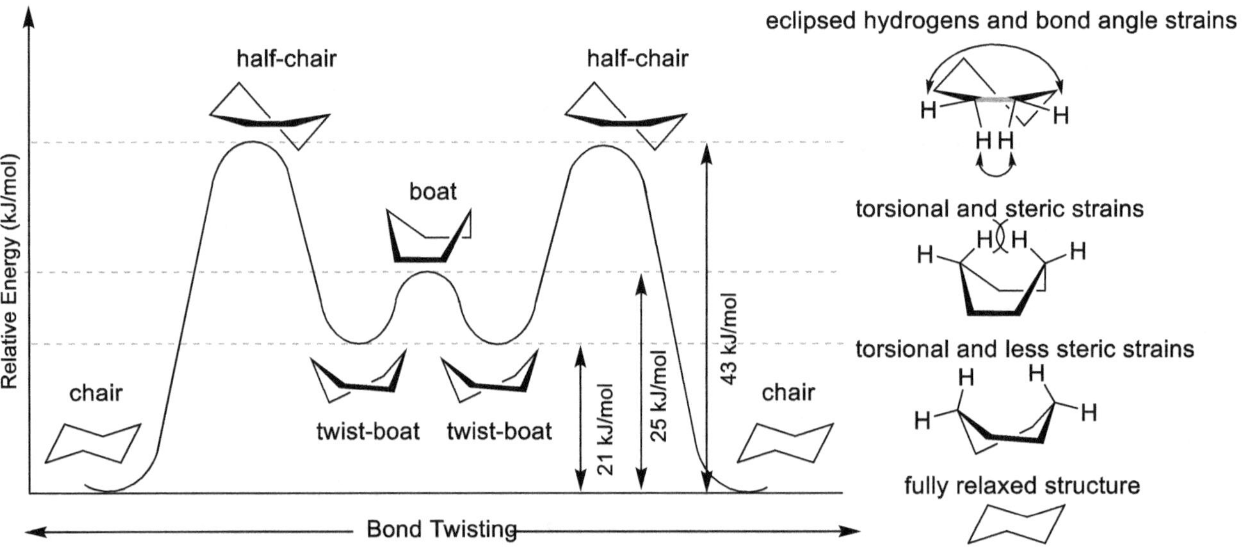

Zimmerman, H. E.; Schuster, D. I. *J. Am. Chem. Soc.* **1962**, *84*, 4527.

Question No-22: The correct order of stability for the following conformations of cyclohexane is

I	II	III

A. I > II > III   **B.** I > III > II   **C.** II > I > III   **D.** III > I > II

Answer: A. Among these, half chair conformer of cyclohexane is with high energy because the two carbons are in the eclipsed relation whereas the twist boat conformer is with low energy than the boat due to less steric strains associated with it.

The correct order of stability for the given conformations of cyclohexane: half chair (III) < boat (II) < twist boat (I) < chair.

Clayden, J.; Greeves, N.; Warren, S. Conformational Analysis. In *Organic chemistry*; 2nd Ed.; Oxford University Press, 2012, p 373.

Question No-23: The major product formed in the following reaction is

$$\text{cyclopentadiene} + \;=\!\bullet\!=\!\!\!\begin{array}{c}\text{COOMe}\end{array} \quad \xrightarrow{\text{TiCl}_4}$$

A

B

C

D

Answer: C. The regioselective concerted thermal [4+2]-cycloaddition of cyclopentadiene with ketene derivative is shown below.

Question No-24: The overall yield (in %) for the following reaction sequence is…….……..

$$\text{Ph-CHO} \xrightarrow[90\%]{\text{MeMgBr}} \underset{\text{Ph}\quad\text{Me}}{\overset{\text{OH}}{\diagup}} \xrightarrow[80\%]{\text{Jones reagent}} \underset{\text{Ph}\quad\text{Me}}{\overset{\text{O}}{\diagup}} \xrightarrow[80\%]{\text{PhCHO, aq. NaOH}} \underset{\text{Ph}\qquad\text{Ph}}{\overset{\text{O}}{\diagup}}$$

Answer: 57.6%. The overall yield (in %) for the given reaction sequence can be calculated below

	Step I	**Step II**	**Step III**

$$\text{Ph-CHO} \xrightarrow[90\%]{\text{MeMgBr}} \underset{\text{Ph}\quad\text{Me}}{\overset{\text{OH}}{\diagup}} \xrightarrow[80\%]{\substack{\text{Jones'}\\\text{reagent}}} \underset{\text{Ph}\quad\text{Me}}{\overset{\text{O}}{\diagup}} \xrightarrow[80\%]{\substack{\text{PhCHO}\\\text{aq. NaOH}}} \underset{\text{Ph}\qquad\text{Ph}}{\overset{\text{O}}{\diagup}}$$

The overall yield of reaction $= \left(\dfrac{90}{100} \text{ of step I} \times \dfrac{80}{100} \text{ of step II} \times \dfrac{80}{100} \text{ of step III}\right) \times 100 = 57.6\,\% \approx \mathbf{58\%}.$

Question No-25: The most suitable reagent combination to effect the following conversion is

A.   i. NaH, CS$_2$, then MeI; ii. Bu$_3$SnH, AIBN, C$_6$H$_6$, reflux

B.   i. I$_2$, PPh$_3$, imidazole; ii. H$_2$, 10% Pd-C, AcOH, high pressure

C.   i. Me$_3$SiC*l*, pyridine, DMAP; ii. Bu$_3$SnH, AIBN, C$_6$H$_6$, reflux

D.   i. Me$_3$SiC*l*, pyridine, DMAP; ii. LiA*l*H$_4$, THF, reflux

Answer: A. The most suitable reagent combination to effect the given synthetic transformation is i. NaH, CS$_2$, then MeI and ii. Bu$_3$SnH, AIBN, C$_6$H$_6$, reflux. This reaction is known as Barton–McCombie deoxygenation which furnishes major product (2*S*,4*S*)-2-((benzyloxy)methyl)-3,4-dihydro-2*H*-pyran-4-yl benzoate.

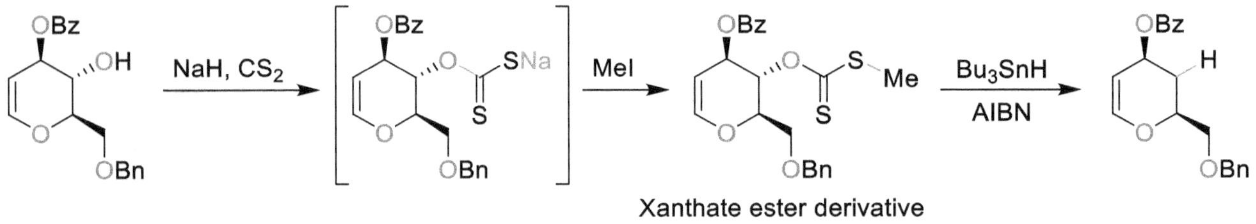

Note. The pyrolytic intramolecular *syn*-Ei-reaction of Xanthate ester in the absence of TBTH/AIBN gives olefin derivative and this reaction is known as Chugaev elimination.

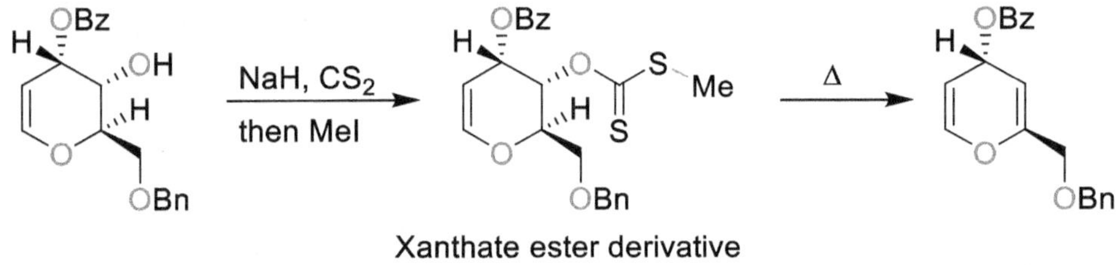

Question No-46: Formation of the ketone from the diazo ketone involves

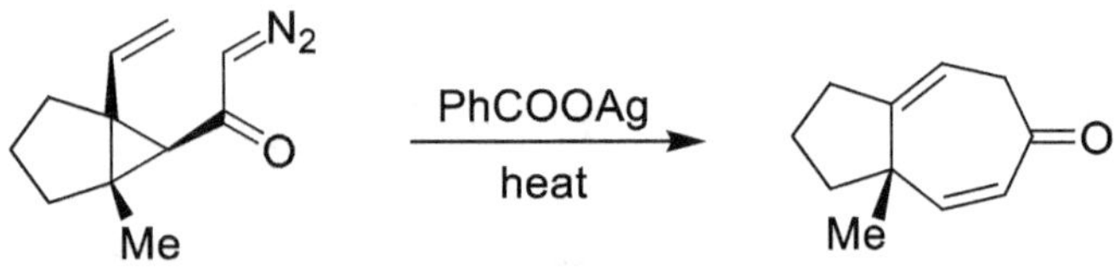

A.   generation of carbene and a [2,3]-sigmatropic rearrangement

B.   generation of carbene and an electrocyclic ring-closing reaction

C.   generation of ketene and a [2+2] cycloaddition

D.   generation of ketene and a [3,3]-sigmatropic rearrangement

Answer: D. The thermal Wolff rearrangement of the given α-diazo ketone compound with silver benzoate generates carbene intermediate which is further rearranged into ketene derivative. Furthermore, it undergoes thermal [3,3]-sigmatropic shift (Cope rearrangement) produces major product (*S*)-3a-methyl-2,3,3a,7-tetrahydroazulen-6(1*H*)-one.

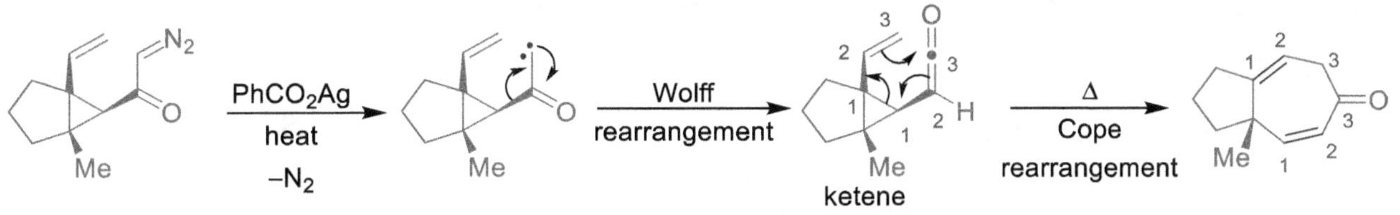

Question No-47: The major products **X** and **Y** formed in the following reaction sequence are

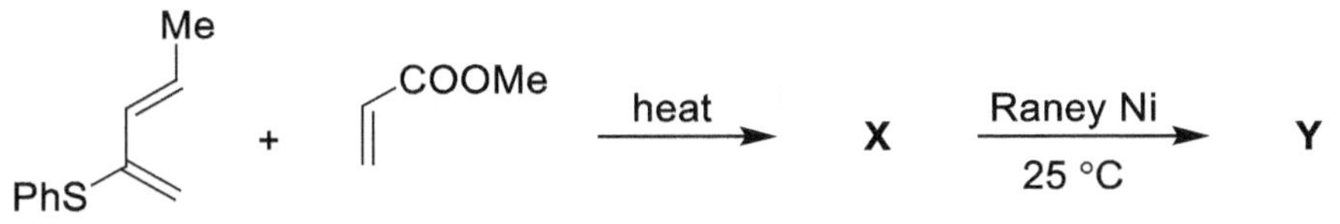

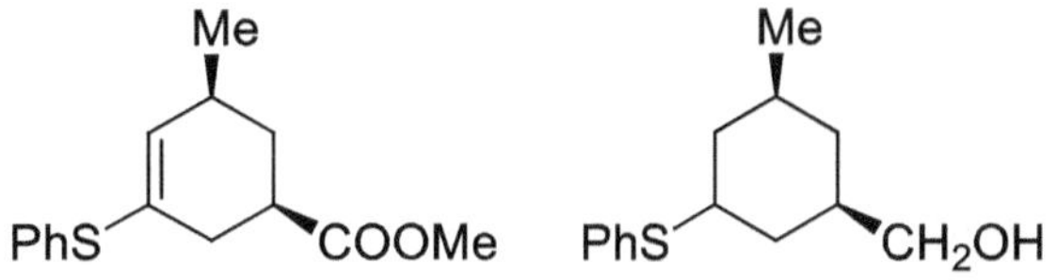

Answer: A. The concerted stereospecific [4+2]-cycloaddition reaction of a diene with methyl acrylate offers *ortho-/para-*substituted cyclohexene derivative **X**. Next, the chemoselective reduction of thiophenyl group without affecting double bond gives reduced product **Y**.

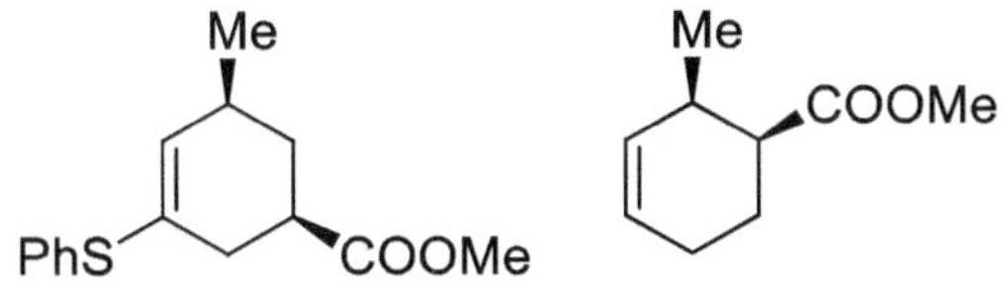

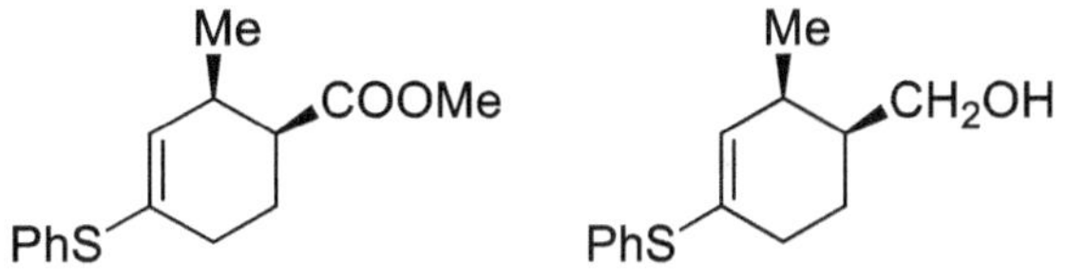

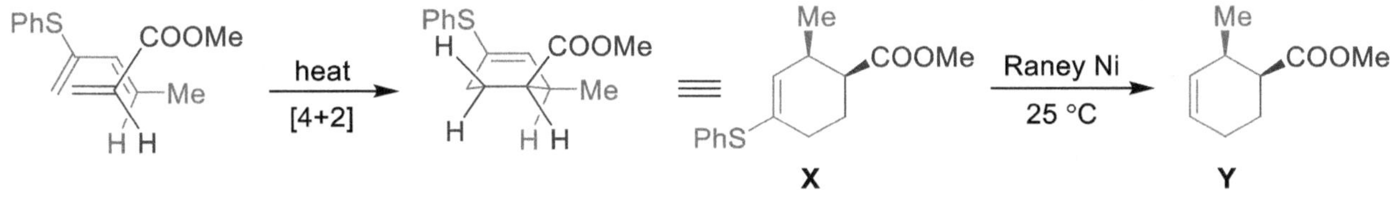

Question No-48: The major products **X** and **Y** formed in the following reactions are

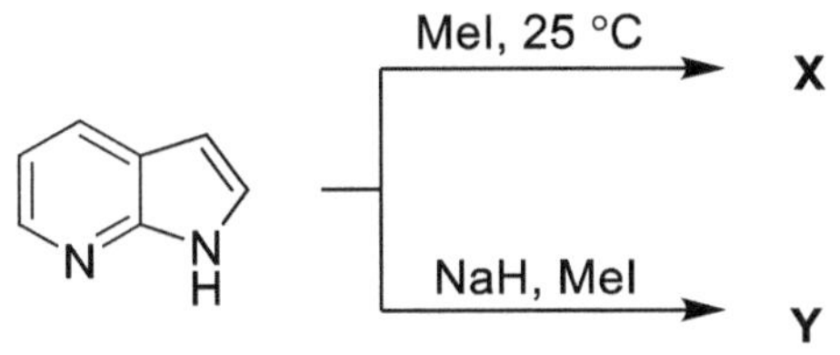

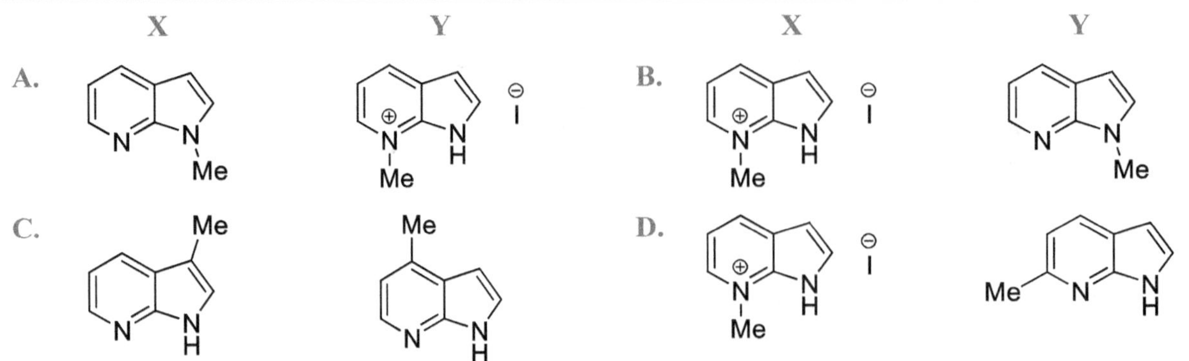

Answer: B. The reaction of 1*H*-pyrrolo[2,3-*b*]pyridine with methyl iodide gives 7-methyl-1*H*-7λ^4-pyrrolo[2,3-*b*]pyridine due to the attack of a freely available one pair of the fused pyridine ring. On the other hand, the presence of sodium hydride abstracts an acidic proton from the fused pyrrole ring which yields a methylated product of the five-member ring.

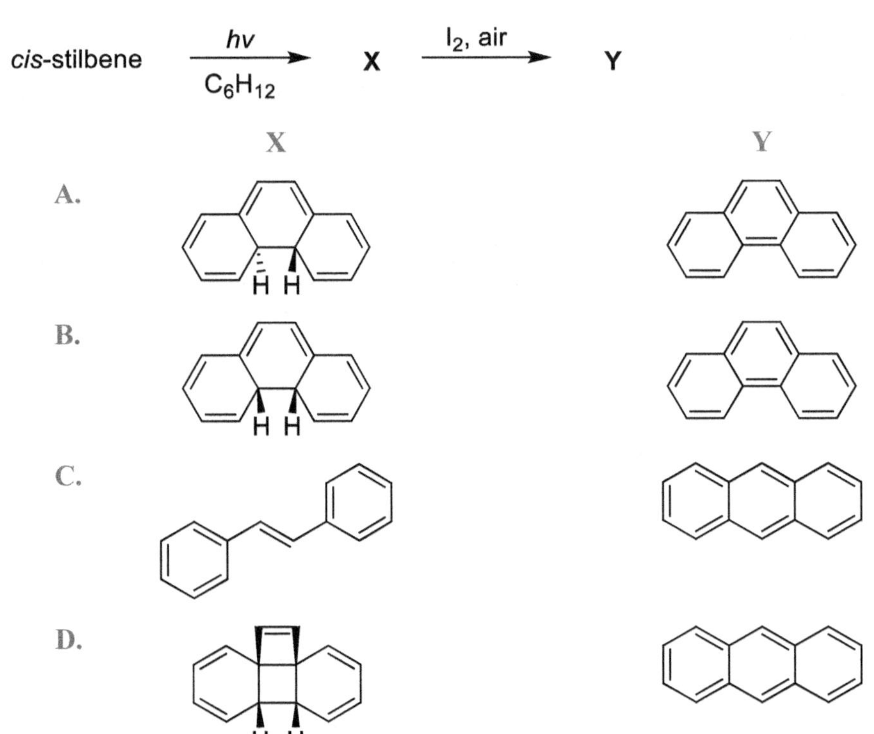

Question No-49: The major products **X** and **Y** formed in the following reaction sequence are

$$\text{cis-stilbene} \xrightarrow[\text{C}_6\text{H}_{12}]{h\nu} \textbf{X} \xrightarrow{\text{I}_2,\ \text{air}} \textbf{Y}$$

Answer: A. The photochemical excitation of *cis*-stilbene undergoes electrocyclic 6π-electron ring closure reaction produces *trans*-4a,4b-dihydrophenanthrene **X**, which on further reaction with molecular iodine undergoes areal oxidation in free radical manner furnishing the end product phenanthrene **Y**.

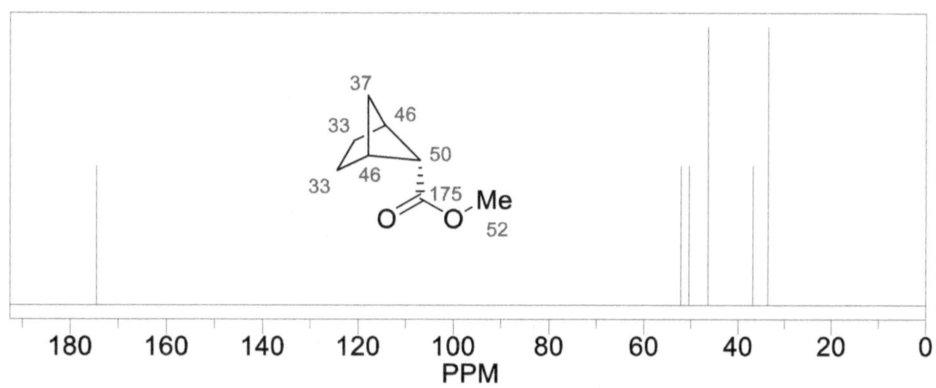

Question No-50: The product of the following reaction gave 6 lines ^{13}C NMR spectrum with peaks at δ 175, 52, 50, 46, 37, 33 ppm. The structure of the product is

Answer: C. The thermal or photochemical reaction of the α-diazo carbonyl compound gives carbene intermediate which later converts into ketene derivative. Further, it undergoes nucleophilic addition with methanol producing bicyclic ester derivative. This reaction is known as the Wolff rearrangement.

The software predicted ^{13}C NMR data shown below

Carruthers, W.; Coldham, I. Radical and Carbene Chemistry. In *Modern Method of Organic Synthesis*, 4th Ed.; Cambridge University Press, 2004; p 310.

Question No-51: The major product formed in the following reaction is

Answer: C. The major product formed in the given thermal *syn*-elimination (pericyclic *syn*-elimination or Ei-reaction) is (E)-stilbene-d_1.

Note. A thermal/photochemical intramolecular/intermolecular elimination reaction in the absence of acid or base is known as pericyclic *syn*-elimination or Ei-reaction.

Question No-52: The major products **X** and **Y** formed in the following reaction sequence are

Answer: A. The major products **X** and **Y** formed in the given reaction sequence are 3-(1-nitroethyl)cyclohexan-1-one and 3-acetylcyclohexan-1-one, respectively.

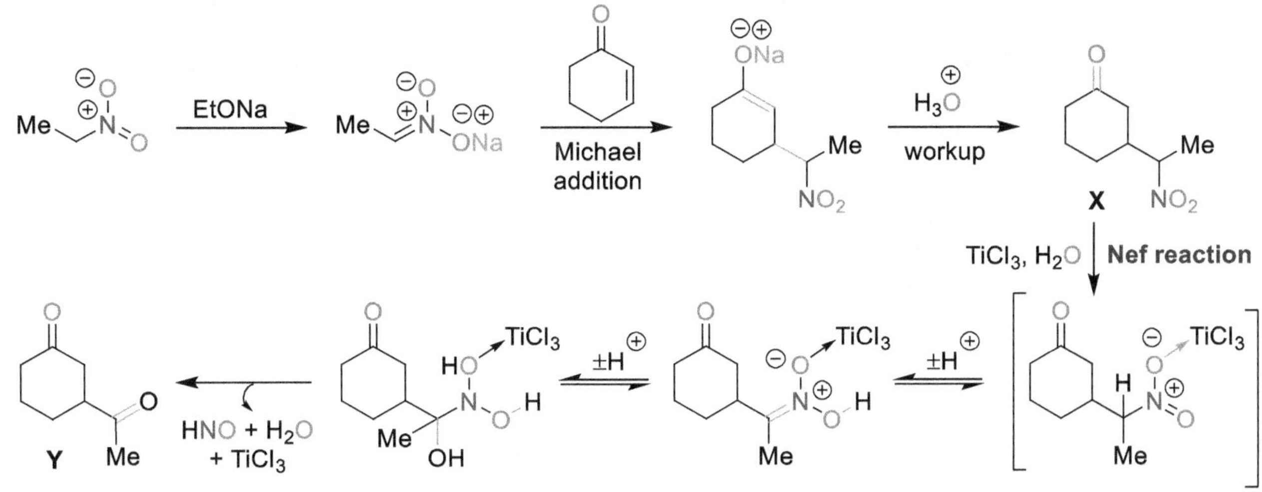

Question No-53: The major products **X** and **Y** formed in the following reaction sequence are

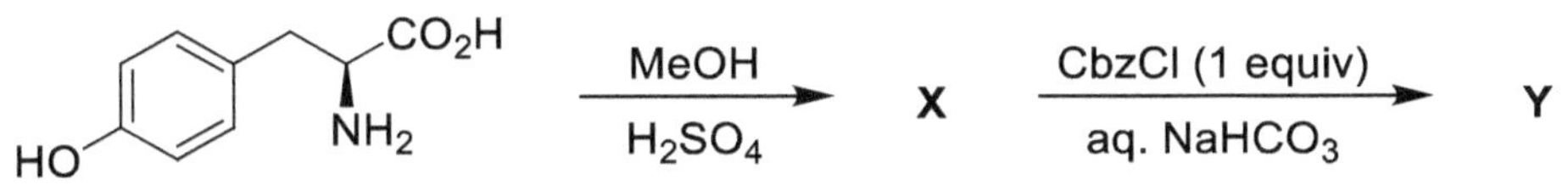

	X	**Y**
A.		
B.		
C.		
D.		

Answer: B. The synthesis of methyl L-tyrosine ester **X** can be achieved from L-tyrosine in the presence of a catalytic amount of sulfuric acid using nucleophilic solvent methanol. The chemoselective –Cbz protection of **X** can be performed using benzyl chloroformate in mild basic media to get –Cbz protected product **Y** as the nucleophilicity of nitrogen is higher than that of oxygen.

Note. L-tyrosine is a non-essential amino acid as our body can synthesize it from the precursor i.e. essential (unable to synthesize) L-phenyl alanine.

Baldini, L.; Lenci, E.; Bianchini, F.; Trabocchi, A. *Molecules* **2022**, *27*, 1249.

Question No-54: Given the fact that 1,3-butadiene has a UV absorption of 217 nm, the absorption wavelength (in nm) for the conjugated system shown below is..................

(Use these absorption values for auxochromic groups: alkyl: +5; *exo*-cyclic double bond: +5; every additional conjugated C=C: +30)

Answer: 282 nm. The absorption wavelength for the conjugated system is calculated as below:

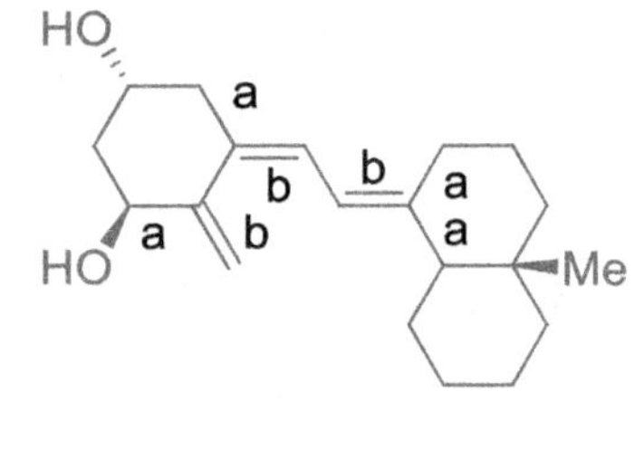

1,3-butadiene has a UV absorption =	217 nm
Total no of additional conjugated C=C (2b+b) = 1 × 30 = 30 nm	
Total no of alkyl substituents (4a) = 5 × 4 =	20 nm
Total no of exo-cyclic double bond (4b) = 5 × 3 =	15 nm
Total absorption wavelength =	**282 nm**

Question No-55: The m/z value of the detectable fragment formed by McLafferty like rearrangement of the following compound in mass spectrometer is...............

Answer: 41. The m/z value of the detectable fragment formed by McLafferty rearrangement is 41.0265 (heteroatomic fragment major) and (aliphatic fragment 56.0626) minor.

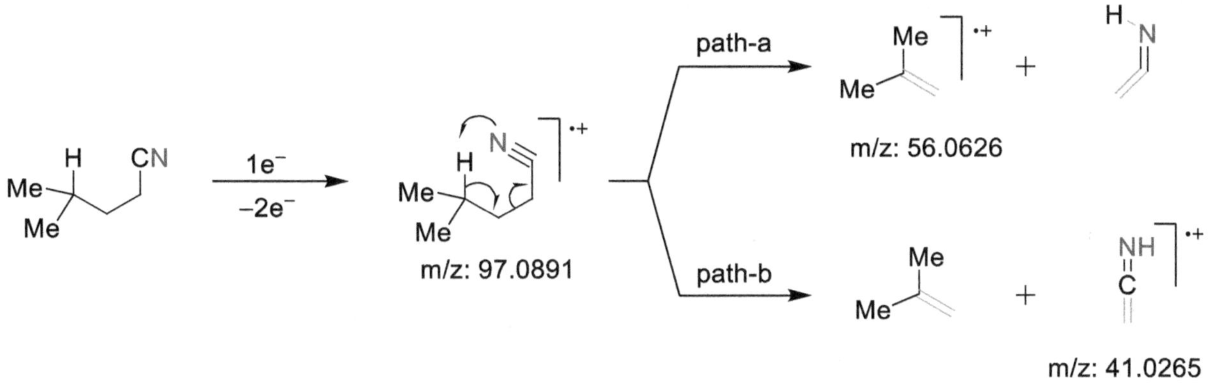

Question No-17: The absolute configuration of C2 and C3 in the following compound is

A. 2R, 3S   B. 2S, 3R   C. 2S, 3S   D. 2R, 3R

Answer: D. The absolute configuration of C2 and C3 in the given compound is 2R and 3R.

Question No-18: Among the following compounds, the one that is non-aromatic is

A. 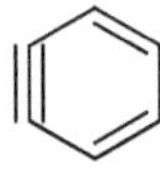   B. 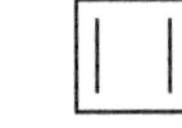   C.   D. 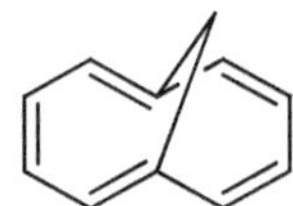

Answer: A. Huckel's rule of aromaticity. According to this rule, the molecule should be cyclic, planner, sp^2-hybridized, resonance stabilized and follows the $(4n + 2)\pi$-electron rule.

➢ Cycloocta-1,3,5,7-tetraene is non-aromatic. It follows the Huckel rule with $(4n)\pi$-electron rule [except $(4n + 2)\pi$-electron rule] and has a non-planar tub shape structure.

➢ Benzyne and bicyclo[4.4.1]undeca-1,3,5,7,9-pentaene both follow the Huckel rule of aromaticity.

➢ Cyclobut-1,3-diene obeys the Huckel rule of aromaticity with $(4n)\pi$-electron system, thus it is antiaromatic.

Question No-19: The correct order of reactivity of *p*-halonitrobenzenes in the following reaction is

(X = F, Cl, Br, I)

A. *p*-chloronitrobenzene > *p*-iodonitrobenzene > *p*-fluoronitrobenzene > *p*-bromonitrobenzene

B. *p*-fluoronitrobenzene > *p*-chloronitrobenzene > *p*-bromonitrobenzene > *p*-iodonitrobenzene

C. *p*-iodonitrobenzene > *p*-bromonitrobenzene > *p*-chloronitrobenzene > *p*-fluoronitrobenzene

D. *p*-bromonitrobenzene > *p*-fluoronitrobenzene > *p*-iodonitrobenzene > *p*-chloronitrobenzene

Answer: B. In the case of *p*-fluoronitrobenzene, C-F i.e. *ipso*-carbon is more electrophilic due to the presence of strong electron-withdrawing group fluorine as well as by the nitro group. The effect of nitro group is common for all thereby making reactivity order with NaOMe dependent on the electronegativity order of halogens i.e. F > Cl > Br > I.

p-fluoronitrobenzene > *p*-chloronitrobenzene > *p*-bromonitrobenzene > *p*-iodonitrobenzene

Question No-20: Tollen's test is *negative* for

A. mannose   B. maltose   C. glucose   D. sucrose

Answer: D. Tollen's test is *negative* for sucrose due to the absence of hemiacetal group at the anomeric carbon.

Question No-21: The compound given below is a

A. sesterterpene   B. monoterpene   C. sesquiterpene   D. triterpene

Answer: C. Isoprene is a monomer unit (2-methyl butadiene) of the terpenoids. The given compound Hirsutene consists of 15 carbon atoms thus, it is recognized as sesquiterpene (equivalent to the three units of isoprene).

S.N.	Terpenoids term	Number of C
1	Hemiterpene	5
2	Monoterpene	10
3	Sesquiterpene	15
4	Diterpene	20
5	Sesterterpene	25
6	Triterpene	30
7	Tetraterpene	40
8	Polyterpene	C_n

Question No-22: Amongst the following, the compound that DOES NOT act as a diene in Diels-Alder reaction is

A. 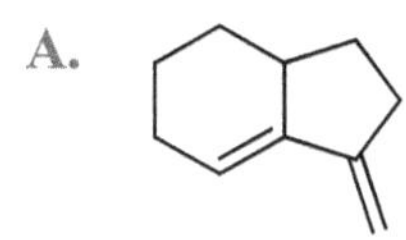 B. 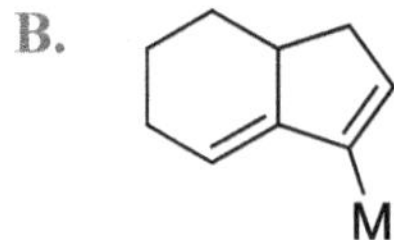 C. 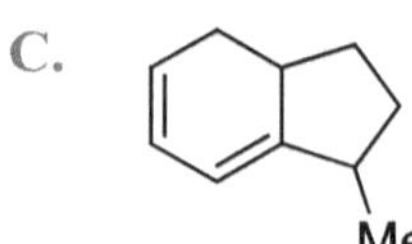 D. 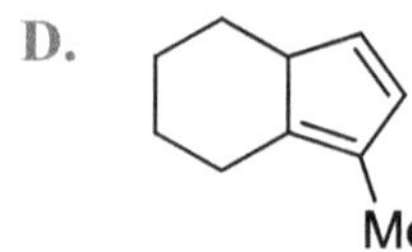

Answer: B. Flexible geometry of *cis-*/*trans*-diene can isomerize to each other. The reaction of rigid geometry of *cis*-diene with dienophile can give the Diels-Alder product, while rigid geometry of *trans*-diene (3-methyl-5,6,7,7a-tetrahydro-1*H*-indene) cannot, because dienophile will not be able to overlap with both terminal ends of the diene.

Question No-23: The following conversion is an example of

A. Arndt-Eistert homologation
C. Michael addition

B. Mannich reaction
D. Chichibabin amination reaction

Answer: B. The given above conversion is an example of a Mannich reaction.

Question No-24: The mass spectrum of a dihalo compound shows peaks with relative intensities of 1:2:1 corresponding to M, [M + 2] and [M + 4] (M is the mass of the molecular ion), respectively. The compound is

Answer: A. In the given EI-mass spectrum (*m/z*), the presence of corresponding M, [M + 2] and [M + 4] peaks reveals that compounds have two bromine groups, which suggests the relative intensity 1:2:1.

Compound	Dibromo-mass peaks	Intensity	Calculation based on $(a+b)^n$
	$[M] = 247.8836$ ($^{79}Br = ^{79}Br$)	1	Here, n = 2 Bromine
	$[M + 2] = 249.9330$ ($^{79}Br = ^{81}Br$)		$(a + b)^2 = a^2 + 2ab + b^2$
	$[M + 2] = 249.9330$ ($^{91}Br = ^{79}Br$)	2	The abundance of a and b i.e. ^{79}Br
	$[M + 4] = 251.8795$ ($^{81}Br = ^{81}Br$)	1	and ^{81}Br are approximately equal.
			Then, $1^2 + 2(1 \times 1) + 1^2 = $ **1:2:1.**

Question No-25: Reaction of benzaldehyde and *p*-methylbenzaldehyde under McMurry coupling conditions (TiCl_3 and LiA/H$_4$) gives a mixture of alkenes. The number of alkenes formed is……………

Answer: 6. Reaction of benzaldehyde and *p*-methylbenzaldehyde under McMurry coupling conditions (TiCl_3 and LiA/H$_4$) are shown below:

Question No-46: The number of possible stereoisomers obtained in the following reaction is……… ……

Answer: 8. In the given sequence of reaction, the end product has two chiral centers and one axial chirality i.e. $(2)^3$ stereoisomers = 8 stereoisomers.

Explanation. As it can be seen above, two aliphatic carbon center (pink and green color) each has two chiral enantiomeric antipodes (each chiral carbon can exhibits S and R configurations).

Thus, the two chiral aliphatic carbons = $(2)^2$ = 4 stereoisomers.

These, 4-stereoisomers again multiplied with 2 due to axial chirality (S and R configurations) = $4 \times 2 = 8$ stereoisomers.

Chart eight stereoisomers are shown below

Axial chirality	R				S			
1st C aliphatic	R		S		R		S	
2nd C aliphatic	R	S	R	S	R	S	R	S
Stereoisomer	*RRR*	*RRS*	*RSR*	*RSS*	*SRR*	*SRS*	*SSR*	*SSS*

Configurations of eight stereoisomers are shown below

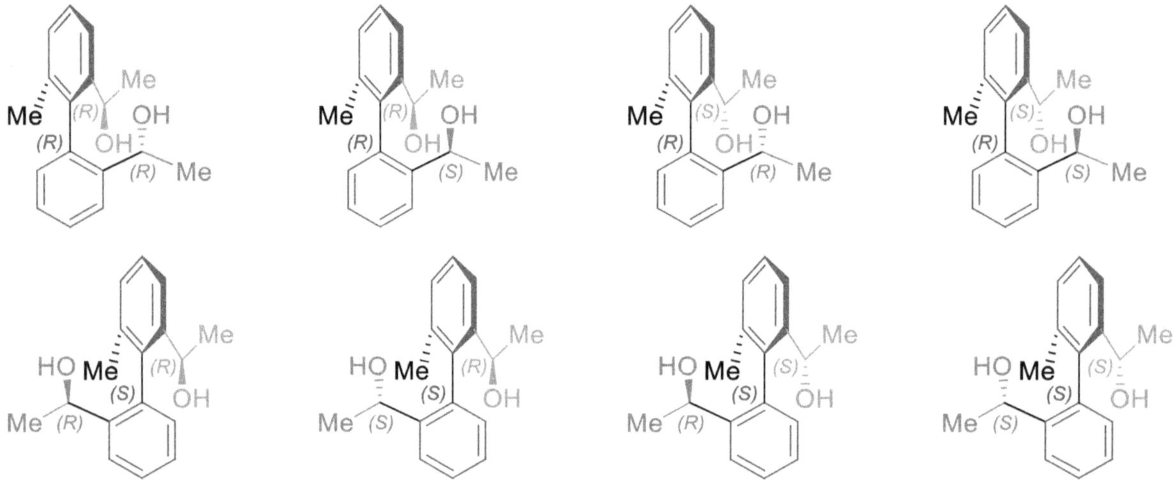

Question No-47: The major product formed in the following reaction is

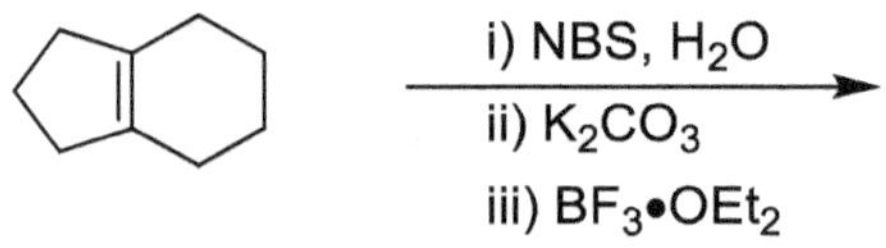

i) NBS, H_2O
ii) K_2CO_3
iii) $BF_3 \bullet OEt_2$

A. 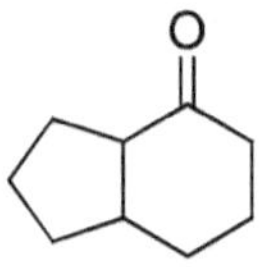   B. 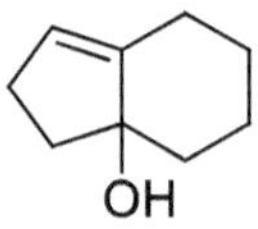   C. 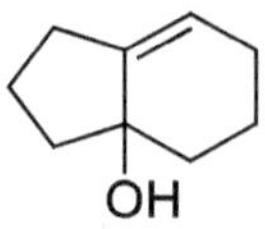   D.

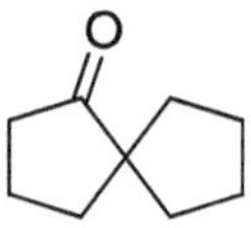

Answer: D. The major product formed in the given sequence reaction is spiro[4.4]nonan-1-one.

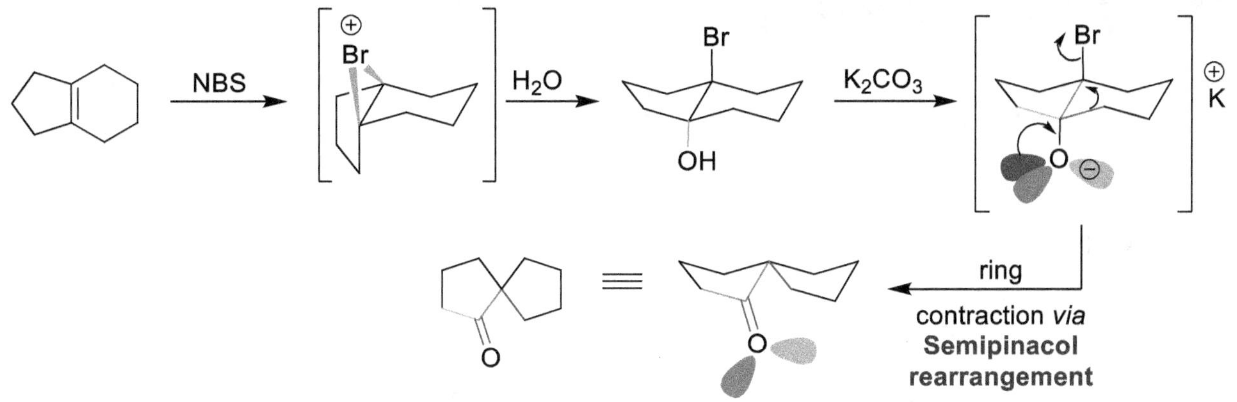

Question No-48: The most suitable reagent(s) to effect the following transformation is

A. N_2H_4, KOH, Δ B. TsNHNH$_2$, TFA   C. LiAlH$_4$ D.   Na/liq. NH$_3$

Answer: A. The most suitable reagent for the give transformation is N_2H_4/KOH, Δ and the reaction is known as Wharton reaction.

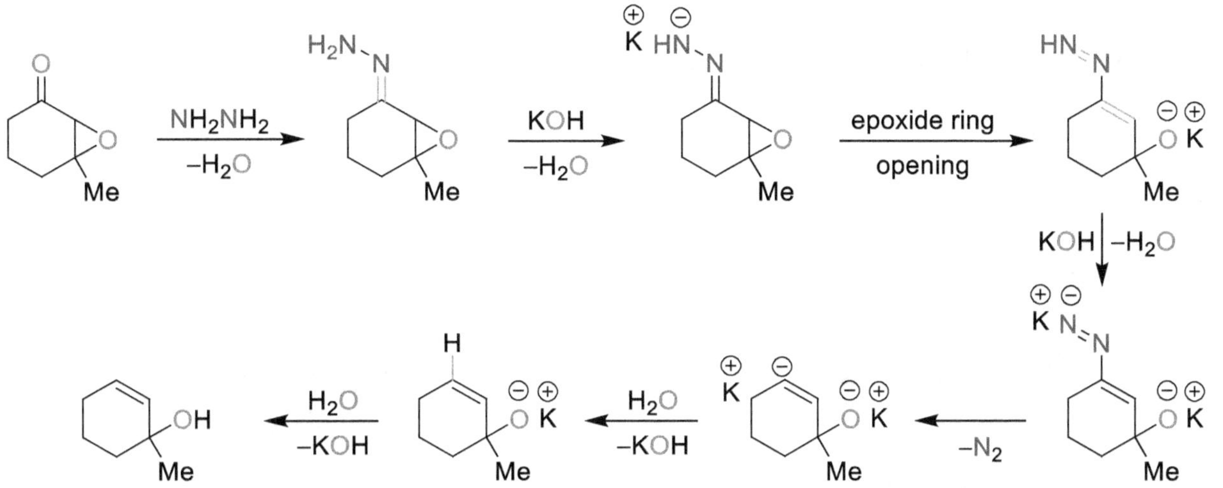

Note. The reaction of α,β-epoxy ketone of a cyclic derivative with hydrazine having a good leaving group (Ts), catalyzed by acid (TFA/AcOH) or base (KOH/LDA) then the reaction proceeds through a fragmentation pathway producing keto-alkynes derivative as the end product. The given below reaction is known as Echenmoser fragmentation reaction.

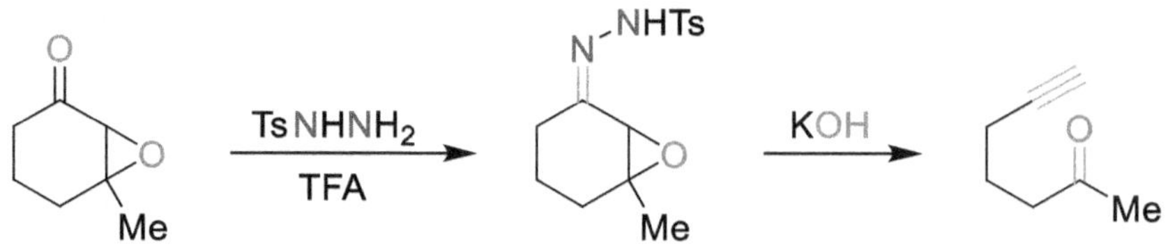

Question No-49: The major product formed in the following reaction is

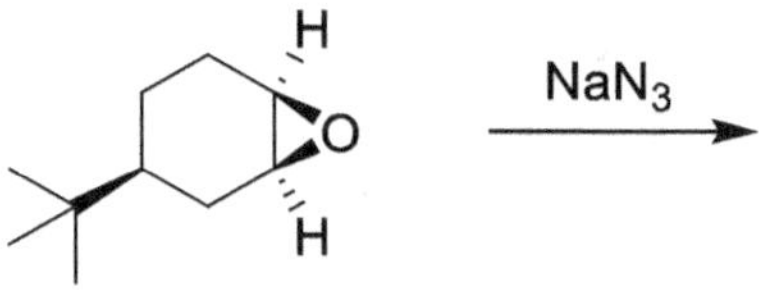

A.

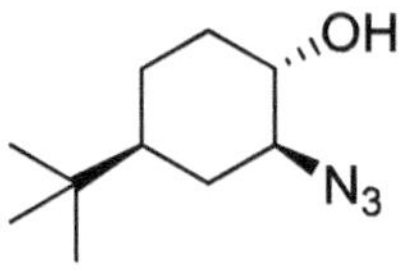

B.

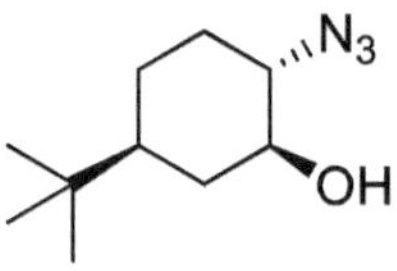

C.

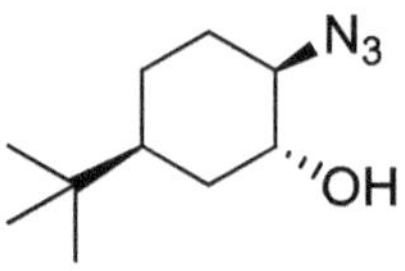

D.

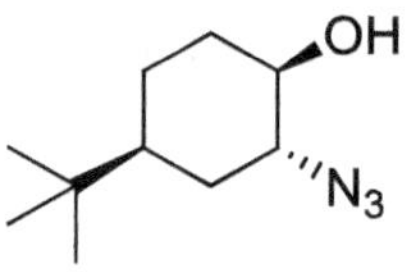

Answer: D. The major product formed in the given reaction *via* axial attack of sodium azide is (1*R*,2*R*,4*S*)-2-azido-4-(*tert*-butyl)cyclohexanol-1.

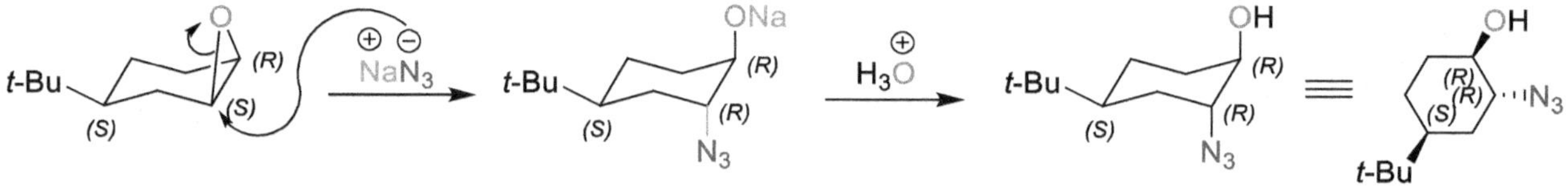

Question No-50: Solvolysis of the optically active compound **X** gives mainly

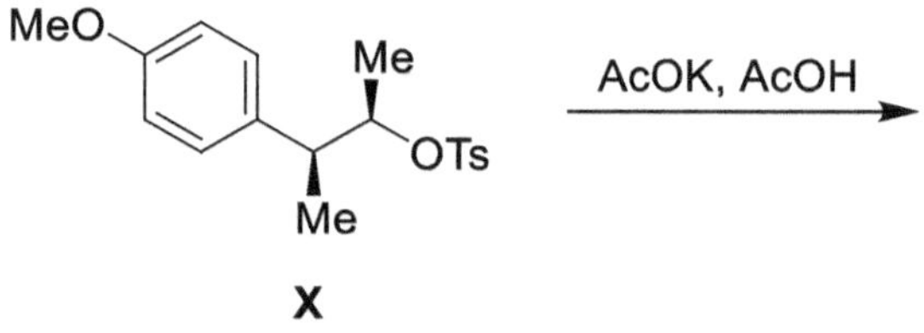

A.

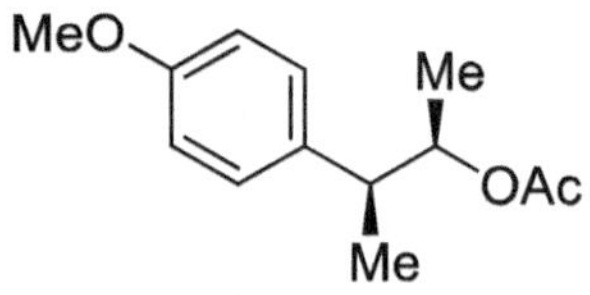

(Optically Active)

B.

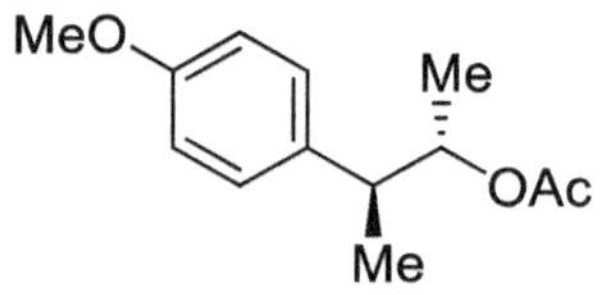

(Optically Active)

C.

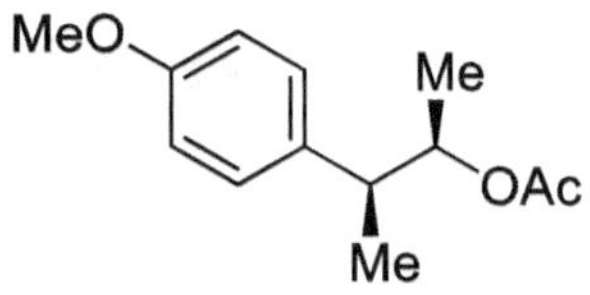

recemic

(Optically Inactive)

D.

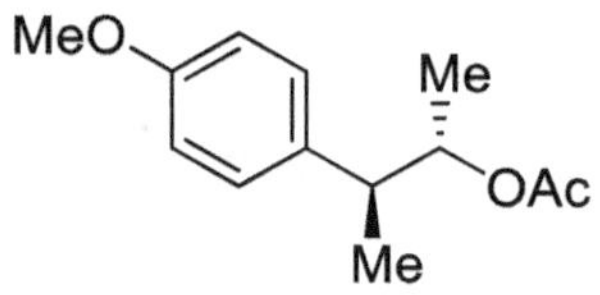

recemic

(Optically Inactive)

Answer: C. Solvolysis of the given optically active compound **X** yields a racemic product. During the course of reaction, *p*-methoxyphenyl group shows anchimeric assistance (NGP) due to the strong +*R*-effect of a methoxy group. As a result, the acetoxy group attacks equally at both ends of the three-membered cyclic ring.

Ring-opening path 'a' and 'b' gives racemic mixture 1:1, i.e. formation of each enantiomers 'a' and 'b' forms equally 50%. Thus, the net optical rotation of the racemic products is zero (optically inactive).

Question No-51: The major product formed in the following reaction is

Answer: D. The reaction of sulfoxide derivative with Ac_2O or $AcCl$ in presence of base (absence also), forms α-acetoxy thioether takes place, which on hydrolyzed gives carbonyl compound (due to that, some places sulfoxide and sulfide groups can also be considered as the precursor of carbonyls). The given reaction is an example of Pummerer rearrangement.

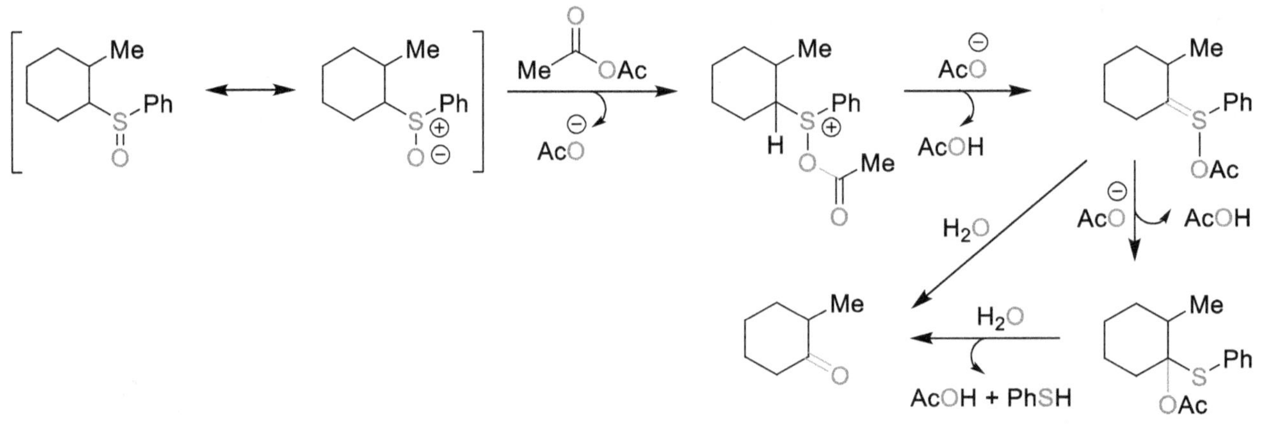

Laleu, B.; Machado, M. S.; Lacour, J. *Chem. Commun.* **2006**, 2786.

Question No-52: The tetrapeptide, Ala-Val-Phe-Met, on reaction with Sanger's reagent, followed by hydrolysis gives

A.

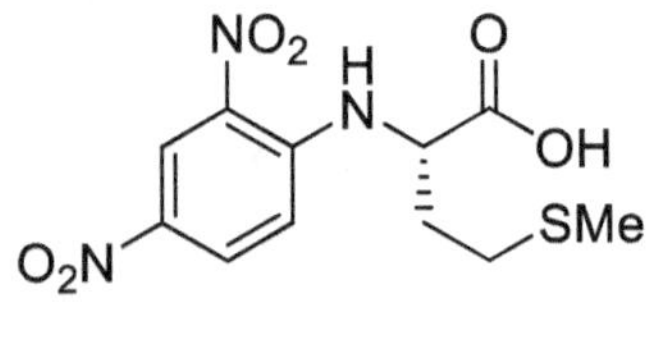

B.

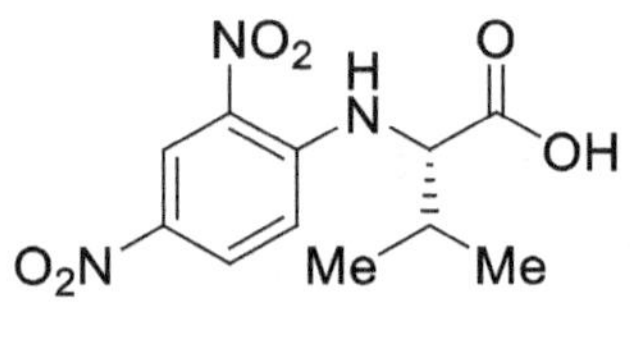

C.

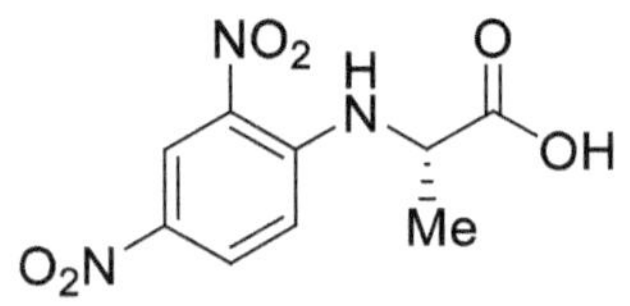

D.

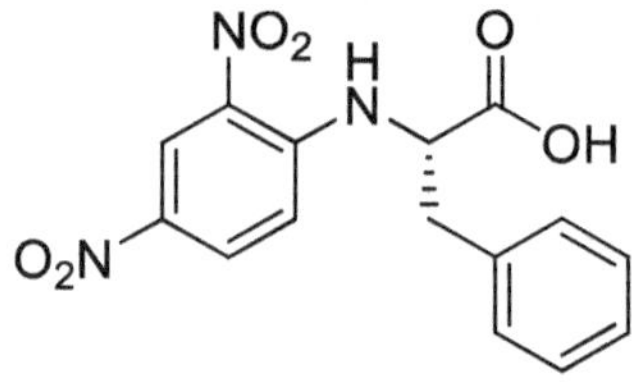

Answer: C. The tetrapeptide Ala-Val-Phe-Met on reaction with Sanger's reagent, followed by hydrolysis gives *N*-2,4-dinitrophenyl alanine.

Ala-Val-Phe-Met

Sanger's reagent
−HF

Hydrolysis

N-2,4-dinitrophenyl alanine   Val   Phe   Met

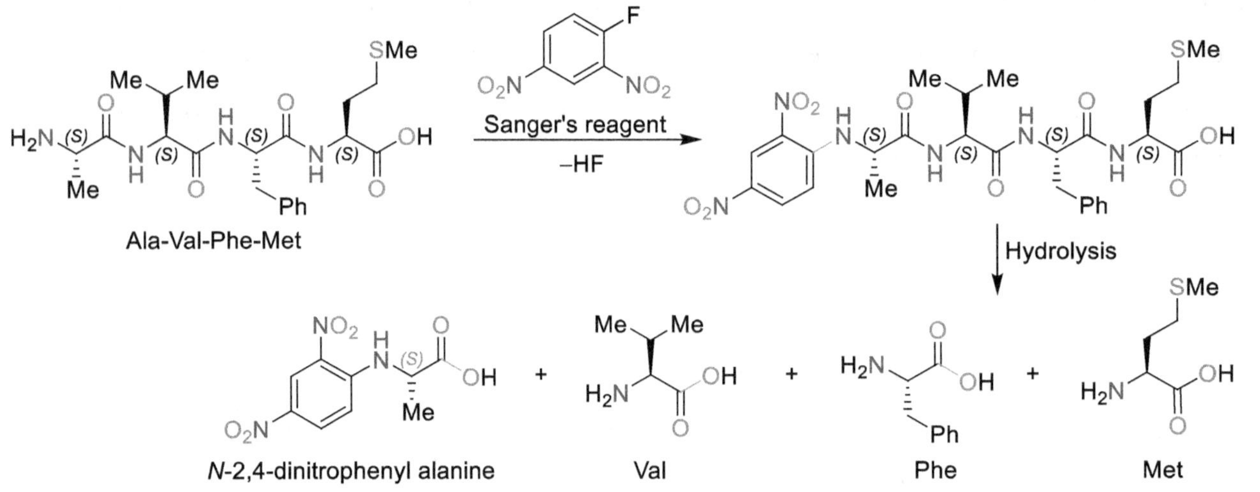

Note. Sanger's reagent (1-fluoro-2,4-dinitrobenzene) is used for the detection of *N*-terminus amino acid from a peptide chain by hydrolysis producing *N*-2,4-dinitrophenyl substituted amino acid analog.

Question No-53: The major product formed in the following reaction is

A. B. C. D.

Answer: B. Allyl methyl benzobutane derivative undergo thermal electrocyclic ring-opening reaction offering products **A and B.** In the case of **A,** both the terminal carbons show clockwise rotation while **B** exhibits counter-clockwise rotation.

A
HOMO
Ψ_2, C_2(s) and m(a)

B
HOMO
Ψ_2, C_2(s) and m(a)

The intermediate product **A** unable to proceed through a 6π-electron ring-closing reaction (**Torquoselectivity:** selectively preferred electrocyclic ring opening product based on the substituent) while product **B** offers trimethyl dihydronaphthalene (the geometry product **B** is facile for the ring closure reaction).

B
HOMO
Ψ_3, C_2(a) and m(s)

Fleming, I. Thermal Pericyclic Reactions. In *Molecular Orbitals and Organic Chemical Reactions*; Student Ed..; John Wiley & Sons Ltd., 2009; pp 267-270.

Question No-54: The Beckmann rearrangement of a bromoacestophenone oxime (C_8H_8BrNO) gives a major product having the following ^{1}H NMR (δ, ppm): 9.89 (s, 1H), 7.88 (s, 1H), 7.45 (d, 1H, J = 7.2 Hz), 7.17 (m, 1H), 7.12 (d, 1H, J = 7.0 Hz), 2.06 (s, 3H). The structure of the product is

A. 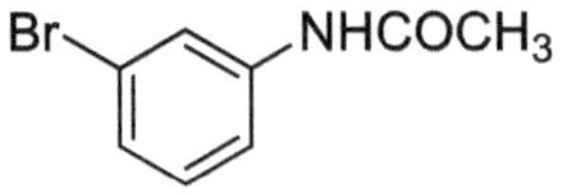
Br
NHCOCH3

B. 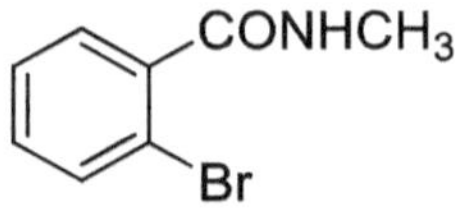
CONHCH3
Br

C. 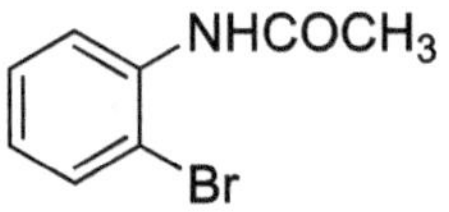
NHCOCH3
Br

D. 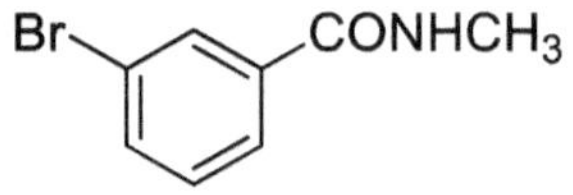
Br
CONHCH3

Answer: A. The given reaction and spectroscopic data analysis reveal that the compound is 3-bromoacetanilide

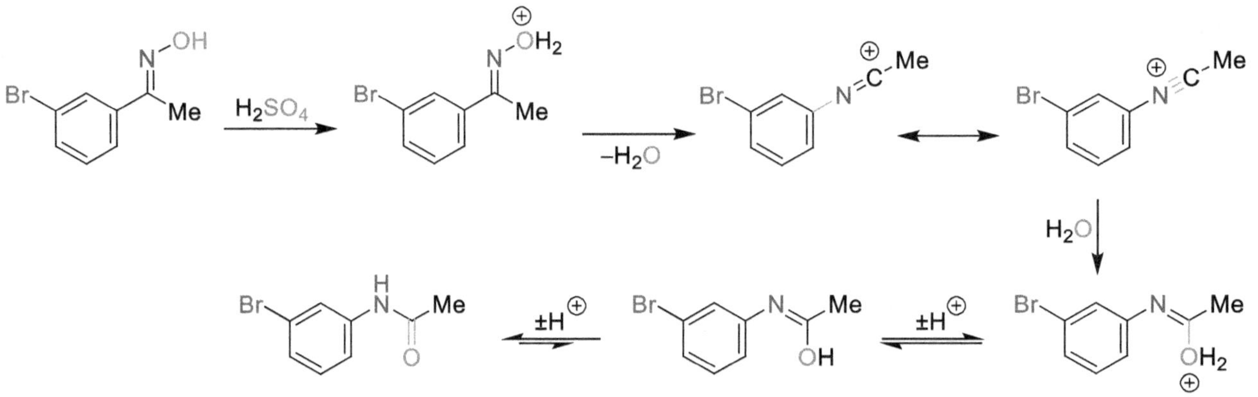
H2SO4
−H2O
H2O
±H⊕
±H⊕

Question No-55: The major products, **K** and **L** formed in the following reactions are

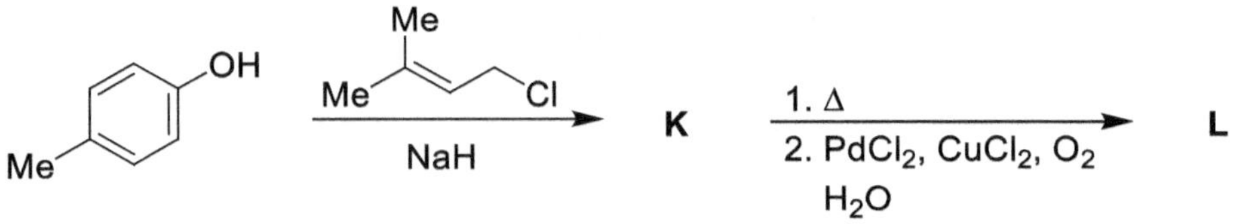
NaH
K
1. Δ
2. PdCl2, CuCl2, O2
H2O
L

	K	L
A.	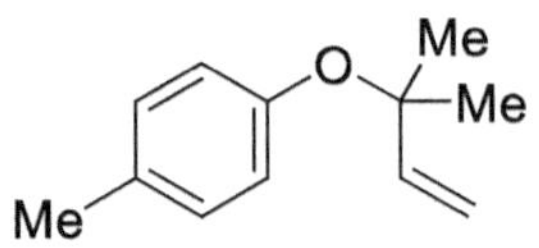	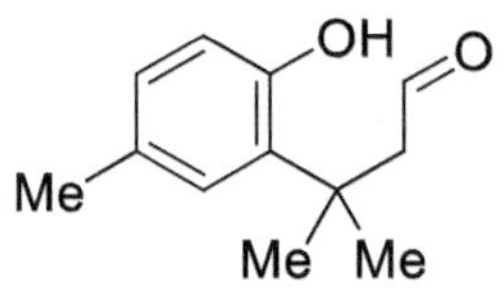

B.

C.

D.

Answer: B. The major product **K** is formed *via* S_N2 reaction of *p*-cresol with dimethyl allyl chloride in the presence of sodium hydride. Further, product **K** transformed into product **L** *via* Claisen rearrangement followed by Wacker oxidation process.

Question No-1: The total number of lines expected (due to spin-spin coupling of a proton with Fluorine and Deuterium nuclei) in ^1H NMR spectrum of the following compound is

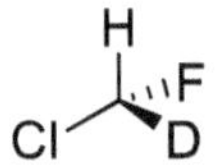

Answer: 6. The total number of the lines of the given compound can be calculated by using the formula $(2nI + 1)$ as follows.

Total number of the lines = $[(\text{for } 1H = 2 \times \frac{1}{2} \times 1 + 1)(\text{for } 1D = 2 \times 1 \times 1 + 1)] = 6$ (sextet).

Question No-4: The compound in 'R' configuration is_

A. 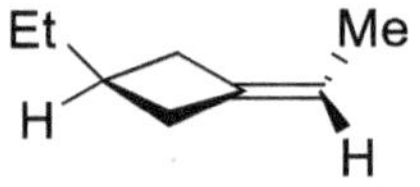 B. 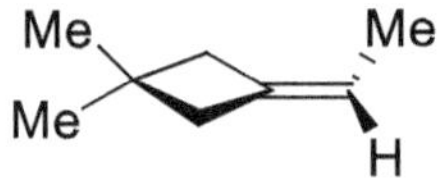 C. 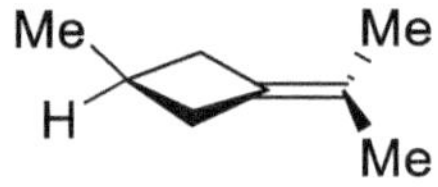 D.

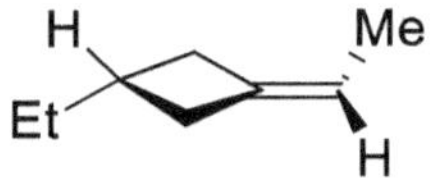

Answer: A. The compound in 'R' configuration is as follows.

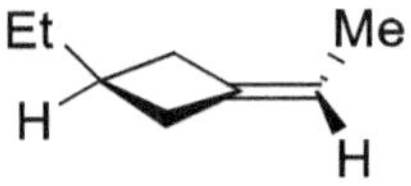

Question No-5: The major product formed in the following reaction, is

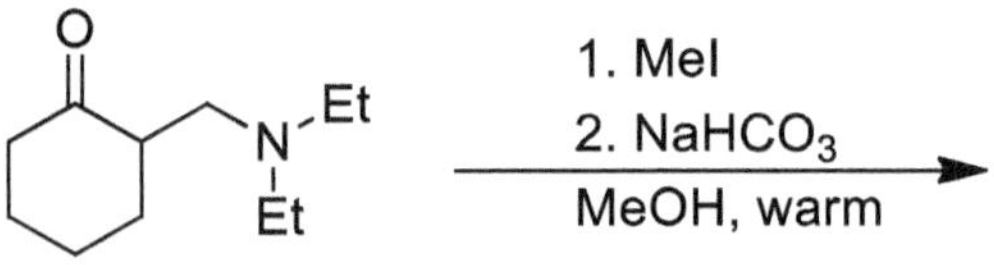

1. MeI
2. $NaHCO_3$
MeOH, warm

A. 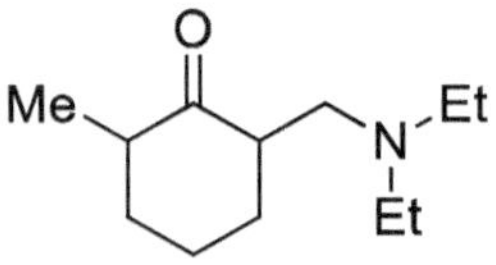 B. 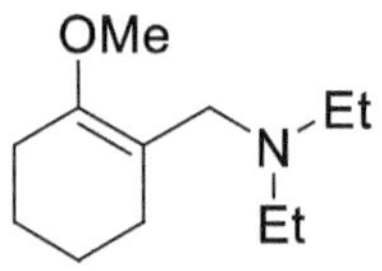 C. 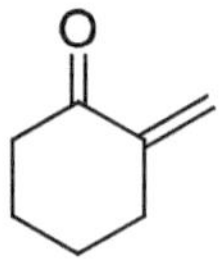 D.

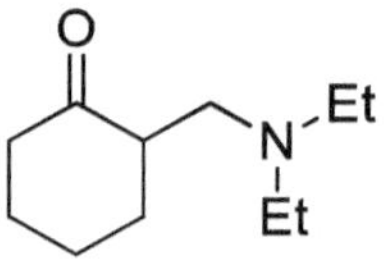

Answer: C. The major product formed in the given reaction is 2-methylenecyclohexan-1-one, which is proceeding through the E1cB-reaction pathway.

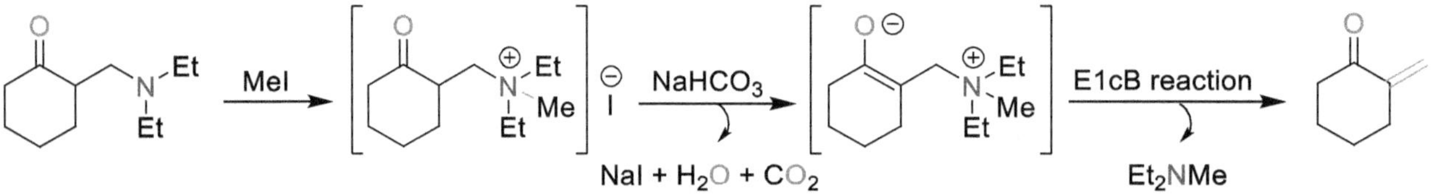

Question No-6: Ring flipping of the compound in the following conformation leads to

A. Br–…–Me (OH) **B.** …Me, Br (OH) **C.** OH…Br…Me **D.** HO…Br…Me

Answer: C. Ring flipping of the compound in the given conformation are shown below.

$$\text{(R,S,R)} \xrightarrow{\text{ring flipping}} \text{(S,R,R)}$$

Question No-7: The major product obtained in the following reaction is

$$\text{H}-\!\!\!\equiv\!\!\!-\text{OH} \quad \xrightarrow[\text{iii. H}^+/\text{H}_2\text{O}]{\substack{\text{i. Li/NH}_3 \text{ (excess)} \\ \text{ii. EtBr (1 equiv)}}}$$

A. $CH_3CH_2-\!\!\!\equiv\!\!\!-CH_2OH$

B. $H-\!\!\!\equiv\!\!\!-CH_2OCH_2CH_3$

C. $CH_3CH_2-\!\!\!\equiv\!\!\!-CH_2NH_2$

D. $H-\!\!\!\equiv\!\!\!-CH_2NHCH_2CH_3$

Answer: A. Thus, the major product obtained in the given reaction is pent-2-yn-1-ol.

$$H-\!\!\!\equiv\!\!\!-CH_2OH \xrightarrow{\text{Li/NH}_3 \text{ (1 equiv)}} H-\!\!\!\equiv\!\!\!-CH_2\overset{\ominus}{O}\overset{\oplus}{\text{Li}} \xrightarrow{\text{Li/NH}_3 \text{ (excess)}} \overset{\oplus}{\text{Li}}\overset{\ominus}{\text{C}}\!\!\equiv\!\!C-CH_2\overset{\ominus}{O}\overset{\oplus}{\text{Li}}$$

$$\downarrow \text{EtBr (1 equiv)}$$

$$\text{Et}-\!\!\!\equiv\!\!\!C-CH_2OH \xleftarrow{\text{H}^+/\text{H}_2\text{O}} \text{Et}-\!\!\!\equiv\!\!\!C-CH_2\overset{\ominus}{O}\overset{\oplus}{\text{Li}}$$

Note. The acidity of –OH group is greater than that of the terminal methyne ($\equiv$CH) group. Thus, the first equivalent of sodamide abstracts the proton from the oxygen atom and then from the carbon. The regioselectively alkylation occurs at the C-terminal carbon than oxygen due to the high nucleophilicity of carbon.

Question No-13: The major product of the following reaction is

$$\text{furan} \xrightarrow[\text{Et}_2\text{O.BF}_3]{(\text{MeCO})_2\text{O}}$$

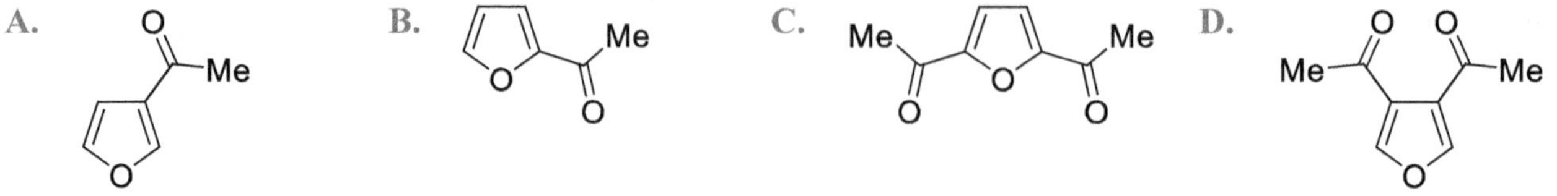

A. **B.** **C.** **D.**

Answer: B. The electrophilic aromatic substitution reaction of furan with acetic anhydride or acetyl chloride in presence of $Et_2O.BF_3$ produces major product 2-acyl furan.

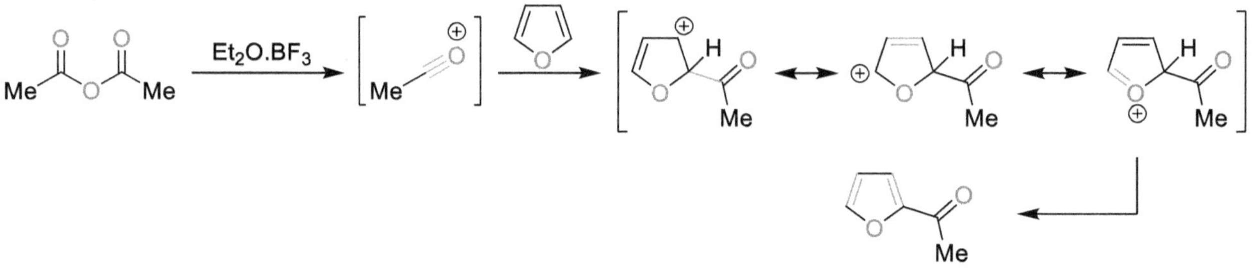

Question No-14: The most suitable reagent for performing the following transformation is

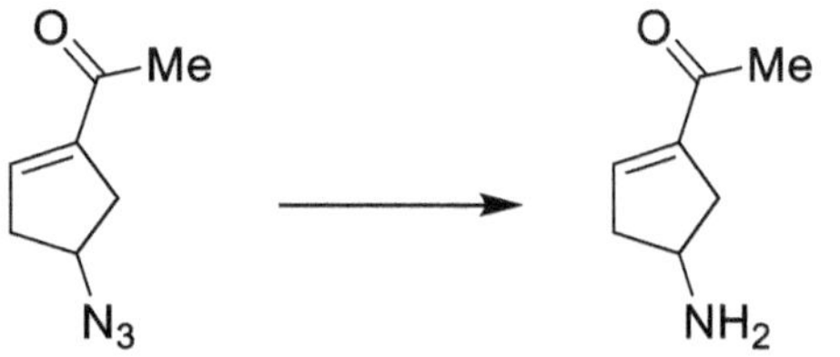

A. $LiAlH_4$ 	 B. H_2/Pd-C 	 C. H_2O/PPh_3 	 D. Li/liq. NH_3

Answer: C. The most suitable reagent for performing the given transformation is H_2O/PPh_3 which is known as Staudinger reaction.

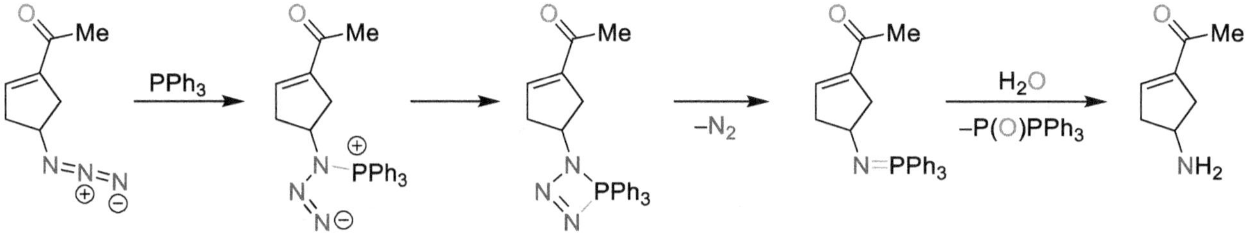

Staudinger, H.; Meyer, J. *Helv. Chim. Acta* **1919**, *2*, 635.

Question No-14: The favorable transition state leading to the formation of the product in the following reaction is

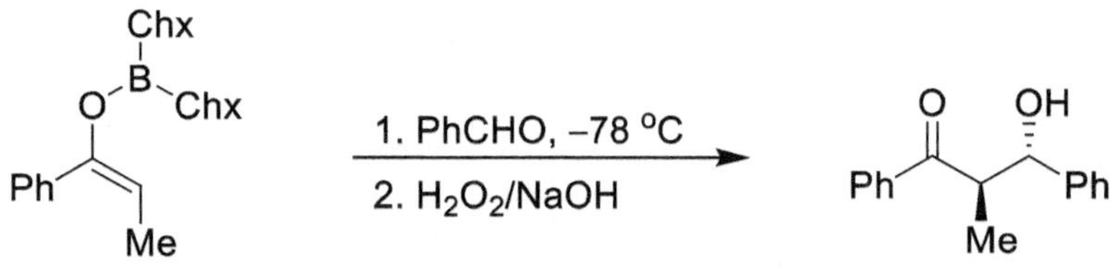

1. PhCHO, −78 °C

2. $H_2O_2/NaOH$

A.

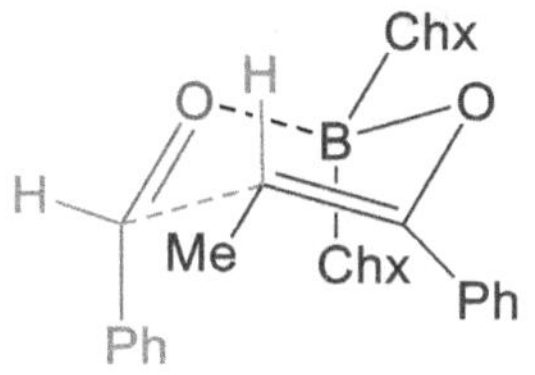

B.

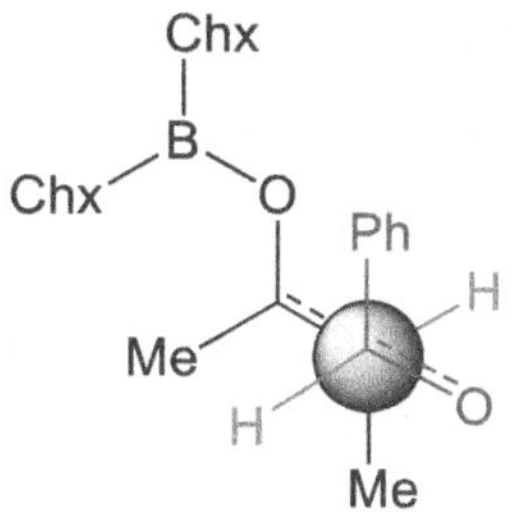

C.

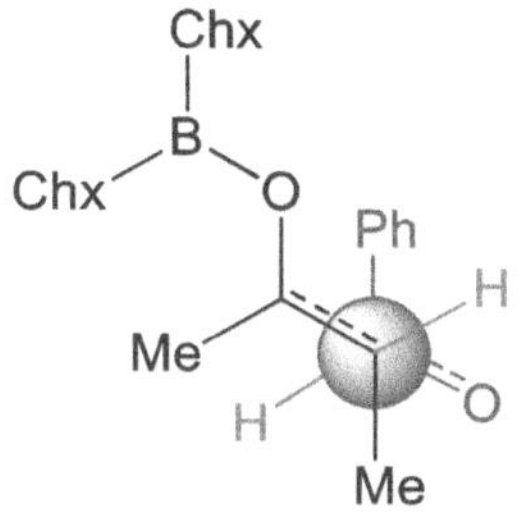

D.

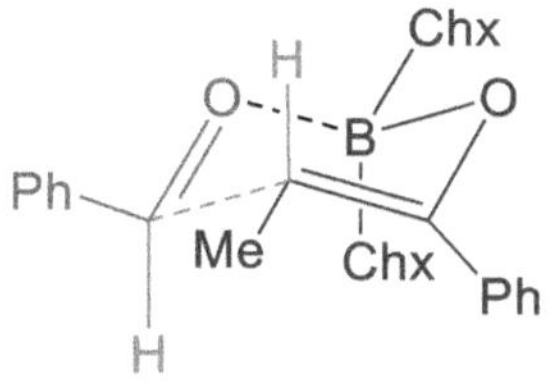

Answer: D. The Zimmerman-Traxler transition state helps in the prediction of the stereochemistry of the aldol reactions *via* the formation of preferred six-membered cyclic chair-like transition state-I. In the transition state, it can be seen that both the aldehydic hydrogen and *E*-enolate hydrogen are axial (*trans*-to each other) and have less 1,3-diaxial interactions with the cyclohexyl group than in transition state-II.

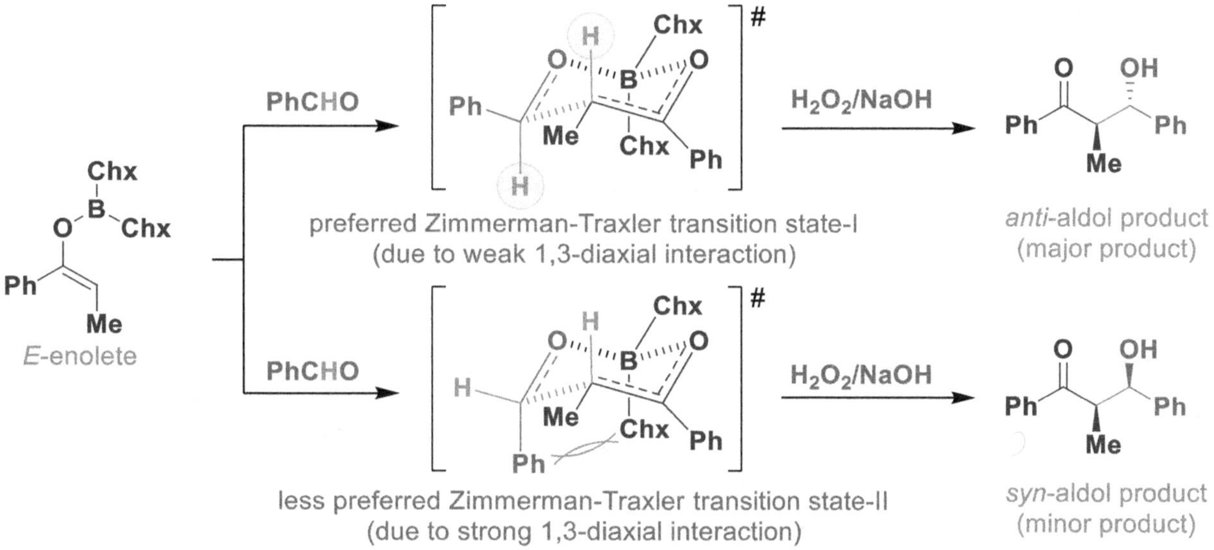

Important points.

- ❖ At first check the stereochemistry of the borane enolate (*syn/anti*- or *Z*-/*E*-enolate).
- ❖ *Z*-enolate and *E*-enolate gives *syn*-aldol and *anti*-aldol product, respectively.
- ❖ The geometry of enolate should be fixed in the preferred Zimmerman-Traxler transition and it should be proceeding through less/least 1,3-diaxial interaction(s).

- ❖ Necked enolate reverses the stereoselectivity of the aldol product i.e. necked *E*-enolate offers *syn*-product and *Z*-enolate gives *anti*-product. In such a case transition state is predicted using the Felkin model.

- ❖ Stereospecifically, Zirconium metal catalyzed aldol reaction does not depend on the geometry of enolate and always ends up with the *syn*-aldol product.

Question No-25: The major product obtained in the following reaction is

$$\xrightarrow[\substack{\text{acetophenone} \\ \text{(as sensitizer)}}]{h\nu}$$

A. **B.** **C.** **D.**

cis-trans mixture

Answer: D. The major product obtained in the given [2+2]-cycloaddition reaction in the presence of sensitizer produces the mixture of both *cis-* and *trans*-1,2-divinyl cyclobutane which is proceeding through a stepwise radical manner.

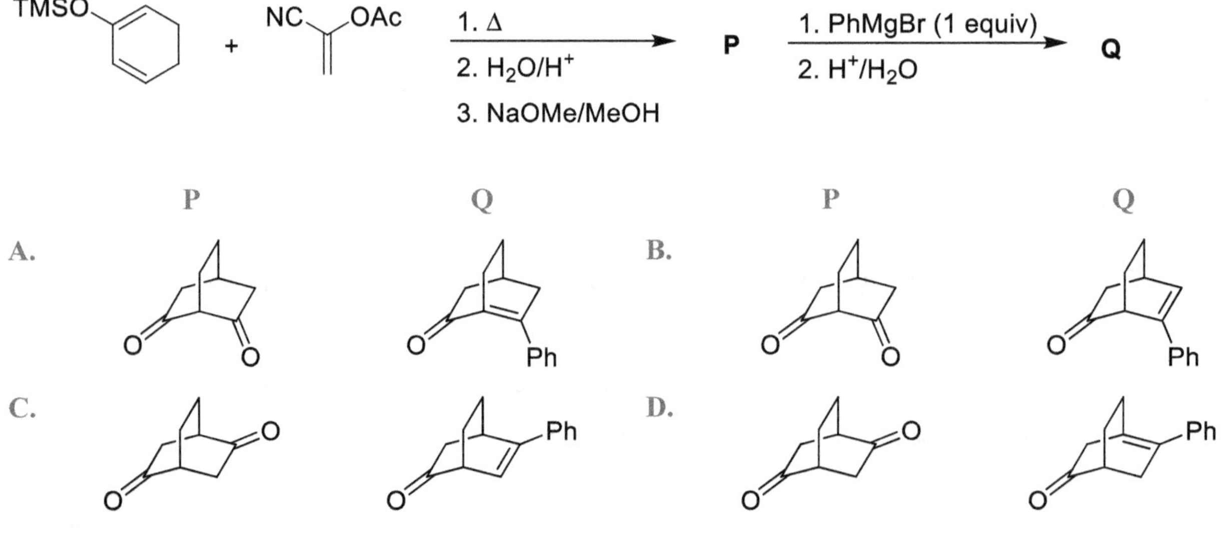

Question No-28: The major products **P** and **Q** in the following reaction sequence are

$$\text{TMSO} + \text{NC}\diagup\text{OAc} \xrightarrow[\substack{\text{2. } H_2O/H^+ \\ \text{3. NaOMe/MeOH}}]{\text{1. } \Delta} \textbf{P} \xrightarrow[\text{2. } H^+/H_2O]{\text{1. PhMgBr (1 equiv)}} \textbf{Q}$$

	P	Q			P	Q
A.			**B.**			
C.			**D.**			

Answer: C. The major products **P** and **Q** in the given reaction sequence are (1*S*,4*S*)-bicyclo[2.2.2]octane-2,5-dione and (1*S*,4*S*)-5-phenylbicyclo[2.2.2]oct-5-en-2-one, respectively.

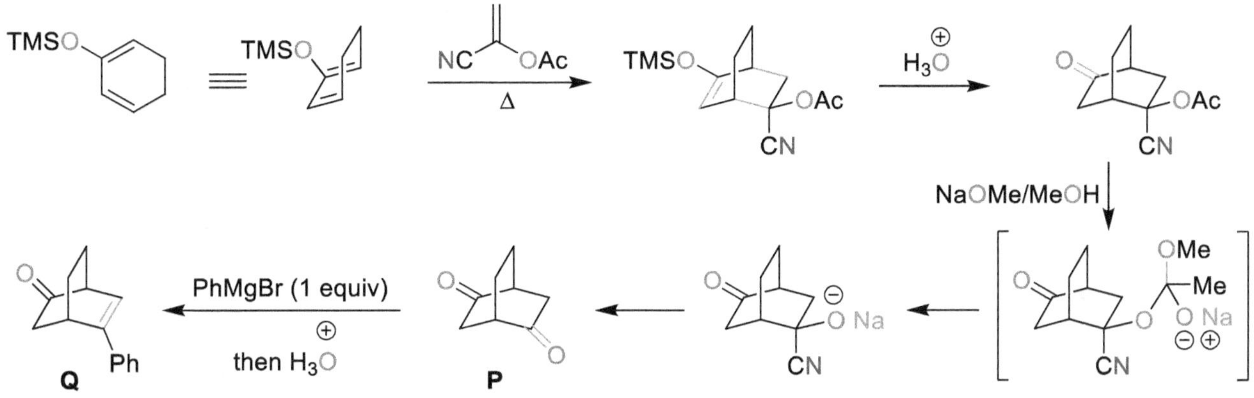

Question No-38: The major products **X** and **Y** in the following synthetic scheme are

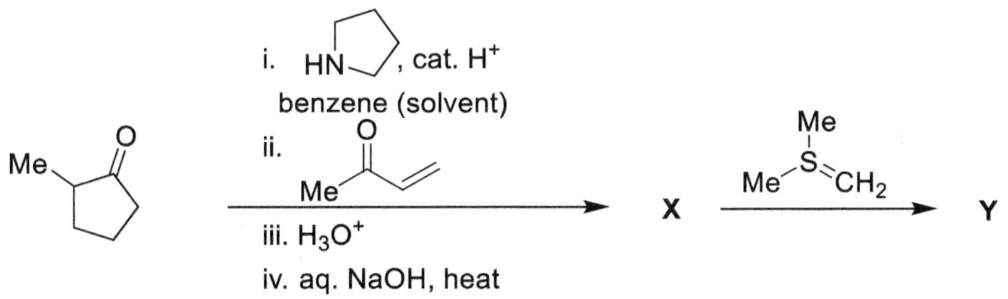

Answer: B. In the first step of the reaction, 2-methylcyclopentanone reacts with methyl vinyl ketone in the presence of pyrrolidine (Stark-enamine type reaction) followed by protonation and aldol condensation produces product **X** (Robinson annulation reaction = Michael addition then aldol condensation). Next, compound **X** reacts with sulfonium ylide (Corey-Chaykovsky reagent) then it offers a major product spiro oxirane derivative **Y**.

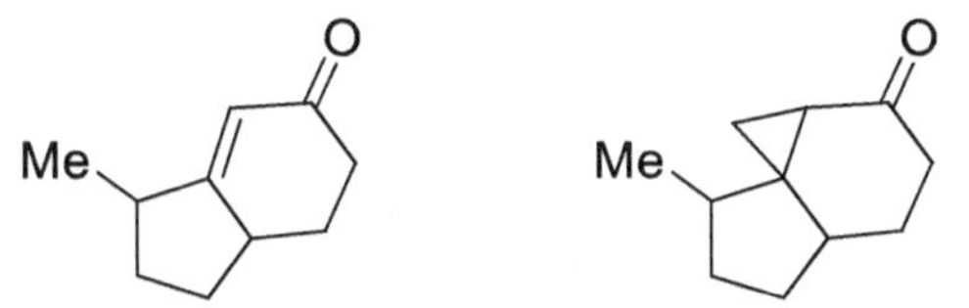

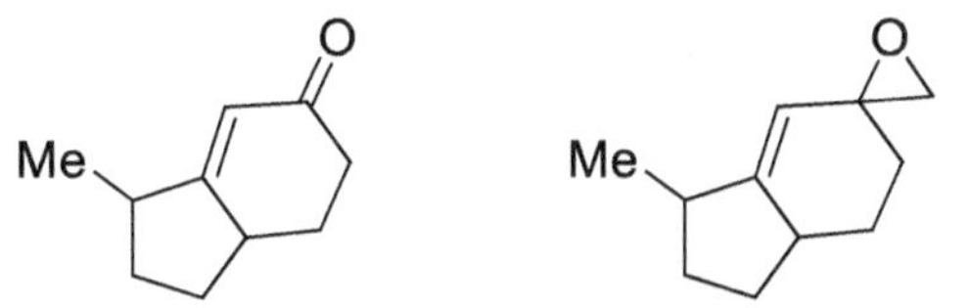

Question No-39: The major product formed in the following reaction is

PhBr (1 equiv)

(Ph$_3$P)$_4$Pd (cat.)

KOAc, DMF

A.

B.

C.

D.

Answer: B. The Heck-coupling of 6-methyl 3,4-dihydropyran with bromobenzene in the presence of a catalytic amount of Pd(0) complex in basic media produces a major product 6-methyl-6-phenyl-3,6-dihydro-2H-pyran.

Pd(0) complex

oxidative insertion

Pd(II) complex

Pd(II) forms π-complex

1,2-migratory insertion

Heck-coupling reaction

reductive elimination

syn-β-hydride elimination

Pd(II) complex

Pd(II) forms σ-complex

Question No-41: The major products **M** and **N** in the following reaction sequence are

$$\text{(epoxirane)} \xrightarrow{\text{LiPPh}_2} \mathbf{M} \xrightarrow{\text{MeI}} \mathbf{N} \;+\; \text{O=PPh}_2\text{Me} \;+\; \text{Li-I}$$

A.

B.

C.

D.

Answer: A. The nucleophilic addition reaction of lithium diphenylphosphide on epoxirane derivative gives intermediate **M**. Next, treatment of **M** with methyl iodide produces betaine derivative and it later forms oxaphosphetane intermediate (like Wittig reaction) at the loss of methyl diphenylphosphine oxide and produces deoxygenated major product **N**.

Question No-45: The following synthetic transformation can be achieved reaction using

Reagents

p) (i) NH_2OH/H^+, (ii) H_2SO_4 **q)** NaN_3/H^+ **r)** (i) NH_2OH/H^+, (ii) NaOH

Codes

A. (p) only   B. (p) and (q) only   C. (q) and (r) only   D. (r) only

Answer: B. The given synthetic transformation can be achieved by both **p)** (i) NH_2OH/H^+, (ii) H_2SO_4 (Beckmann rearrangement) and **q)** NaN_3/H^+ (Schmidt reaction). On the other hand, the sequence of reactions of cyclohexanone with (i) NH_2OH/H^+ then (ii) NaOH gives major product 2-aminocyclohexanone *via* Neber rearrangement.

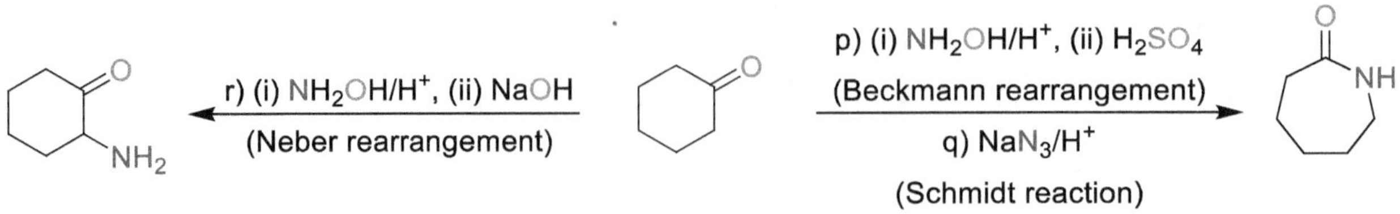

r) (i) NH_2OH/H^+, (ii) NaOH
(Neber rearrangement)

p) (i) NH_2OH/H^+, (ii) H_2SO_4
(Beckmann rearrangement)
q) NaN_3/H^+
(Schmidt reaction)

Question No-49: A disaccharide does NOT give a positive test for Tollen's reagent. Upon acidic hydrolysis, it gives an equimolar mixture of two different monosaccharides, both of which can be oxidized by bromine water. This disaccharide is

A.

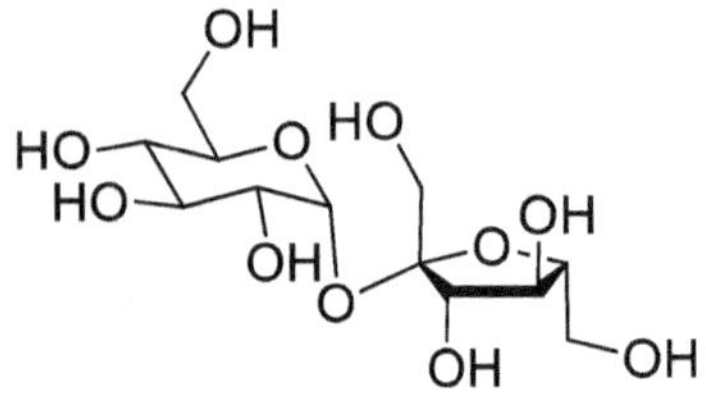

B.

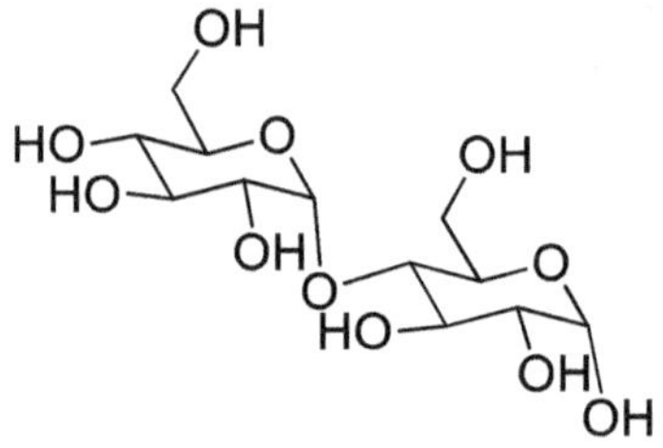

C.

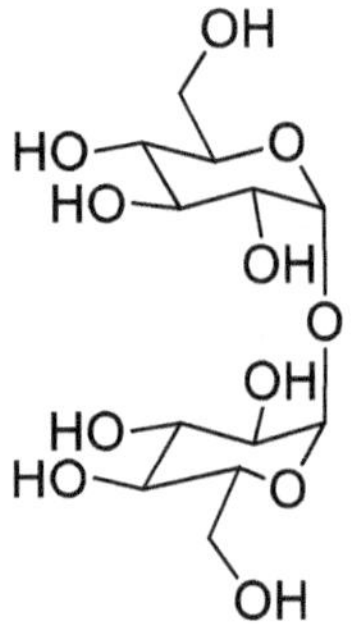

D.

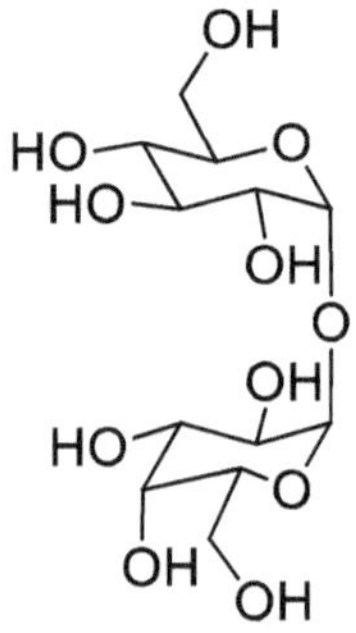

Answer: D. Sucrose **A** cannot be reduced by Tollen's reagent due to the lack of hemiacetal group at the anomeric carbon. Next, the hydrolysis of it produces two different monosaccharides, namely; glucose and fructose. Further, the oxidation of glucose using Br_2/H_2O gives gluconic acid, while fructose remains intact.

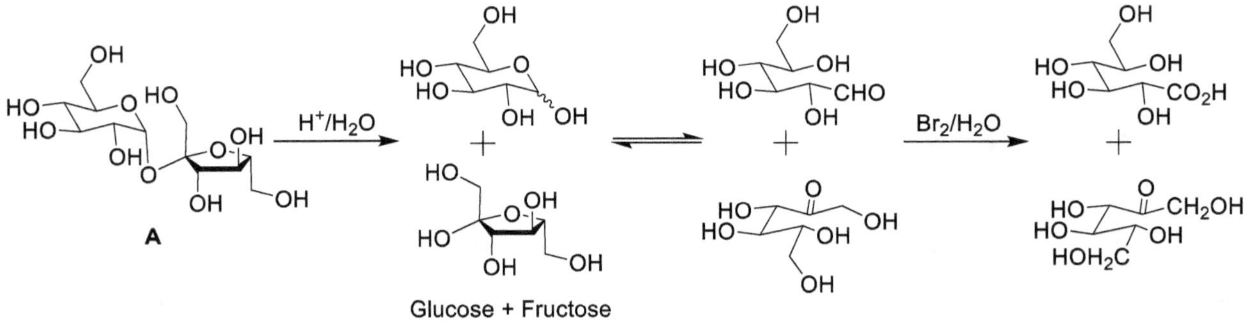

Glucose + Fructose

Maltose **B** and Compound **C** on oxidation using bromine water produces only one type of monosaccharide, i.e. gluconic acid which is shown below.

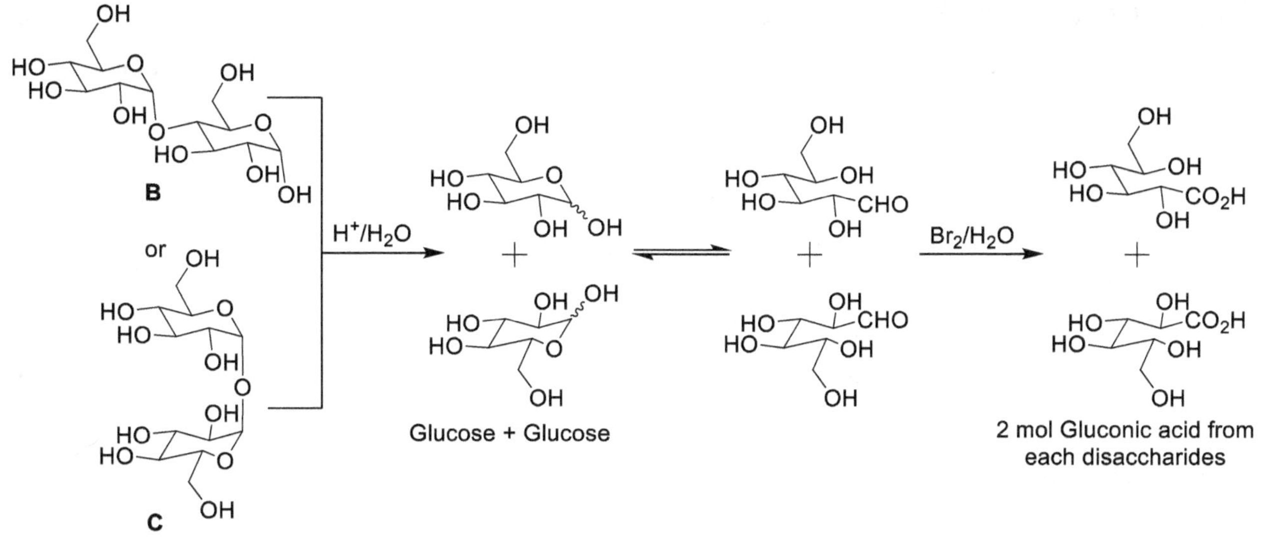

Glucose + Glucose

2 mol Gluconic acid from each disaccharides

The acidic hydrolysis of the given compound **D** (Lactose) offers two different types of monosaccharides, i.e. one mole of each glucose and galactose. As it can be seen both the molecule have a hemiacetal group at the anomeric carbon. Thus, it can easily be oxidized by Br_2/H_2O to give gluconic acid and galactonic acid, respectively.

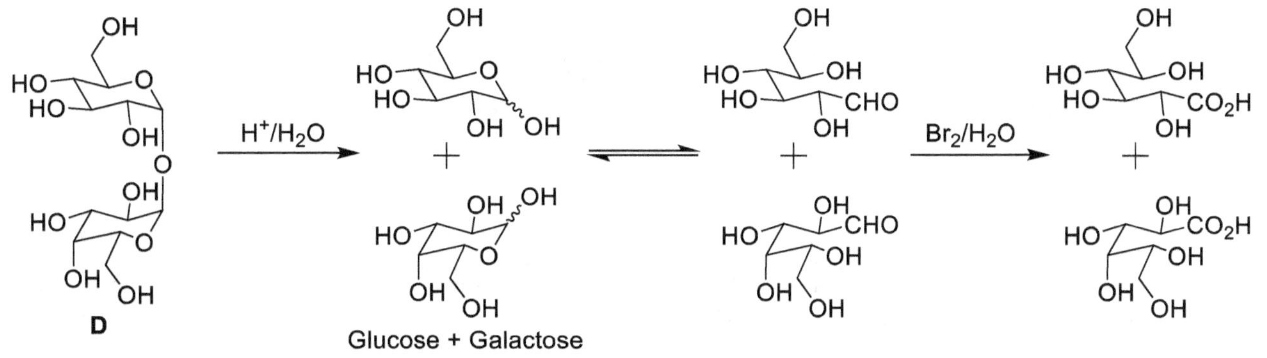

Glucose + Galactose

Question No-50: Among the following, the transformation(s) that can be accomplished using the *umpolung* concept

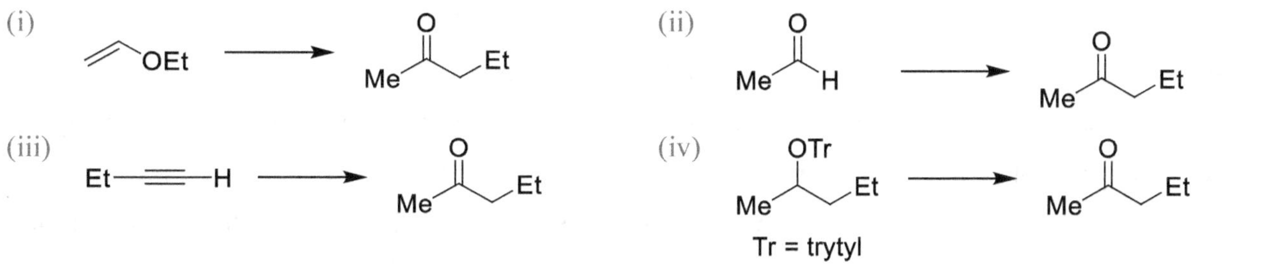

(i)

(ii)

(iii)

(iv)

Tr = trytyl

Codes

A. (i) and (iii) B. (ii) and (iv) C. (ii) only D. (i) and (ii)

Answer: B. Corey-Seebach reaction is one of the best synthetic reactions based on the umpolung concept, and is largely employed for the synthesis of lower aldehydes to give corresponding higher aldehydes/ketones.

The selective oxidative transformation of the given reaction having trityloxy group with one α-hydrogen undergoes facile oxidation with triphenylcarbenium tetrafluoroborate yields ketone derivative *via* hydride transfer mechanism.

Question No-52: The major products **S** and **T** in the following synthetic scheme are

Answer: B. The Horner–Wadsworth–Emmons (HWE) reaction is widely employed for the synthesis of *E*-selective olefins from the stabilized phosphonate carbanions with aldehydes/ketones. In the given reaction, the *in situ*-generated phosphonate using sodium hydride which abstracts methylene proton and then reacts with 2,2-dimethylcyclohexanone furnishing ethyl (*E*)-2-(2,2-dimethylcyclohexylidene)acetate. Further, reduction with LAH produces (*E*)-2-(2,2-dimethylcyclohexylidene)ethan-1-ol as the major product **S**. Next, the Sharpless asymmetric epoxidation of **S** using (-)-DET produces the major product ((2*R*,3*R*)-4,4-dimethyl-1-oxaspiro[2.5]octan-2-yl)methanol **T**.

Note. HWE reaction is a modified version of the Wittig reaction. This modified reaction has the least solubility and selectivity issues than the Wittig reaction.

Question No-55: The structure of the compound having the following characteristic data is

IR: 1690 cm^{-1}

^{1}HNMR: δ 1.30 (3H; t, J = 7.2 Hz); 2.41 (2H; q, J = 7.2 Hz); 2.32 (3H; s,); 7.44 (1H; q, J = 7.0 Hz); 7.57 (1H; dt, J = 7.0, 3.0 Hz); 7.77 (1H; t, J = 3.0 Hz); 7.90 (1H; dt, J = 7.0, 3.0 Hz).

EI Mass: m/z 119 (100%), 57 (80%).

A.

B.

C.

D.

Answer: A. The given spectroscopic data revealed that the compound should be 1-(*m*-tolyl)propan-1-one.

Question No-2: The ^{13}C NMR spectrum of acetone-d_6 has a signal at 30 ppm as a septate in the intensity ratio

A. $1:6:15:20:15:6:1$

B. $1:3:6:7:6:3:1$

C. $1:2:3:5:3:2:1$

D. $1:3:7:10:7:3:1$

Answer: B. The ^{13}C NMR spectrum of acetone-d_6 has a signal at 30 ppm as a septate in the intensity ratio of Pascal's triangle for deuterium is shown below.

Solvents	Structure	Shift(ppm)	Lines	Intensity	J_{CD} (Hz)
Chloroform-*d*	CDCl$_3$	77.0	3	1:1:1	32
Dichloromethane-*d$_2$*	CD$_2$Cl$_2$	54.0	5	1:2:3:2:1	27.2
Acetone- *d$_6$*	CD$_3$COCD$_3$	29.9, 207.0	7	1:3:6:7:6:3:1	19.4
Acetonitrile- *d$_3$*	CD$_3$CN	1.39, 118.69	7	1:3:6:7:6:3:1	24.3
DMSO- *d$_6$*	CD$_3$SOCD$_3$	39.51	7	1:3:6:7:6:3:1	21.0
Methanol- *d$_4$*	CD$_3$OD	49.15	7	1:3:6:7:6:3:1	21.4
Benzene- *d$_6$*	C$_6$D$_6$	128.4	3	1:1:1	24.3
Pyridine-*d$_5$*	C$_5$D$_5$N	150.4	3	1:1:1	27.2
Pyridine-*d$_5$*	C$_5$D$_5$N	136.0	3	1:1:1	24.9
Pyridine-*d$_5$*	C$_5$D$_5$N	124.0	3	1:1:1	24.9

Concern in this book for the calculation of Pascal's Triangle intensity ratio of deuterium (For Deuterium I $= 1$; $2nI + 1 = 2 \times 3 \times 1 + 1 = 7$, septate lines).

Jacobsen, N. E. NMR Hardware and Software. In *NMR Data Interpretation Explained: Understanding 1D and 2D NMR Spectra of Organic Compounds and Natural Products*; John Wiley & Sons, 2012; p 130.

Question No-3: The number of possible stereoisomers for cyclononene is_________

Answer: 3. The possible stereoisomers of cyclononene is three, as shown below

Question No-4: The major product formed in the following reaction is

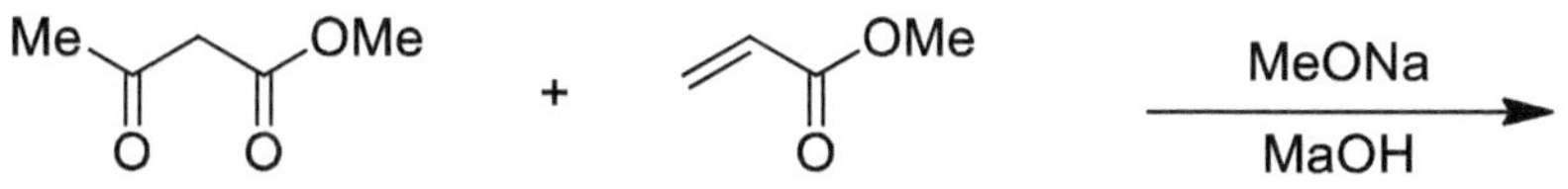

A.

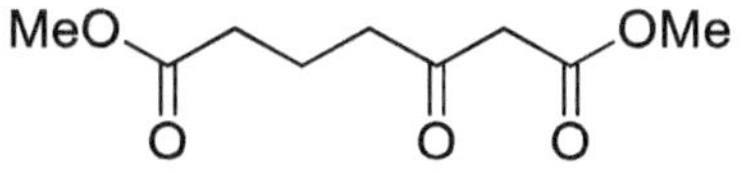

B.

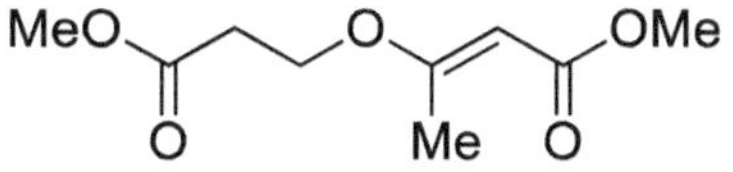

C.

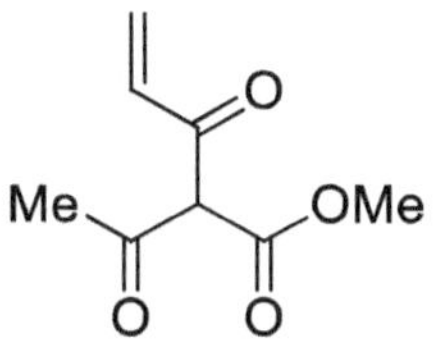

D.

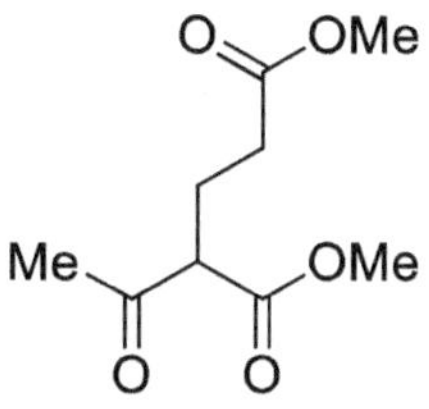

Answer: D. The major product formed in the given reaction *via* Michael addition is dimethyl 2-acetylpentanedioate.

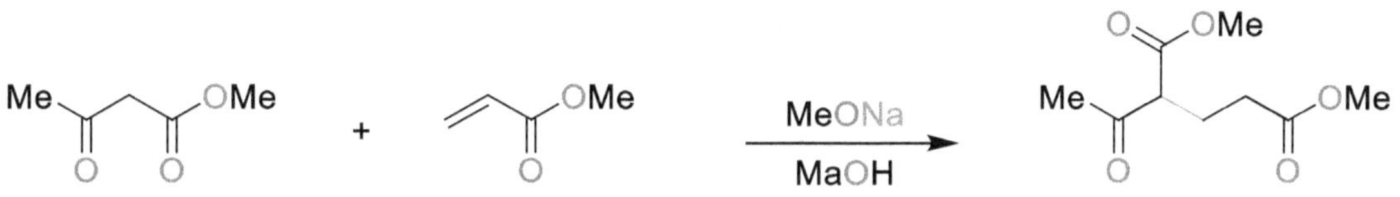

Question No-9: The major product formed in the following photochemical reaction is

A.

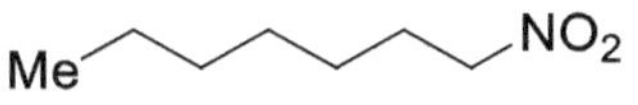

B.

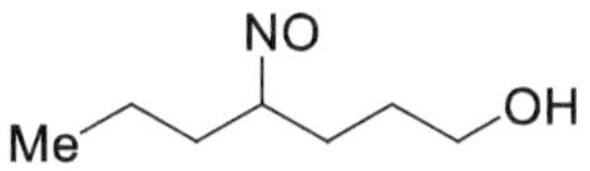

C.

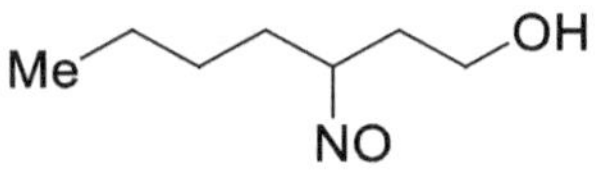

D.

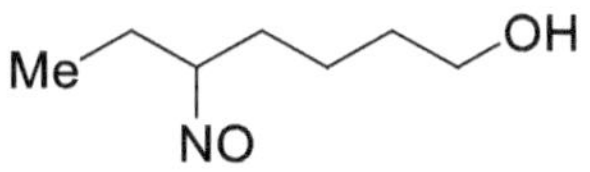

Answer: B. The major product formed in the given photochemical Barton reaction is 4-nitrosoheptan-1-ol.

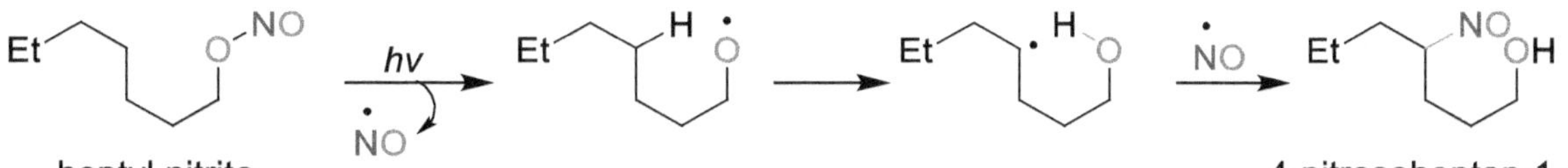

heptyl nitrite

4-nitrosoheptan-1-ol

Note. In this photochemical reaction, the functionalization of unactivated δ-carbon of nitrous acid ester to corresponding nitroso alcohols takes place by abstraction of δ-proton in a free radical manner.

Question No-11: The most suitable reagent for the following transformation is

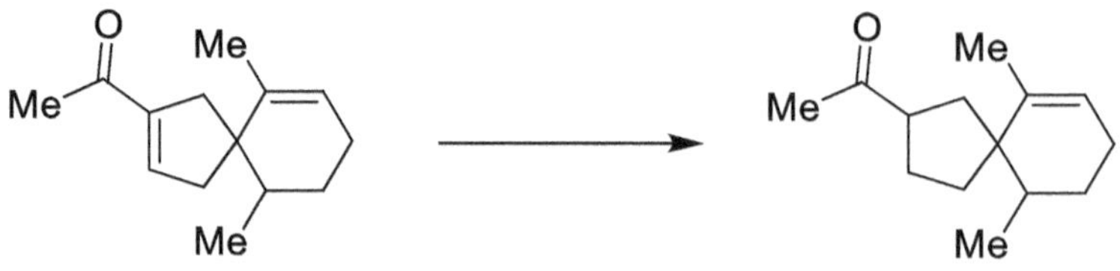

A. Li/NH$_3$ B. PtO$_2$/H$_2$ C. LiAlH$_4$ D. B$_2$H$_6$

Answer: A. The most suitable reagent for the given transformation is the Birch reagent (Li/NH$_3$).

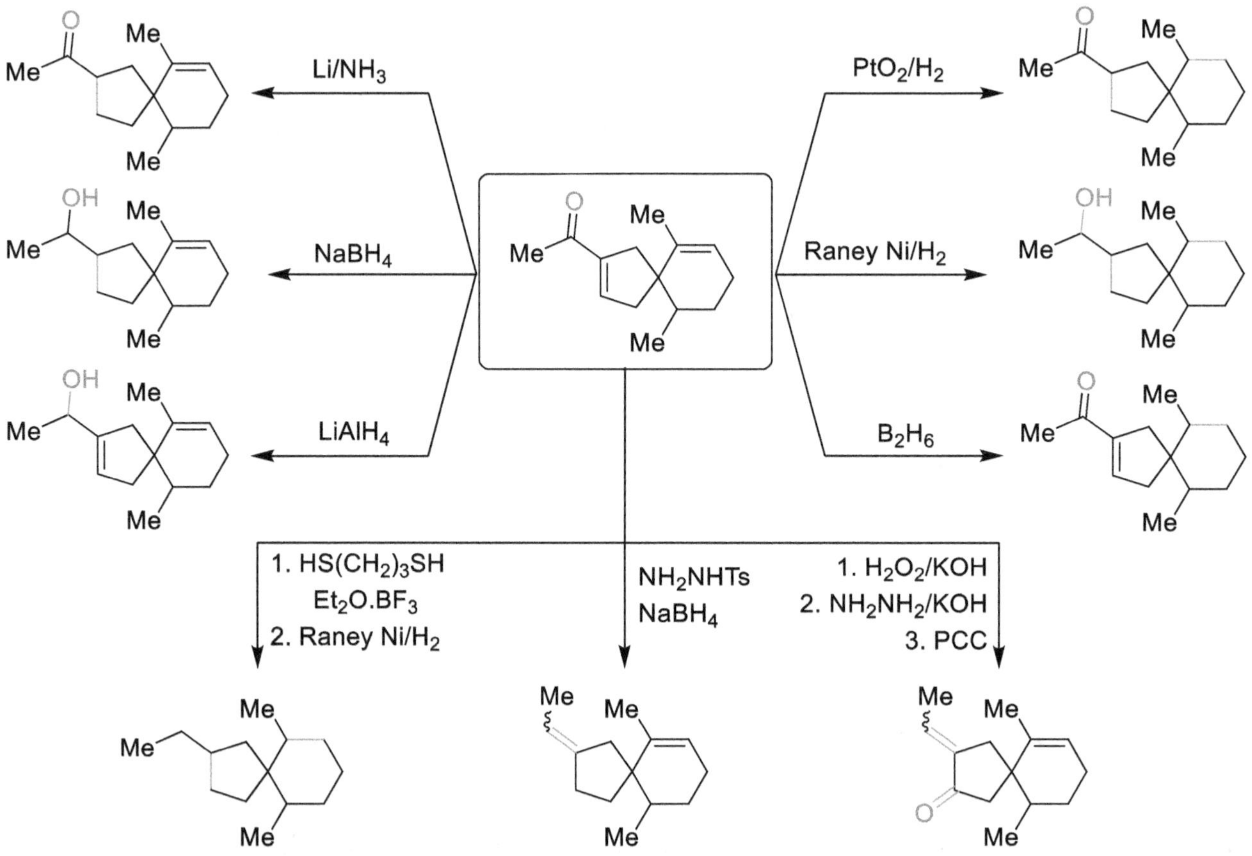

Question No-12: The major products **M** and **N** are formed in the following reactions, are

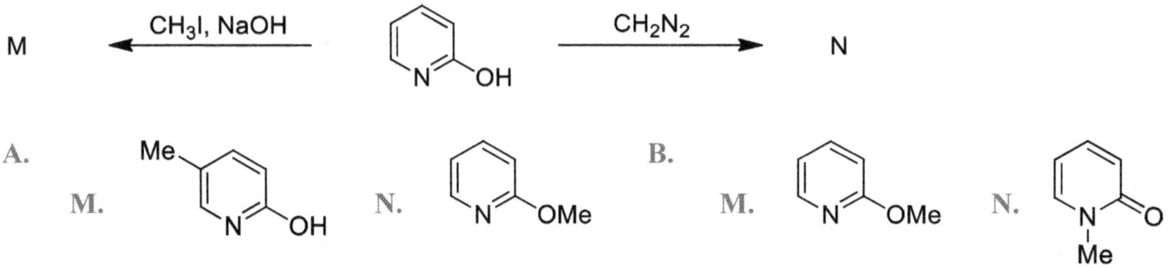

C.

M.

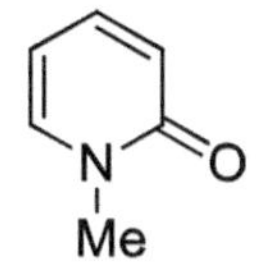

N.

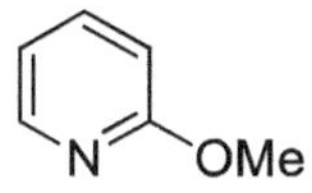

D.

M.

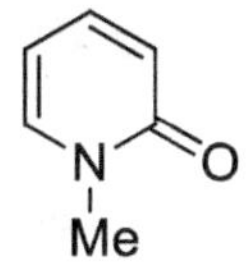

N.

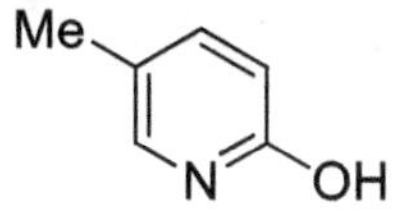

Answer: C. The major products **M** and **N** are formed in the given chemoselective protection reactions are 1-methylpyridin-2(1H)-one and 2-methoxypyridine, respectively.

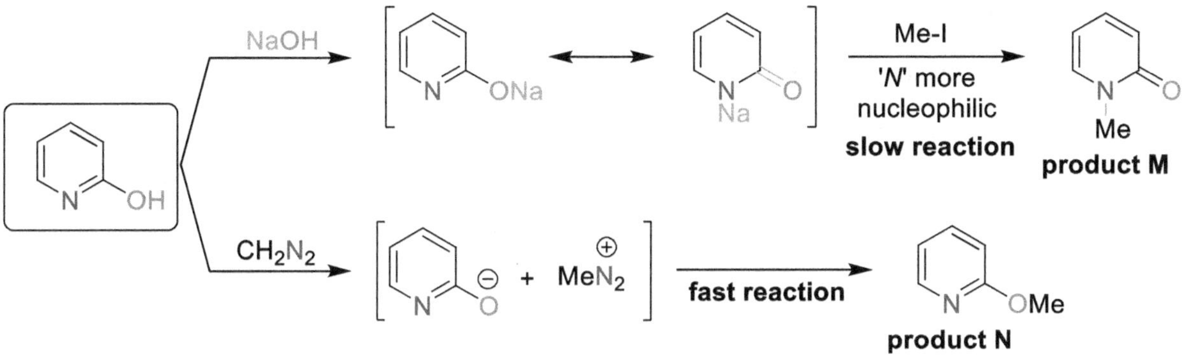

Question No-13: The major product formed in the following reaction, is

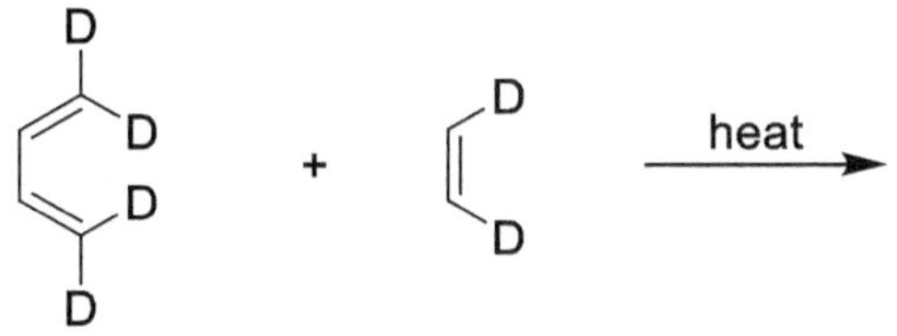

A.

a 1:1 mixture of 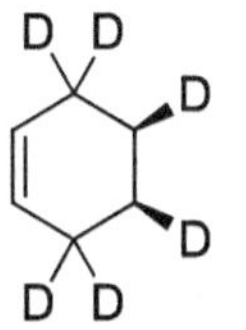   and

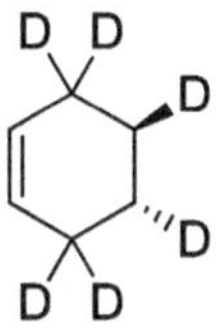

B.

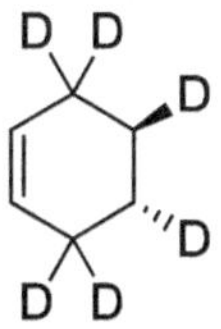

C.

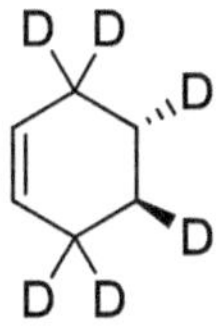

D.

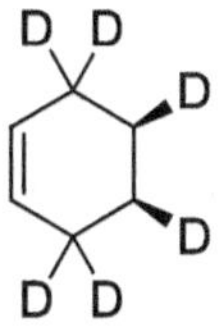

Answer: D. The major product formed in the given concerted thermal [4+2]-cycloaddition reaction, is cyclohex-1-ene-3,3,4,5,6,6-d_6.

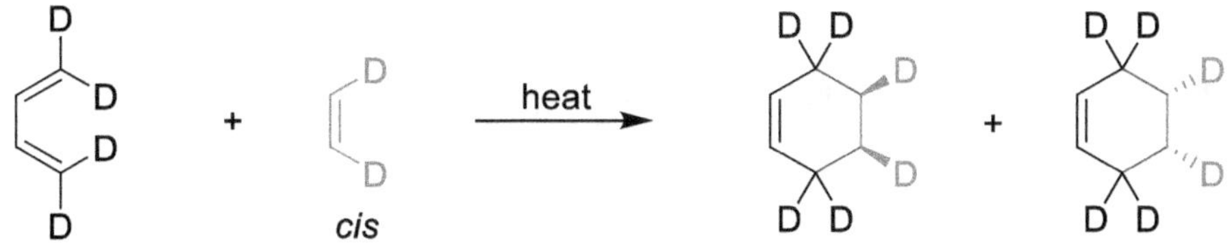

Question No-19: In the two step reaction sequence given below, the starting *bis*-sulfone act as

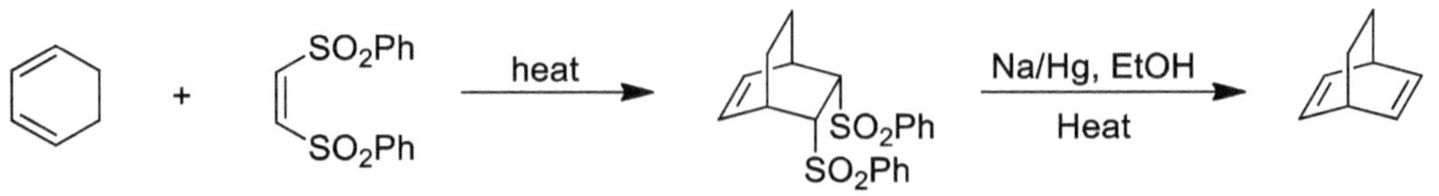

A. A dienophile and synthetic equivalent of acetylene

B. A dienophile and synthetic equivalent of ethylene

C. A dipolarophile and synthetic equivalent of acetylene

D. A dipolarophile and synthetic equivalent of ethylene

Answer: A. The given cascade of reaction proceeds through a concerted [4+2]-cycloaddition reaction followed by reduction using sodium-amalgam which offers a major end product bicyclo[2.2.2]octa-2,5-diene.

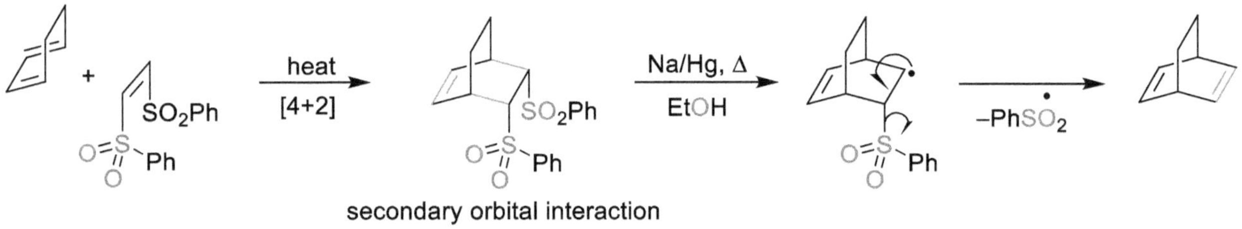

secondary orbital interaction

Note. The newly generated double bond in the first step have strong secondary orbital interaction with sulphone groups that help in getting selective exclusively with an *endo*-product.

Cossu, S.; Battaggia, S.; De Lucchi, O. *J. Org. Chem.* **1997**, *62*, 4162.

Question No-22: The major product obtained in the following reaction, is

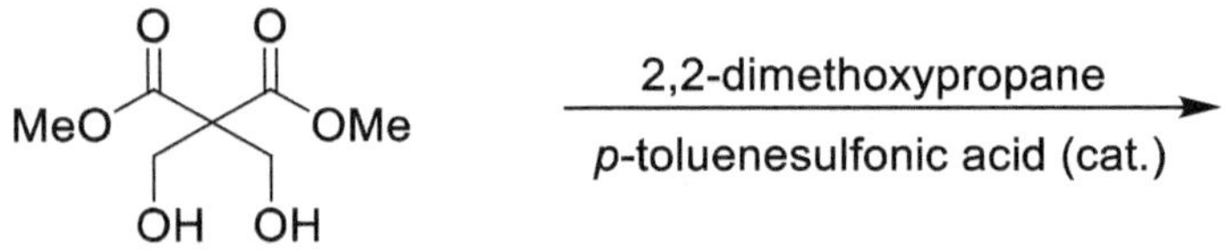

2,2-dimethoxypropane

p-toluenesulfonic acid (cat.)

A.

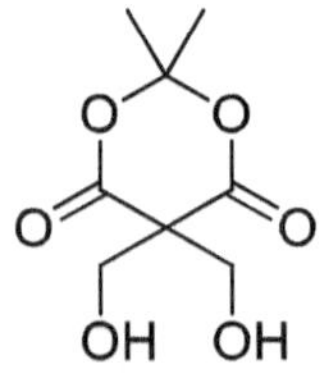

B.

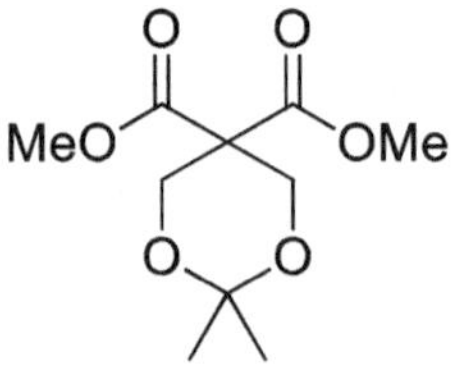

C.

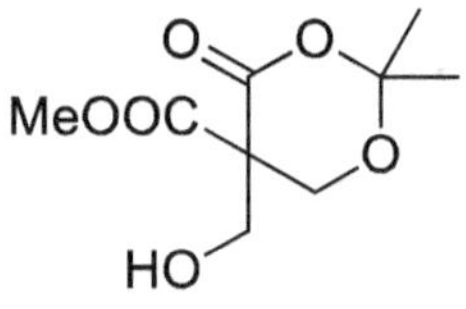

D.

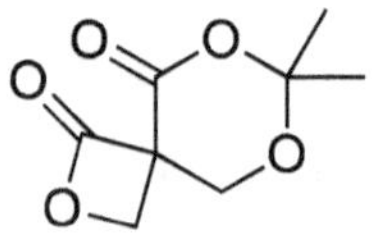

Answer: B. The major product obtained in the given reaction is dimethyl 2,2-dimethyl-1,3-dioxane-5,5-dicarboxylate.

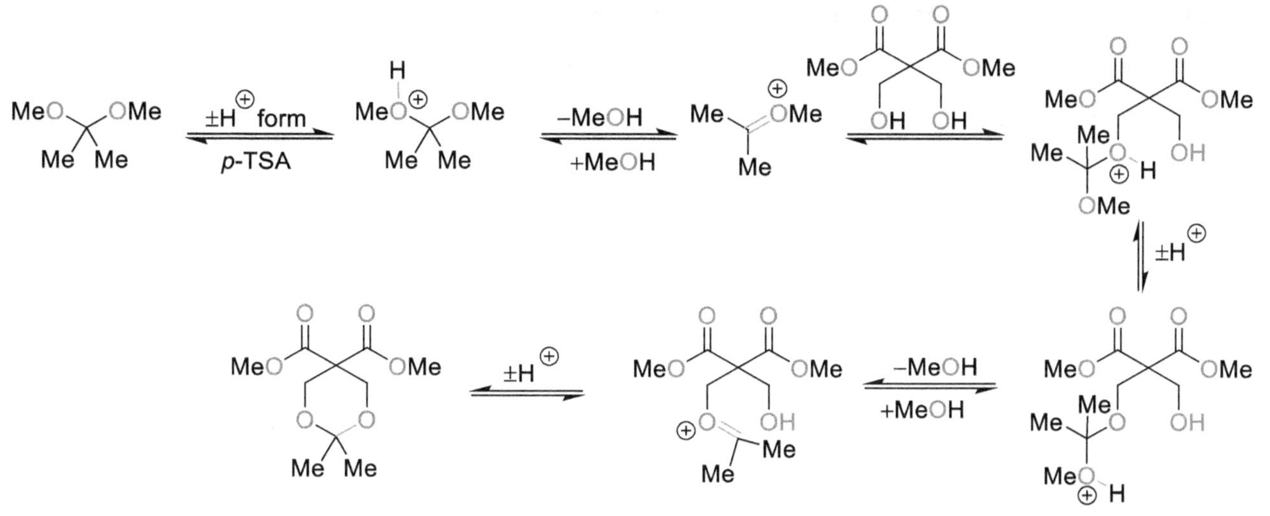

Question No-26: The structures of the intermediate **[P]** and major product **Q** formed in the following reaction sequence are

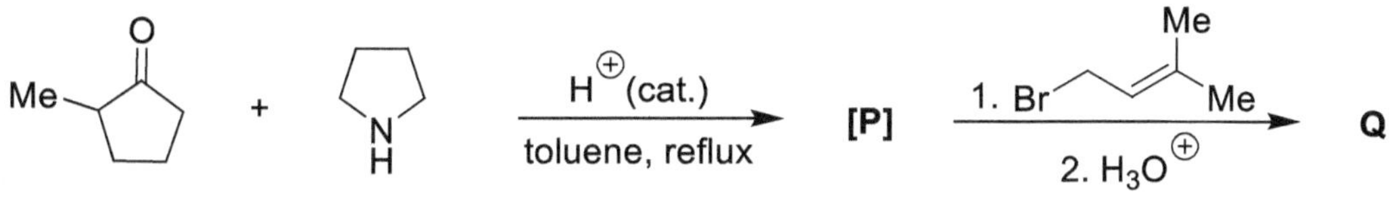

A.

P. 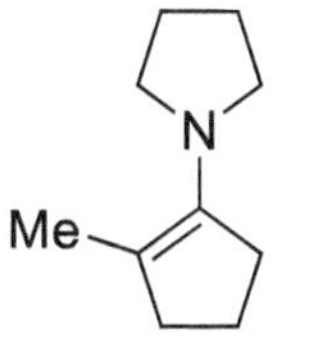 Q.

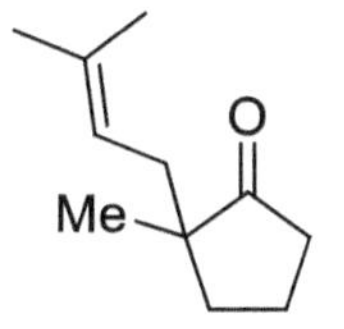

B.

P. 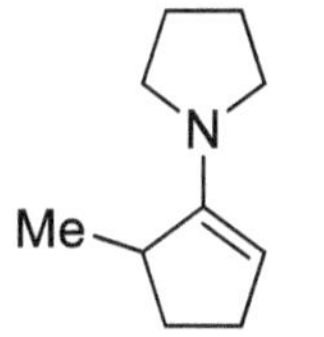 Q.

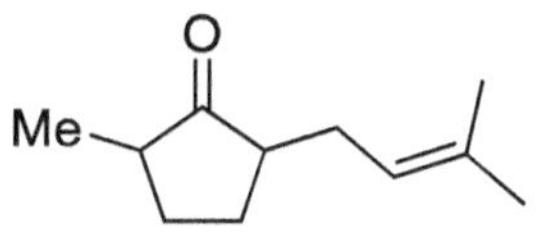

C.

P. 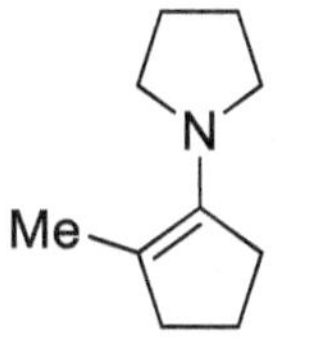 Q.

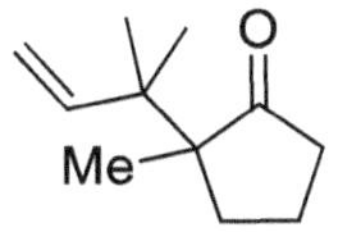

D.

P. 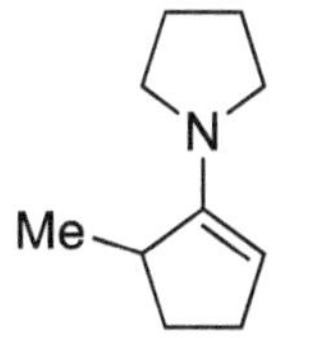 Q.

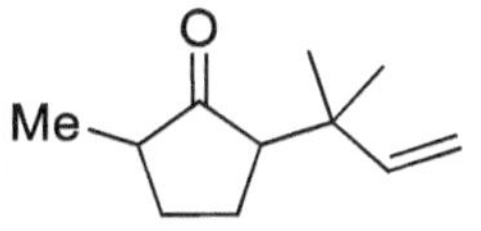

Answer: B. In the first step of the reaction, pyrrolidine reacts with 2-methylcyclopentanone and produces kinetically controlled intermediate **[P]**. In the next step, it reacts with 1-bromo-3-methylbut-2-ene in S$_N$2 manner produces major product 2-methyl-5-(3-methylbut-2-en-1-yl)cyclopentan-1-one **Q**. The given reaction is known as Stork enamine allylation reaction.

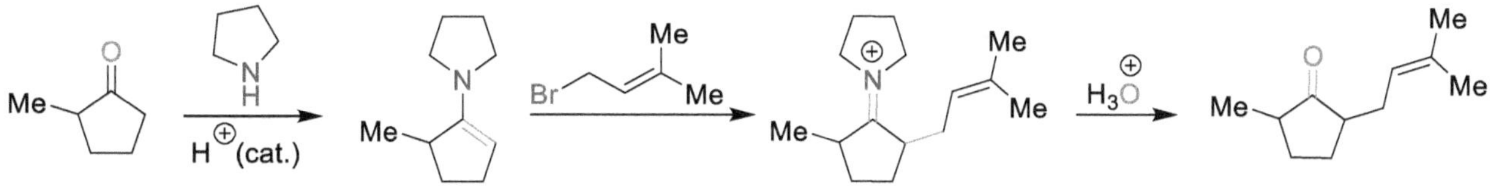

[P]

Q

Note. Usually, Stark-enamine reactions are proceeding through intermediate **[P]** due to the absence of $A^{1,3}$-allylic strain with it, which selectively offers kinetically controlled major product **Q**. On the other hand, the more substituted thermodynamically controlled intermediate **[R]** is formed by isomerization of kinetically controlled intermediate **[P]** when the reaction is carried out without addition of allyl bromide derivative for a longer time duration.

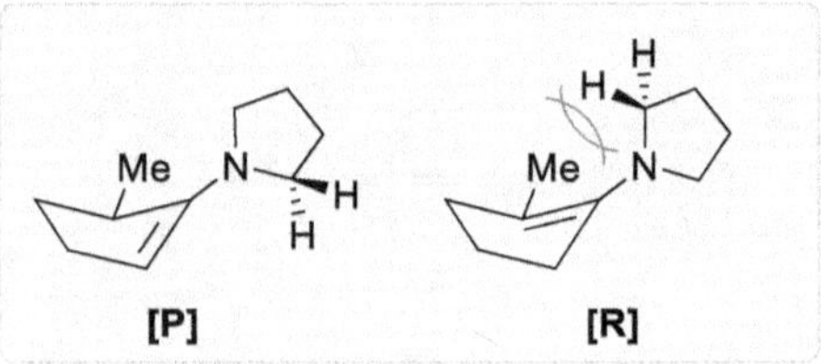

Question No-27: The structures of the major products **W** and **X** in the following synthetic scheme are

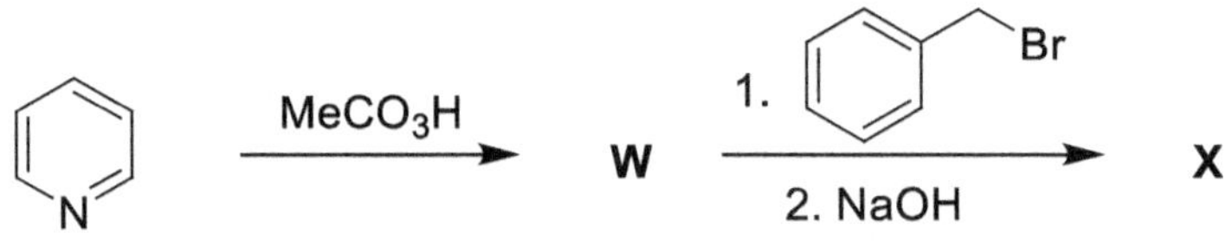

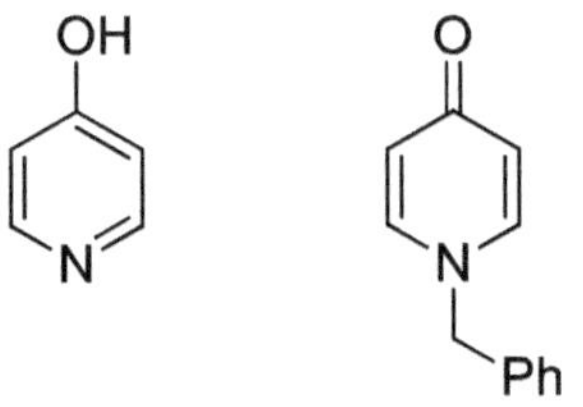

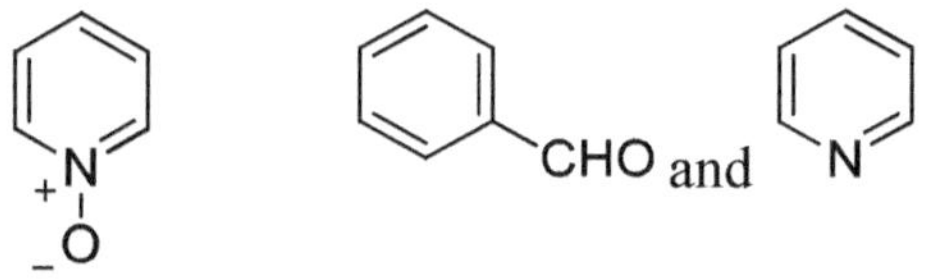

Answer: D. The reaction of per-acetic acid with pyridine produces pyridinium-N-oxide **W** which on further reaction with benzyl bromide in the presence of basic media furnishes the end product benzaldehyde and pyridine **X**. Similarly, 2-methyl pyridine also converts benzyl bromide to benzaldehyde but, the mechanism is different than the prior one which is also shown below.

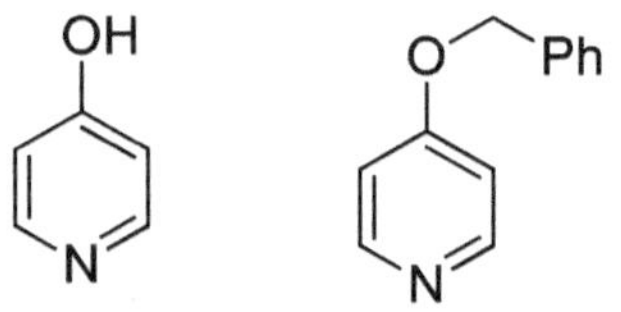

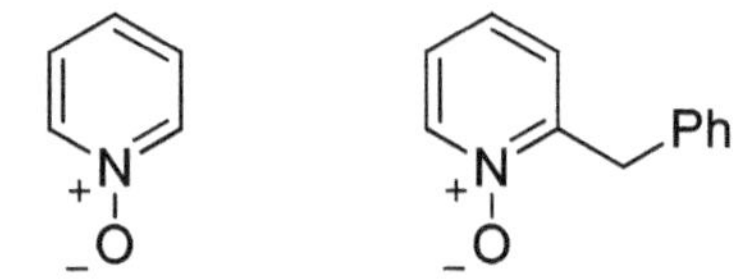

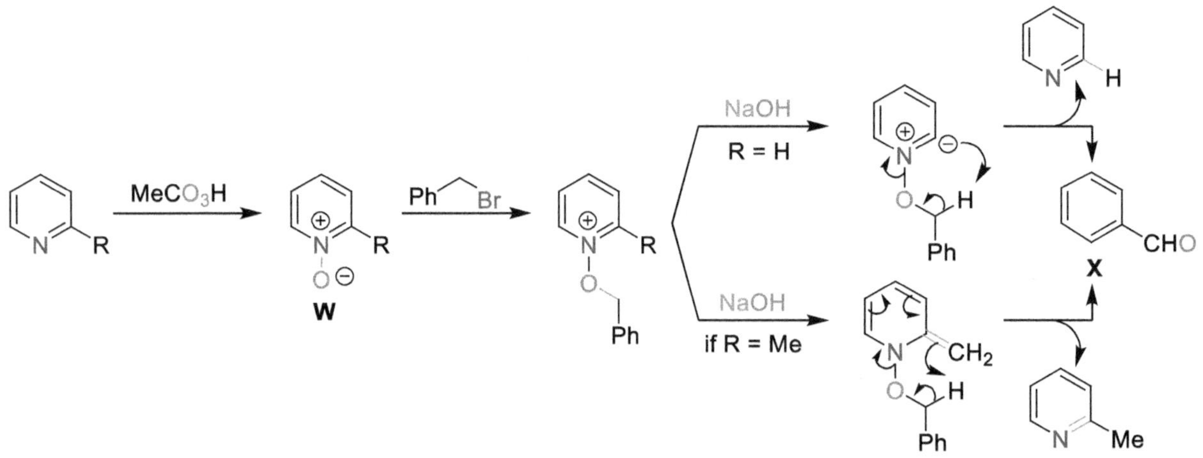

Itoh, A.; Miura, T.; Tada, N. Oxidation of Carbon–Halogen Bonds. In *Comprehensive Organic Synthesis*; Vol. 7; Knochel, P.; Molander, G. A. Eds.; Elsevier, 2014; pp 744-769. DOI: 10.1016/B978-0-08-097742-3.00728-X.

Question No-28: Among the following decahydroquinoline tosylsulfonates (Ts), the one that yields 9-methylamino-*E*-non-5-enal as a major product upon aqueous solvolysis is

A. 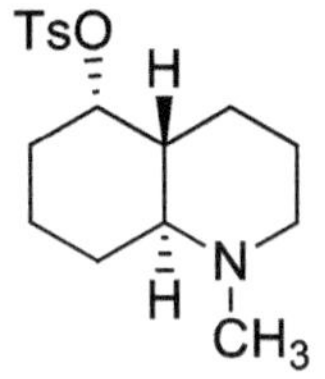

B. 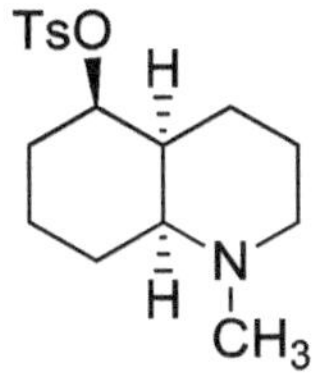

C. 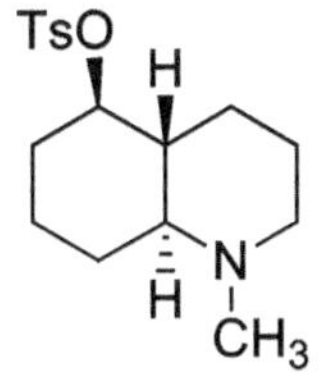

D. 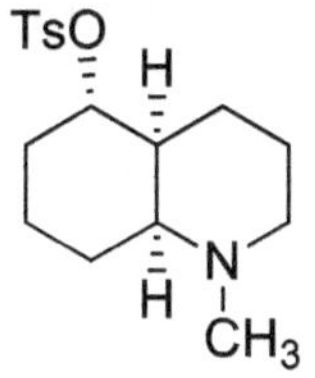

Answer: C. Among these, the two diastereomers of *N*-methyl decahydroquinoline tosylsulfonates **2** and **3** have antiperiplanar relation with the lone pair of nitrogen which helps in faster fragmentation. Decahydroquinoline tosylsulfonates **2** gives '*Z*'-isomers while another configurational isomer **3** yields desired product 9-methylamino-*E*-non-5-enal.

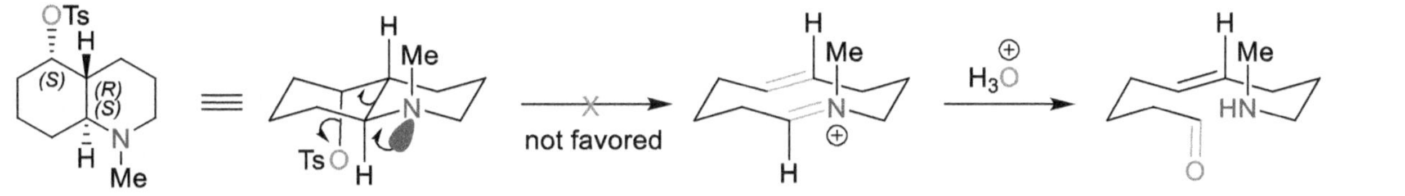

N-methyl decahydroquinoline tosylsulfonate **1** (*E*)-9-(methylamino)non-5-enal

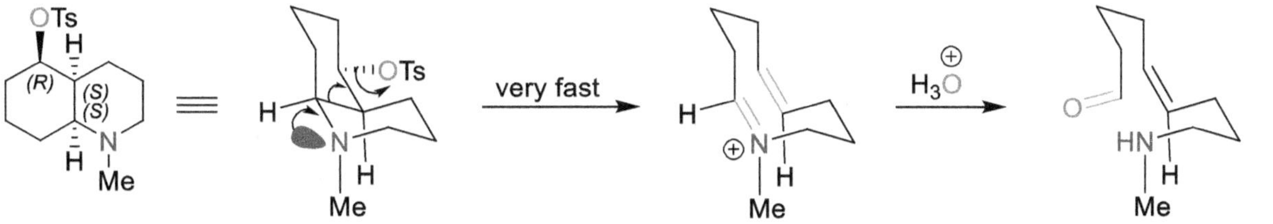

N-methyl decahydroquinoline tosylsulfonates **2** (*Z*)-9-(methylamino)non-5-enal

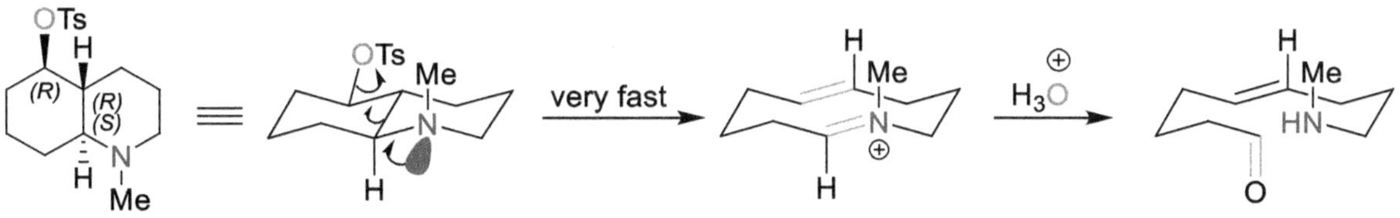

N-methyl decahydroquinoline tosylsulfonates **3** (*E*)-9-(methylamino)non-5-enal

N-methyl decahydroquinoline tosylsulfonates **4**

not favored

(*Z*)-9-(methylamino)non-5-enal

Question No-30: The products formed in the following photochemical reaction, is

$$h\nu$$

A.

B.

C.

D.

Answer: D. The photochemical irradiation of the given compound in the presence of sensitizer undergo di-π-methane rearrangement which offers major product dimethyl of vinyl cyclopropane derivative.

less stable radical intermediate

resonance stabilized radical intermediate

path a

path b

X

Y

minor product

major product

Note. In the case of path b, the intermediate **Y** is more stable and offers a major product than path a through intermediate **X**.

Klán, P.; Wirz, J. Chemistry of Excited Molecules. In *Photochemistry of Organic Compounds: From Concepts to Practice*; 1ˢᵗ Ed.; John Wiley & Sons Ltd. 2009; p 249.

Question No-32: The product obtained in the following solvolysis reaction is

enantiomerically pure compound

A. a racemic mixture of *trans*-1,2-diacetoxycyclohexane

B. enantiomerically pure *trans*-1,2-diacetoxycyclohexane

C. racemic *cis*-1,2-diacetoxycyclohexane

D. a mixture of *cis*- and *trans*-1,2-diacetoxycyclohexane

Answer: A. The product obtained in the given solvolysis reaction offered a racemic mixture of *trans*-1,2-diacetoxycyclohexane. It is due to the reversible flipping of reaction intermediates **I** to **II**.

Clayden, J.; Greeves, N.; Warren, S. Participation, Rearrangement, and Fragmentation. In *Organic Chemistry*, 2ⁿᵈ Ed.; Oxford University Press, 2012; p 932 & p 937.

Question No-37: The major product formed in the following reaction, is

Answer: C. As in the case of manganese dioxide, a chemoselective oxidative transformation of allylic alcohol to corresponding conjugated aldehyde derivative is achieved with silver carbonate which further on cyclization and oxidation gives major product 3-methylenedihydrofuran-2(3*H*)-one.

Question No-40: For the following three alkenes, the rate of hydrogenation using Wilkinson's catalyst at 25 °C, vary in order,

1.	2.	3.

Code

A. $1 > 3 > 2$ B. $1 > 2 > 3$ C. $2 > 1 > 3$ D. $2 > 3 > 1$

Answer: B. For the given three alkenes, the rate of hydrogenation using Wilkinson's catalyst at 25 °C, vary in order $1 > 2 > 3$.

Note. The least substituted olefins undergo a faster hydrogenation reaction than more substitute with Wilkinson's catalyst and also the *cis*-olefins undergoes faster hydrogenation than *trans*-olefins.

Question No-41: The spectroscopic data for an organic compound with molecular formula $C_{10}H_{12}O_2$ are given below:

IR band around 1750 cm^{-1}, **^{1}H NMR:** δ 7.3 (m, 5H); 5.85 (q, 1H, $J = 7.2$ Hz); 2.05 (s, 3H); 1.5 (d, 3H, $J = 7.2$ Hz) ppm. The compound is

A. Methyl 2-phenylpropionate   B. 1-(phenyethyl) acetate

C. 2-(phenyethyl) acetate   D. Methyl 3-phenylpropionate

Answer: B. The given ^{1}H NMR data revealed that the compound should be 1-(phenyethyl) acetate.

Methyl 2-phenylpropionate   **1-(phenyethyl) acetate**

IR band around 1738 cm^{-1}, ^{1}H NMR: δ 1.50 (d, 3H, $J = 7.2$ Hz); 3.66 (s, 3H); 3.73 (q, 1H, $J = 7.2$ Hz); 7.24 - 7.35 (m, 5H).

IR band around 1750 cm^{-1}, ^{1}H NMR: δ 1.49 (d, 3H, $J = 6.8$ Hz); 1.98 (s, 3H) 5.86 (q, 1H, $J = 6.8$ Hz); 7.22-7.33 (m, 5 H).

Iinuma, M.; Moriyama, K.; Togo, H. *Tetrahedron* **2013**, *69*, 2961.

Ma, S.; Toy, P. H. *Synlett* **2016**, *27*, 1207.

Question No-43: Hydroboration of 2-butyne with $(C_6H_{11})_2BH$ yields the intermediate **U**, which on treatment with I_2 and NaOMe at -78 °C, gives product **V**. The structures of **U** and **V** are

	U	V		U	V

A. Me, B(C₆H₁₁)₂ / H, Me — Me, Me / H, C₆H₁₁

B. Me, Me / H, B(C₆H₁₁)₂ — Me, Me / H, C₆H₁₁

C. Me, B(C₆H₁₁)₂ / H, Me — Me, C₆H₁₁ / H, Me

D. Me, Me / H, B(C₆H₁₁)₂ — Me, C₆H₁₁ / H, Me

Answer: D. Hydroboration of 2-butyne with dicyclohexyl borane gives stereospecific *anti*-Markovnikov *syn*-addition product intermediate **U**.

The obtained above product intermediate **U** reacts with molecular iodine in the presence of sodium methoxide which activates the intermediate **U1** and then simultaneous elimination of borane and iodide offers *cis*-olefin **V**.

Carruthers, W.; Coldham, I. Formation of Carbon-Carbon Double Bonds. In *Modern Method of Organic Synthesis*, 4th Ed.; Cambridge University Press, 2004; p 127.

Question No-44: The major products **Y** and **Z** in the following reaction sequence are

A.

B.

C.

D.

Answer: D. In Curtius rearrangement, the reaction of acryloyl chloride with sodium azide gives intermediate acryloyl azide which undergoes rearrangement on heating and converts into vinyl isocyanate intermediate **Y**. This reactive intermediate product **Y** undergoes nucleophilic addition reaction with benzyl alcohol furnishes major product benzyl vinyl carbamate **Z**.

Question No-44: Hydration of fumaric acid gives malic acid as shown below. Assume that the addition of water takes place specifically from **a** face or **b** face. The correct statement pertaining to the stereochemistry of malic acid formed is

A.   Addition specifically from **a** face gives S isomer of malic acid

B. Addition specifically from **b** face gives *S* isomer of malic acid

C. Addition specifically from **a** face gives *R* isomer of malic acid

D. Addition specifically from **b** face gives a racemic mixture of malic acid

Answer: B. The hydration of fumaric acid gives malic acid in the presence of fumarase enzyme; specifically from **a** face gives *S*-isomer of malic acid. Where zero (0) and eight (8) are the conformation state of the fumarase enzyme, '0' and '8' shows the addition of fumarate and elimination of (*S*)-malate.

$$[CaCO_3.fumarase] + fumaric\ acid \longrightarrow Ca[fumarate] + fumarase + byproduct \quad (Biological\ system)$$

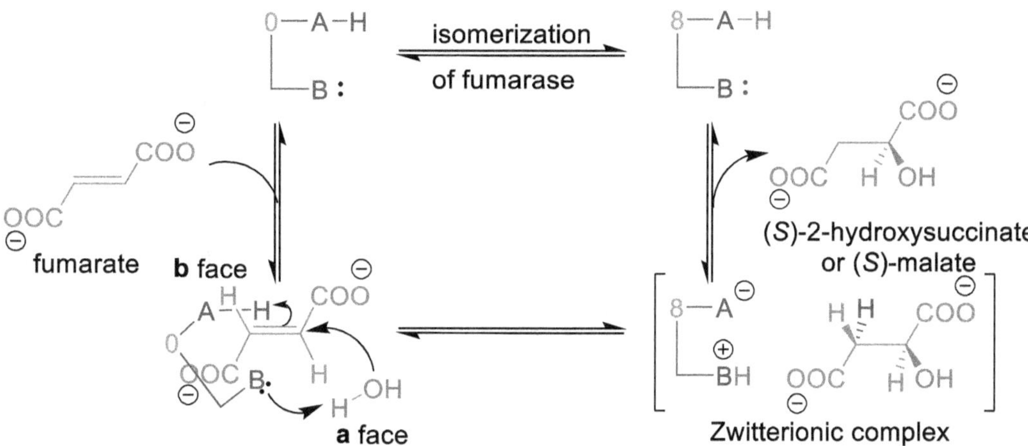

Jin J.; Hanefeld, U. *Chem. Commun.* **2011**, *47*, 2502.

Question No-3: The major product formed in the following reaction is

$$Ph{-}CHO \ + \ \text{(ethyl acetoacetate)} \ + \ NH_3 \xrightarrow[\text{EtOH}]{\text{pH 8.5}}$$

A.

B.

C.

D.

Answer: D. The major product formed in the given reaction *via* Hantzsch-dihydropyridine synthesis is diethyl 2,6-dimethyl-4-phenyl-1,4-dihydropyridine-3,5-dicarboxylate.

Mechanism of reaction. Step I: The condensation of ethyl acetoacetate (EAA) and benzaldehyde is known as Knoevenagel condensation.

Step II: The condensation of EAA and ammonia is useful for the generation of enamine reagent.

Step III: At last, enamine reagent undergoes Michael addition with Knoevenagel condensed product followed by intramolecular cyclization reaction offering Hantzsch-Dihydropyridine product.

Alvim, H.G. O.; Júnior, E. N. S.; Neto, B. A. D. *RSC Adv.* **2014**, *4*, 54282-54299.

Question No-4: For the radioactive isotope ^{131}I, the time required for 50% disintegration is 8 days. The time required for 99.9% disintegration of 5.5 g of ^{131}I is……………. Days. (Up to one decimal place)

Answer: 79.7 Days. Let the initial concentration of a = 100%

$$k = \frac{2.303}{t} log\ (a/a\text{-}x) = \frac{2.303}{t} log\ (a/a'')$$

Given a'' (100-50) = 50% remaining concentration after t = 8 days and by putting it into the expression

$$\text{value of k} = \frac{2.303}{8} log\ (100/50) = \frac{2.303}{8} (log\ 2) = \frac{2.303}{8} (0.3010) \qquad \textbf{(eq. 1)}$$

Now after 99.9% completion a'' = 0.1%

$$k = \frac{2.303}{t} log\ (100/0.1) = \frac{2.303}{t} log\ 10^3 = \frac{2.303}{t} 3log\ 10 \qquad \textbf{(eq. 2)}$$

Putting the value of $k = \frac{2.303}{t} 3log\ 10$ in (eq. 1) from (eq. 2)

$$\frac{2.303}{t} 3log\ 10 = \frac{2.303}{8} (0.3010)$$

$$\textbf{t} = \frac{3 \times 8}{0.3010} = 79.7 \text{ days} \approx \textbf{80.0 days.}$$

Question No-5: The major product of the following reaction is

A.

B.

C.

Me—(structure: epoxide with two propyl chains)—Me

D.

SiMe₃

Me—(structure: alkene with SiMe₃)—Me

Answer: B. The major product of the given Peterson olefination is (*Z*)-octene-4.

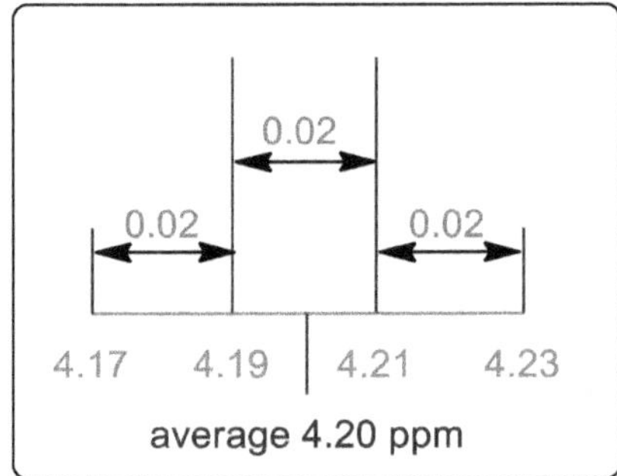

Question No-10: In the ¹H NMR spectrum of an organic compound recorded on a 300 MHz instrument, a proton resonates as a quartet at δ 4.20 ppm. The individual signals of the quartet appear at δ 4.17, 4.19, 4.21 and 4.23 ppm. The coupling constant *J* in Hz is................

Answer: 6 Hz. The individual signals of the quartet appear at δ 4.17, 4.19, 4.21 and 4.23 ppm.

Each peak has a 0.02 ppm difference at 300 MHz.

So the coupling constant $J = 0.02 \times 10^{-6} \times 300 \times 10^{+6}$

The coupling constant **$J = 6$ Hz**

For the quartet peak the peak intensity ratio is 1 : 3 : 3 : 1; and it can be calculated by Pascal's triangle.

Question No-19: The major product of the following intramolecular cycloaddition reaction is

A.

B.

C.

D.

Answer: D. The major product formed in the given intramolecular photochemical [2+2]-cycloaddition reaction is octahydrocyclopenta[1,4]cyclobuta[1,2]benzen-5(6*H*)-one.

Pirrung, M. C. *J. Am. Chem. Soc.*, **1981**, *103*, 82–87.

Question No-20: The major product formed in the following reaction sequence is

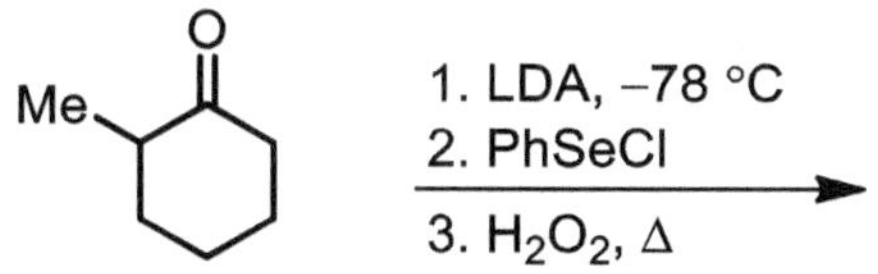

1. LDA, –78 °C
2. PhSeCl
3. H_2O_2, Δ

A.

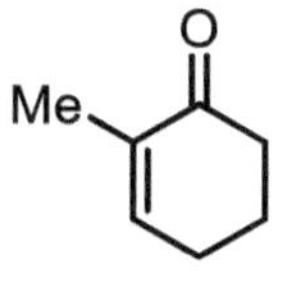

B.

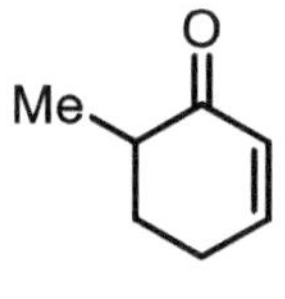

C.

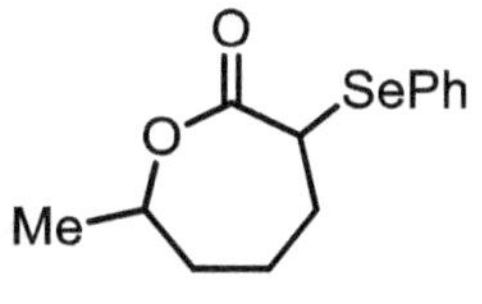

Me   SePh

D.

PhSe

Me

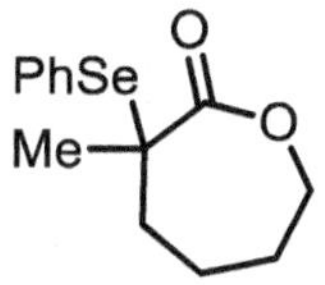

Answer: B. Lithium diisopropylamide (LDA) is a strong and bulky hindered base. It will abstract a proton from the less hindered site and produces a kinetically controlled product (KCP).

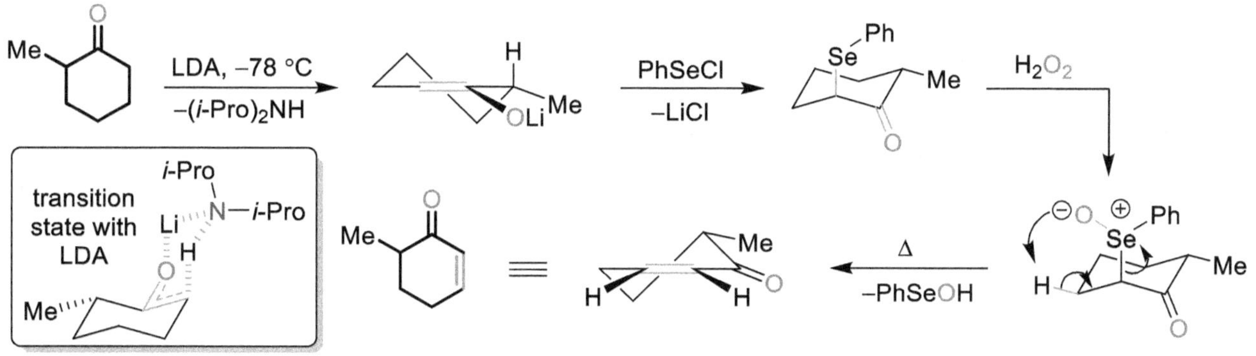

LDA, –78 °C / –(*i*-Pro)$_2$NH   PhSeCl / –LiCl H_2O_2

transition state with LDA

i-Pro — N — *i*-Pro

Δ / –PhSeOH

Question No-23: In the electron ionization (EI) mass, methyl hexanoate, methyl heptanoate and methyl octanoate give the same base peak. The m/z value of the base peak is.................

Answer: 73.8 to 74.2. The m/z value of the base peak is, which is obtained by McLafferty rearrangement.

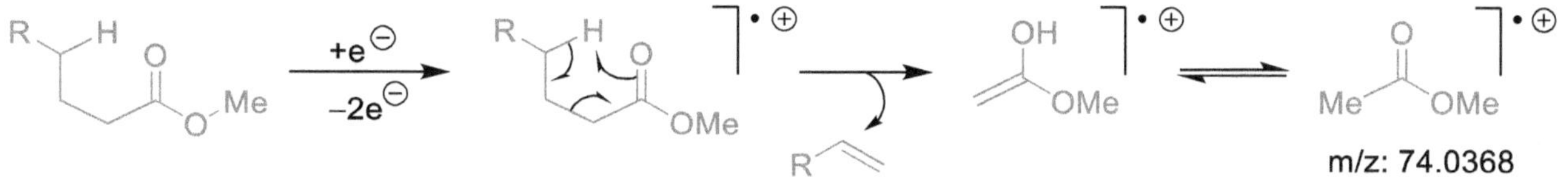

$+e^{\ominus}$ / $-2e^{\ominus}$

m/z: 74.0368

Where, R = Ethyl (methyl hexanoate,), Propyl (methyl hexanoate,), Butyl (methyl octanoate).

Question No-24: The major product formed in the following reaction is

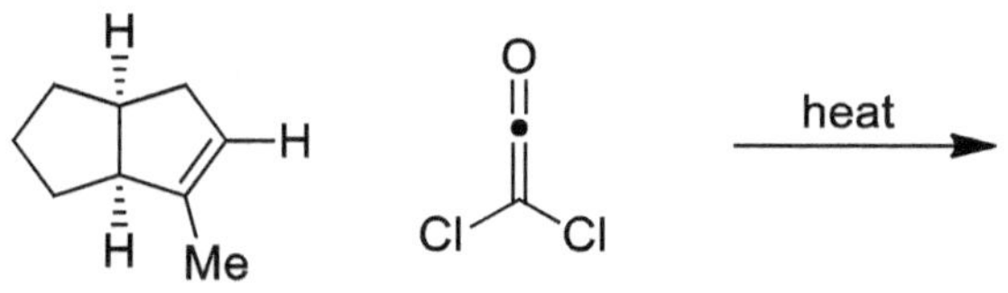

heat

A.

B.

C.

D.

Answer: B. The bicyclic fused cyclopentene derivative reacts regioselectively with ketene furnishes thermal concerted [2+2]-cycloadduct product.

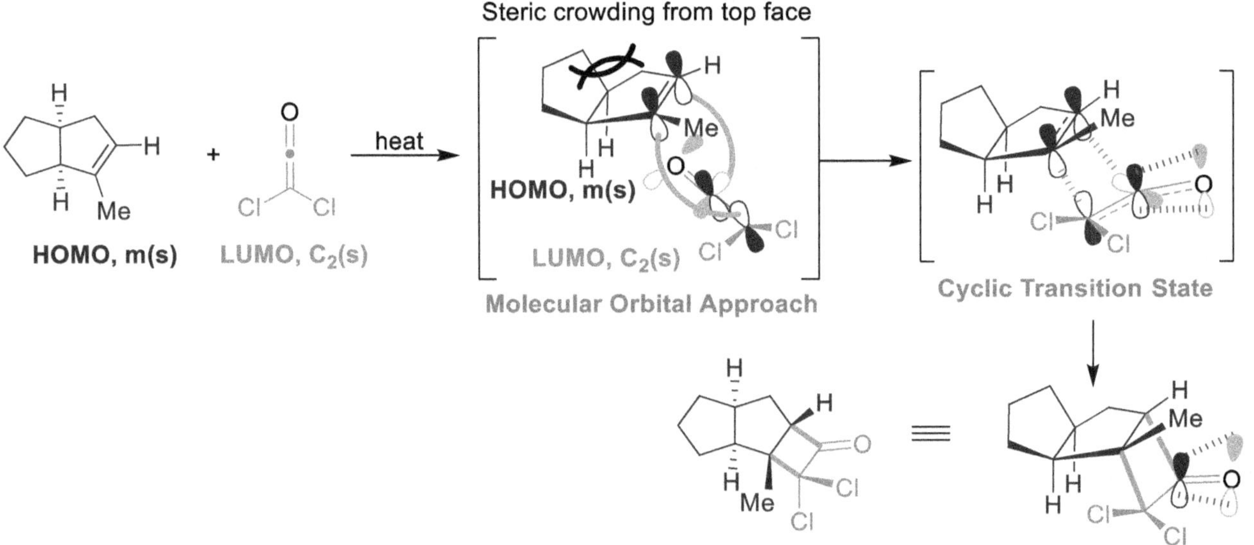

Question No-25: The major product formed in the following reaction sequence is

1. Me—⟨ ⟩—SO₂N₃
2. Ru₂(OAc)₄

A   B   C   D

Answer: A. The reaction of a β-ketoester derivative with tosyl azide produces an α-diazo-β-ketoester derivative.

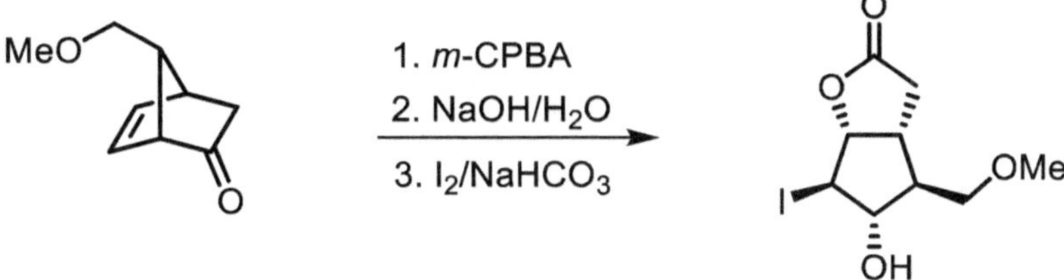

Further, the above-achieved α-diazo-β-ketoester derivative undergoes thermal decomposition and produces carbene which later reacts with Ru$_2$(OAc)$_4$ to produce a fused bicyclic β-lactam derivative.

Hendrickson, J. B.; Wolf, W. A. *J. Org. Chem.* **1968**, *33*, 3610–3618.

Question No-30: The major product formed in the following reaction sequence is

A.

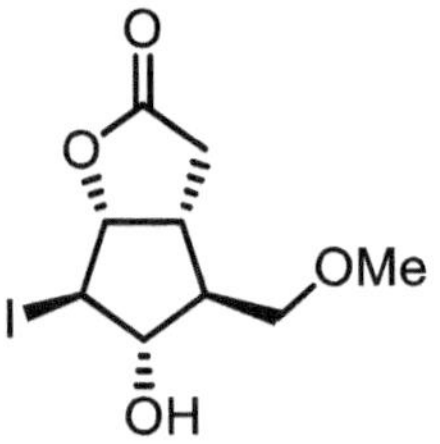
O
O
OMe
I
OH

B.

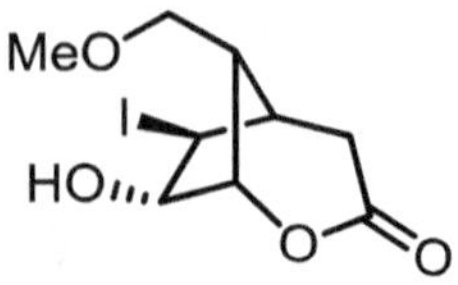
MeO
I
HO
O
O

C.

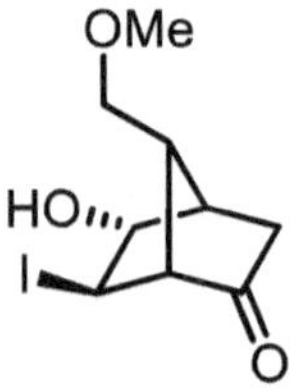
OMe
HO
I
O

D.

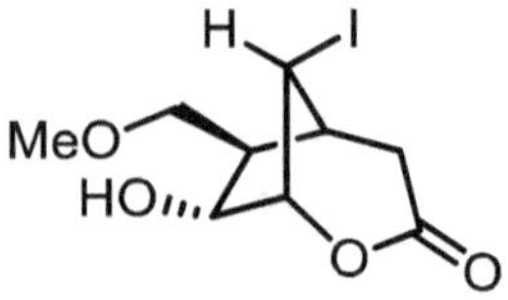
H
I
MeO
HO
O
O

Answer: A. The major product formed in the given reaction proceeds *via* epoxidation, hydration followed by iodolactonization reaction offers bicyclic fused lactone derivative.

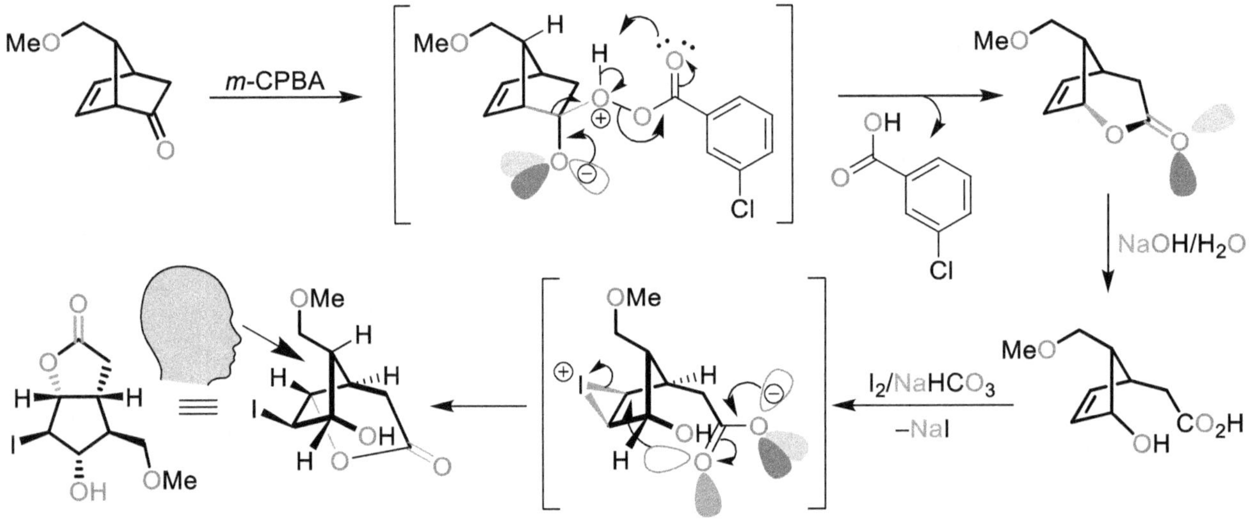
MeO
m-CPBA
NaOH/H2O
I2/NaHCO3
–NaI
Cl
OMe
OH
CO2H

A detail of this is available in this book, GATE-2010, Question Answer No-37.

Question No-31: The major product formed in the following reaction sequence is

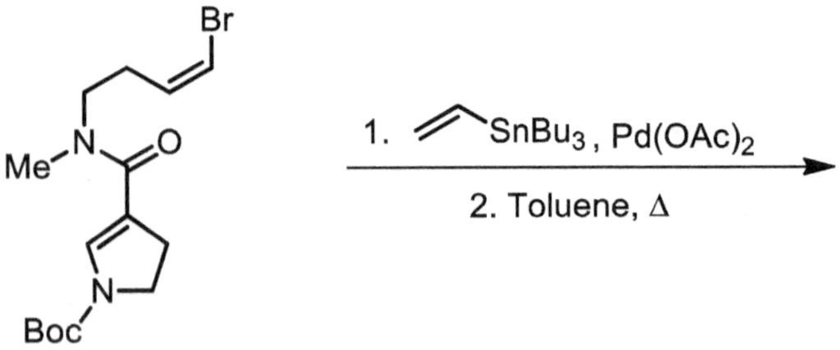
Br
Me
N
O
N
Boc
1. SnBu3, Pd(OAc)2
2. Toluene, Δ

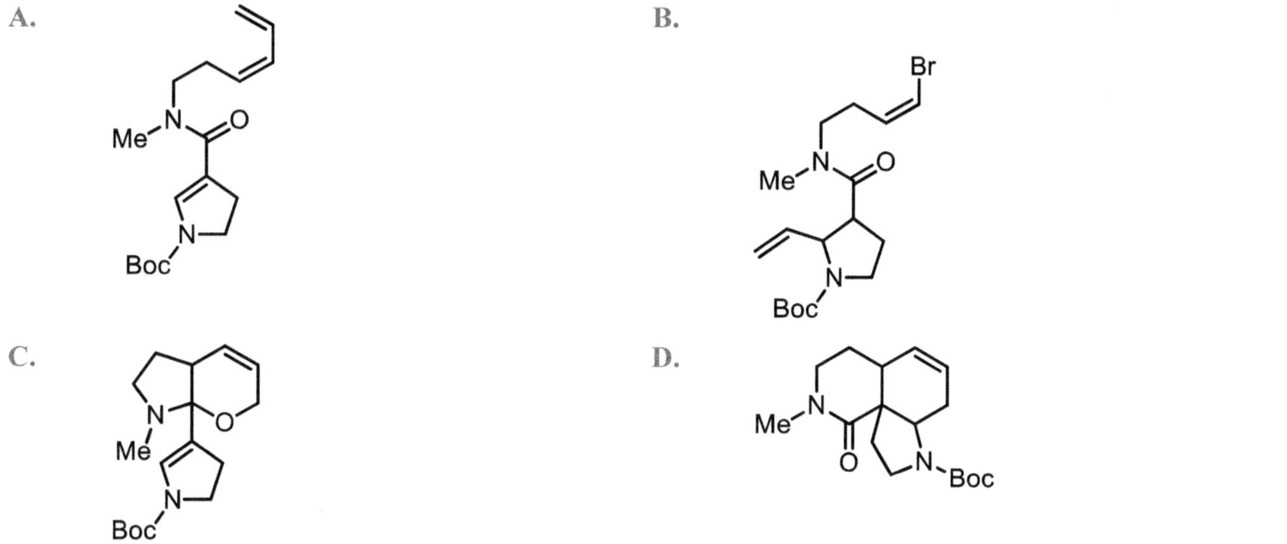

A.

B.

C.

D.

Answer: D. The stereocontrolled transfer of vinyl group using Stille coupling protocol and then simultaneous, thermal concerted [4+2]-cycloaddition reaction offers fused tricyclic derivative.

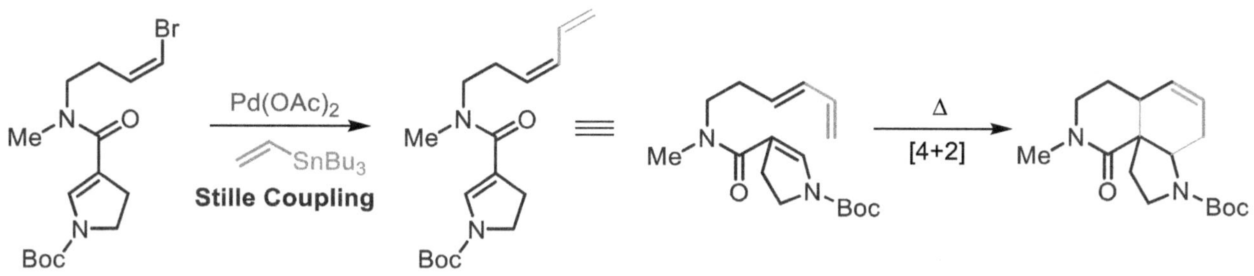

Question No-35: The number of carbonyl groups present in the final product of the following reaction sequence is................

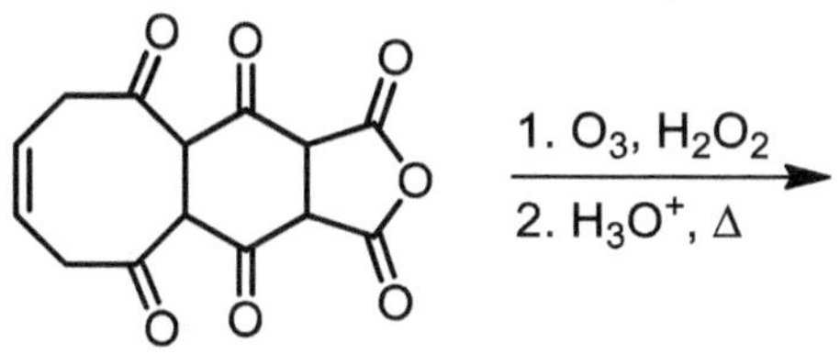

Answer: 4. The number of carbonyl groups present in the final product of the given reaction is four as shown below.

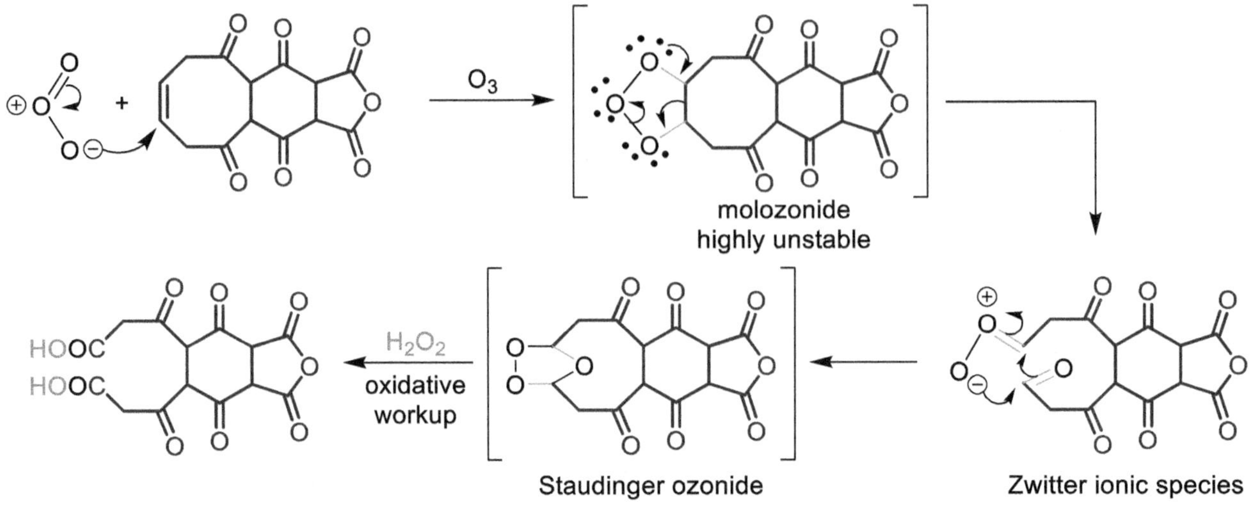

Bailey, P. S. Ozonation in Organic Chemistry; Vol. 1; Elsevier Inc., 1978; pp 1-265.

Question No-36: The major product formed in the following reaction sequence is

i) *t*-BuOK
ii) Raney Ni
EtOH

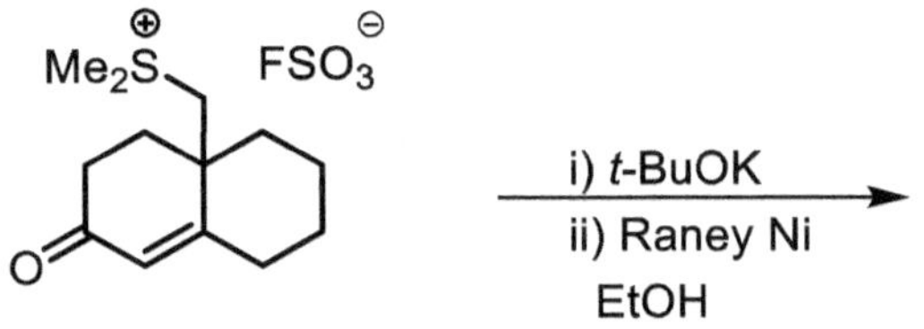

A. 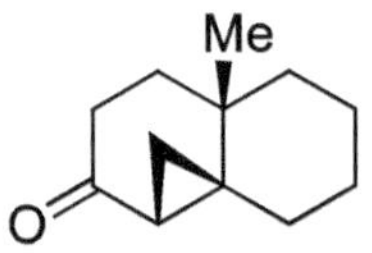   B. 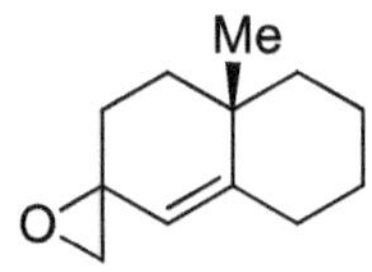   C. 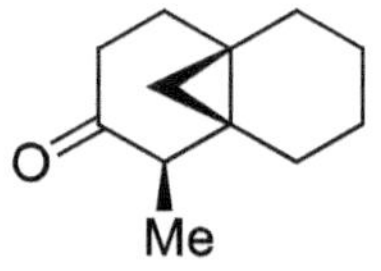   D.

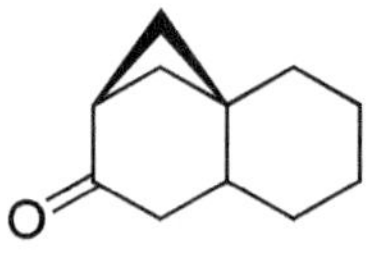

Answer: A. Generally, sulphonium ylide gives 1,2-addition with conjugated carbonyl compounds. Herein, the reaction is proceeding in a conjugate manner due to the rigidity of the given skeleton.

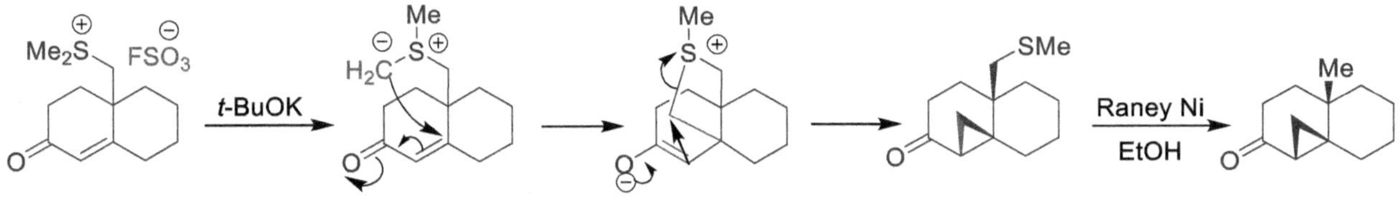

t-BuOK

Raney Ni
EtOH

Matthews, R. S.; Meteyer, T. E. *Chem. Commun.* **1971**, 1576.

Question No-37: The major product formed in the following reaction sequence is

1. CF$_3$COOH

2. BH$_3$ (1 equiv)

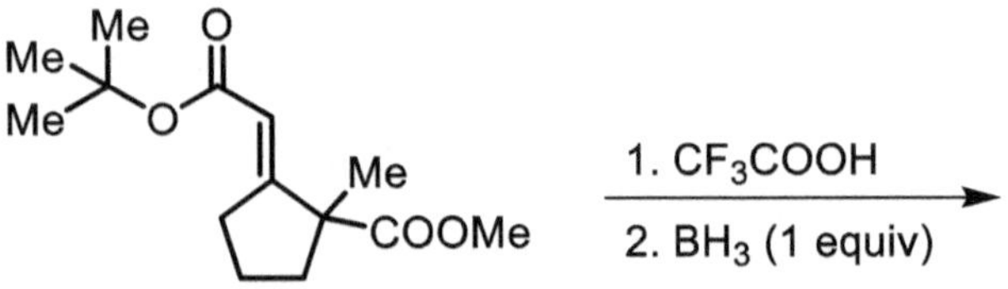

A.

B.

C.

D.

Answer: A. In the first step of the reaction, chemoselective hydrolysis of *t*-butyl ester gives corresponding carboxylic acid while methyl ester is intact. In the next step of the reaction, again borane reduces carboxylic acid in presence of ester, chemoselectively.

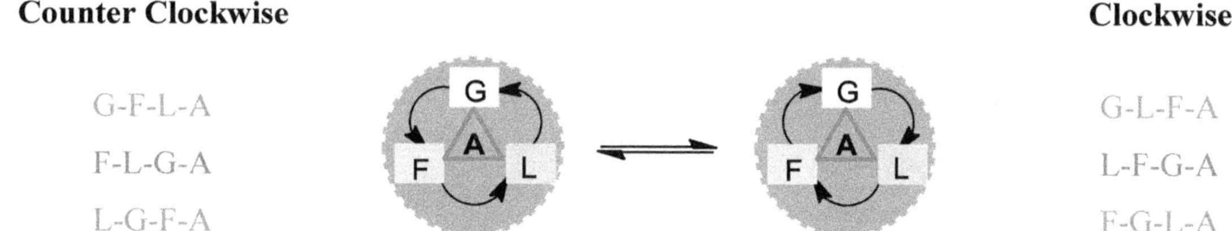

A detail of this is available in this book, GATE-2010, Question Answer No-34.

Question No-41: A tetrapeptide made up of natural amino acids, has alanine as the *N*-terminal residue which is coupled to a chiral amino acid. Upon complete hydrolysis, the tetrapeptide gives glycine, alanine, phenylalanine and leucine. The number of possible sequences of the tetrapeptide is................

Answer: 4. A single word code of glycine, alanine, phenylalanine and leucine are G, A, F and L, respectively. If a tetrapeptide has alanine as the *N*-terminal residue, then the number of possible sequences of the tetrapeptide is six.

Counter Clockwise   **Clockwise**

G-F-L-A   G-L-F-A

F-L-G-A   L-F-G-A

L-G-F-A   F-G-L-A

According to the given question, the alanine as the *N*-terminal residue which is coupled to a chiral amino acid, then only four tetrapeptides are acceptable and the two tetrapeptides **F-L-G-A** and **L-F-G-A** are unacceptable, as glycine doesn't have any chiral carbon center.

Question No-43: The strongest band observed in the IR spectrum of the final product of the following reaction appears, approximately, at............... $\times 100$ cm^{-1}. (Up to one decimal place)

Answer: 16.99-17.31. The strongest band observed in the IR spectrum of the final product in the given reaction appears, approximately, at $(16.99$ to $17.31) \times 100 = 1699$ to 1731 cm^{-1}.

Question No-44: The reaction of PCl_5 with PhLi in 1:3 molar ratio yields **X** as one of the products, which on further treatment with CH$_3$I gives Y with *n*-BuLi gives product **Z**. The products **X**, **Y** and **Z** respectively, are

A.   [PPh$_4$]Cl, Ph$_2$P=CH$_2$ and Ph$_2$P(*n*-Bu)
B.   PPh$_3$, [Ph$_3$PI](CH$_3$) and Ph$_2$P(*n*-Bu)$_3$
C.   PPh$_3$, [Ph$_3$P(CH$_3$)]I and Ph$_3$P=CH$_2$
D.   [PPh$_4$]Cl, Ph$_2$P=CH$_2$ and [Ph$_3$P(*n*-Bu)]Li

Answer: C. The given sequence of reactions is widely employed for the synthesis of methylene phosphonium ylide (Wittig reagent).

Question No-48: The major product formed in the following retro-aldol reaction is

Answer: B. The protonation of the given compound undergoes retro-aldol reaction which further converts into fragmented product 2-((1S,2R)-2-(hydroxymethyl)-4-oxo-2-vinylcyclohexyl)acetaldehyde.

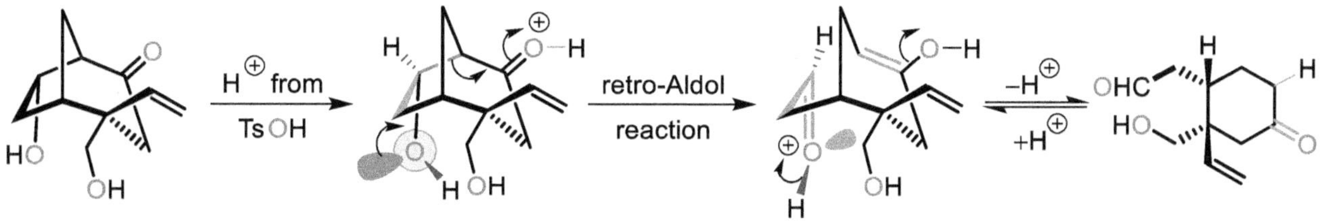

Question No-48: The enantiomeric pair, among the following is

A.

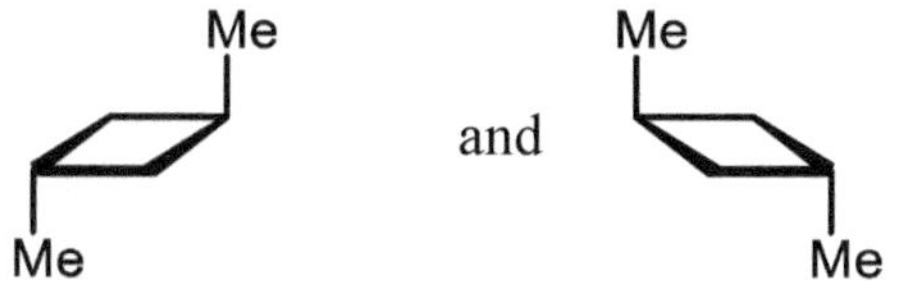

B.

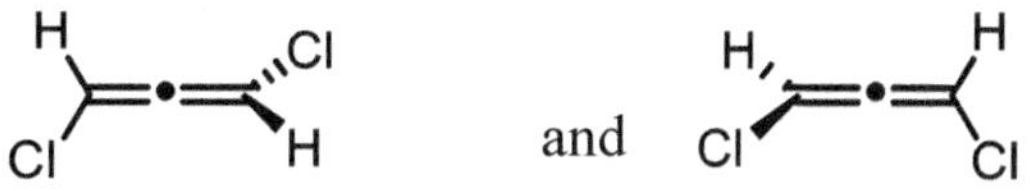

C.

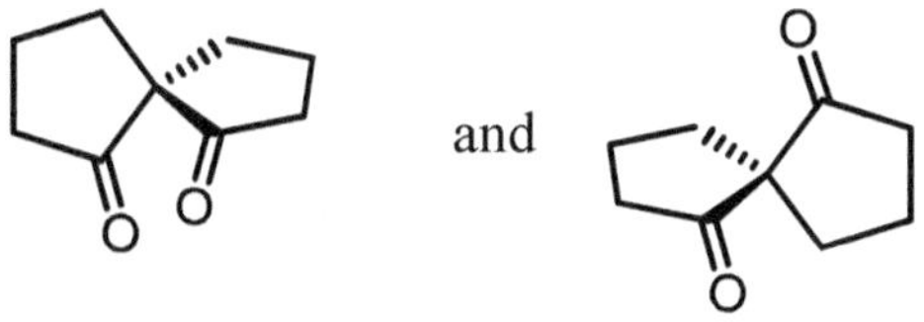

D.

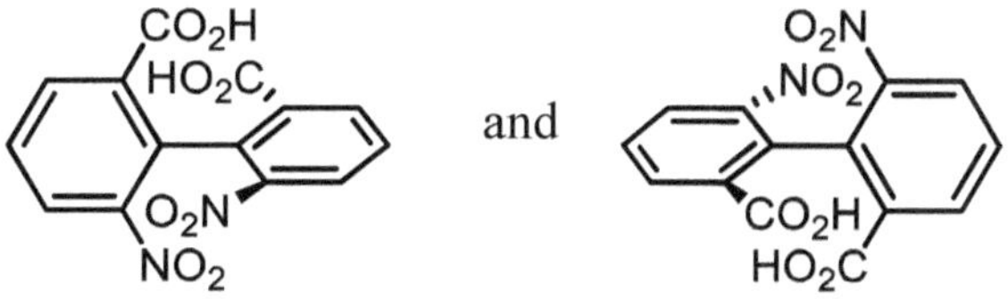

Answer: D. Among these, 6,6'-dinitro-[1,1'-biphenyl]-2,2'-dicarboxylic acid is present in the form of enantiomeric pair.

A.

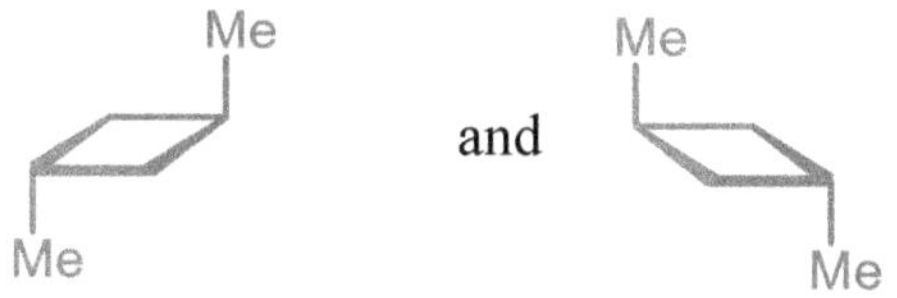

B.

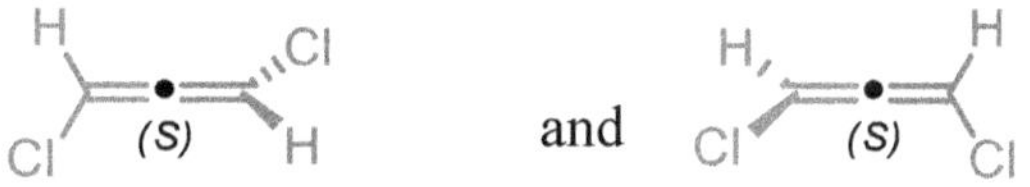

C.

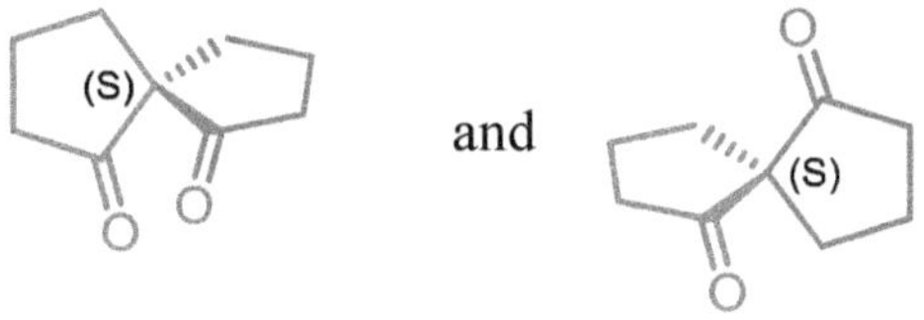

D.

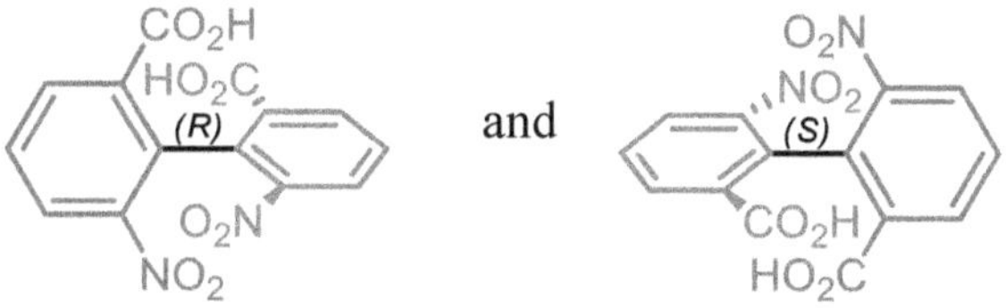

Question No-49: In the following reaction is

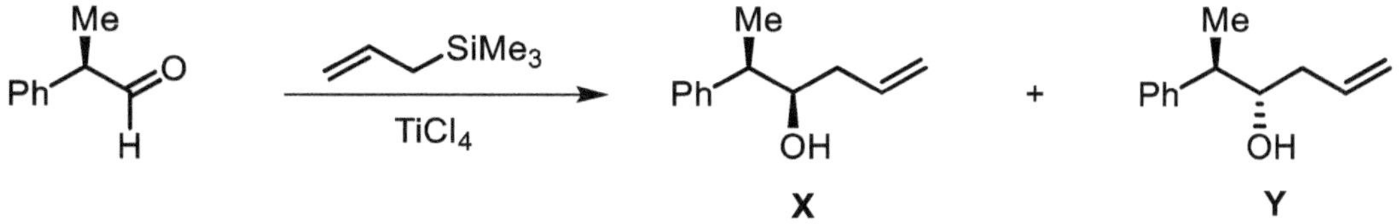

A. **X** is the major product and **Y** is the minor product

B. **X** is the only product

C. **Y** is the only product

D. **X** is the minor product and **Y** is the major product

Answer: A. The formation of major and minor products can easily be visualized by the Felkin-Anh model which is shown as follows.

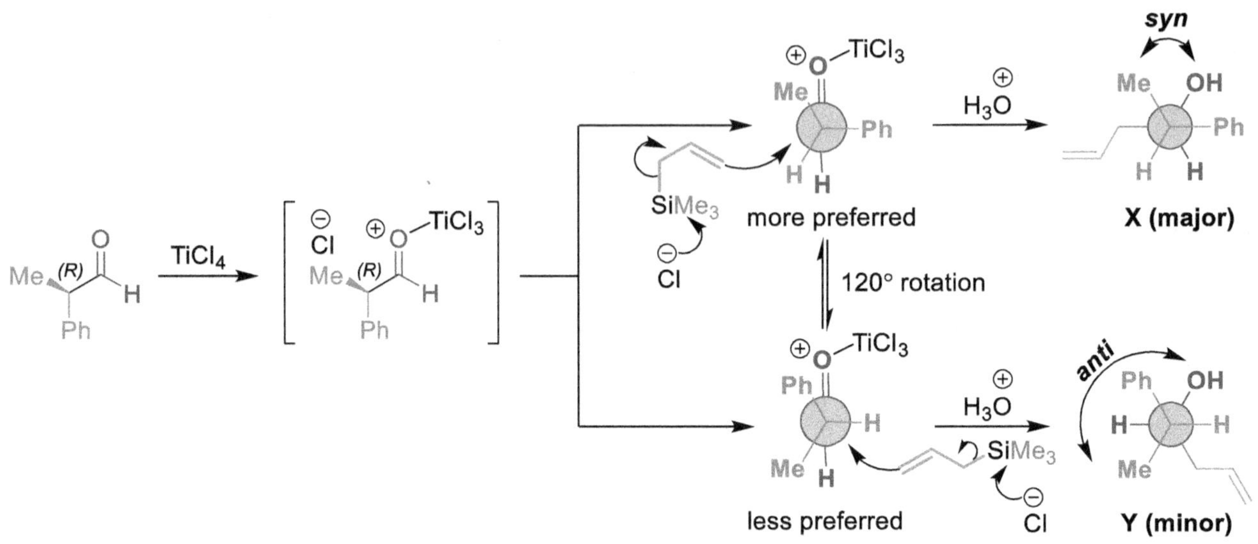

Note. The attack of allyl-silane (activated by chloride ion) occurred from the less substituted site when the larger substituents having a perpendicular relationship with carbonyl offer a major product (**X**) that can be seen in the case of the more preferred conformational transition state pathway.

Question No-3: Among the following carbon allotropes, the one that discrete molecular structure is

A. Diamond   **B.** α-Graphite   **C.** β-Graphite   **D.** Fullerene

Answer: D. Among these the one that discrete molecular structure is fullerene.

Question No-9: The major product formed in the following reaction is

A.   **B.**   **C.**   **D.**

Answer: B. The major product formed in the given reaction *via* neighboring group participation (NGP or anchimeric assistance) of double bond which leads to the formation of *syn*-attacked product.

Question No-10: The Woodward-Hoffmann condition to bring out the following transformation is

A. Δ, conrotatory   **B.** Δ, disrotatory   **C.** *hv*, disrotatory   **D.** *hv*, conrotatory

Answer: D. The Woodward-Hoffmann condition to bring out the given transformation is an example of photochemical (*hv*) 6π-electrons electrocyclic conrotatory ring closer reactions (clockwise as well as anticlockwise).

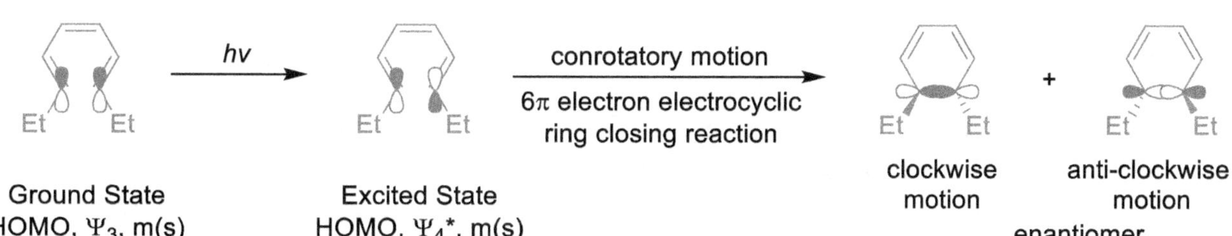

Question No-11: The major product formed in the following reaction is

$$\text{(}\beta\text{-lactone, } Cl_3C\text{ substituted)} \xrightarrow[\text{Benzene, 5 °C}]{Et_2AlCl}$$

A.

$$\underset{Cl_3C}{\overset{OH \quad O}{\diagdown}}Ph$$

B.

$$\underset{Cl_3C}{\overset{OH \quad O}{\diagdown}}Ph$$

C.

$$\underset{Cl_3C}{\overset{Ph \quad O}{\diagdown}}OH$$

D.

$$\underset{Cl_3C}{\overset{Ph \quad O}{\diagdown}}OH$$

Answer: B. The major product formed in the given reaction is (R)-4,4,4-trichloro-3-hydroxy-1-phenylbutan-1-one.

Question No-12: In the following reaction, the stereochemistry of the major product is predicted by the

$$Ph-\underset{Et}{\overset{O}{\underset{|}{C}}}-\underset{}{\overset{Ph}{\underset{}{C}}}-OMe \xrightarrow{EtLi} \text{(Newman projection product)}$$

A. Cram's model

B. Cram's chelation model

C. Felkin model

D. Felkin-Anh model

Answer: B. In the given reaction, the stereochemistry of the major product is predicted by Cram's chelation model.

Cram's chelation model

Question No-13: The product(s) formed in the following reaction is(are)

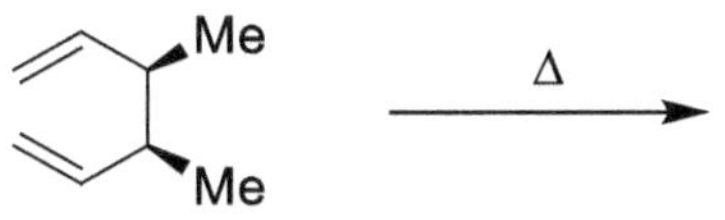

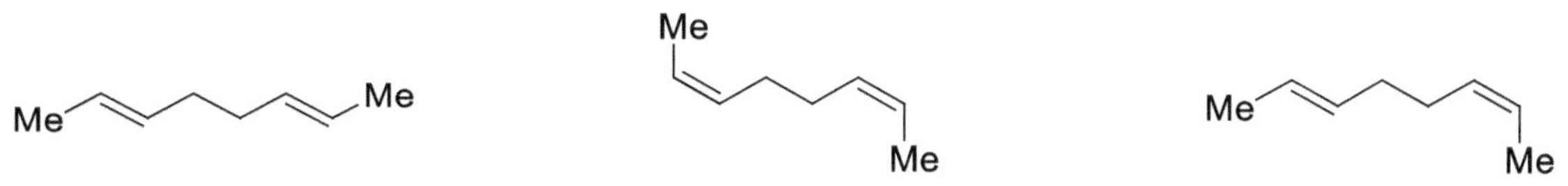

I   II   III

Codes

A.   **I** only   B.   **II** only   C.   **III** only   D.   mixture of **I** and **II**

Answer: C. The product formed in the given reaction is (2Z,6E)-octa-2,6-diene *via* 6π-electrons i.e. [4π + 2σ]e⁻-system having non-degenerate thermal [3,3]-sigmatropic shift (Cope rearrangement).

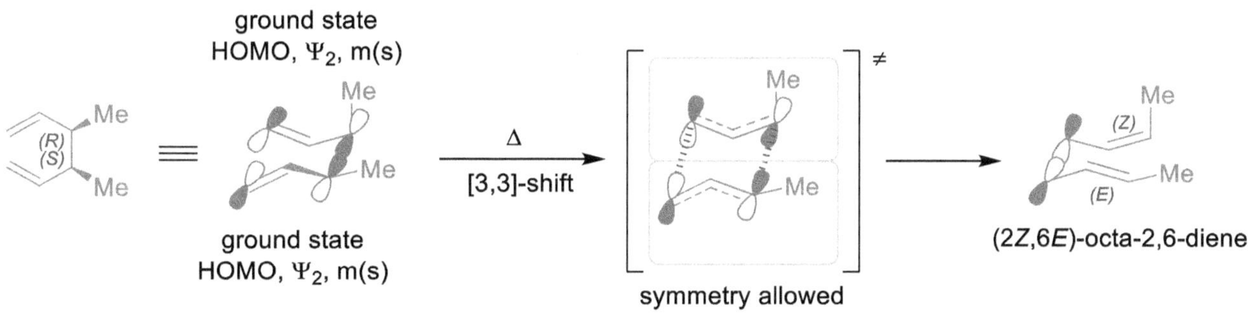

Question No-14: Among the following compounds, the number of compounds that *do not* exhibit optical activity at room temperature is______________

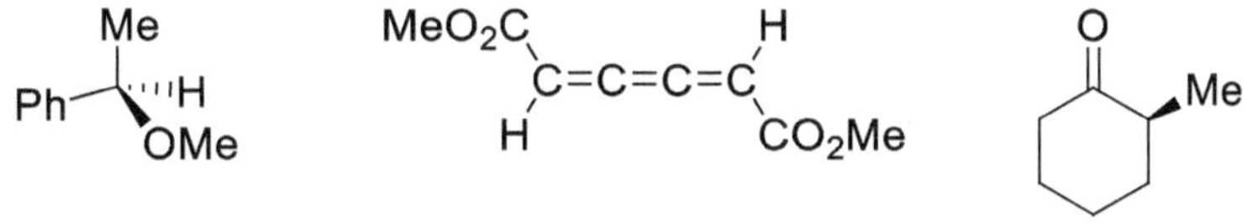

A   B   C

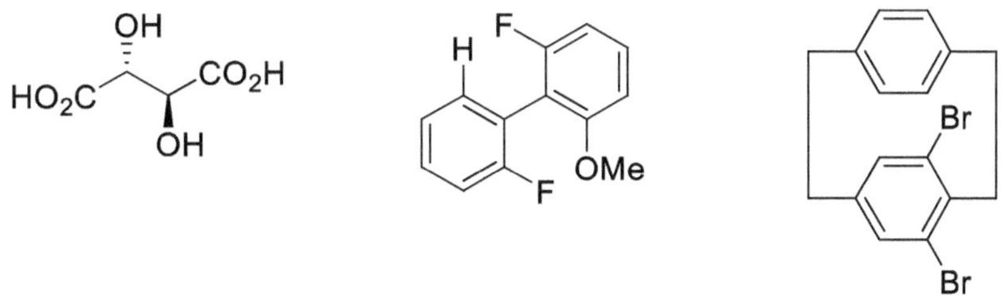

D   E   F

Answer: 4. Among these, the number of compounds **B, D, E** and **F** do not exhibit optical activity at room temperature is *four*.

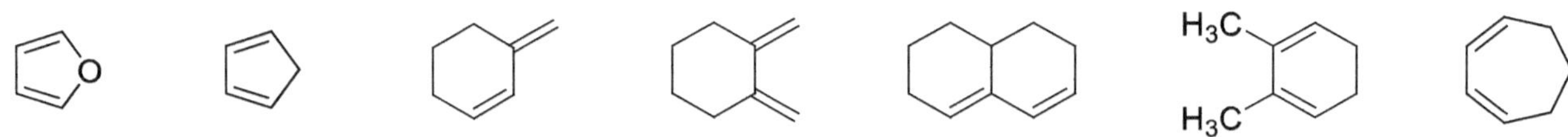

Question No-15: The number of following diene(s) that undergo Diels-Alder reaction with methyl acrylate is_______________

Answer: 5. The number of given *cis*-dienes I, II, IV, VI and VII that undergo Diels-Alder reaction with methyl acrylate is *five*.

I	II	III	IV	V	VI	VII

Question No-16: The number of ^{1}H NMR signals observed for the following compound is_______________

Answer: 5. The number of ^{1}H NMR signals observed for the following compound is *five*.

Question No-24: In a 400 MHz ^{1}H NMR spectrometer, a proton resonates at 1560 Hz higher than that of tetramethylsilane. The chemical shift value of this proton is________ppm. (Round off to one decimal place)

(Chemical shift of tetramethylsilane is fixed at zero ppm)

Answer: 3.9. The chemical shift value of this proton = 1560Hz/400MHz = **3.9** ppm.

Question No-34: The major product formed in the following reaction is

$$n\text{-Bu}_3\text{SnH, AIBN} \quad \xrightarrow{\text{Benzene, }\Delta}$$

(AIBN = azobisisobutyronitrile)

A.

B.

C.

D.

Answer: A. The major product formed in the given reaction is methyl 5-oxocyclodecane-1-carboxylate.

Question No-35: The major product formed in the following reaction is

$$\xrightarrow[\text{2. H}^{\oplus}]{\text{1. B}_2\text{H}_6}$$

A.

B.

C.

D.

Answer: B. The chemoselective reduction of the carbonyl group of a carboxylic acid in presence of an ester with diborane produces intermediate **B** which upon treatment with acid produces a major product (*R*)-4-isopropyltetrahydropyran-2-one.

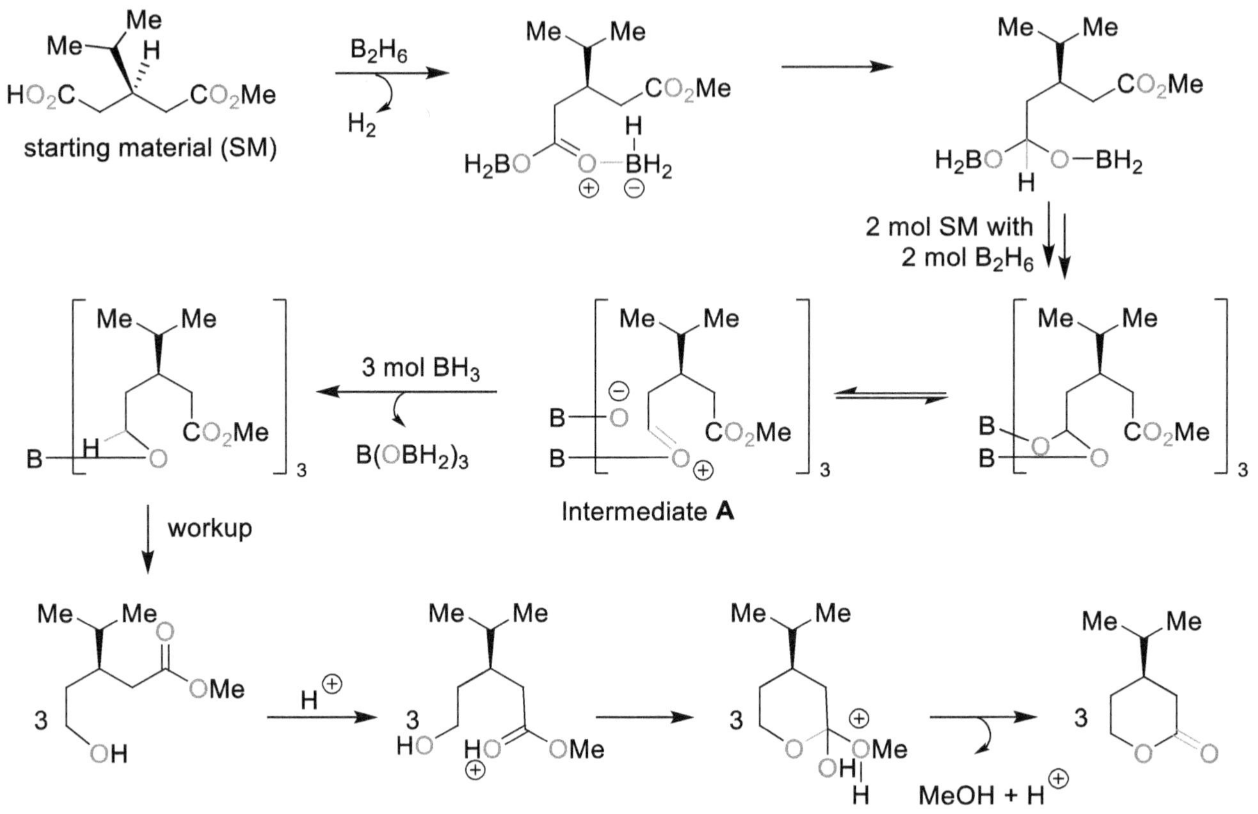

Question No-36: The major product formed in the following reaction is

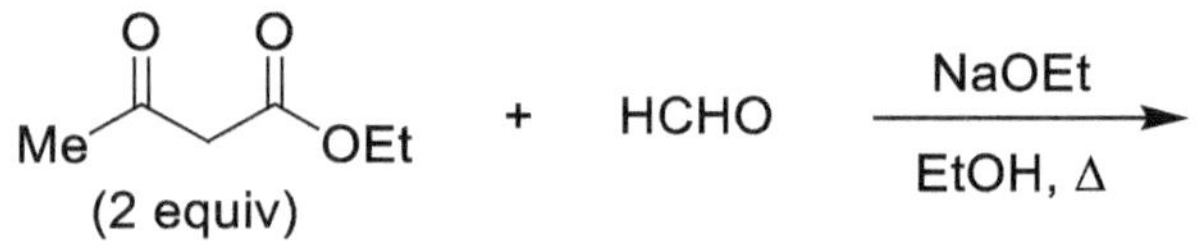

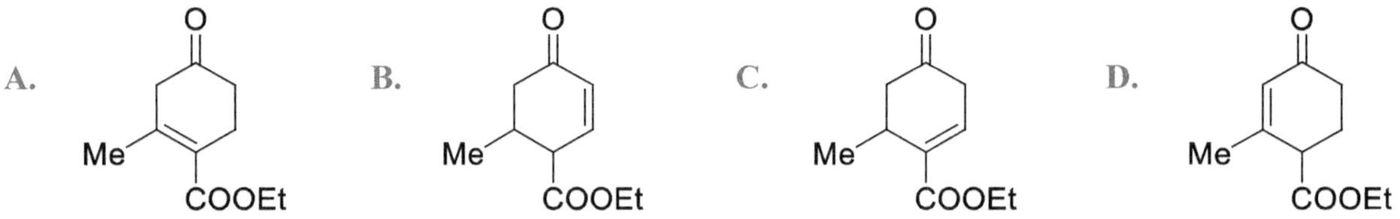

$$\text{Me-C(O)-CH}_2\text{-C(O)-OEt} \quad (2 \text{ equiv}) \quad + \quad \text{HCHO} \xrightarrow[\text{EtOH, } \Delta]{\text{NaOEt}}$$

A.

B.

C.

D.

Answer: D. The major product formed in the given Claisen condensation is ethyl 2-methyl-4-oxocyclohex-2-ene-1-carboxylate.

Question No-37: The major product formed in the following reaction is

$$\text{(cyclobutanecarbaldehyde)} \xrightarrow[\text{2. HCl}]{\text{1. MeMgCl}}$$

A. (1-chloroethyl)cyclobutane

B. (1-chloro...)cyclobutane

C. 1-chloro-2-methylcyclopentane

D. 1-chloro-1-methylcyclopentane

Answer: D. The major product formed in the given reaction is 1-chloro-1-methylcyclopentane.

Question No-38: In the following reaction sequence, the products **P** and **Q** are

$$\text{(reaction scheme with Pd(OAc)}_2 \text{ (cat.), PPh}_3 / \text{Ag}_2\text{CO}_3, \text{DMSO}, \Delta \rightarrow P \xrightarrow[\text{2. Ac}_2\text{O, Et}_3\text{N}]{\text{1. LiAlH}_4, \text{ether}} Q)$$

A. P / Q

B. P / Q

C. P / Q

D. P / Q

Answer: C. In the given reaction sequence, the products **P** and **Q** are 2-(9-tosyl-1,2,9,9a-tetrahydro-4a*H*-carbazol-4-a-yl)acetonitrile   and   *N*-(2-(9-tosyl-1,2,9,9a-tetrahydro-4a*H*-carbazol-4a-yl)ethyl)acetamide, respectively.

Question No-39: The major product formed in the following reaction is

$$\xrightarrow[\text{2. ZnBr}_2]{\text{1. PCC}}$$

(PCC = pyridinium chlorochromate)

A. **B.** **C.** **D.**

Answer: C. The oxidation of the given alcohol followed by $ZnBr_2$ catalyzed Metallo-ene reaction yields a major product of a monoterpenoid (+)-isopulegol in *trans*-relation with hydroxyl and isopropenyl group.

Sousa, C.; Leitão, A. J.; Neves, B. M.; Judas, F.; Cavaleiro, C.; Mendes, A. F. *Scientific Reports* **2020**, *10*, 7199. https://doi.org/10.1038/s41598-020-64032-1.

Question No-40: In the following reaction sequence, the products **P** and **Q** are

$$Q \xleftarrow[\substack{\text{benzene, 0 °C} \\ R = H}]{PhCO_3H} \qquad \xrightarrow[\substack{\text{benzene, 0 °C} \\ R = COEt}]{PhCO_3H} P$$

P **Q** **P** **Q**

A. **B.**

C. **D.**

Answer: B. The diastereoselective major product of the epoxidation of cyclohexenol-2 with *m*-CPBA produces an epoxide ring with *syn*-selectivity **Q** (hydroxyl group), whereas in the case of the protected hydroxyl group it ends up with the *anti*-selectivity **P**.

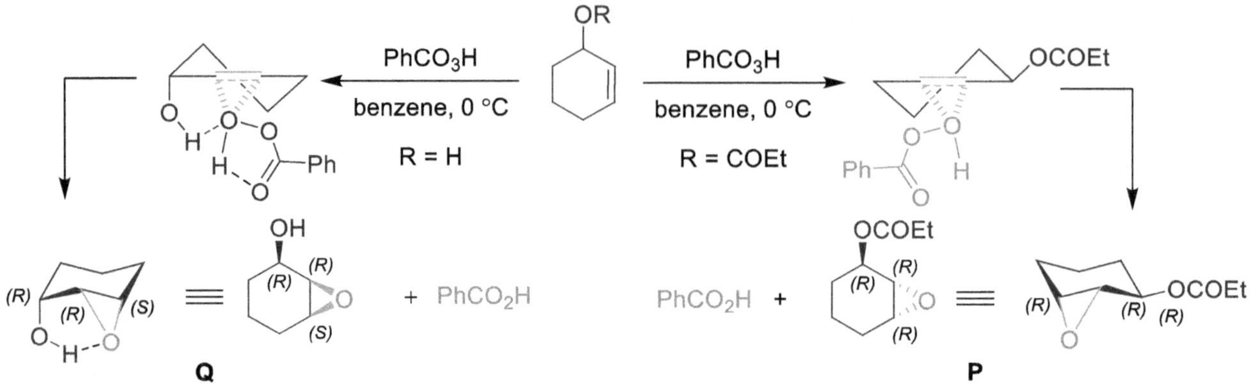

Question No-41: In the following reaction sequence, the products **P** and **Q** are

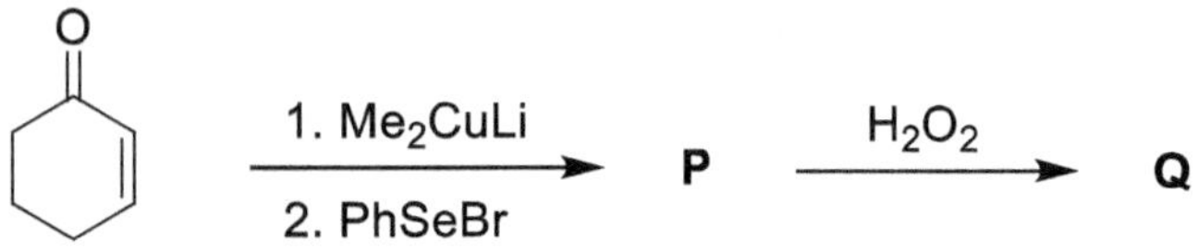

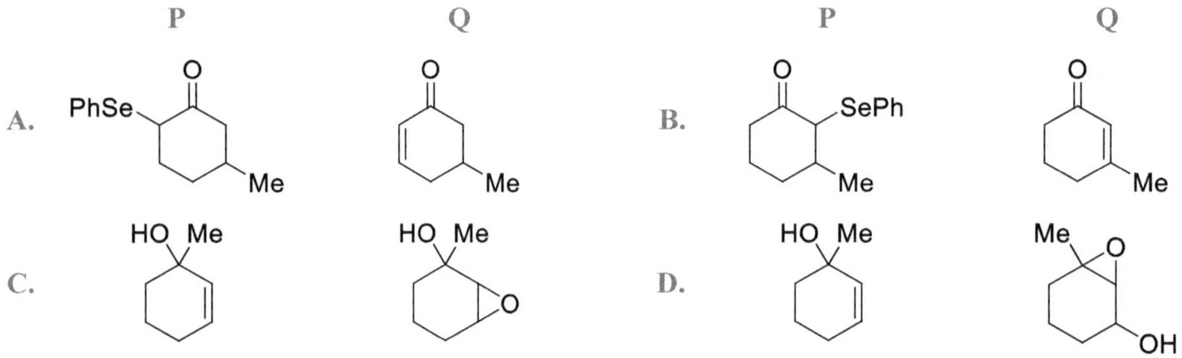

P — 1. Me$_2$CuLi / 2. PhSeBr → **P** — H$_2$O$_2$ → **Q**

	P	**Q**		**P**	**Q**
A.			B.		
C.			D.		

Answer: B. The conjugate nucleophilic addition of a given Gillman reagent with cyclohexenone-2 then reaction with phenylselenyl bromide offers *trans*-3-methyl-2-(phenylselanyl)cyclohexan-1-one. At last, it undergoes selenium oxidation with H$_2$O$_2$ and intramolecular pericyclic *syn*-elimination yields 3-methylcyclohex-2-en-1-one.

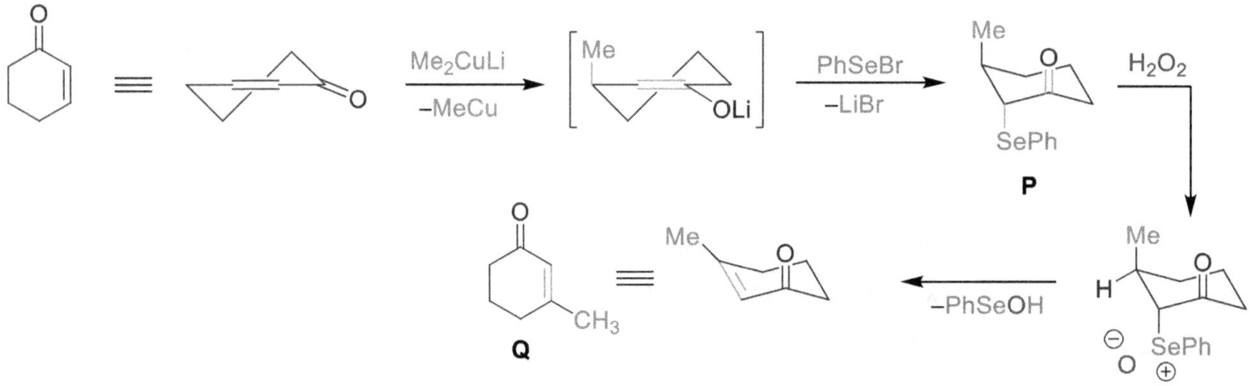

Question No-42: The major product formed in the following reaction is

$$\text{(pyridine N-oxide with CH}_3\text{)} \xrightarrow{(CH_3CO)_2O}$$

A. (structure: pyridine N-oxide with CH₂COCH₃) **B.** (structure: COCH₃ substituted pyridine N-oxide with CH₃) **C.** (structure: pyridine with CH₂OCOCH₃) **D.** (structure: OCOCH₃ substituted pyridine with CH₃)

Answer: C. The major product formed in the given reaction is pyridin-2-ylmethyl acetate.

$$\text{(pyridine N-oxide, CH}_3) \xrightarrow[-AcO^{\ominus}]{(MeCO)_2O} \left[\text{intermediate} \right] \xrightarrow[-AcOH]{AcO^{\ominus}} \text{intermediate} \xrightarrow[\text{[3,3]-shift}]{\Delta} \text{pyridin-2-ylmethyl acetate}$$

Question No-46: The specific rotation of optically pure (R)-2-bromobutane is -112.00. A given sample of 2-bromobutane exhibited a specific rotation of -82.88. The percentage of (S)-(+)-enantiomer present in this sample is______________

Answer: 13%. The % pure enantiomeric excess of (R)-2-bromobutane in the sample mixture i.e. the

$$\text{optical purity of the sample} = \left[\frac{\text{specific rotation exhibited by sample mixture } (-82.88)}{\text{the specific rotation of optically pure compound } (-112.0)} \right] \times 100 = 74\%$$

The total amount of enantiomer of any sample $= 100\%$

The equimolar mixture of R and S-2-bromobutane of enantiomer $= 100 - 74 = 26\%$

Thus, the concentration of (R) enantiomer is 13% and (S) enantiomer is also 13% i.e. 13% of each isomer in an equal amount.

Question No-1: Among the following, the suitable reagent for the given transformation is

A. H_2, Pd/C B. H_2N-NH_2/KOH, Δ C. $NaBH_4$/CeCl$_3$.7H$_2$O D. Li/Liq. NH$_3$

Answer: C. The major reduced product obtained in the given reaction *via* using $NaBH_4$/CeCl$_3$.7H$_2$O regent system (Luche reduction) is 3-cyclopentene-1-ol.

Note. The coordination of oxygen of ketone with Cerous chloride or Cerium trichloride makes it more hard center (more electrophilic) of the carbonyl carbon that helps to get an exclusive major 1,2-addition product with sodium borohydride.

Gemal, A. L.; Luche, J.-L. *J. Am. Chem. Soc.* **1981**, *103*, 5454.

Question No-2: Major product formed in the following reaction sequence is

(i) Li/Liq. NH$_3$, *t*-BuOH

(ii) O$_3$ (1 equiv), MeOH, Me$_2$S

A.

B.

C.

D.

Answer: C. The Birch reduction of 2-ethyl-4-methylanisole offered 2-ethyl-1-methoxy-4-methylcyclohexa-1,4-diene as a major product. Next, it reacts with ozone and dimethylsulfide in methanol to give methyl (Z)-4-methyl-6-oxooct-3-enoate. This transformation proceeds *via* chemoselective oxidative cleavage of electron-rich carbon-carbon double bond.

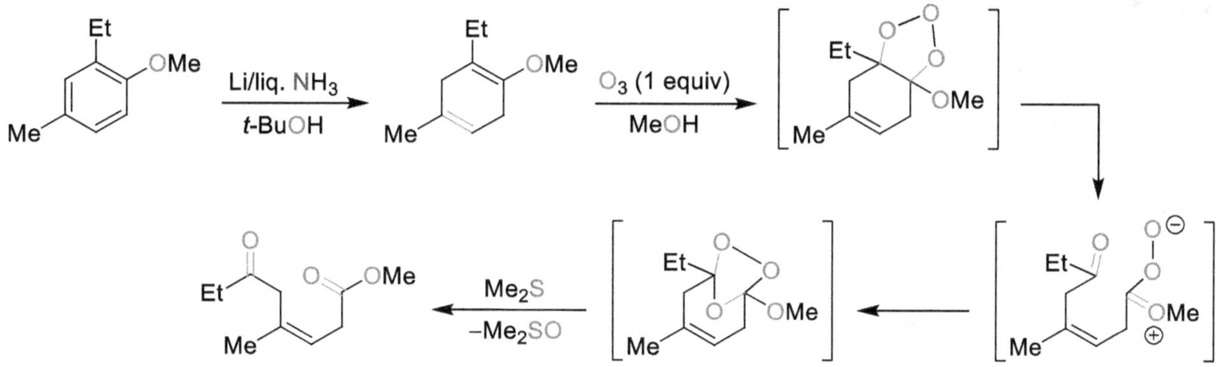

Question No-3: The major product formed in the following reaction is

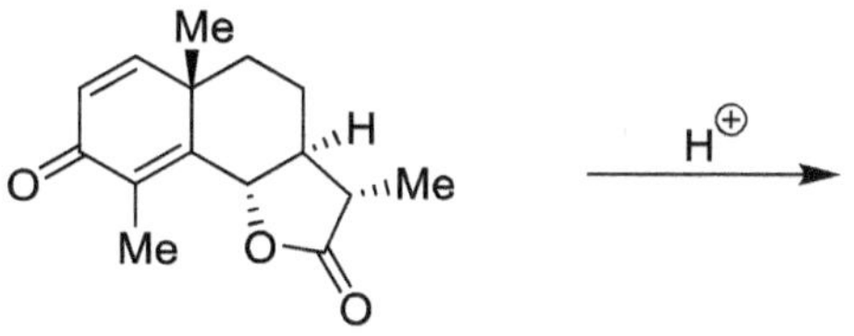

A.

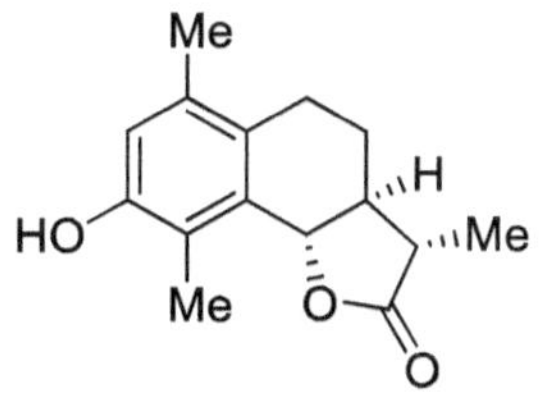

B.

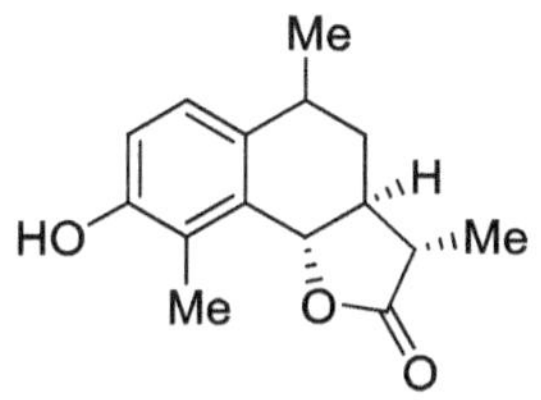

C.

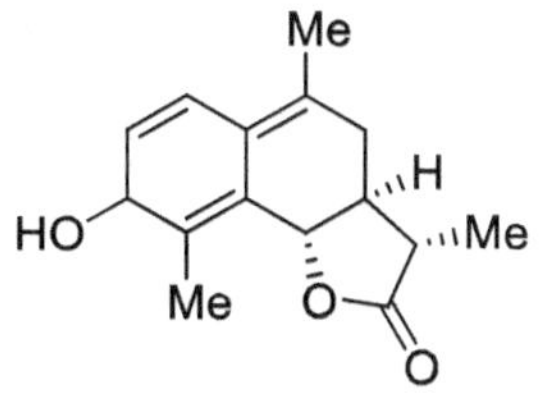

D.

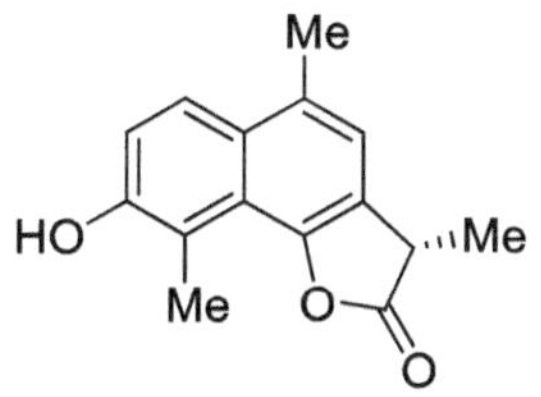

Answer: A. The major product formed in the given reaction is the phenol derivative which proceeds through Dienone–Phenol rearrangement.

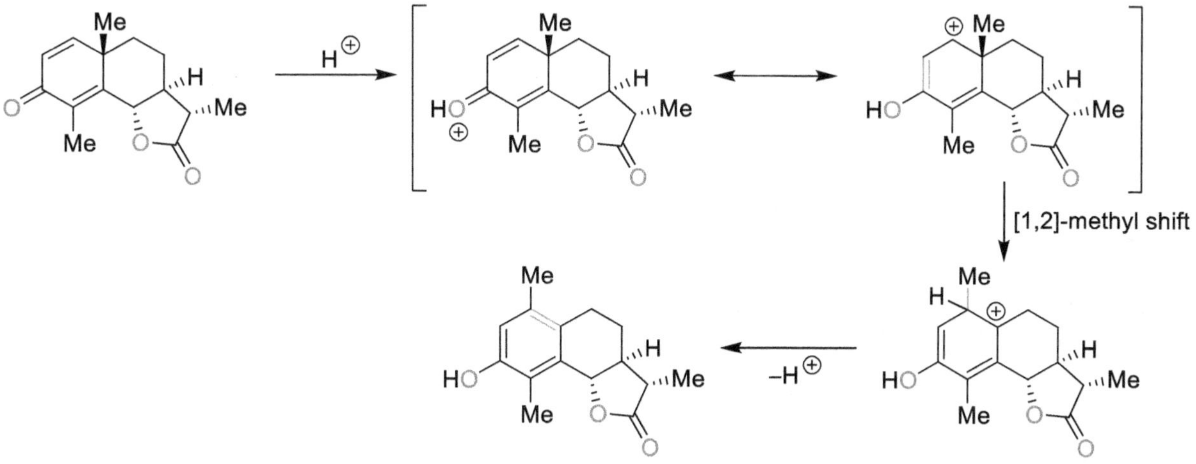

[1,2]-methyl shift

Question No-4: Major product formed in the following transformation is

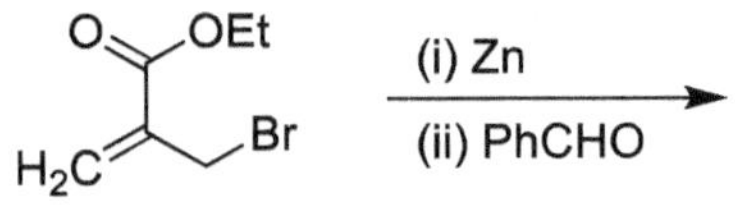

(i) Zn
(ii) PhCHO

A. 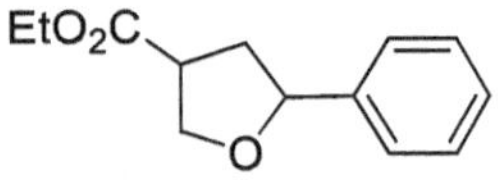 B. 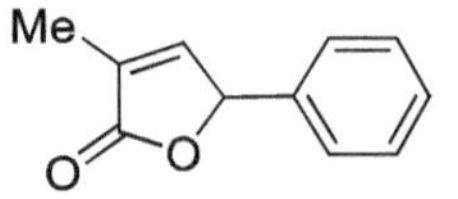 C. 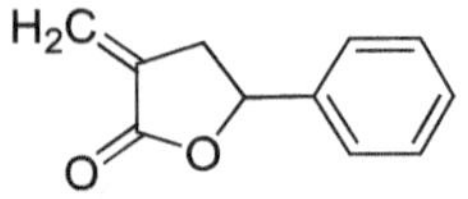 D.

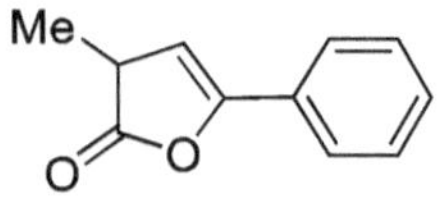

Answer: C. The reaction of allyl bromide with zinc offered organozincbromide derivative which further reacts with benzaldehyde yields a five-membered cyclic ring derivative.

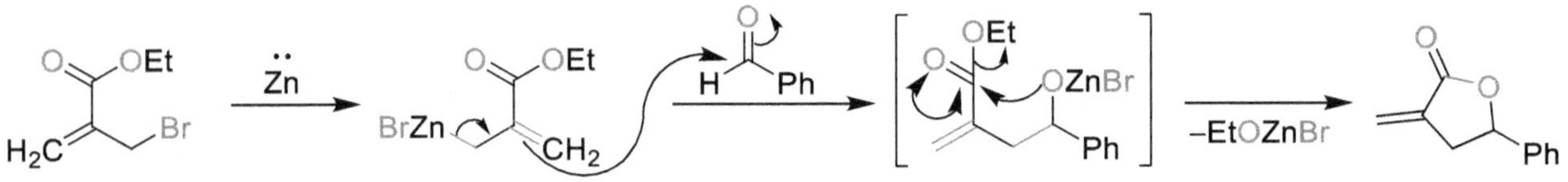

Question No-5: Absolute configuration of the given compound is

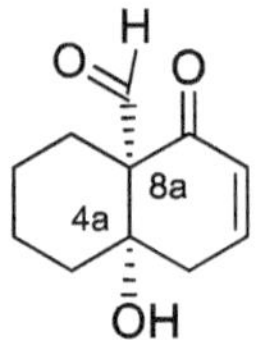

A. 4aR, 8aS B. 4aR, 8aR C. 4aS, 8aS D. 4aS, 8aR

Answer: D. The absolute configuration of the above compound is 4a (S) and 8a (R).

Question No-6: In the following reaction sequence

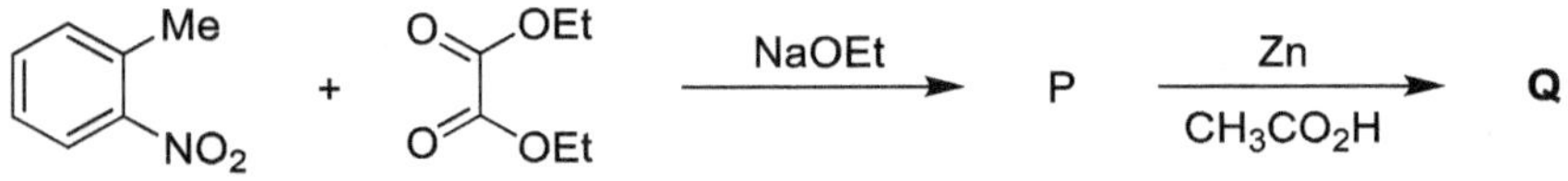

$$\text{NaOEt} \longrightarrow P \xrightarrow{\text{Zn}, \ \text{CH}_3\text{CO}_2\text{H}} Q$$

the major products **P** and **Q** are

A.   B.

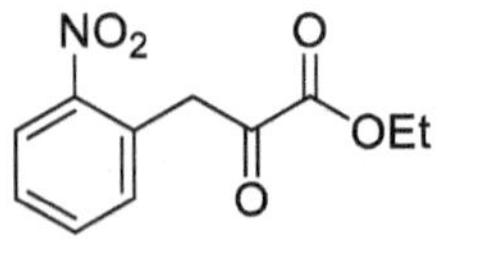

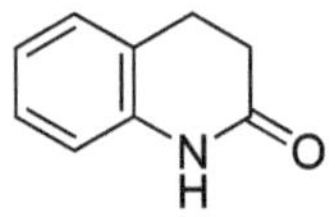

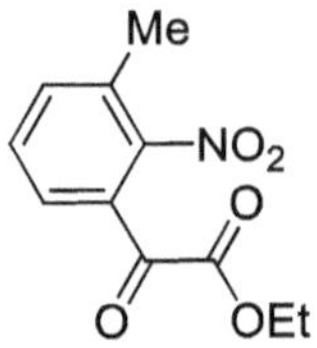

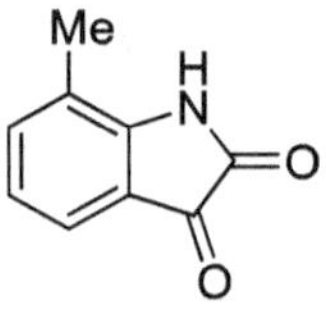

C.

D.

Answer: C. The reaction of 1-methyl-2-nitrobenzene with diethyl oxalate in the presence of sodium ethoxide gives ethyl 3-(2-nitrophenyl)-2-oxopropanoate (compound **P**). Furthermore, in situ-generated compound **P** was reduced to ethyl 3-(2-aminophenyl)-2-oxopropanoate using Zn/AcOH. Finally, condensation with carbonyl group and [1,5]-sigmatropic shift leads to ethyl indole-2-carboxylate as a major product **Q**.

Question No-7: The major product formed in the given reaction is

$$\alpha\text{-D-glucose} \xrightarrow[\text{H}^+]{\text{acetone (excess)}}$$

A.

B.

C.

D.

Answer: B. The reaction of α-D-glucose with acetone in the presence of acid provides a nonreducing sugar furanose derivative of diacetonide i.e. 1,2,5,6-dioxopropylidene glucose.

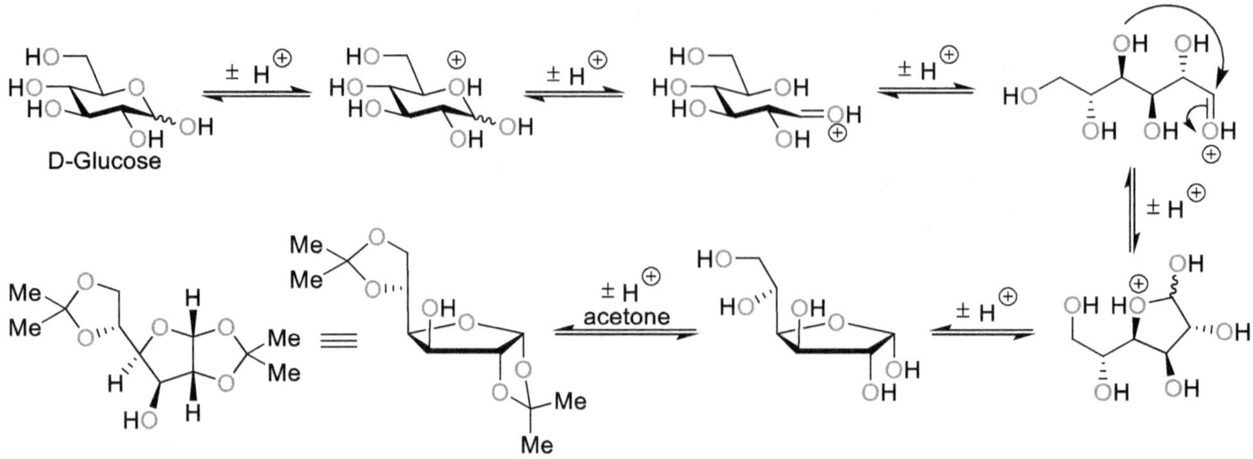

Note. The absence of acetal group in the sugars at the anomeric carbon belongs to the category of non-reducing sugars.

Question No-16: In the following reaction:

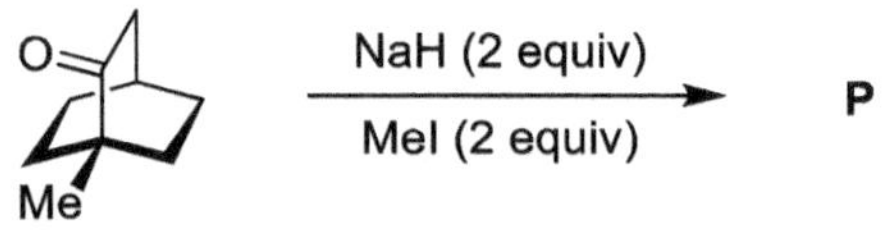

P

the number of peaks exhibited by the major product **P** in its broadband proton decoupled ^{13}C NMR spectrum is______

Answer: 8. In the given reaction, the total number of peaks exhibited by the major product **P** in its broadband proton decoupled ^{13}C NMR spectrum is **8** (eight).

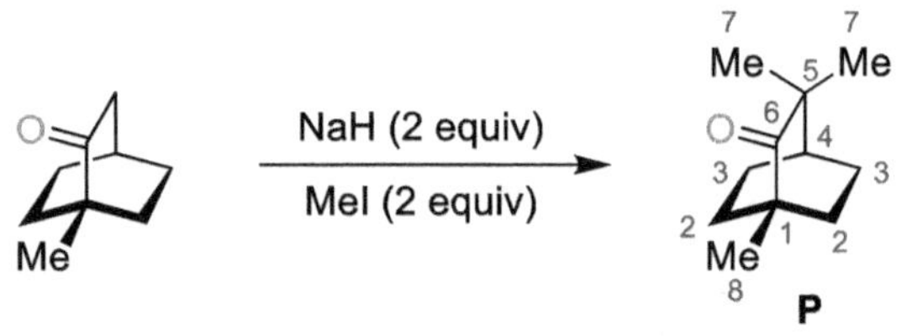

Question No-16: Among the following,

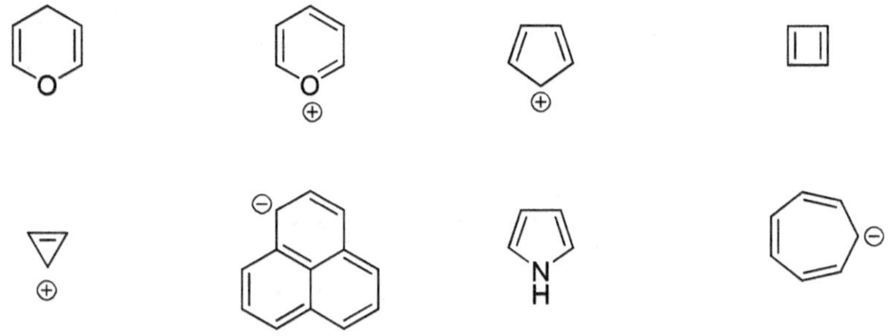

the total number of aromatic species is______

Answer: 4. Among these, the total number of aromatic species is **four**. The compound **A** (4*H*-pyran) in an aliphatic cyclic compound. The compounds **B** (pyrylium), **E** (2-cyclopropen-1-ylium), **F** (1*H*-phenalenide-1) and **G** (pyrrole) are aromatic [obeys (4n + 2)π electron rule] and compounds **C** (2,4-cyclopentadien-1-ylium), **D** (1,3-cyclobutadiene) and **H** (2,4,6-cycloheptatrien-1-ide) are antiaromatic [obeys (4n)π electron rule].

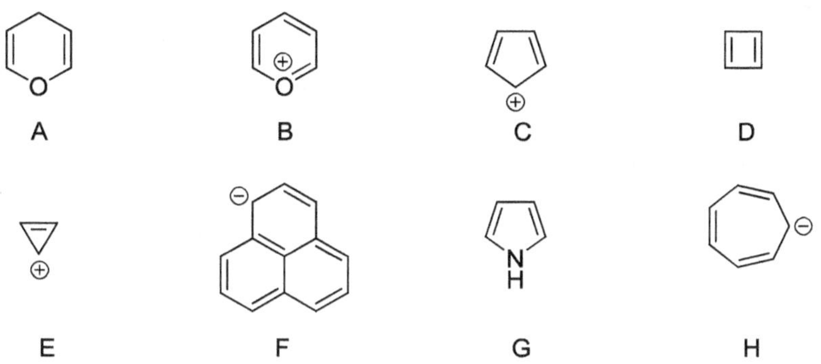

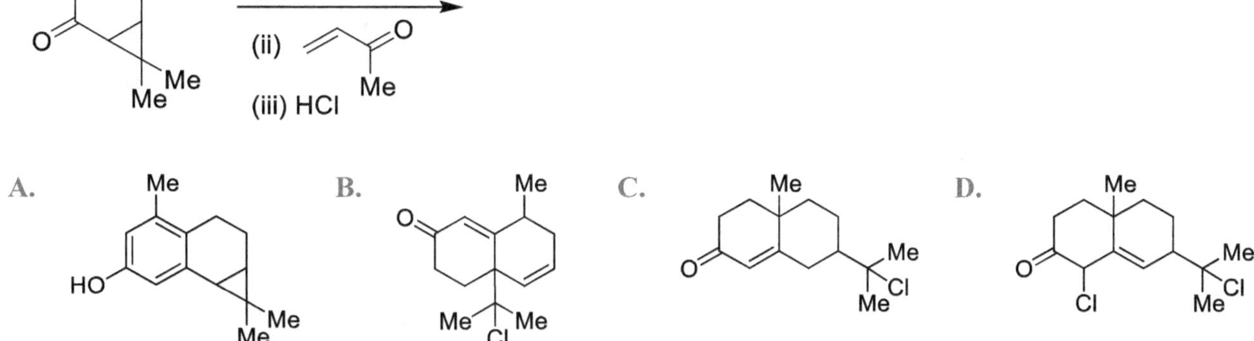

Question No-26: The major product form in the following reaction sequence is

A. B. C. D.

Answer: C. The major product form in the given reaction proceeds *via* Michael addition followed by aldol condensation (Robinson annulation) is 7-(2-chloropropan-2-yl)-4a-methyl-4,4a,5,6,7,8-hexahydronaphthalen-2(3*H*)-one.

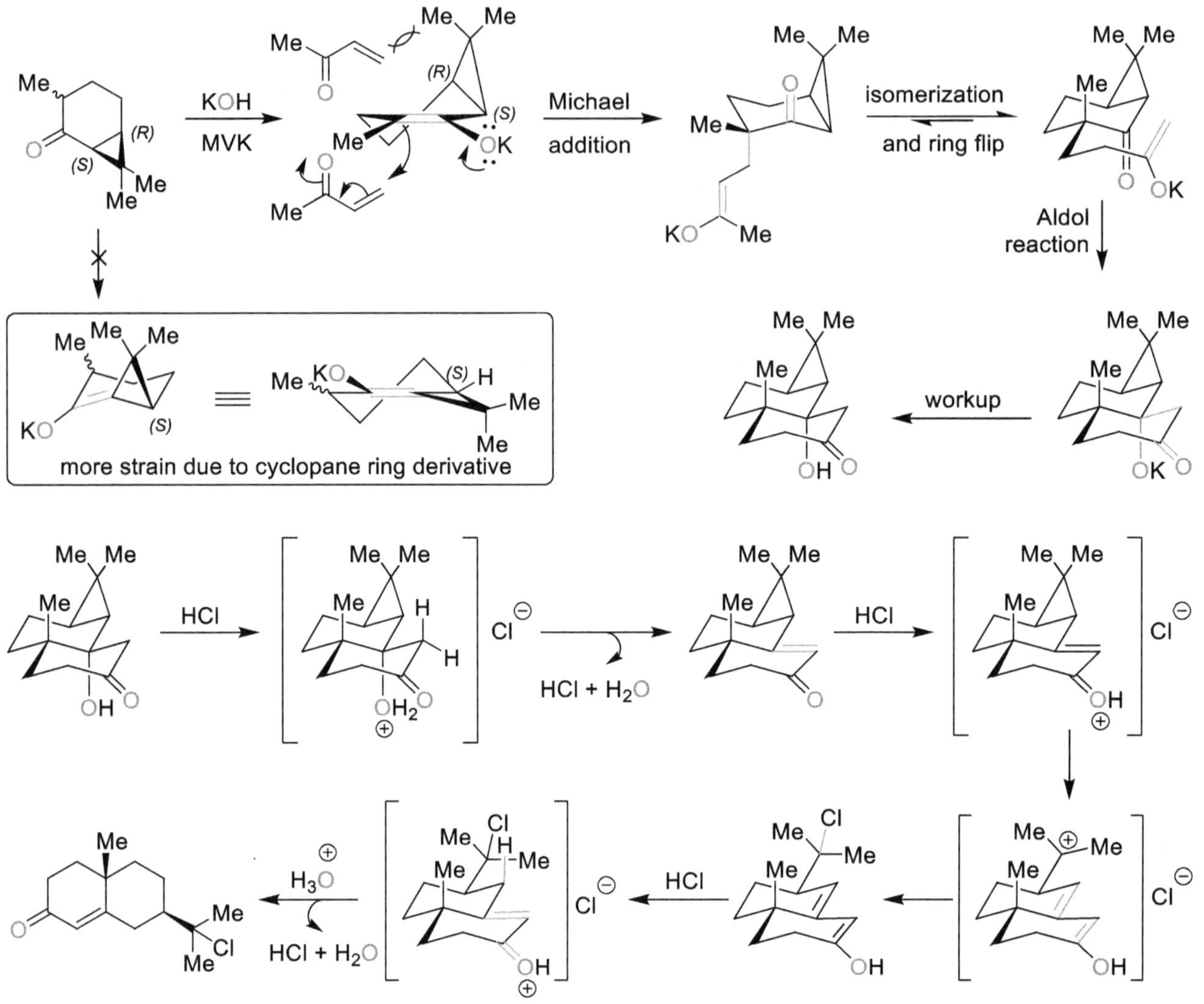

Clayden, J.; Greeves, N.; Warren, S. Participation, Rearrangement, and Fragmentation. In *Organic Chemistry*; 2nd Ed.; Oxford University Press **2012**, pp 966-967.

Question No-27: The major products **P** and **Q**, in the given reaction sequence are

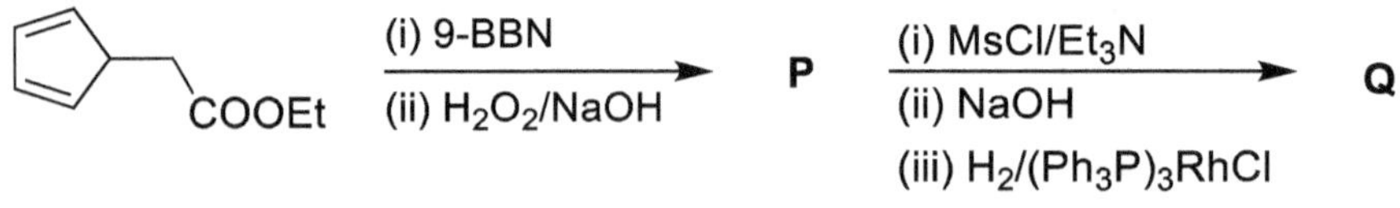

(i) 9-BBN
(ii) H_2O_2/NaOH → **P**

(i) MsCl/Et_3N
(ii) NaOH
(iii) H_2/$(Ph_3P)_3RhCl$ → **Q**

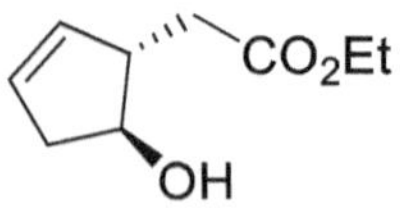

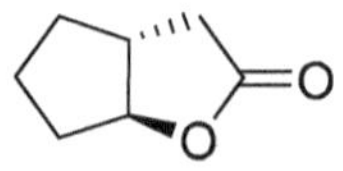

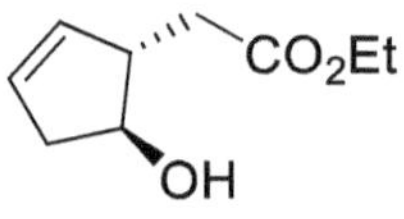

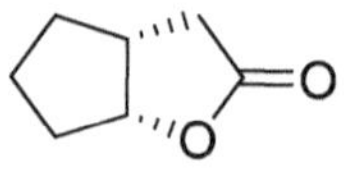

C.

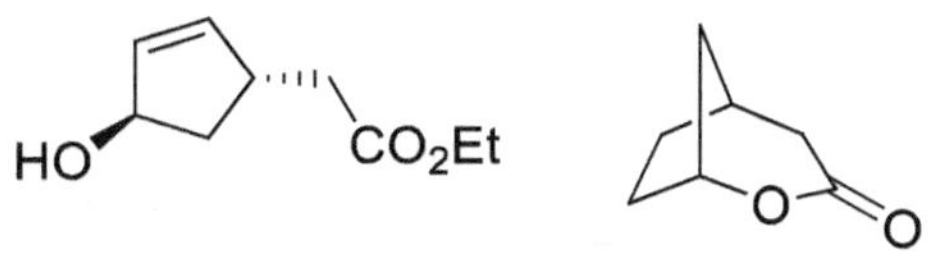

D.

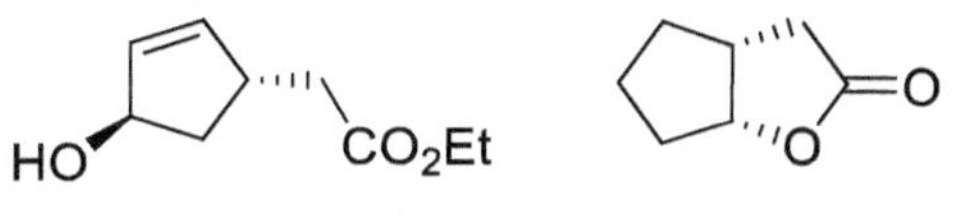

Answer: B. The reaction starts with chemo- and regioselective reduction of the given cyclopentadiene derivative with 9-borabicyclo 3.3.1 nonane (9-BBN) followed by oxidation giving hydroxylated product **P**. Later on, it reacts with MsC*l* in the presence of triethyl amine (TEA) and then with NaOH produces a fused bicyclic five-membered product. Upon reduction with Wilkinson's catalyst offers compound **Q**.

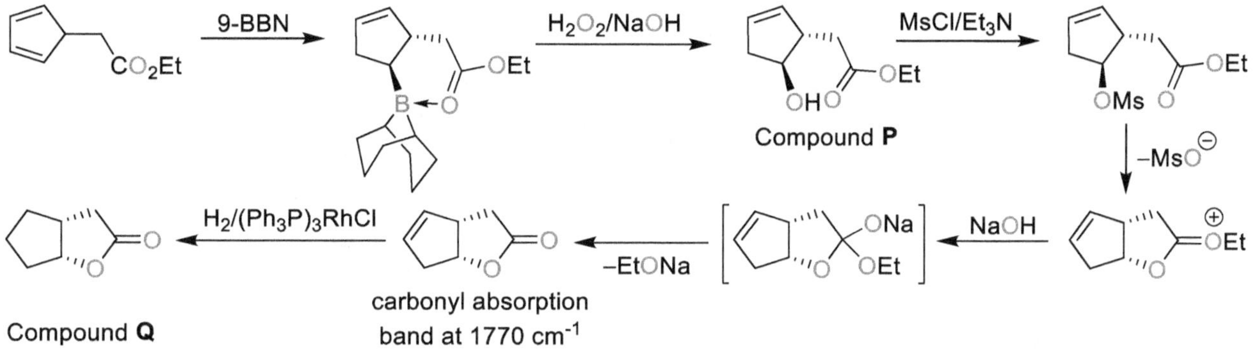

Compound **P**

Compound **Q**

carbonyl absorption
band at 1770 cm^{-1}

Question No-28: The major products P and Q, formed in the reactions given below are

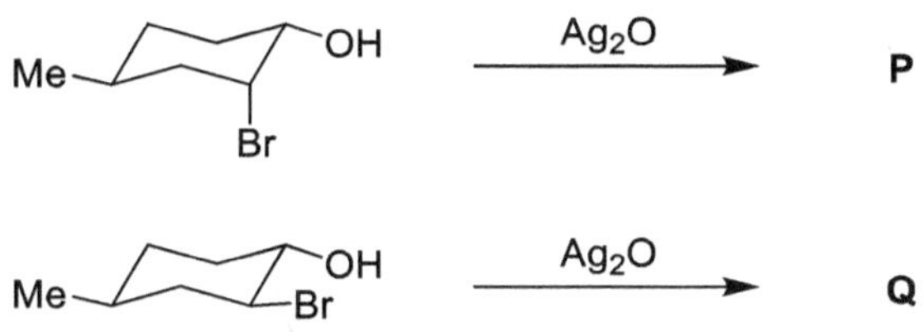

P

Q

A.

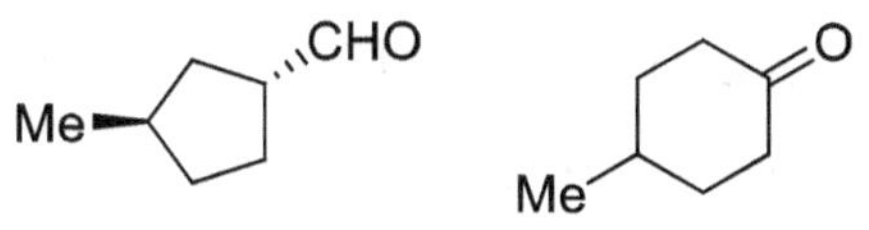

B.

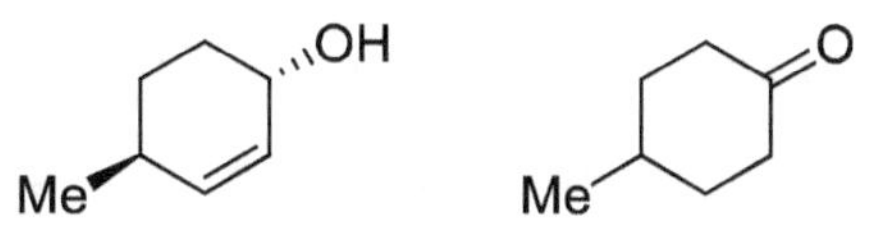

C.

D.

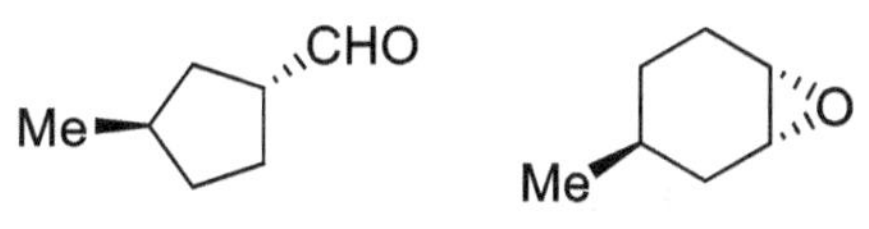

Answer: C. The major products **P** and **Q**, formed in the given reactions are 4-methylcyclohexanone (*via* antiperiplanar migration of hydride group) and *cis*-3-methylcyclopentanecarbaldehyde (*via* antiperiplanar migration of ring methylene group).

$$Ag_2O + H_2O \rightarrow 2AgOH$$

Question No-29: A compound with molecular formula $C_{10}H_{12}O_2$, showed a strong IR band at ~1720 cm^{-1}, a peak at *m/z* 122 in the mass spectrum and the following ^{1}H NMR signals: δ 8.1-8.0 (2H, m), 7.6-7.5 (1H, m), 7.5-7.3 (2H, m), 4.3 (2H, t), 1.8 (2H, sextet) and 1.0 (3H, t). The structure of a compound is

A.

B.

C.

D.

Answer: B. The compounds, propyl benzoate and ethyl 2-phenylacetate have five aromatic peaks. In both the case, methylene protons can easily be correlated as follows

Propyl benzoate

Ethyl 2-phenylacetate

^{1}**H NMR signals:** δ 8.1-8.0 (2H, m), 7.6-7.5 (1H, m), 7.5-7.3 (2H, m), 4.3 (2H, t), 1.8 (2H, sextet) and 1.0 (3H, t).

IR band ~1720 cm^{-1} and *m/z* 122

^{1}**H NMR signals:** δ 7.27 (2H, m), 7.24 (2H, m), 7.22 (1H, m), 3.71 (2H, s), 4.13 (2H, q) and 1.21 (3H, t).

IR band ~1736 cm^{-1} and *m/z* 136

Mc-Lafferty Fragmentation. The γ-hydrogen abstraction of propyl benzoate offers benzoic acid with *m/z* 122 while ethyl 2-phenylacetate corresponds to *m/z* 136.

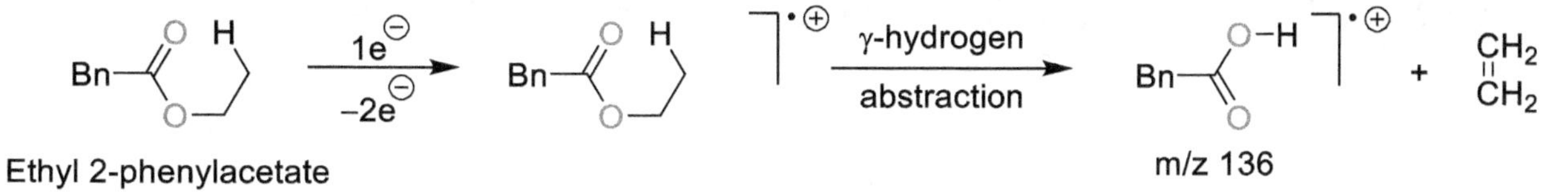

Ethyl 2-phenylacetate

m/z 136

The above data analysis supports the possible structure of the compound must be propyl benzoate.

Question No-30: The major product formed in the following synthetic sequence is

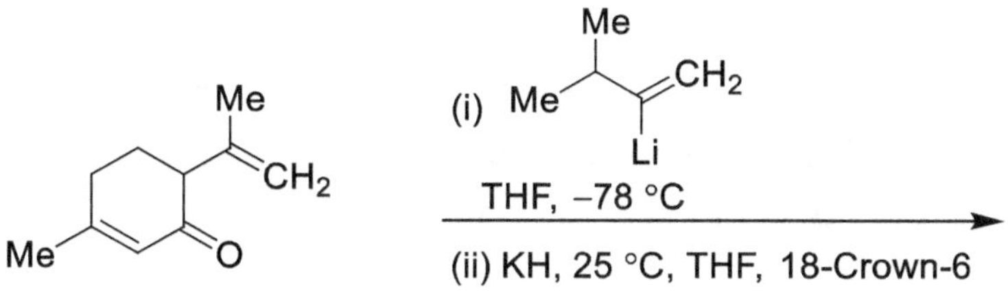

(i) THF, −78 °C

(ii) KH, 25 °C, THF, 18-Crown-6

A.

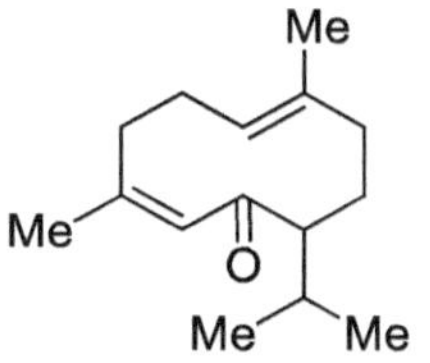

B.

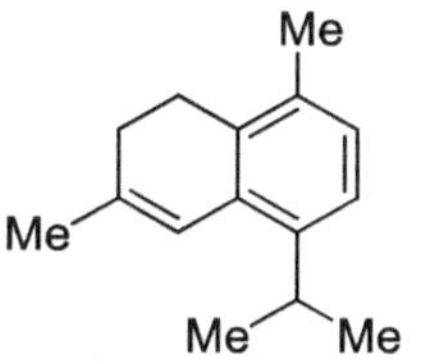

C.

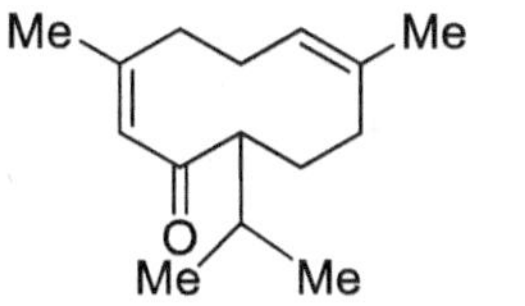

D.

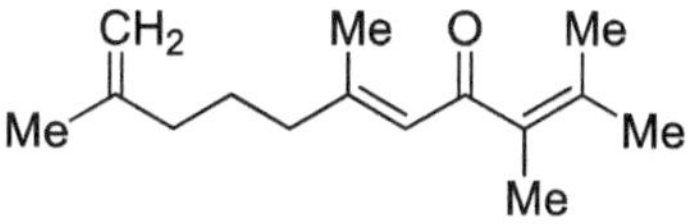

Answer: A. The major product formed *via* nucleophilic addition followed by [3,3]-sigmatropic shift (Oxy-Cope rearrangement) and then workup is (2Z,6E)-10-isopropyl-3,7-dimethylcyclodeca-2,6-dien-1-one.

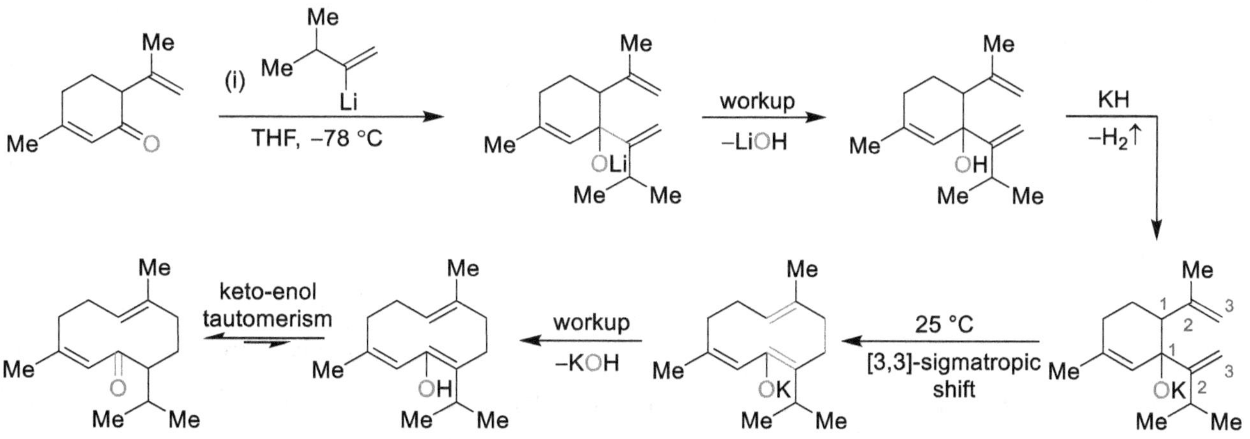

Question No-31: The correct statement with respect to the stereochemistry of α-hydroxyacids **P** and **Q** formed in the following reactions is

A. Both **P** and **Q** are formed with retention of configuration.

B. Both **P** and **Q** are formed with inversion of configuration.

C. **P** is formed with retention of configuration and **Q** is formed with inversion of configuration.

D. **P** is formed with inversion of configuration and **Q** is formed with retention of configuration.

Answer: D. The stereochemistry of α-hydroxy acids **P** and **Q** formed in the following reactions are as follows.

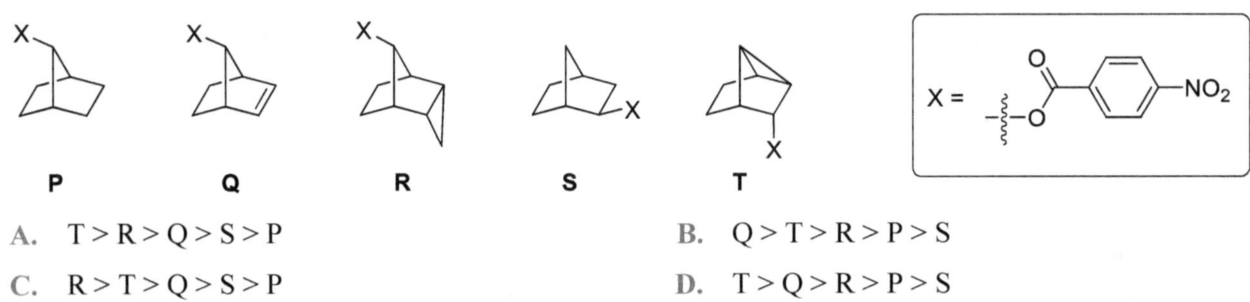

NGP = Neighboring Group Participation

Clayden, J.; Greeves, N.; Warren, S. Participation, Rearrangement, and Fragmentation. In *Organic Chemistry*; 2nd Ed.; Oxford University Press **2012**, pp 933-934.

Question No-32: The rate of solvolysis of the given compounds is in the order

A. $T > R > Q > S > P$ B. $Q > T > R > P > S$

C. $R > T > Q > S > P$ D. $T > Q > R > P > S$

Answer: A. As we know that three-membered cyclic compounds are relatively more reactive than the double bonds due to a high ring strain associated with them. However, a sigma bond is less reactive than a double bond. Hence, the rate of solvolysis of the given compounds is in the increasing order $= T > R > Q > S > P$.

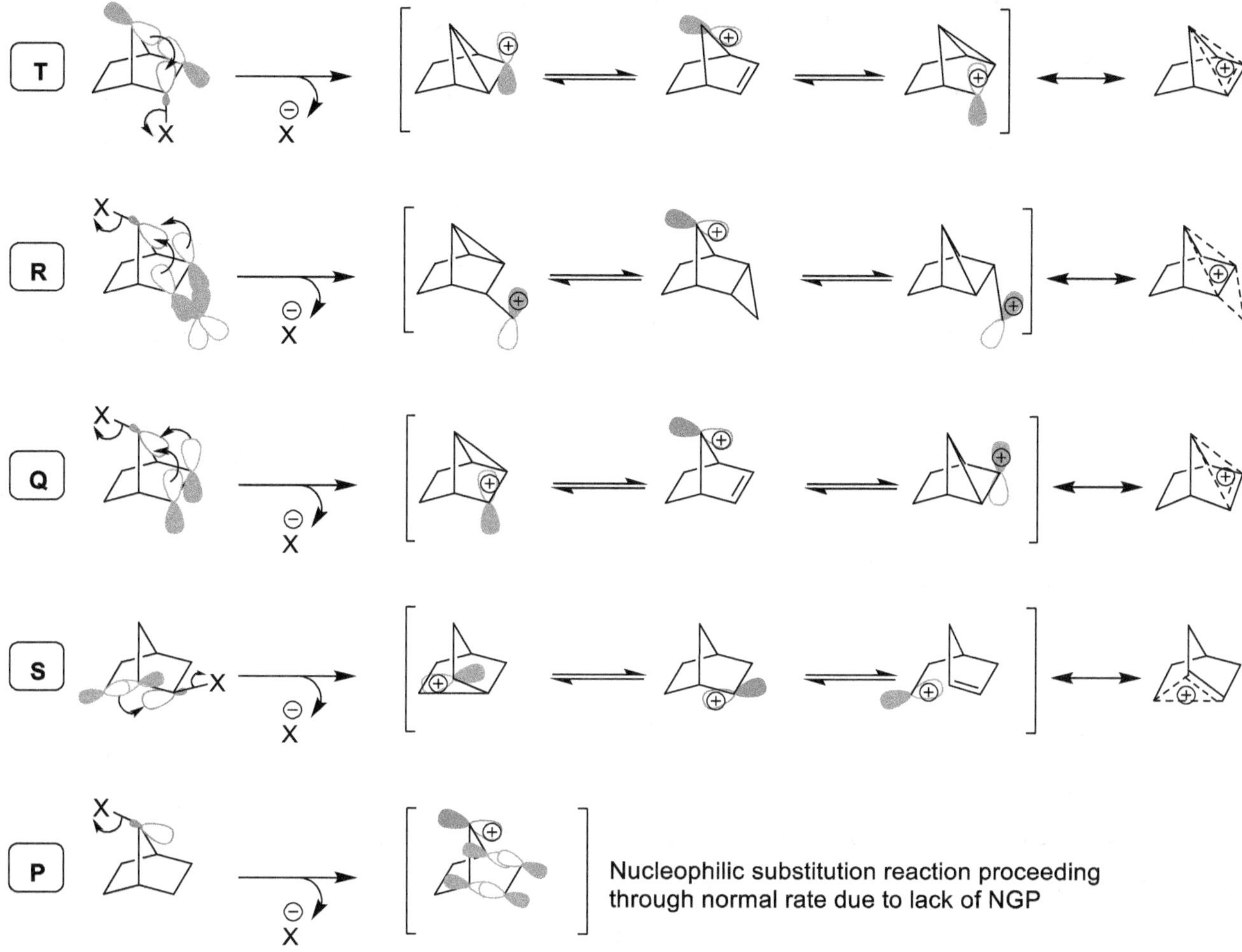

Note. The rate of solvolysis of leaving group (**X**) depends on the ability of a neighboring group to participate along with/or antiperiplaner nature of migrating groups such as lone pair donating heteroatoms, cyclopropyl ring, double bond, sigma bonds, etc.

Question No-33: In the following reaction sequence, the major products **Q** and **R** are

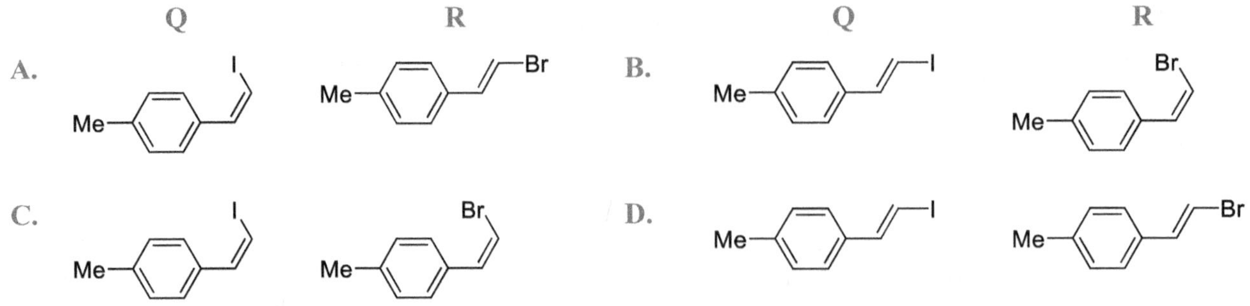

Answer: B. The Sonogashira cross-coupling of the given alkyne with 4-iodotoluene followed by desilylation reaction and then the regioselective hydroboration produces *trans*-organoborane derivative **P**.

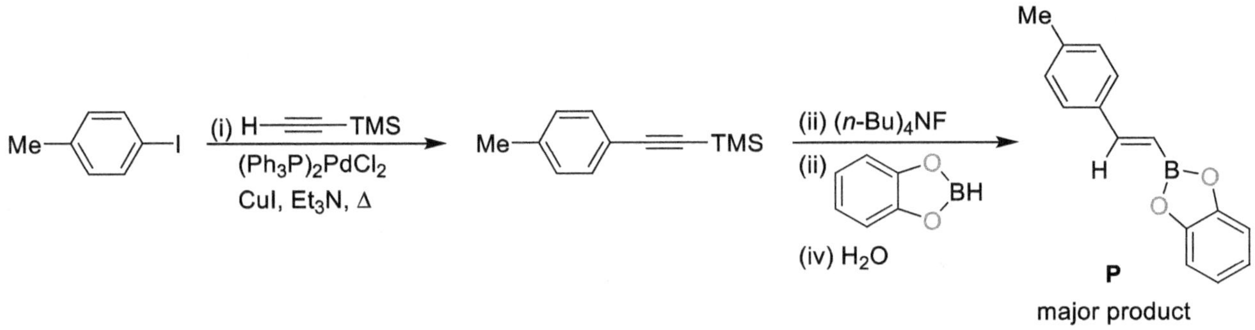

Furthermore, stereoselective halogenation reactions of **P** gives **Q** and **R**. The formation of *trans*-olefin **Q** occurs when P is treated with sodium hydroxide and molecular iodine, and *cis*-olefin **R** is obtained when it reacts with molecular bromine and sodium methoxide.

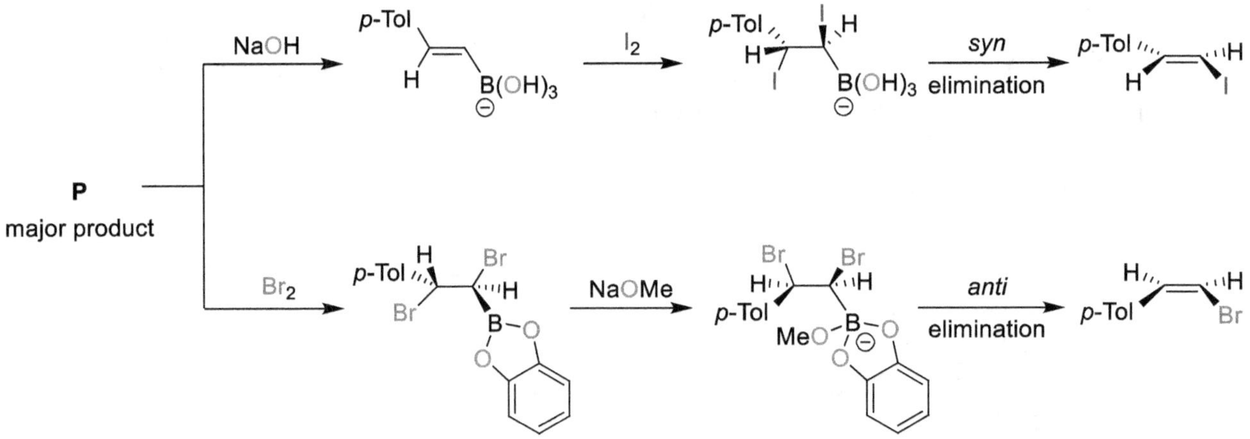

Brown, H. C.; Subrahmanyam, C.; Hamaoka, T.; Ravindran, N.; Bowman, D. H.; Misumi, S.; Unni, M. K.; Somayaji, V.; Bhat, N. G. *J. Org. Chem.* **1989**, *54*, 6068.

Question No-44: Among the following sets,

the total number of set(s) of diastereomeric pair(s) is/are________

Answer: 4. In the given above compounds, the total number of sets of diastereomeric pairs are *four*.

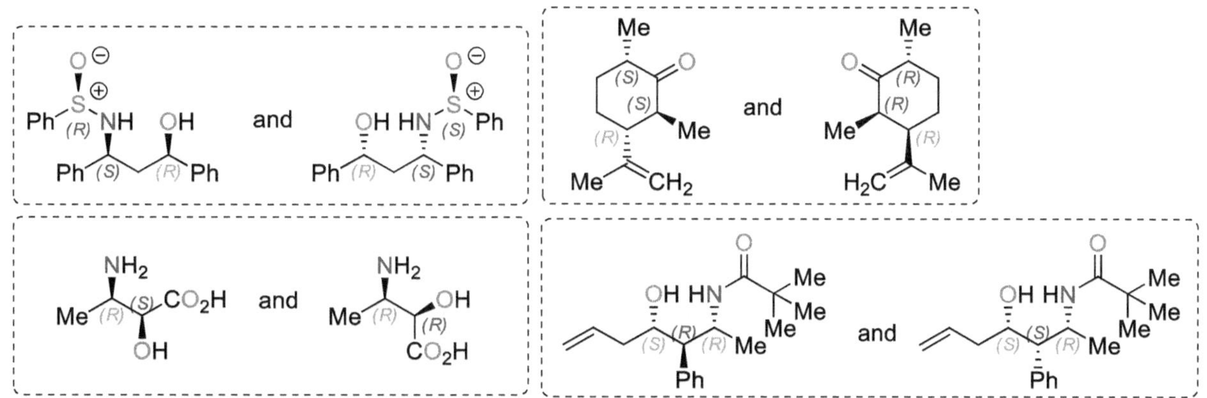

Question No-45: Among the following,

The total number of compounds showing characteristics of carbonyl stretching frequency less than 1700 cm^{-1} in their IR spectra is_______

Answer: 3. In the given above compounds, only _three_ compounds are showing characteristics carbonyl stretching frequency value which is less than 1700 cm^{-1} in their IR spectra; namely _m_-tolyl methylketone, methyl salicylate (oil of wintergreen) and 3-methyl-2-cyclohexenone.

Question No-1: The rates of alkaline hydrolysis of the compounds shown below

follow the order

A. I > II > III   **B.** II > I > III   **C.** II > III > I   **D.** III > I > II

Answer: C. The conjugation of amine with carbonyl in amide makes it more difficult to undergo hydrolysis than an ester. Among two given stereoisomers of esters, the formation of the tetrahedral hydrated complex is facile in the case of equatorially oriented ester than axial.

compound II   facile tetrahedral complex

compound III   1,3-diaxial interactions occur during the formation of tetrahedral complex

Hence, the correct order of hydrolysis is II > III > I.

Question No-2: Major product formed in the following reaction is

Answer: A. Herein, a transition state formed from the less hindered face with Simmons–Smith reagent and offered the major product dimethyl((R)-1-(($1S,2R$)-2-methylcyclopropyl)ethyl)(phenyl)silane.

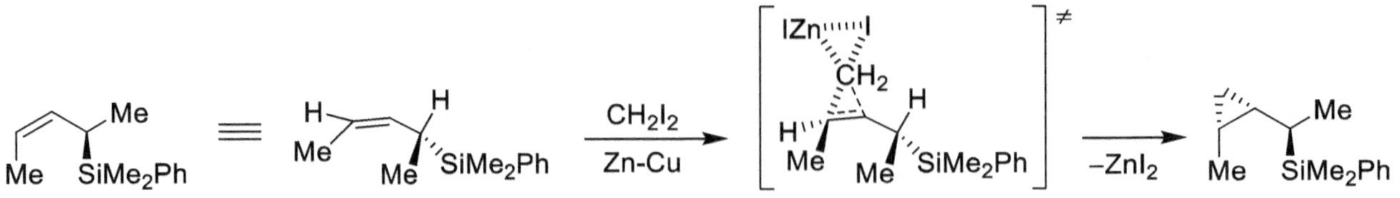

Question No-3: The major product formed in the following reaction

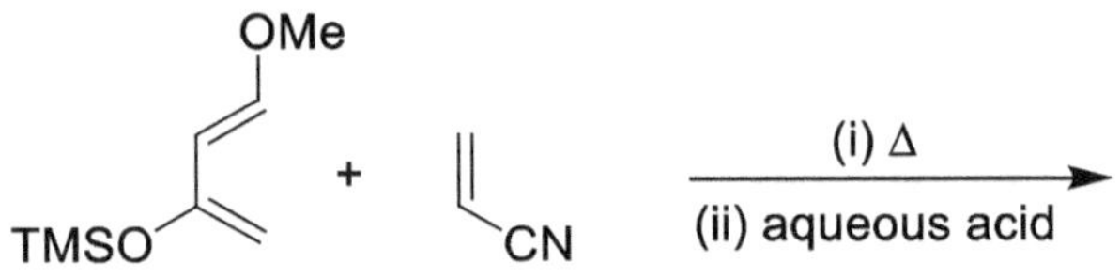

A.

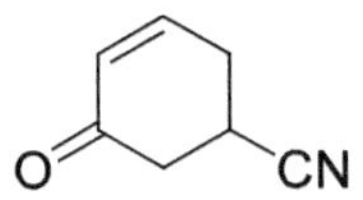

B.

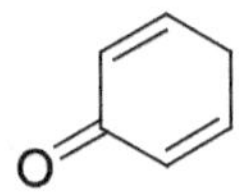

C.

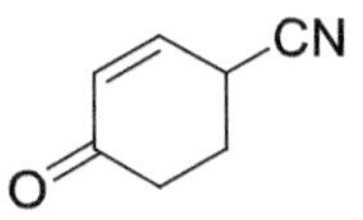

D.

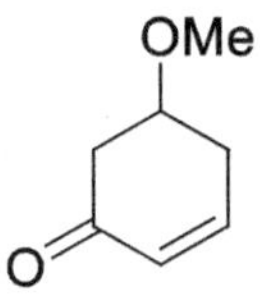

Answer: C. The given sequence of reaction offers 3-cyano-cyclohexenone-2.

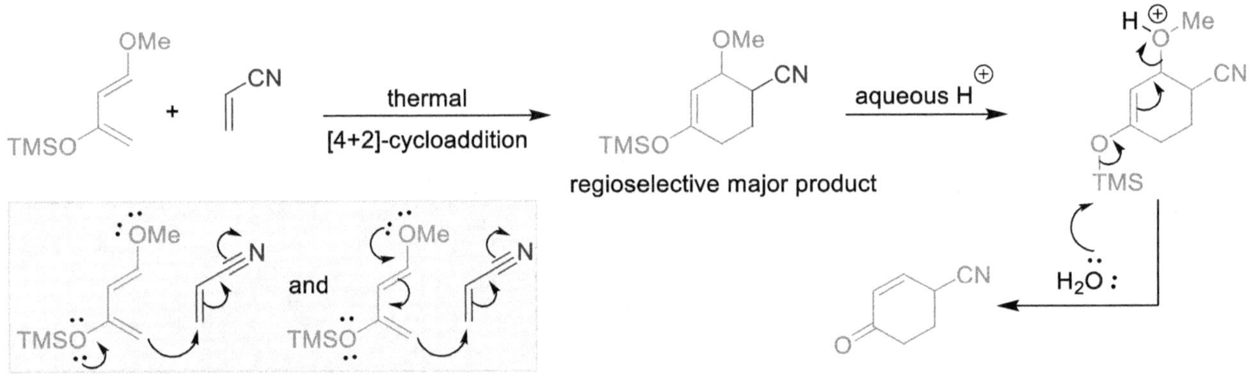

regioselective major product

Question No-4: The least acidic among the following compounds

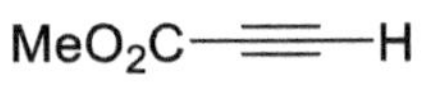

M

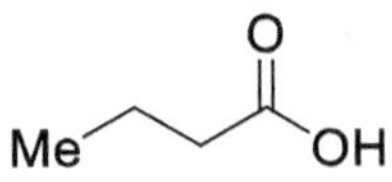

N

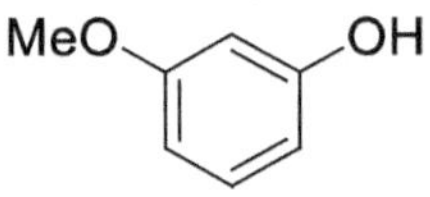

O

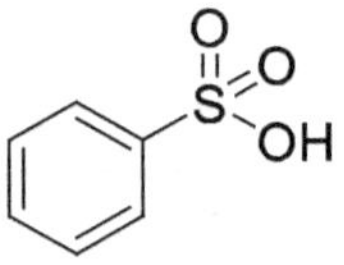

P

A. M

B. N

C. O

D. P

Answer: A. Among these, methyl propionate is the least acidic compound and the most acidic is sulfonic acid.

The increasing order of the acidity will be $M < N < O < P$.

Question No-5: The major product formed in the following reaction is

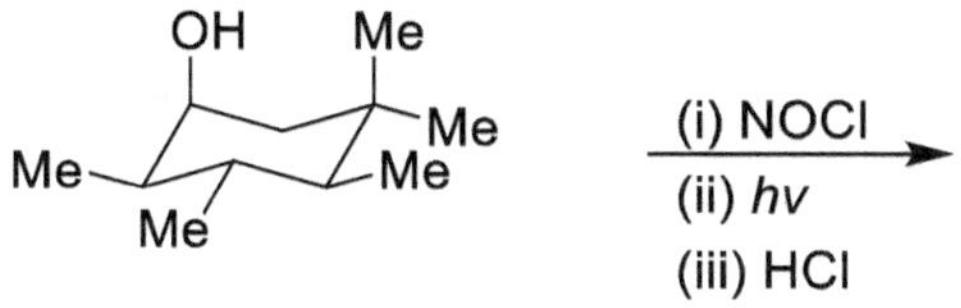

OH   Me

(i) NOCl

(ii) *hv*

(iii) HCl

A 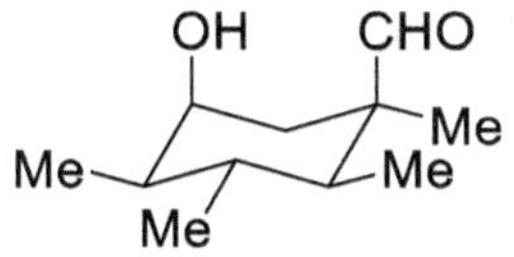   OH   CHO   B 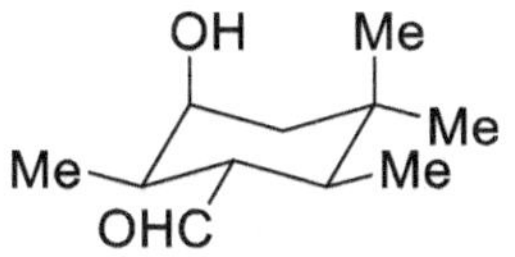   OH   Me   C   OH   Me   D   OH   CHO

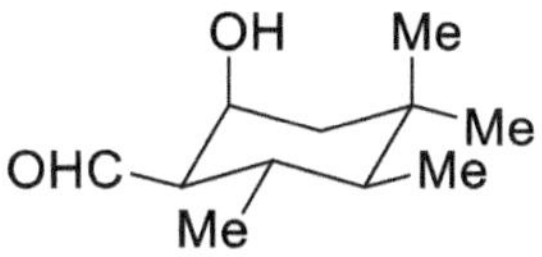

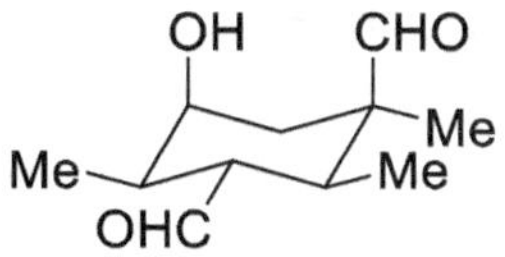

Answer: A. Barton reaction is a photochemical reaction that is widely employed for the δ-functionalization through *syn*-oriented R-O-NO of inactive sp^3-carbon in a radical manner.

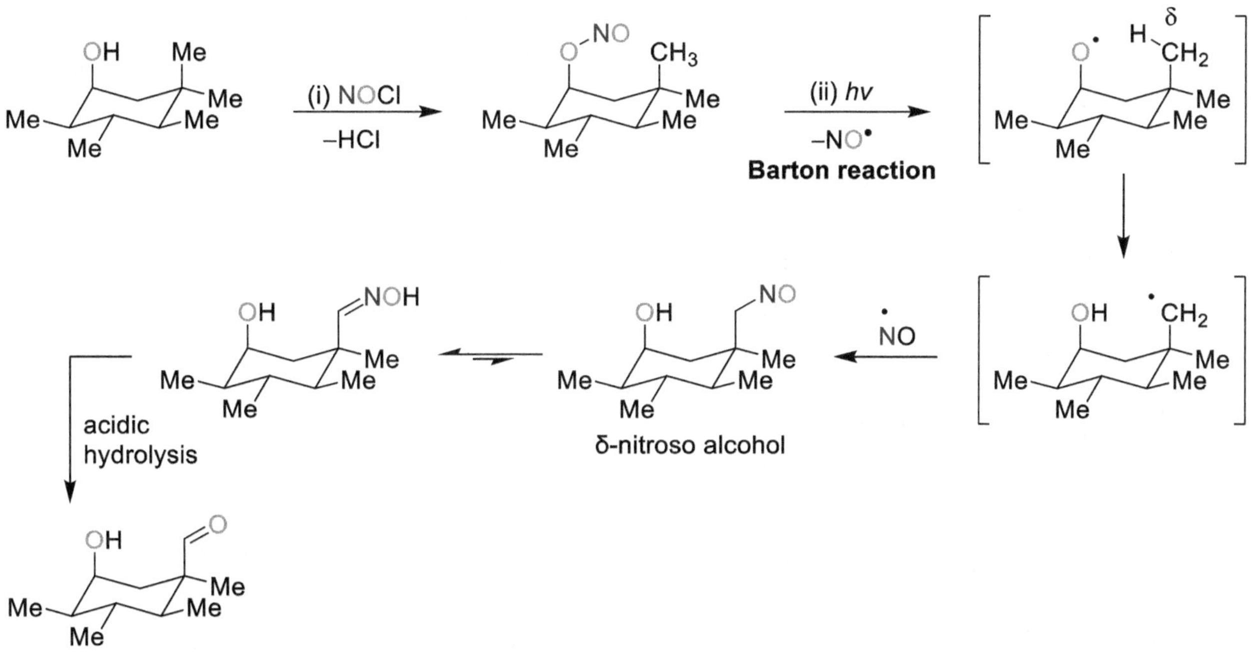

(i) NOCl   −HCl

(ii) *hv*   −NO$^\bullet$ **Barton reaction**

$\bullet$ NO

δ-nitroso alcohol

acidic hydrolysis

Question No-6: The reagent(s) required for the conversion of hex-3-yne to (*E*)-hex-3-ene is/are

A. H$_2$, Pd/BaSO$_4$ B. Bu$_3$SnH   C. Li/liquid NH$_3$ D. LiAlH$_4$

Answer: C. Birch reagent, stereospecifically as well as stereoselectively, reduces triple bond (hexyne-3) to corresponding double bond (*trans*-hexene-3).

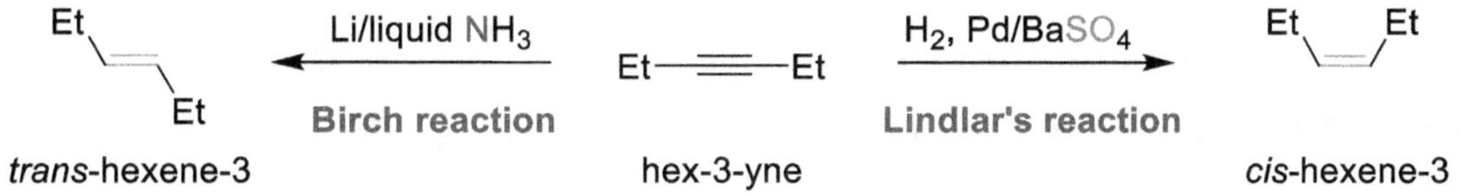

Li/liquid NH$_3$

Birch reaction

Et——Et

H$_2$, Pd/BaSO$_4$

Lindlar's reaction

trans-hexene-3   hex-3-yne   *cis*-hexene-3

Question No-7: An organic compound exhibits the $[M]^+$, $[M + 2]^+$ and $[M + 4]^+$ peaks in the intensity ratio 1:2:1 in the mass spectrum, and shows a singlet at δ 7.49 in the ^{1}H NMR spectrum in $CDCl_3$. The compound is

A. 1,4-dichlorobenzene

B. 1,4-dibromobenzene

C. 1,2-dibromobenzene

D. 1,2-dichlorobenzene

Answer: B. The given data analysis reveals that the compound is 1,4-dibromobenzene.

^{1}H NMR spectrum	Mass analysis	Intensity
	$[M]^+ = 233$ $(Br^1 = Br^2 = 79)$	1
	$[M + 2]^+ = 235$ $(Br^1 = 79$ and $Br^2 = 81)$	2
	$[M + 2]^+ = 235$ $(Br^1 = 81$ and $Br^2 = 79)$	
	$[M + 4]^+ = [M]^+ = 233$ $(Br^1 = Br^2 = 81)$	1

Question No-8: Reaction of $LiAlH_4$ with one equivalent of $Me_3N \cdot HCl$ gives a tetrahedral compound, which reacts with another equivalent of $Me_3N \cdot HCl$ to give compound **N**. The compound **N** and its geometry, respectively, are

A. $LiAlH_4NMe_3$ and trigonal bipyramidal

B. Li_2AlH_4Cl and square pyramidal

C. $AlH_3(NMe_3)_2$ and trigonal bipyramidal

D. $AlH_3(NMe_3)_2$ and pentagonal

Answer: C. The compound **N** is $AlH_3(NMe_3)_2$ and it has trigonal bipyramidal geometry.

tetrahedral (sp^3)   tetrahedral (sp^3)   trigonal bipyramidal (sp^{3}d)

Question No-9: Which one of the following is a non-heme protein?

A. Hemoglobin   B. Hemocyanin   C. Myoglobin   D. Cytochrome P-450

Answer: B. Like hemoglobin (Hb), hemocyanin is also a non-heme copper-containing respiratory pigmented protein that is found in lower organisms invertebrates such as arthropods, mollusks, etc. The oxygenated form of hemocyanin is blue in color while colorless is deoxygenated once.

Question No-10: A correct example of a nucleotide is

A. AMP   B. RNA   C. Uridine   D. DNA

Answer: A. The correct example of a nucleotide is adenosine monophosphate (AMP).

Question No-20: Among the following eight compounds

the number of compound(s) which can exhibit stereoisomerism is _________.

Answer: 6. Among these, six compounds can exhibit stereoisomerism except 1,7-dioxaspiro[5.5]undecane and 1-bromo-3-methylbuta-1,2-diene.

Question No-23: The number of signal(s) in the ^{1}H NMR spectrum of the following compound

recorded at 25 °C in CDCl_3 is ___________

Answer: 3. In ^{1}H NMR spectrum gives triacyl bromobenzene at 25 °C in CDCl_3 is 3.

Question No-30: The major product formed in the following reaction is

A. non-6-yn-2-one   B. non-3-yn-8-one   C. non-2-yn-6-one   D. non-3-en-8-one

Answer: A. The major product formed in the given Eschenmoser fragmentation is non-6-yn-2-one.

Question No-31: The major product formed in the following reaction is

(i) KNH$_2$ (2 equiv)

(ii) *n*-BuBr (1 equiv)

(iii) NaOH

A.

B.

C.

D.

Answer: A. The major product formed in the following reaction is 2-butyl-6-methylcyclohexan-1-one.

Question No-32: The major product formed in the following reaction is

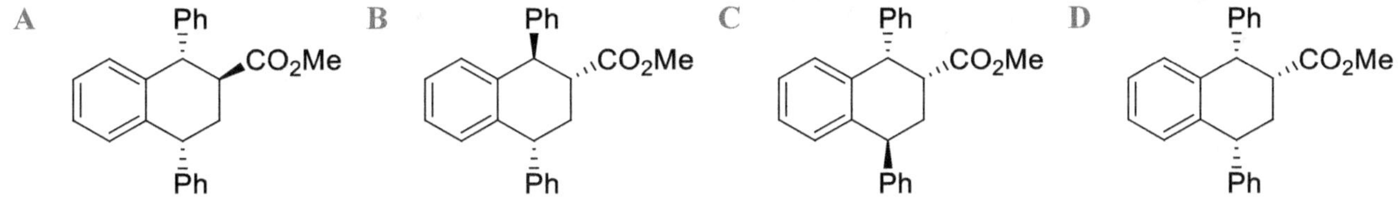

Answer: A. Diphenyl benzocyclobutene derivative under thermal condition proceeds through regioselective 4π-electron conrotatory ring opening (both the phenyl group moves outward to relieve the strain) in C_2-symmetric fashion to give *trans*-diene. Next, the formed *trans*-diene reacts with methyl acrylate in a thermal [4+2] manner to give a stereospecifically *trans*-stereogenic product with respect to phenyl and ester due to the secondary orbital interaction.

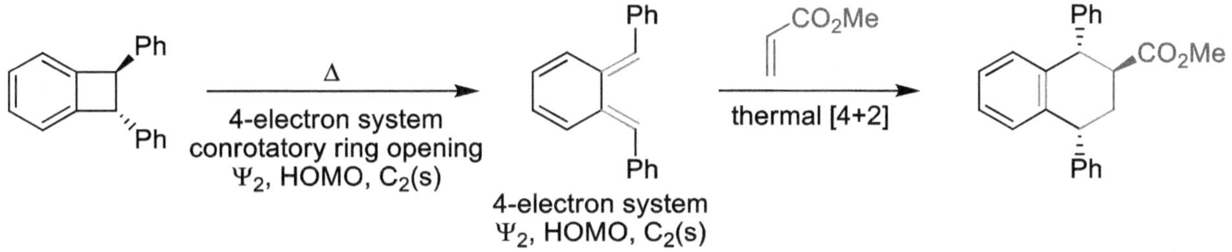

Question No-33: In the following reaction sequence,

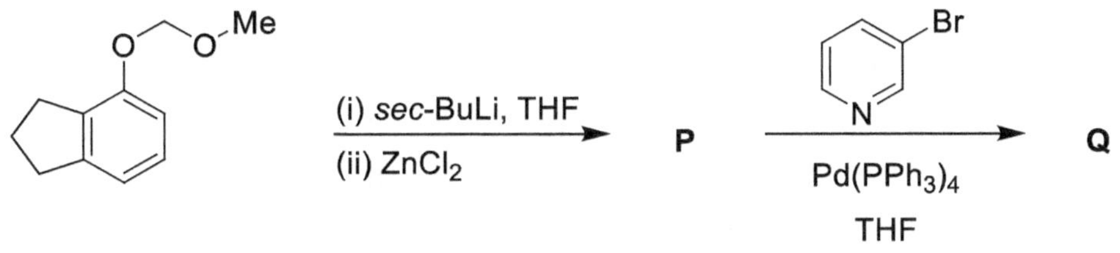

the major products **P** and **Q**, respectively are

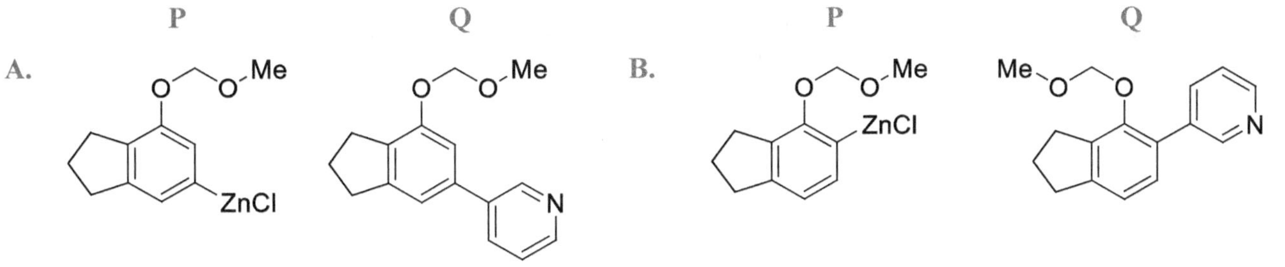

C.

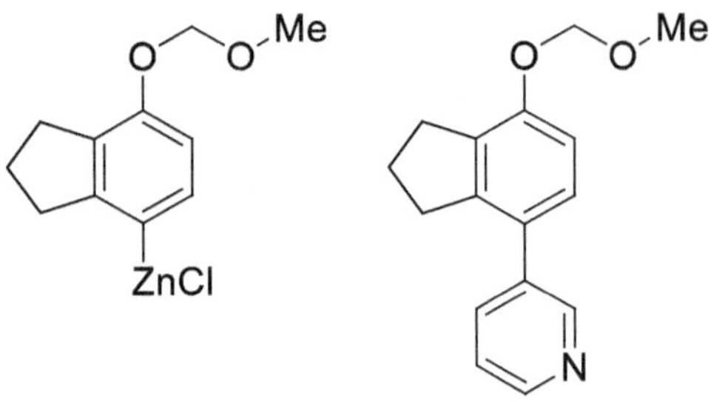

D.

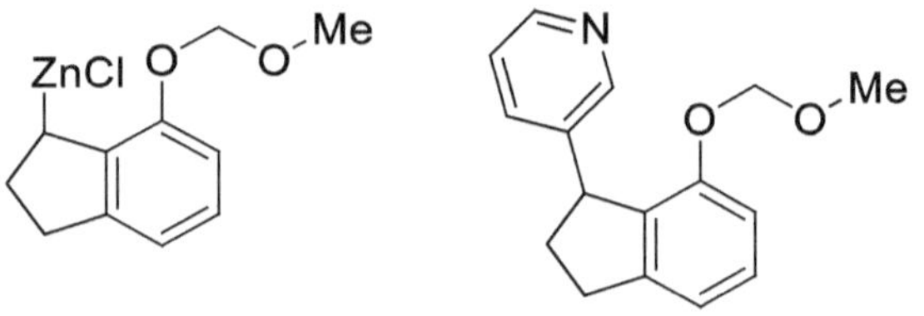

Answer: B. The given starting material was used for the synthesis of organozinc compound **P** *via* ortho-lithiation reaction. Finally, it was subjected to the Negishi coupling with 3-bromopyridine using Pd(0) complex.

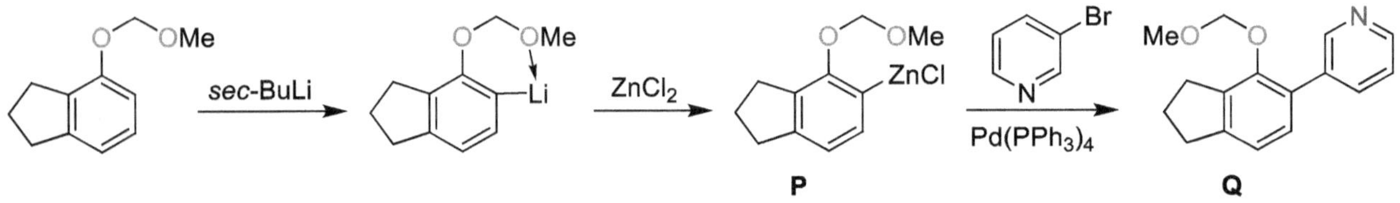

Question No-35: Among the following sets,

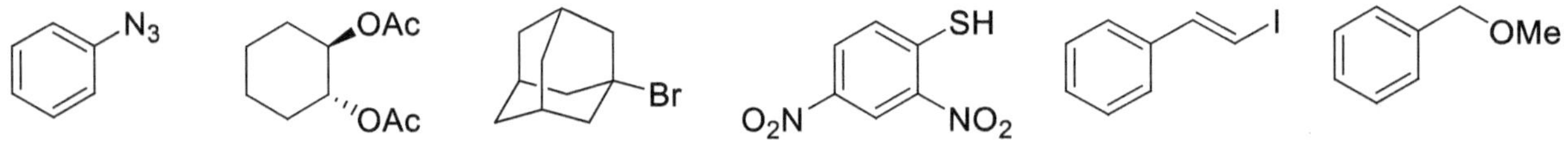

I	**II**	**III**	**IV**	**V**	**VI**

the compounds which can be prepared by nucleophilic substitution reaction are________

A. III, IV, and V   B. I, II, and VI   C. II, IV, and VI   D. I, III, and V

Answer: C. The compounds II, IV and VI can be prepared by nucleophilic substitution reaction.

Question No-36: In the following reaction,

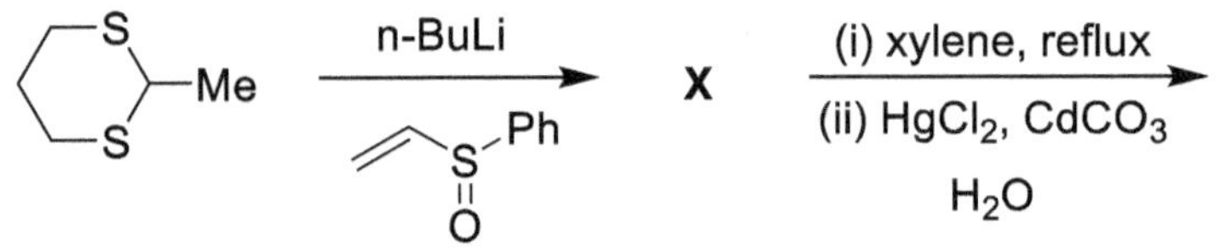

the major products **X** and **Y**, respectively, are

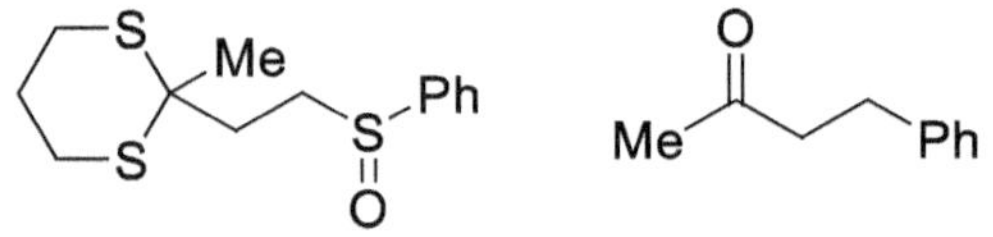

C.

D.

Answer: C. The given sequence of reactions is used for the synthetic utility of phenyl vinyl sulphoxide to methyl vinyl ketone.

Question No-37: In the major products **P** and **Q** formed in the following reactions, respectively are

	P	Q		P	Q
A.			**B.**		
C.			**D.**		

Answer: B. In the given reaction, the major products **P** and **Q** are formed, respectively are 4-methyl-7-(prop-1-en-2-yl)-1-oxaspiro[2.5]oct-4-ene and 1-methyl-4-(prop-1-en-2-yl)bicyclo[4.1.0]heptan-2-one.

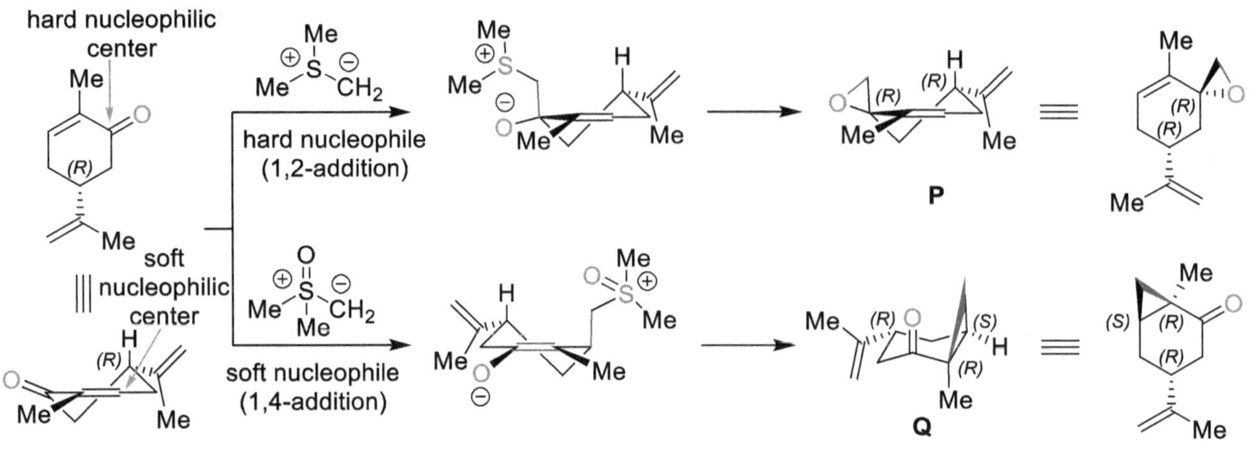

Question No-38: The major product formed in the reaction of $(2R,3R)$-2-bromo-3-methylpentane with NaOMe is

A. (Z)-3-methylpent-2-ene
B. (E)-3-methylpent-2-ene
C. $(2R,3R)$-2-methoxy-3-methylpentane
C. $(2S,3R)$-2-methoxy-3-methylpentane

Answer: B. Saytzeff's elimination of $(2R,3R)$-2-bromo-3-methylpentane with NaOMe produces (E)-3-methylpent-2-ene.

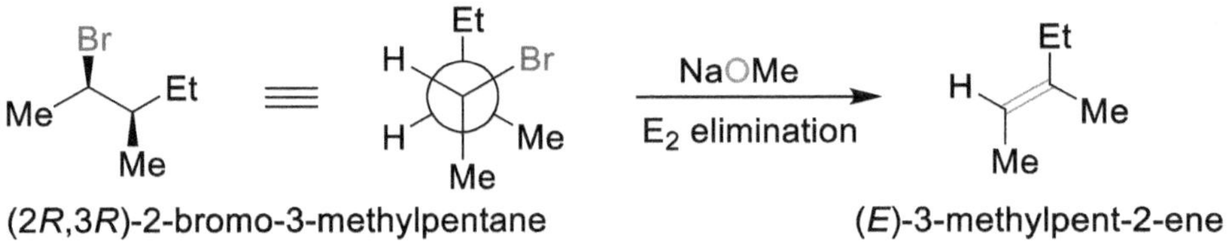

Question No-39: The major product formed in the following reaction is

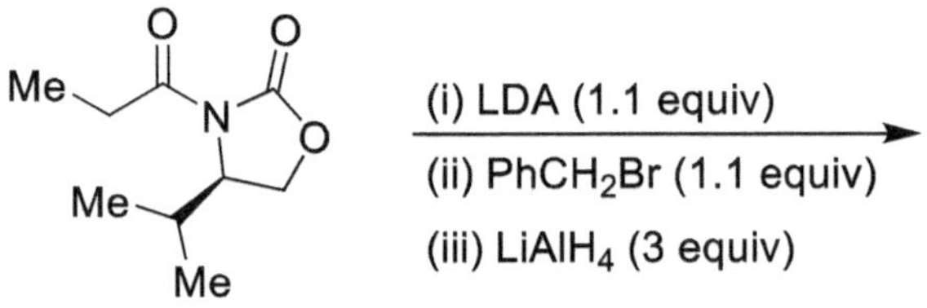

(i) LDA (1.1 equiv)
(ii) PhCH$_2$Br (1.1 equiv)
(iii) LiAlH$_4$ (3 equiv)

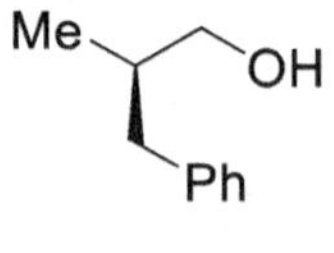

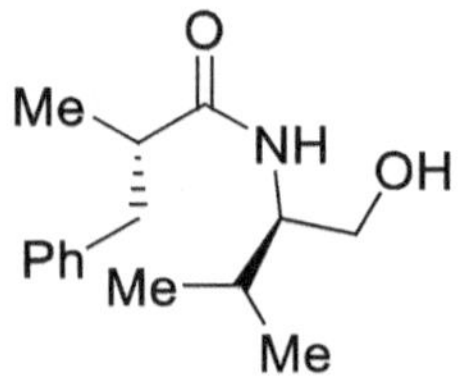

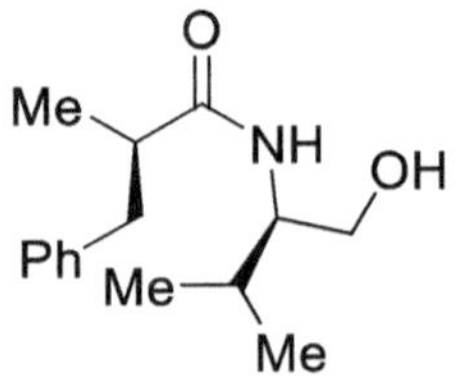

Answer: A. The given substrate having chiral auxiliary reacts with LDA generates *syn*-enolate which undergoes regioselective S$_N$2-reaction (from the bottom-face due to less steric strain) and produces (S)-2-methyl-3-phenylpropan-1-ol on reduction with LAH stereoselectively.

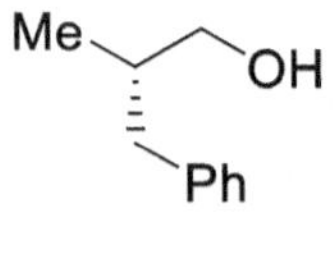

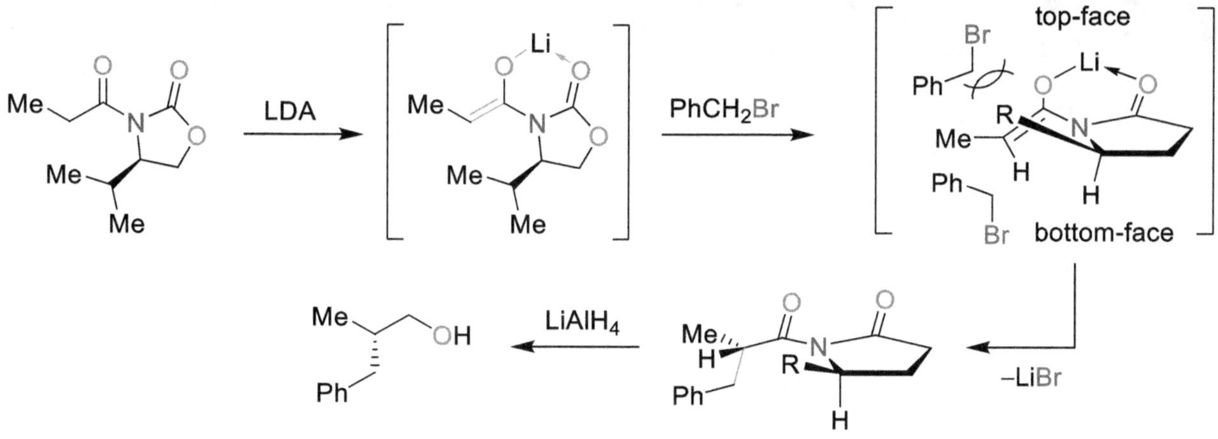
Me
O
O
N
O
Me
Me
LDA
Li
Me
O
O
N
O
Me
Me
PhCH$_2$Br
Br
top-face
Ph
Li
O
O
R
N
Me
H
H
Ph
Br
bottom-face
–LiBr
Me
O
O
H
N
R
Ph
H
LiAlH$_4$
Me
OH
Ph

Question No-11: The major product **M** formed in the following reaction is

$$\text{(cyclodeca-diene)} \xrightarrow[\text{CuSO}_4,\ O_2]{\text{N}_2\text{H}_4\ (1\ \text{equiv})}$$

A.

B.

C.

D.

Answer: B. The major product **M** formed in the given reaction is (*Z*)-cyclodecene.

$$\xleftarrow[\text{Benzene}]{\text{Rh(PPh}_3)\text{Cl, H}_2} \qquad \xrightarrow[\text{CuSO}_4,\ O_2]{\text{N}_2\text{H}_4\ (1\ \text{equiv})}$$

Question No-12: The starting material **Y** in the following reaction is

$$\textbf{Y} \ + \ \underset{(3\ \text{equiv})}{\diagup\!\!\!\diagdown\text{MgBr}} \xrightarrow[-40\ ^\circ\text{C}]{\text{THF}}$$

A. NH_2, Br

B. NO_2, Br

C. N_3, Br

D. pyrrole with Br, Br

Answer: B. The starting material **Y** in the given reaction is 1-bromo-2-nitrobenzene and reaction is known as Bartoli indole synthesis (Bartoli reaction).

Dobbs, A. *J. Org. Chem.* **2001**, *66*, 638–641.

Question No-13: The major product in the given reaction is **Q**. The mass spectrum of **Q** shows {[M] = molecular ion peak}

A.   [M], [M + 2] and [M + 4] with relative intensity of 1:2:1

B.   [M] and [M+2] with the relative intensity of 1:1

C.   [M], [M + 2] and [M + 4] with relative intensity of 1:3:1

D.   [M] and [M + 2] with relative intensity of 2:1

Answer: A. The major product in the given reaction is 1,1-dibromo-5-methylhex-1-ene **Q**. It can be used as a synthon for the synthesis of terminal alkyne derivative in the Corey-Fuchs reaction.

The mass spectrum of **Q** shows [M], [M + 2] and [M + 4] with relative intensity of 1:2:1.

Compound	Mass analysis	Intensity
	$[M]^+ = 233$ ($Br^1 = Br^2 = 79$)	1
	$[M + 2]^+ = 235$ ($Br^1 = 79$ and $Br^2 = 81$)	2
	$[M + 2]^+ = 235$ ($Br^1 = 81$ and $Br^2 = 79$)	
	$[M + 4]^+ = [M]^+ = 233$ ($Br^1 = Br^2 = 81$)	1

Question No-14: A tripeptide on treatment with PhNCS (pH = 8.0) followed by heating with dilute HC*l* afforded a cyclic compound **M** and a dipeptide. The dipeptide on treatment with PhNCS (pH = 8.0) followed by heating with dilute HC*l* afforded a cyclic compound **N** and an acyclic compound **O**. The correct sequence (from *N*- to *C*-terminus) of the tripeptide is

M = (structure) **N =** (structure) **O =** (structure)

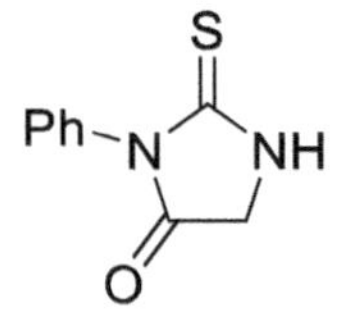

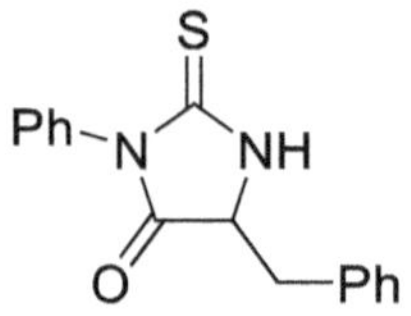

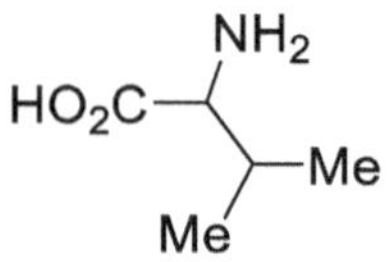

A. glycine-phenylalanine-valine

B. valine-phenylalanine-glycine

C. glycine-tyrosine-valine

D. glycine-phenylalanine-alanine

Answer: A. Edman degradation method is an experimental technique that helps to determine the sequence of amino acids in a polypeptides chain. This degradation starts from the *N-* and ends at the *C-*terminus with the help of phenyl isothiocyanate (PhNCS at pH = 8.0).

As per the given statements in the Question:

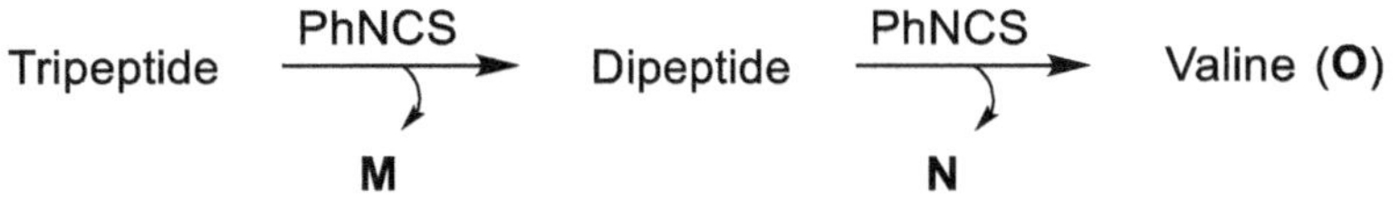

Tripeptide $\xrightarrow[\textbf{M}]{\text{PhNCS}}$ Dipeptide $\xrightarrow[\textbf{N}]{\text{PhNCS}}$ Valine (**O**)

From the above reaction, dipeptide and tripeptide sequences will be **N-O** and **M-N-O**, respectively. The structure of **M** and **N** form when Ph-N=C=S (at pH = 8.0) reacts with glycine and phenylalanine, respectively. Thus, the structure of tripeptide **M-N-O** should be glycine-phenylalanine-valine.

gly-phe-val (M-N-O)

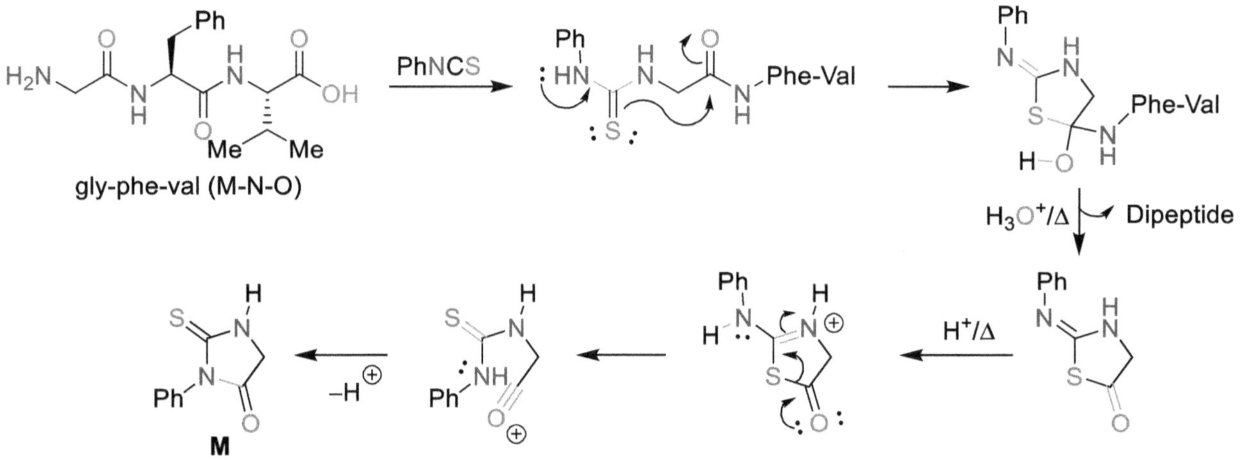

Note. As shown above, a similar repetitive reaction with dipeptide i.e. Phe-Val offers **N** and **O** compounds.

Question No-15: The major product **M** in the following reaction is

$\xrightarrow{h\nu}$ **M**

$Ar = $ (4-cyanophenyl) —CN

A. Me, Me / Ar–, Ar– cyclopropyl; Ph, Ph vinyl

B. Me, Me / Ar–, Ph cyclopropyl; Ar, Ph vinyl

C. Me, Me / Ph–, Ph cyclopropyl; Ar, Ar vinyl

D. Me, Ar / Me–, Ar cyclopropyl; Ph, Ph vinyl

Answer: A. The photochemical irradiation of the given compound undergoes *Di-π-methane rearrangement* producing (diphenyl)vinyl cyclopropane derivative as the major product. The formation of cyclopropyl ring occurs at the double bond of cyanophenyls site because the formed radical intermediate is stabilized by the conjugation associated with the electron-withdrawing group (Intermediates II, III and IV).

intermediate I

intermediate II

intermediate III

intermediate IV

Note. When –CN is replaced by –OMe group, the formation of cyclopropyl ring takes place on the di-phenyl substituted double bond.

Zimmerman, H. E.; Armesto, D. *Chem. Rev.* **1996**, *96*, 3065.

Question No-16: The major product **T** formed in the following reaction is

$$\text{(2,5-dibromo-6-methoxypyridine)} \quad \xrightarrow[\text{(b) PhCHO, }-78\,°\text{C}]{\text{(a) }n\text{-BuLi, Et}_2\text{O, }-100\,°\text{C}} \quad \textbf{T}$$

A (5-bromo-2-methoxypyridin-3-yl)(phenyl)methanol

B

C

D

Answer: A. The major product **T** formed in the given reaction *via* the *ortho*-lithiation process is (5-bromo-2-methoxypyridin-3-yl)(phenyl)methanol.

$$\text{aryl bromide} \xrightarrow{n\text{-BuLi}} \left[\text{lithiated intermediate} \right] \xrightarrow{-n\text{-BuBr}} \text{aryllithium} \xrightarrow[\text{then H}_3\text{O}^{\oplus}]{\text{PhCHO}} \text{product}$$

Question No-18: The $\nu_{\text{O–O}}$ resonance Raman stretching frequency (cm^{-1}) of the coordinated dioxygen in oxy-hemoglobin and oxy-hemocyanin appears, respectively, nearly at

A.   1136 and 744   B.   1550 and 744   C.   744 and 1136   D.   744 and 1150

Answer: A. The stretching frequencies for the given statements will be 1136 and 744, respectively.

Question No-26: The correct reagent(s) for the given reaction is(are)

A. H_2O_2, NaOH

B.   dimethyldioxirane (DMDO)

C.   DIBAL-H, then *m*-CPBA

D. $SO_3 \cdot$ pyridine, Me$_2$SO

Answer: A & B. The reagents for the given transformations are H_2O_2/NaOH and dimethyldioxirane (DMDO), independently.

Question No-27: The correct statement(s) about the ^{1}H NMR spectra of compounds **P** and **Q** is (are)

A. **P** shows a sharp singlet at $\delta = 3.70$ ppm (for H_a and H_b)

B. **Q** shows a sharp singlet at $\delta = 3.70$ ppm (for H_a and H_b)

C. **P** shows a AB-quartet centered at $\delta = 3.63$ ppm (for H_a and H_b)

D. **Q** shows a AB-quartet centered at $\delta = 3.63$ ppm (for H_a and H_b)

Answer: A & D. The correct statements about the ^{1}H NMR spectra of compounds **P** and **Q** are (i) **P** shows a sharp singlet at $\delta = 3.70$ ppm (for H_a and H_b) and (ii) **Q** shows an AB-quartet centered at $\delta = 3.63$ ppm (for H_a and H_b).

Question No-30: Match the correct option(s) from column **A** with column **B** according to the metal centre present in the active site of metalloenzyme

	A			B
P	Cu	**I**		B12-coenzyme
Q	Mo	**II**		Carboxypeptidase
R	Co	**III**		Nitrate reductase
S	Zn	**IV**		Cytochrome P-450
		V		Tyrosinase

Code

A. P-V, Q-III, R-I, S-II

B. P-IV, Q-II, R-I, S-III

C. P-II, Q-IV, R-V, S-III

D. P-V, Q-III, R-II, S-IV

Answer: A. The correct match of column **A** and column **B** is P-V, Q-III, R-I, S-II.

Question No-33: The number of peaks exhibited by **T** in its broadband proton decoupled ^{13}C NMR spectrum recorded at 25 °C in CDCl_3 is

Answer: 8. In the proton decoupled ^{13}C NMR spectrum of 2,7-dimethylphenanthrene gives **8** peaks at 25 °C in CDCl_3.

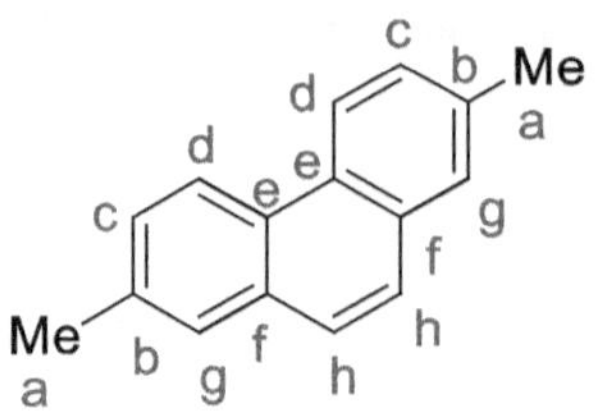

Question No-36: The major product **P** obtained in the following reaction sequence is

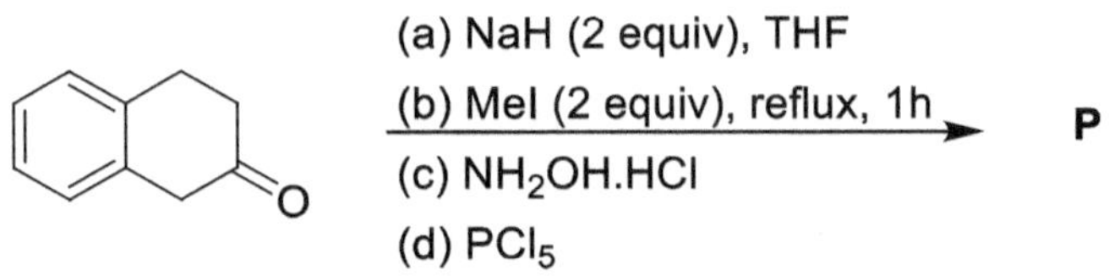

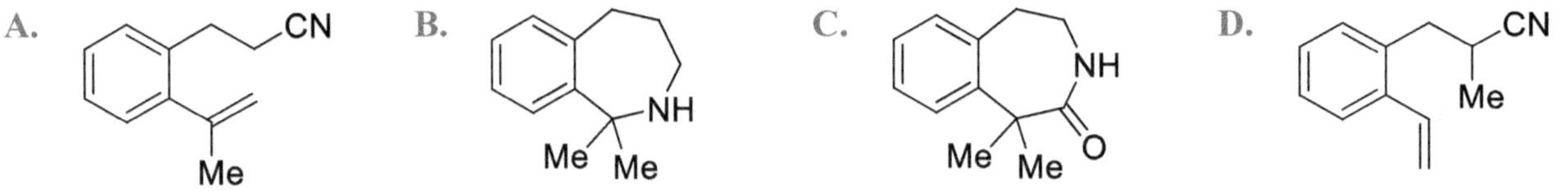

(a) NaH (2 equiv), THF
(b) MeI (2 equiv), reflux, 1h
(c) NH$_2$OH.HCl
(d) PCl$_5$

$\longrightarrow$ **P**

A. **B.** **C.** **D.**

Answer: A. The major product formed in the given reaction is 3-(2-(prop-1-en-2-yl)phenyl)propanenitrile.

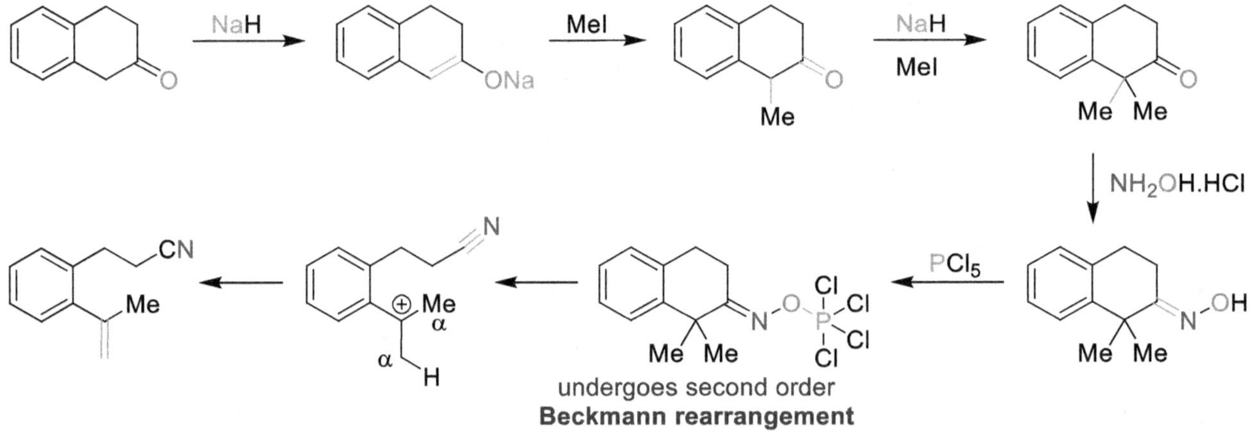

undergoes second order
Beckmann rearrangement

Note. The formation of highly stabilized carbocation intermediate during the reaction gives fragmentation product, which upon elimination of α-hydrogen produces a second order Beckmann rearrangement product.

Question No-37: The major product **Q** in the given reaction is

$\xrightarrow[\text{MeCN, 0 °C}]{\text{ZnCl}_2}$ **Q**

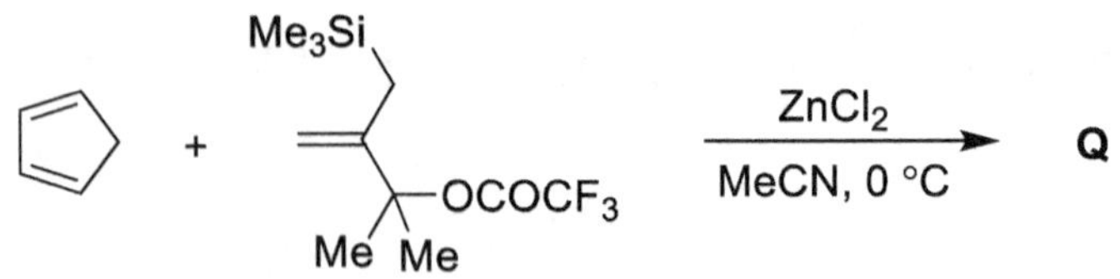

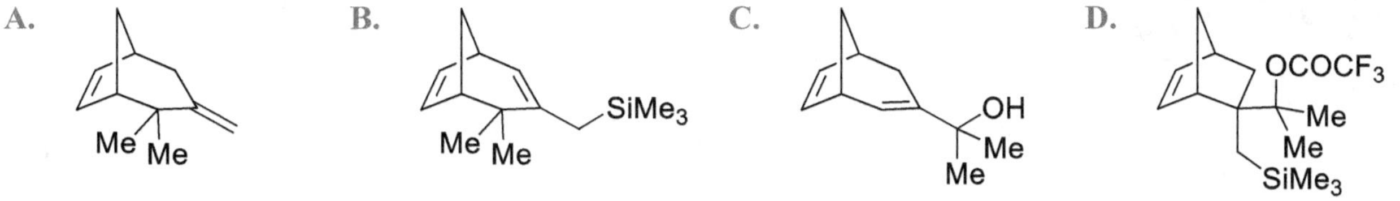

A.

B.

C.

D.

Answer: A. The major product **Q** in the given reaction is 2,2-dimethyl-3-methylenebicyclo[3.2.1]oct-6-ene.

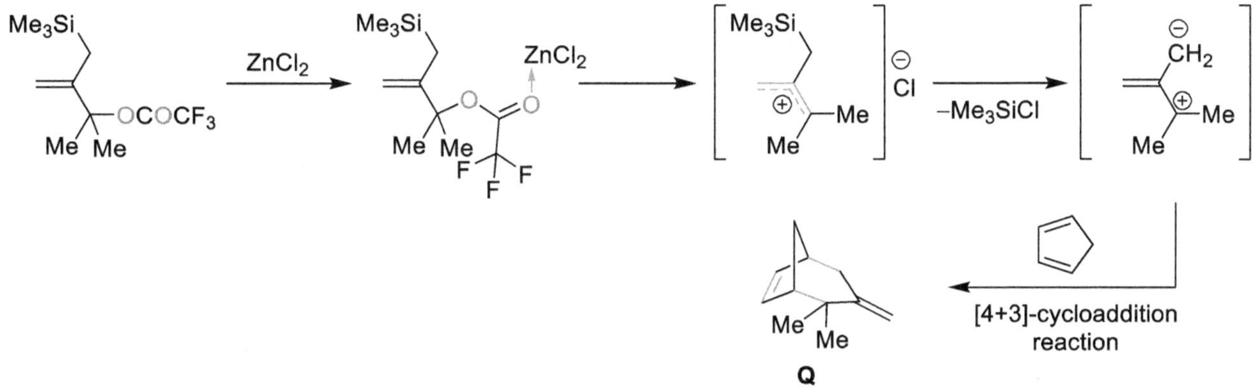

[4+3]-cycloaddition reaction

Q

Henning, R.; Hoffman, H. M. R. *Tetrahedron Lett.* **1982**, *23*, 2305-2308.

Question No-38: The major product **P** in the following reaction is

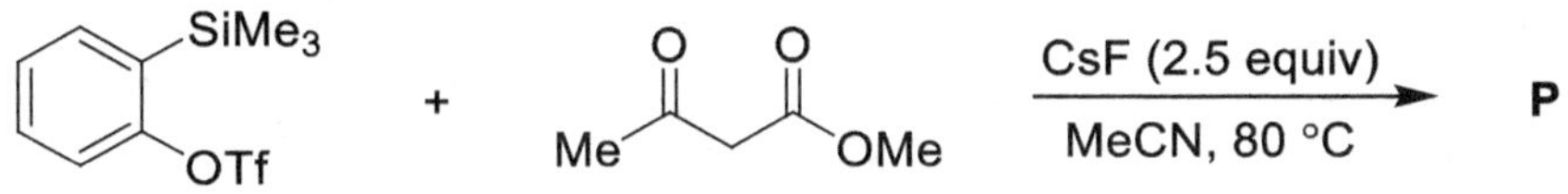

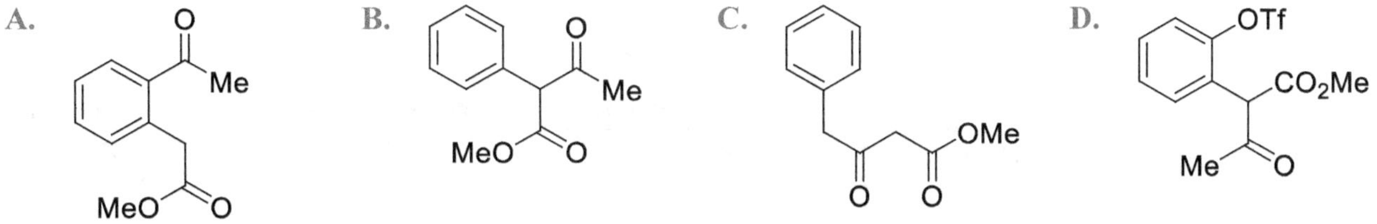

$$\text{CsF (2.5 equiv)}$$
$$\text{MeCN, 80 °C}$$

P

A.

B.

C.

D.

Answer: A. The major product **P** in the given reaction is methyl 2-(2-acetylphenyl)acetate.

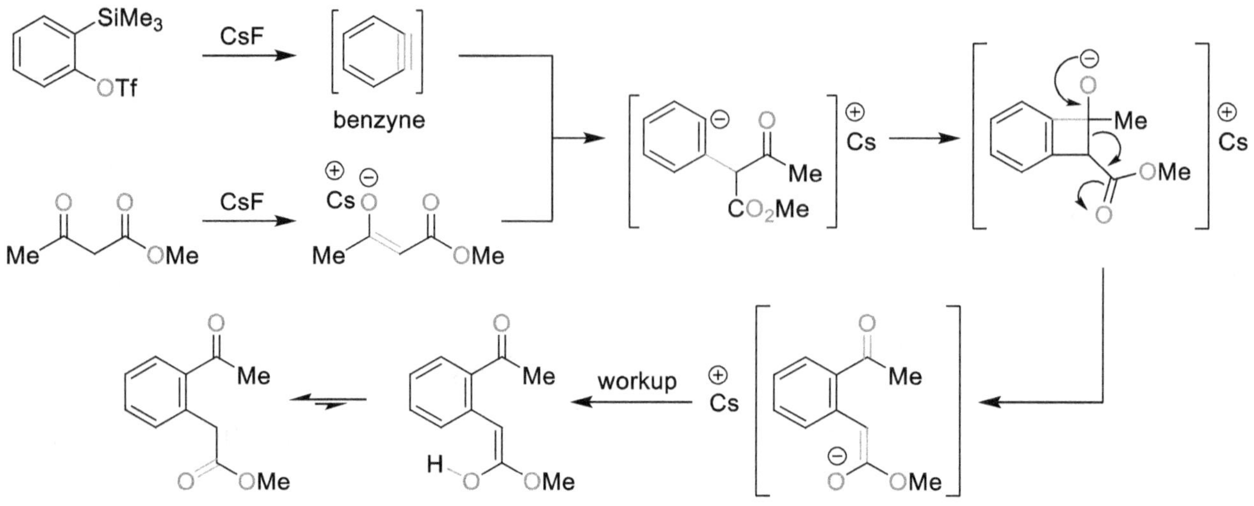

Zahid, M.; Ibal, M. F.; Abilov, Z. A.; Langer, P. *J. Fluor. Chem.* **2013**, *146*, 80.

Question No-39: The major product **P** in the reaction sequence is

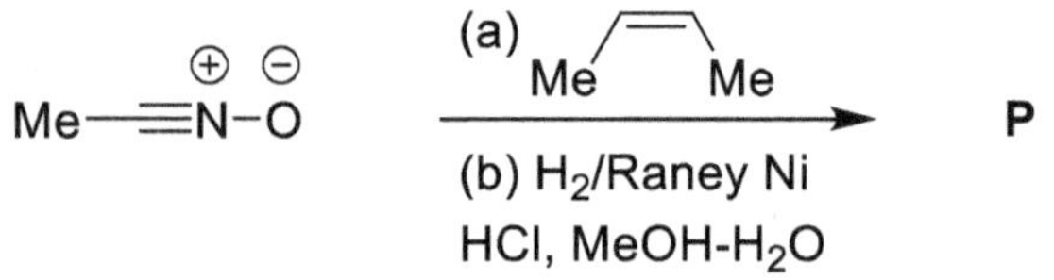

$$Me-\overset{\oplus}{\equiv}N-\overset{\ominus}{O} \quad \xrightarrow[\substack{\text{(b) } H_2/\text{Raney Ni} \\ \text{HCl, MeOH-H}_2\text{O}}]{\text{(a) } Me\diagup\diagdown Me} \quad P$$

A. 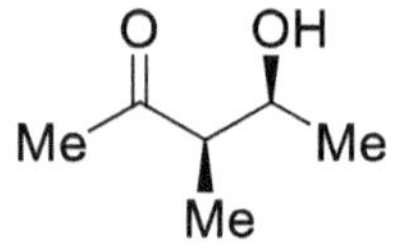   B. 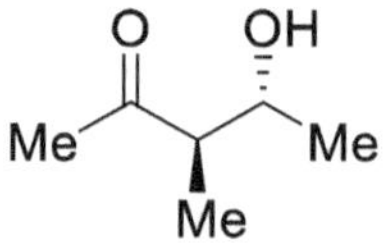   C. 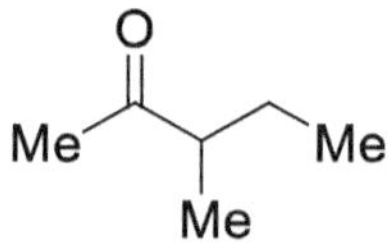   D.

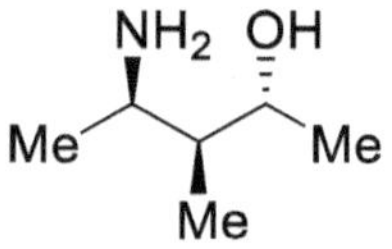

Answer: A. The major product **P** in the given reaction sequence is *syn*-4-hydroxy-3-methylpentan-2-one.

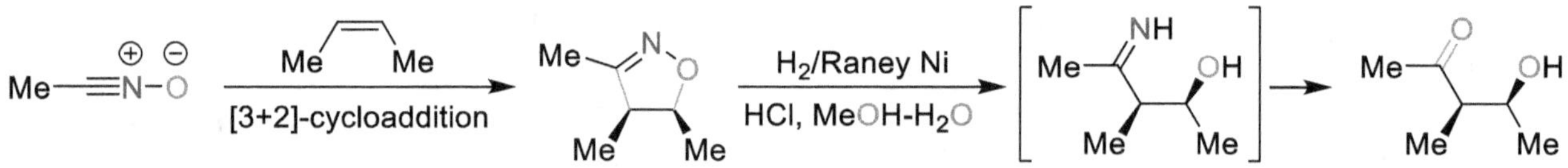

$$Me-\overset{\oplus}{\equiv}N-\overset{\ominus}{O} \quad \xrightarrow[\text{[3+2]-cycloaddition}]{Me\diagup\diagdown Me} \quad \xrightarrow[\text{HCl, MeOH-H}_2\text{O}]{H_2/\text{Raney Ni}} \quad$$

Note. The above method can also be useful for the synthesis of stereoselective Aldol products.

Question No-40: The major products **P** and **Q** in the following reaction sequence are

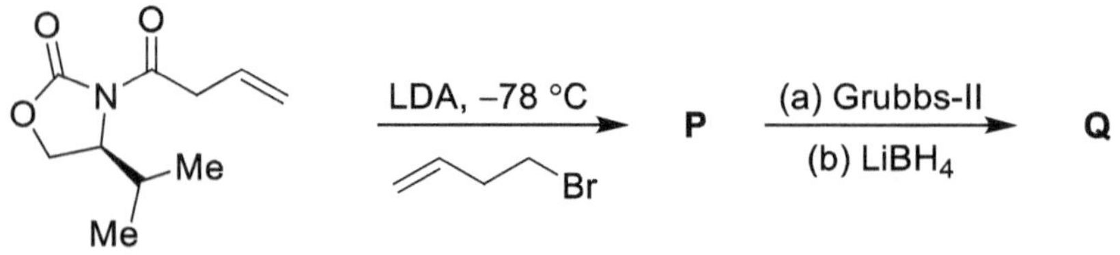

$$\xrightarrow[\substack{\diagup\diagdown\diagup \text{Br}}]{\text{LDA, } -78\ ^\circ\text{C}} \quad P \quad \xrightarrow[\text{(b) LiBH}_4]{\text{(a) Grubbs-II}} \quad Q$$

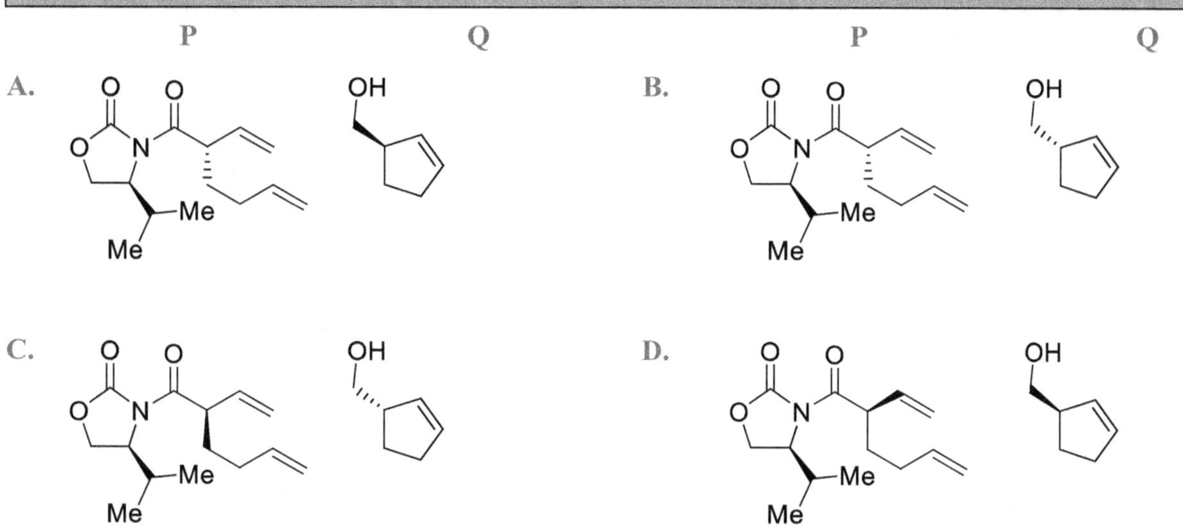

Answer: B. The major products **P** and **Q** in the given reaction sequence are shown below,

Question No-41: The major products **M** and **N** in the given reaction sequence are

	(a) NaH, $(MeO)_2CO$, benzene		DIBAL-H (excess)	
	(b) Br_2 (2 equiv), Et_2O	**M**		**N**
	(c) NaOMe, MeOH			

C.

D.

Answer: B. The major products **M** and **N** formed in the given reaction sequence are dimethyl 4-ethylcyclopent-1-ene-1,2-dicarboxylate and (4-ethylcyclopent-1-ene-1,2-diyl)dimethanol, respectively.

Note. Favorskii rearrangement of 1,1-/1,3-dibromo ketones produces bromocyclopropane intermediate, which on further reaction with alkoxide base offers corresponding unsaturated esters.

Question No-51: The reaction(s) that yield(s) 3-phenylcyclopentanone as the major product is(are)

A.

(a) Ph_2CuLi

(b) H_3O^+

B.

PhI, $Pd(OAc)_2$ (cat.)

$KOAc$, DMF, 60 °C

C.

(a) $PhLi$

(b) H_3O^+

D.

(a) LDA, THF, −78 °C

then $PhSeBr$

(b) H_2O_2

Answer: A & B. Gillman reagent i.e. Ph₂CuLi is the best choice to get the desired product from the starting material 2-cyclopentenone.

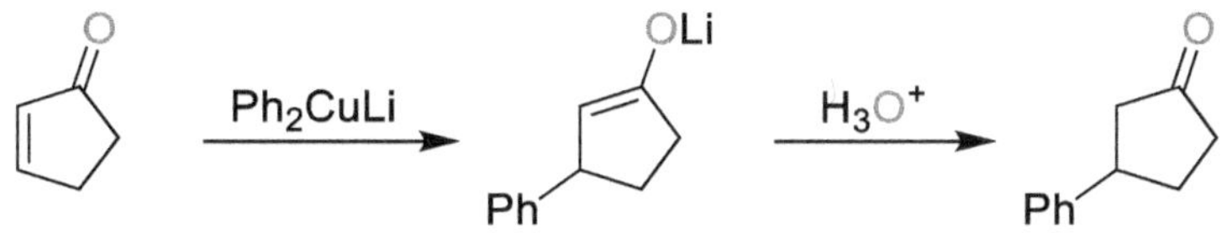

Heck arylation of 2-cyclopentenol followed by *syn-β*-hydride elimination gives enol derivative which isomerizes into desired target molecule.

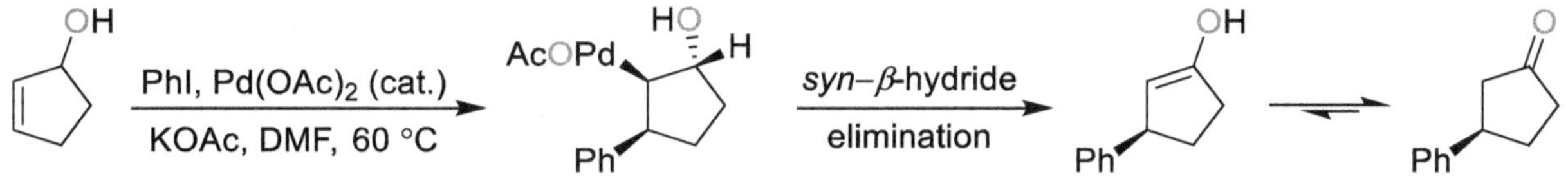

Calo, V.; Nacci, A.; Monopoli, A.; Ferola, V. *J. Org. Chem.* **2007**, *72*, 2596-2601.

Question No-52: The reaction(s) that yield(s) **M** as the major product is(are)

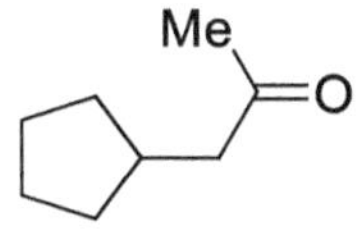

M

A. (a) *t*-BuLi, THF, −65 °C (b) 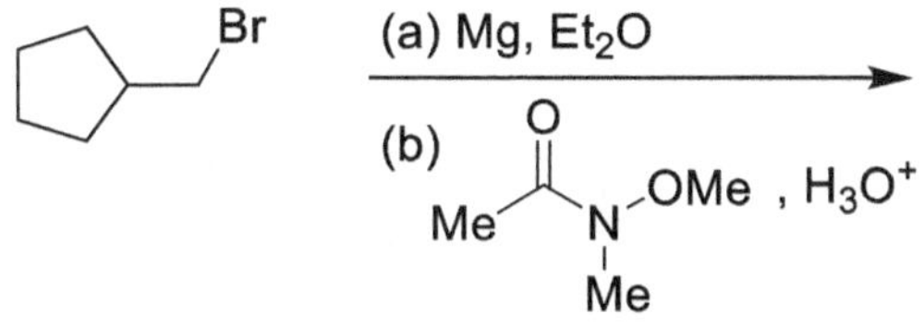 (c) H₃O⁺

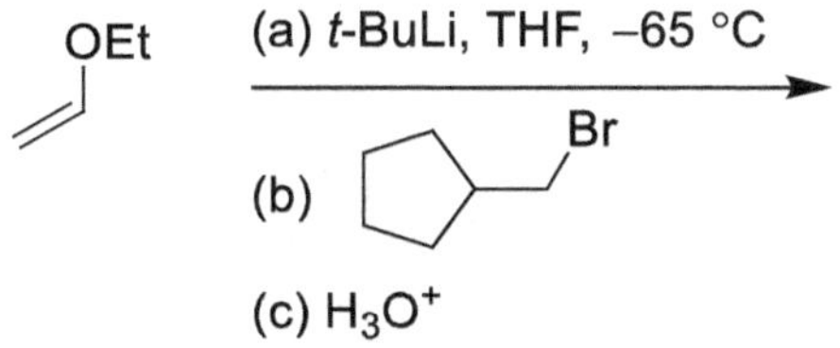

B. (a) Mg, Et₂O (b) , H₃O⁺

C. Li≡Me (a) (b) HgSO₄ (cat.) H₂SO₄, H₂O

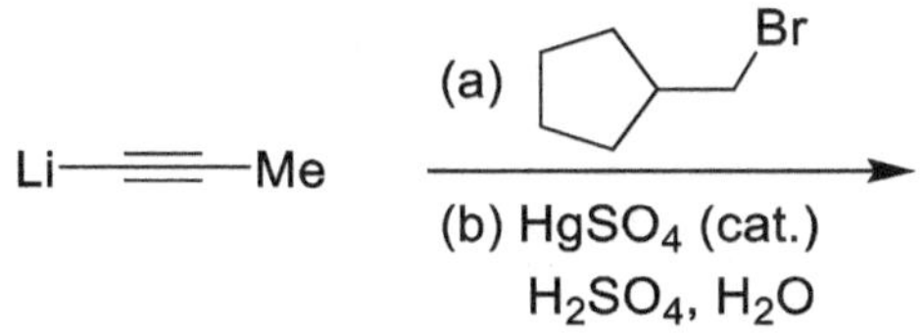

D. Me–NO₂ (a) NaOMe, (b) 10N H₂SO₄, −10 °C

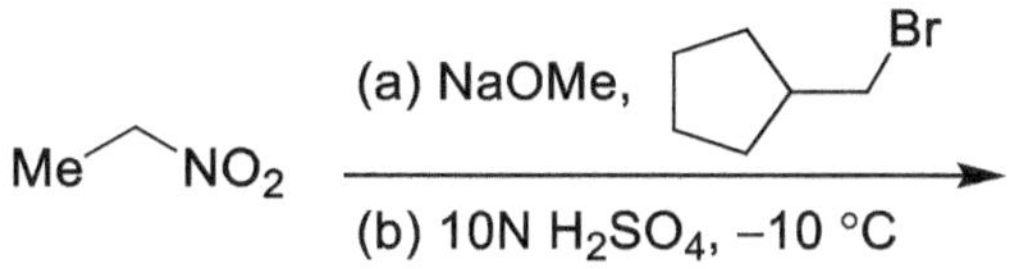

Answer: A, B & D. The reaction of ethyl vinyl ether with butyl lithium generated a new organolithium derivative, which reacts with cyclopentyl carbyl bromide and then acidic workup furnishes desired product 1-cyclopentylpropan-2-one **M**.

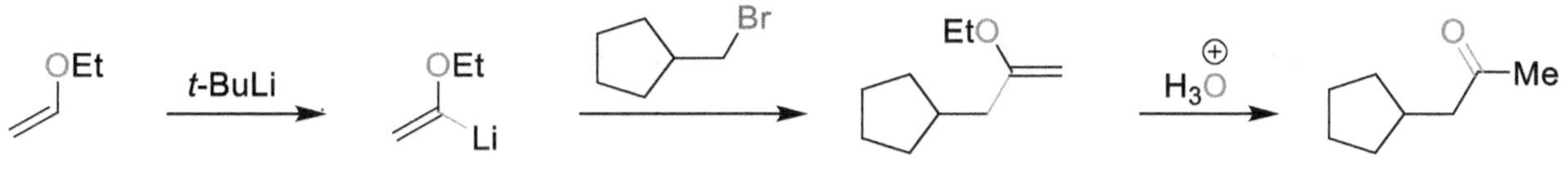

The synthesis of fresh Grignard reagent from cyclopentyl carbyl bromide using magnesium turning and then the addition of Weinreb amide gives an unstable tetrahedral intermediate. Finally, acidic hydrolysis produces the major product 1-cyclopentylpropan-2-one **M**.

The direct displacement of bromine from the cyclopentyl methyl bromide with prop-1-yn-1-yllithium, followed by the Kucherov reaction unable to produce the desired product. Instead, a homologous product is formed with one more carbon.

The S_N2 reaction of nitroethane with (bromomethyl)cyclopentane in the presence of sodium methoxide gives (2-nitropropyl)cyclopentane, which on further oxidation (Nef-oxidation) yielding the target molecule 1-cyclopentylpropan-2-one **M** as the product.

Question No-57: The difference between the number of Gauche-butane interactions present in **P** and **Q** is

Answer: 1. The difference between the number of Gauche-butane interactions present in **P** and **Q** is one $(5 - 4 = 1)$.

Explanation. In the case of *cis*-methyl decalin, gauche-butane interactions are five.

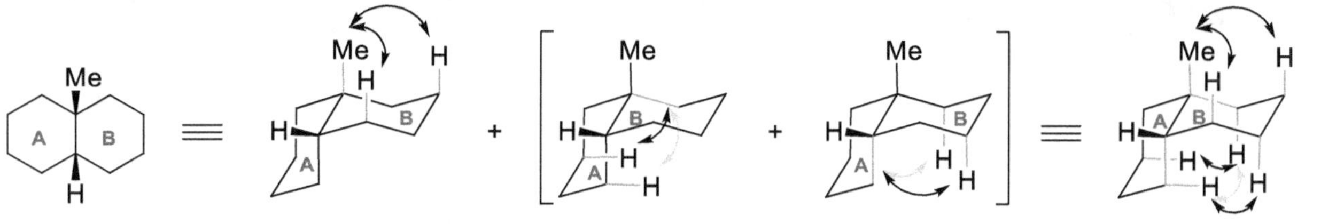

P

P1

1,3-diaxial interactions by
methyl group = 2

P2

1,3-diaxial interactions by
methylene groups = 3

P3

= total 1,3-diaxial
interactions = 2 + 3 = 5

In the case of *trans*-methyl decalin, gauche-butane interactions are four.

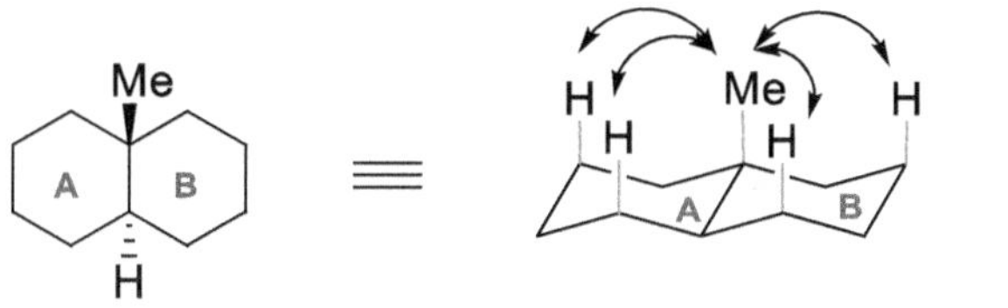

Q

1,3-diaxial interactions by
methyl group = 4

Note. In both the structures **P2** and **P3**, the double-headed light black arrow is of the same type of 1,3-diaxial interaction. Thus, it is considered a single interaction.

www.ingramcontent.com/pod-product-compliance
Lightning Source LLC
LaVergne TN
LVHW060613200726
843510LV00009B/1092